To OMNI Board
of Presidences

1/13/14

B. M

BAMBOO
Prison Without Walls
PROMISE

VICHEARA HOUN

abbott press®
A DIVISION OF WRITER'S DIGEST

Abbott Press books may be ordered through booksellers or by contacting:

Abbott Press
1663 Liberty Drive
Bloomington, IN 47403
www.abbottpress.com
Phone: 1-866-697-5310

Because of the dynamic nature of the Internet, any web addresses or links contained in this book may have changed since publication and may no longer be valid. The views expressed in this work are solely those of the author and do not necessarily reflect the views of the publisher, and the publisher hereby disclaims any responsibility for them.

Any people depicted in stock imagery provided by Thinkstock are models, and such images are being used for illustrative purposes only.

Certain stock imagery © Thinkstock.

ISBN: 978-1-4582-0631-2 (e)
ISBN: 978-1-4582-0630-5 (sc)
ISBN: 978-1-4582-0632-9 (hc)

Library of Congress Control Number: 2012919265

Printed in the United States of America

Abbott Press rev. date: 11/13/2012:

The book intended as a voice for my family, friends, neighbors, and all for Khmers who are no longer able to tell their stories and share their pain. They are not able because they were slaughtered without justice; they were starved in a nation that exported the bounty from its fields; they died from illness easily cured by access to modern medicine; they were permanently traumatized by the war crimes perpetrated by Pol Pot, the Khmer guerilla leader, and his followers.

I will not let this story die because I don't want my children or your children to ever live in a Prison Without Walls, as I did. That is living in Hell. I want my children and yours to live in freedom and peace.

"All the ingredients for total holocaust are here, and the tension is palpable. One can sense a storm coming................ She and the reader have become used to a life of luxury that the jarring scenes, the hunger and the poverty that follow are extreme to the point of horror. The narrative tone is strong, and she keeps a firm grip on her personality through these chapters, even though her perspective on the world changes radically. These pages are truly haunting."

- Editorial desk of Authonomy.com from *Harper Collins*.

"Bamboo Promise - is written by a true Cambodian lady, who was an adult when the Khmer Rouge took her country, and informs how it was betrayed by those in thrall to Mao. Her recollections are vivid, historically accurate and informative, and her words really do burn off the pages like napalm."

-KAY-KRISTINA FENTON, Author of *The Ragged Yellow Ribbon*.

"BAMBOO PROMISE is both a valuable record of the Cambodian genocide and a compelling personal account. The author paints a broad picture--the atrocity, the terror, the attempt by the Khmer Rouge to erase an entire people and their culture. And we experience it all through the eyes of one brave woman who lived it and survived."

-BILL CARRINGTON. Author of *The Doctor of Summitville*

"Anyone who has visited Cambodia or is interested in modern Asian history should read this book. Life under Pol Pot's Maoist dictatorship is vividly described by one who was actually there and who witnessed the horrors of his cruel regime first hand. A really great read...sad, funny, horrific and moving by turn...this story will grip you from start to finish."

-BARRY WENLOCK, Author of *Little Krisna and The Bihar Boy*

"I enjoyed this story. It's written from the heart in such a way that it makes you feel like you are really there. Powerful writing. I can recommend this story without hesitation."

OLGA SEGAL, Author of *Lurking in the Shadows*

"The book opens a window on pre-war (pre-1975) Cambodia where the story starts. Ms. Houn gives detailed and personal description of a society that no longer exists. But the greatest contribution of this book is that it provides an insight on how individuals can survive the greatest and worst imaginable atrocities. The story of Bamboo Promise is a story of hope and inspiration. I highly recommend this book because it taps into mankind's greatest mysteries. How do people endure complete physical, emotional, and psychological destruction? And how do they find the energy and strength to defy all odds? Bamboo Promise belongs in a long line of literature that describes the heroic survival stories of brave individuals."

-PAULETTE KURZER, professor of political science of *University of Arizona*

Introduction

One day, more than ten years after settling in America and struggling every day to begin a new life, I sat alone by a window watching a beautiful little bird pick up a tiny twig in his beak and fly away. I wondered how far that bird had to fly with those twigs, one by one, to make a nest. How remarkable that this bird would be so devoted to his family. The miracle of family, family devotion and sacrifice was symbolized to me by that little bird and his labors.

Although I had lived many years with painful memories, I was suddenly overwhelmed with grief for the loss of my father. The realization my Papa was gone forever was suddenly sharply and acutely painful. I cried aloud for him and asked God why I was left alone without him. I regretted wishing I could live on my own without hearing his voice. I did not value the family values, the advice, discipline, love and caring that Papa gave me then, but now, it all made so much sense.

This book began as a letter to my father. Though he had died years before, I felt his spirit still around me, still there to comfort me and ease my frustration and pain. I longed to tell him once more that I loved him and honored him. I wanted him to know how much I missed him.

My letter began as just a few little scratches. Then, as I wrote, many memories – so long suppressed – returned. My scratches became forty pages, then one hundred, then more and more. My letter to Papa had become "Bamboo Promise", the story of my life and my journey through the Cambodian genocide and its aftermath.

It is my memoir to honor my family who were victims of Pol Pot and his monstrous Khmer Rouge (KR) during the Cambodian Genocide. While members of my large, extended family suffered and died in different areas of Cambodia, my immediate family spent their last miserable days starving to death in a lean-to, next to a bamboo patch, in Battambang Province, District of Preah Netr Preah.

As long as I live, "Bamboo" will remind me of that God-forsaken place where I held my father as he tried to whisper his last words to me. Even though I will never know what he was trying to say, I have tried to guide the rest of my life by the principles that he stressed to me over and over: *"Don't forget who you are and where you come from; Education never can be stolen; and maintain hope – never give up."*

"Promise" is for my assurance to Papa that when, not if, I survived the Pol Pot time, I would finish my pharmacy degree. I kept that promise to honor my father.

This story, including the legends and history, is my personal history as I learned and lived it. It is what I saw, heard, felt, and learned. All the characters are real, although I have changed some names to protect the privacy of other survivors.

I am neither a historian nor a political scientist. I am a survivor and the story I tell is how I and my family experienced the world during this terrible time and what we believed was happening.

My hope is that young Cambodians and Cambodians in the Diaspora will read this, and more erudite texts, to learn more about what happened to their country and its people. I hope all who read will understand how a radical, violent political movement bent on death and destruction, was able to consume nearly two million innocent souls, while the world stood by. It is only when you know why something has happened that you can prevent its re-occurrence.

It is important that the world learns how Cambodians, my family and I included, lived and died through four years of Hell on earth. Nearly two million Cambodians were executed, starved, and tortured to death. All who survived, both victims and victimizers, have been traumatized and permanently scarred.

I also hope that, in some small way, my book will help Cambodians remember the history of their country and not let history repeat itself. I hope it will make young Cambodians more sensitive to the trauma that their parents and grandparents endured. Also, my book shows how naïve many of the most privileged were to believe that nothing so horrible could happen to our country. My father, who had promised me that nothing would happen to us or to Cambodia, is my best example of this blindness. In our case, genocide was the price we paid for ignoring the signs, and assuming that something cannot happen simply because you can't imagine it.

The weaknesses in Cambodian society, in particular our sometimes blind and unquestioning obedience to our leaders; our failure to educate all our citizens; and our acceptance of a society based upon class distinctions rather than the value of all people paved the road for Pol Pot and his angry and vengeful followers. Our neighboring countries and the rest of the world allowed it to happen for a variety of reasons – primarily, of course, self-interest.

Acknowledgements

I would like to give my deeply thanks to:

-My mother-in-law, Carol Matarazzo, has been my partner as we have turned my often inadequate English into a readable story. Because of her commitment and patience, my scratches have been transformed into a book.

-My friends, Charles King, and Dawna Phillips who helped with editing and to my many other friends who have encouraged and supported me as I learned what it takes to change a manuscript into a book on a shoestring budget.

Contents

It was not for nothing that the Khmer Rouge, an army dressed from head to foot in black, with hearts to match, became known to my people as "Black Crows." Later, in my life in the West, I learned the expression "A Murder of Crows." It was so appropriate.

~ONE~

MURDER OF CROWS

On a hot morning, April 17, 1975, the day after our New Year celebrations in Phnom Penh, Cambodia, artillery bombing shook our house like a thunderstorm carried in on a monsoon wind. My little Pekinese dogs barked and raced around the house, alarmed by the sounds that had been far away before this day. Mimi, who rarely barked at anything, was frightened by the loud noises and came to quietly sit by me with his tail between his legs. The other dogs soon gave up challenging the sounds of war and ran to hide underneath the table and chairs. They all sensed something ominous was afoot.

We had endured those distant sounds during my wedding barely four months earlier, but now it seemed as if the war was next door. Mid-morning, the guns gradually fell oddly silent. I went to the garden and peeked out the gate. Neighbors were leaving their houses heading towards the main street, edging past cars backing down our street. When I stepped outside, I saw others waving homemade white flags, dancing, hugging each other and cheering, "Hurrah, Hurrah! We finally have peace. The war is ended! No more rocket shells! No more killing! No more corruption! We are socialist. We are equal."

These people were trying to convince whoever might be watching that they were happy, but in reality, they were as terrified as I was. We had all smelled danger coming. We didn't know what would happen, but many, like my father, still had hope that the KR rebels would settle the regime in a peaceful way when they took over. Papa had left for his job in the national government earlier in the day, so he was not home to help us understand what was happening and we were very worried about him. I felt panic begin to rise in my throat with all the confusing activity in the street. Was it true the communist rebels (Khmer Rouge) had taken over the government? Where was Papa? Who would protect us?

Black-clad KR soldiers began to arrive in the main street. They wore the same hard expressions I had seen when Papa, in his capacity as a top government minister, had invited some KR representatives to our house for a negotiating dinner. My heart dropped at the sight of them. My hands and my feet felt paralyzed. When I recovered from the initial shock, I ran back inside - right into *Eeh*, my stepmother, who was frozen with panic in the doorway. Soon we began to hear vehicles speeding down the street. Riding on them were very young KR soldiers, some as young as ten, and all with the same cold and angry faces.

1

To my relief, Papa then drove up. He also seemed confused with what was going on. He told us that he had changed his mind about trying to get to work and that he had sent Un, our chauffeur, home to be with his family. As Papa stood in the gate, we were surprised to see a man we knew among the black-uniformed KR soldiers. It was Sambath, a man that Papa had hired at his pharmaceutical plant. The truck slowed down a little at the gate and Papa caught Sambath's eye and called to him, "What is going on, *Mit Yeung* (Comrade)?"

It seemed Sambath was no longer Papa's employee, since he did not answer but merely gave Papa an ironic smile. "Why did you call him *Mit Yeung?*" I asked, as we walked back to the house.

Uncharacteristically, Papa ignored my question and instead told our servant, Kilen, to close and lock the gate. He told all of us to get into the house and be quiet. Our family all gathered in the living room – my father and Stepmother, my paternal grandparents and my grandaunt, my uncle Sunthary, my husband and I, as well as Kilen and her toddler son.

Papa appeared very worried, even though he didn't say anything alarming. He couldn't call anybody to get information as the phone had been dead for hours. He impatiently turned on the radio to hear the news, but there was no sound and this seemed to increase his anxiety. However, it soon became clear that the KR had indeed taken Phnom Penh, Cambodia's capital city, when the radio crackled and we heard a very shaky and defeated voice, "I am Hem, Ket Dara. Lon Nol's military are ordered to put down their guns while they are in negotiation with the KR. We….."

Silence.

At that moment, we could hear mechanical sounds of the speaker in the background – clicking noises but no words. Then, the sounds of a struggle … sounds that were quickly interrupted by an angry, aggressive and disrespectful shout, "We are not here for negotiations. We have won the war by force of arms!" We exchanged silent and terrified looks as we waited for whatever might come next.

Now the KR music, very aggressive, fast, sharp and violent, began to play. Following, we heard that Mr. Long, Boreth[1], the foreign minister and acting prime minister of the Khmer Republic, and Prince Sirimatak (Prince Sihanook's cousin) had been arrested and possibly executed.

"Why did Sambath ignore you Papa? What happened to all the KR leaders that you invited to have dinner at our house to negotiate the peace?" I asked, unable to make sense of it all.

Before Papa could answer there was a loud, aggressive banging on the gate door. I followed Kilen as she went to open it. There stood a child soldier, about ten, in a black uniform with the signature KR *krama* – scarf around his neck and

---

[1]   In Cambodian culture, the last name will go first followed by a comma and then the first name.

a black hat. He was holding a very large gun which looked heavy but the boy held it with confidence.

"Leave this house immediately!" he ordered in an angry voice that hadn't yet changed. If it hadn't been for our fear and the gun, it would have been funny, like my cousins playing a war game.

"Why, *Mit Yeung?*"

"We must search for enemies."

"What enemies?"

"Americans!!"

"We haven't seen any Americans?"

"They are hiding among you!"

"They are not in our house. Why must we leave?"

"We must search for ourselves. Leave this house immediately!" His young voice became more irate as I questioned him.

I asked softly, "How long must we be gone?"

"Three days," he said and stalked away. My feet were frozen with fear as I heard we must leave the house.

Trembling, holding back tears, I returned inside with Kilen, "Papa, what is happening? What should we do? They said the Americans were hiding among us. Who are they?" I asked frantically.

"Stay where you are. We won't leave yet," Papa said calmly. "Maybe something will change. I will call my friend, S.E. Phlek, Pheun to find out what should we do." But the phone line was still dead. Papa was worried about his friend and business partner, and also about his nephew, Dr. Thor (Dr. Thor, Peng Thong), and his family. They lived nearby but we could not make contact with them because the road was blocked by KR troops. Although this was so distressing at that time, I believe if Papa had connected with either one of them, especially S.E.Phlek, Pheun, then Papa would have brought all of us to follow them and we would all have been executed within days.

We heard someone shake the door gate again, "Open the door, *Baung* (Older Brother)!" We opened the gate since we recognized the voice of Aunt Sichoeur, Papa's older half-sister. She was there with her whole family.

Her husband, Phan, had panic in his voice as he told Papa, "It was difficult and risky to make the trip here. The KR are everywhere. They have started to expel people from the city. They are arresting anyone in a military or police uniform. They strip off their clothes and tie their hands behind their back. I saw them on the way coming here! The roads are very crowded. Doctors are forced to leave the hospitals and patients are being chased out into the street in their nightgowns; some die on the spot. Currency is being destroyed and many people are senselessly being killed at random."

"What are we supposed to do?" Papa asked. His voice was shaking and this terrified me. My Papa was always in control. I instantly thought of my cousin, Or, who was a police inspector.

"You must destroy your identification cards and anything that could tell the KR who you are," *Pou* (Uncle) Phan said, his voice thick with fear and desperation. "Put on old clothes and make yourselves look poor. You must not look wealthy. Prepare simple food and be prepared to leave the city for a few days. Don't take anything that will identify you as upper class and that includes the dogs. Simple people don't have toy dogs as pets."

"Where will we go?" Papa asked, his voice edged with defeat.

"I am going to Kompong Thom, my natal province. You may be safe there until you can return," *Pou* Phan offered.

We stayed quiet inside the house with the gate closed and locked as the daylight waned. We kept the lights off so the house would seem deserted. We lost our appetites, couldn't sleep; all we could do was wait and see what would happen next. Our neighbor left his house that night without saying goodbye to us. The people across the street had left days before. My newly-wed husband, Leang, and I finally went outside to check on Papa. The moonlight was enough for me to see how nervous and anxious he was as he decided how to best protect his family. We all were waiting for his orders as the leader of the family. Sitting in the dark under the jackfruit tree, we just looked at each other and waited.

As usual, my hated, childless stepmother held our servant Kilen's son on her lap - Papa's son, it was rumored, but I did not believe it. She tried to keep him quiet but he was a toddler and did not understand the dangers that we all faced. When he protested, she squeezed his head to punish him, "Quiet!! KR will kill you if you make a noise." Koy responded by crying loudly and his mother, Kilen, picked him up and covered his mouth to stop the noise.

Papa's Gun and Gold Bars

"Why don't we leave tonight when the weather is cooler?" *Eeh* asked Papa. He got up from the bench, "Not yet. I want to wait a little longer in case the KR leaders decide to let us stay." Papa turned to his much younger half-brother Sunthary and my husband and ordered, "Dig a hole in the little room next to the garage."

As Papa went inside the house, Sunthary, who lived with us, said, "He must keep a lot of gold and money in the house. He wants to hide it in the ground."

Leang started digging the hole while my *Pou* Sunthary was standing with both hands on his hips. "Are you going to help me or just be the boss here?" Leang asked, with mild irritation.

"This is dumb; the KR will discover it," Sunthary replied.

Papa came out with a big box. "Where do you think is the best place to put this?" he asked all of us.

"You must put it in a metal container to protect it from humidity. I saw you have a military box in the garage. That will be perfect," *Pou* Phan assured him and Papa nodded. Papa walked over to me and whispered, "I have hidden American dollars, gold bars and a set of very valuable jewelry."

4

"Is the jewelry mine?" I asked.

"Yes, I've been saving it for you. They are the best quality emeralds. I never let your stepmother know about it; she would want them all."

"Why didn't you give it to me for my wedding? It is not too late to give it to me now. We will need this to survive, Papa, when we leave the house. Take the money, too."

"No, we will leave all here," he insisted. He turned away and told Sunthary to come back inside with him. I did not follow, since I knew Papa wouldn't listen to me.

My husband put his arms around me and said, "Don't get upset with Papa, *Aun* (Honey)! We are all in danger; no one knows what will happen tomorrow."

Then Papa came back with *Pou* Sunthary. "Is everything done, *Kaun* (Son)?" he asked my husband. I looked up to be sure it was Leang that Papa was speaking to so kindly. It was amazing since Papa was usually dismissive and suspicious of my husband and had never approved of my marriage.

"*Bat* (Yes)! Papa," Leang replied, with a wry smile.

"His gun is hidden in a box in the ceiling over the living room," *Pou* Sunthary whispered in my ear.

"Keep silent, shush…" Papa shushed at both of us and then he told Leang, "*Kaun*, take Vicheara and go to sleep. Everything is going to be OK." Leang smiled at him, then at me and we left.

My husband whispered, "Papa called me *Kaun* twice. Did you hear it?" I nodded but it was hard to pay attention to Papa's sudden change in attitude with all the turmoil surrounding us. I remembered the words of *Pou* Ban, the fortuneteller, who had warned us to leave the country before April. He had told me that 'things will be upside down'. Papa dismissed this talk at the time and I wondered if it made sense to him now.

I looked at my dogs that were following me everywhere. I knelt down to respond to their wagging tails, caressing then gently. "Did you have your dinner yet?" The tails were wagging harder and Mimi seemed to look up at me sadly. I felt he was aware of what was going on, based on my tone of voice and my emotions. "Pray with me, Mimi!" I hugged him, "I love you so much. I don't know how to protect you when I cannot even protect myself. I can only hug you and tell you how much I am going to miss you. I have to leave the house and leave you. I will pray for you, Mimi."

I got up and looked out the window for Papa. I tried to imagine what he was thinking as he walked back and forth, head down and hands crossed behind his back. I knew he was worried; thinking to find a way to save the family. He seemed so strong to me. If he was scared, he did not show it to anyone. During that last night in our house, Papa ordered us not to turn on any lights, nor cook food for dinner. We kept our conversation very low to pretend that the house was unoccupied. Papa still hoped that tomorrow might bring better news.

As I walked into my bedroom, I felt it was my last time to sleep in here. I looked at my red blanket, a gift from my cousin, Phach. Should I take it with me? I looked at the picture of my *Mak* (mother) who had died when I was eight, "*Mak*! I will leave you tomorrow. I cannot take you with me as I have nowhere to hide your photo, but I know I take your love with me. I will remember you forever."

Messages from God

I got into bed and hugged my red blanket. My husband held me and told me to forget about everything, just sleep. I felt safe in his arms and soon slept. I dreamed that two men were carrying a throne along the side of a big farm field. I knew the man on the throne was a King. When they got near me, the men stopped and the King left the throne to work in the field. I awoke to my husband shaking me, "*Aun*, what is going on?" he asked.

Confused, I asked, "Where is the King?"

"You were screaming as if someone tortured you."

I shook off the blanket with my feet and sat up, telling him about the dream, "What do you think it means, *Baung* (Darling)?" I asked.

"I don't know. Hopefully, it means something good will happen." My mind was racing to figure out what the dream was telling me. Maybe it was as the fortune teller said, 'things will be upside down'. I fell back to sleep.

"*Aun*, wake up. What is going on? Why are you crying?"

"Oh, I dreamt again. It seems God has important messages to tell me tonight."

"What do you see this time?" He held my hand and kissed me on the cheek.

"I dreamt that all my teeth were falling out," I used my tongue to verify my teeth were still there. I had been superstitious all my life; I knew that dreaming about losing teeth meant that people in my family would die. I began to weep, "I am worried about Papa. Will Papa die?"

"Keep praying, *Aun*," he said. More bad dreams came, even with Leang holding me tight. When I awoke the next morning there was blood on my hand; I never found out what caused it. I did not know then that it was an omen of the rats we would have to live alongside and fight for food. I looked through the windows and went outside to check out the neighborhood. It was very quiet. It seemed we were the last ones to leave. I found Papa outside; apparently he had not slept as he still wore the same clothes. "Are we going to leave the house today, Papa?"

"We are waiting for your cousin, Or." Or was like a son to my father and had lived off and on with us for years. We were especially worried about him because he was a police inspector and *Pou* Phan had said that the KR were arresting, even killing the police. I returned to my room and went through all my cosmetics and all the medicines that I kept in the house – both my husband and I were pharmacy

6

students and my father owned a pharmaceutical production plant. I knew I should bring basic medicines with me to protect the family. It was a decision to be made immediately, as there was no more time. My fear was telling me to take them all, even though my father was still convinced that we would be home in three days. I filled up a large leather bag. The last thing I packed was the embroidered lace blouse I wore at my wedding and some fancy lingerie bought from Paris. I wore a long, green *sampot* and a black, long-sleeved blouse. A *sampot* is like a long skirt – it is a long piece of cloth wrapped around the waist and fastened at the side of the hip with a hook.

I took every piece of quality jewelry that I had and hid it in a bag that I tied around my waist under my clothes. It was a considerable amount since, as in many Cambodian households, the family's wealth was often in gemstones and gold since the banking system could not be trusted.

Cousin Or never came. "I have decided to leave without him," Papa finally made a decision and walked to the car.

My aunt's family decided not to follow us, but to make their own way. "We will be reunited if we are still alive. Please take care of my parents!" My aunt's voice was choked with tears. *Pou* Phan left us with his last words, "Goodbye, *Baung*! God will take care of you all. I hope we will return home in three days."

My grandparents, my father and stepmother, and our servant Kilen and her son were in one car with Papa driving; my husband and I in another car with Grandaunt and *Pou* Sunthary. Before we left home, I brought out a "Le Creuset" pot, food, my favorite red blanket and clothes. I had already packed clothes for Papa in the luggage and slipped them into my trunk. But, Papa caught me with this last load and said, "No, put them back in the house, *Kaun* (Daughter). Silly, do you want to be noticed by KR with luggage and a red blanket?"

I showed him the pot, "This needs to go with us, rice and palm sugar, too."

Papa pushed them away, "Take them back to the house. I don't want to get the car dirty." He walked to the car, "We do not need to take anything; we'll buy food along the way. In three days, we will return home."

"No, keep the pot," *Eeh* made a decision, a good one it would turn out.

Before I got in the car, I went to caress my dogs one last time, "I rather not see you all killed by the KR or die of starvation in front of me. We do not know if we are going to live or die." I said a tearful goodbye to all of them. Having to leave them behind was breaking my heart, but we knew that pet toy dogs would mark us as bourgeoisie and that was far too dangerous. Mimi did not follow me as he usually did, but sat in front of the house, watching us leave. He did not cry as we did, but his beautiful eyes gazed mournfully at us. I was heartbroken as I said goodbye to the house and my dogs. Even though we were supposed to return in three days, I was filled with dread that we wouldn't come back and I would never see my dogs, my best friends, again.

Everyone was quiet, each of us trying to deal with the question of what would happen next. Friday, April 18, 1975, was the day I looked back at my house, at the gate with Papa's initials 'KH', and it would be a very long time before I saw it again. Finding myself at the mercy of Pol Pot's KR and in such fear, not even knowing of the living Hell to come, my privileged childhood in this house seemed to belong to somebody else.

PART I

CHILDHOOD

The year I was born my parents were happily living in a one-floor brick apartment in the center of Phnom Penh. This apartment was built about twenty feet from the road, near the Independence Monument. We had one servant, Choen, who helped clean the house, do dishes, laundry, and grocery shopping. My cousin, Phach, babysat me and cooked for the whole family. She lived with us since her mother, my mother's youngest sister, had died in childbirth.

~TWO~

MY FAMILY HOME

We soon moved from this small apartment in the city center to live in the wonderful house I would come to love, and be forced to leave on that awful day in 1975. The house was given to my parents as a gift by my maternal grandmother, Sem. I called her *Lok Yey* in Khmer. This house was a real family home. Built of a special wood from Kratié province, the house was located on 182 Samdech Ponn Street. The main gate door was stenciled with my Papa's initials, KH, as decoration. The house had about 4,000 square feet on two floors with three big bedrooms, one dining room and big, long living rooms. The kitchen was a separate building in the rear of the house, as was common in many hot climates.

Childhood Fears

When I was around five years old, my Papa took me to his paternal family home in Peam Chileang District, province of Kompong Cham, in the eastern part of Cambodia. The house was unoccupied when we visited. Papa stopped in front of the house and announced, "This is the house where I was born." A man in his late thirties came out to welcome us. "Everything looks good. You've maintained the property very well," Papa said to the man, patting him on the shoulder.

The man smiled back and responded "*Bat.*" Papa and I walked upstairs and the man followed us. I kept looking back. The man smelled of tobacco and sweat and I was suspicious of him. Without looking at the man Papa asked, "Do you have a shovel?"

"*Bat*, we have a very small one downstairs," the man answered, turning back down the steps to retrieve the shovel.

"Not now. I will need it later," Papa said, stopping him. I kept an eye on the smelly man as he continued to follow us up the steps.

The house was built on wooden stilts in Khmer traditional village style with twelve steps up to the main door in the center of the house. There were windows on both sides of the main door, and a large balcony above the entrance. Small rooms downstairs accommodated the servants. Upstairs were three bedrooms, each with one small window. I followed Papa as he checked each room. "This room was my bedroom, next to your grandpa's," he said, as we entered a small room. "Your aunt's room was in back, next to the kitchen."

I followed him from one room to another as he pointed out the purpose of each room, until we reached the kitchen. It was dirty and the unsealed wood floor was covered with dust. The kitchen was merely an overhang from the house – really just a floor and a roof. There were no walls, so some of the floor boards had begun to rot in the elements. I was afraid to enter, but I was more afraid to lag behind with the smelly man. A big earthenware jar sat at one corner of the room. Papa walked toward the jar and I followed cautiously.

"Stay back! The jar is filthy, do not get too close!" Papa said. Without listening to Papa, I slipped behind him as he walked away and bent over the jar to check what it was in there. A spider suddenly emerged to greet me. I jumped away, grabbing Papa's hand. Papa laughed at me and explained, "The water from the jar was used for cooking and bathing. He turned to the caretaker, "The outside of the house also needs to be kept clean," Papa said, in his booming, authoritative voice. "I pay you to do a good job. I pay you to keep the house clean inside and out. If you cannot do the job, I will find someone who can and I will kick your ass out of here!"

The man shrank at the sound of Papa's voice, nodded his head and said nothing other than "*Bat, Bat.*" I looked at him, as I wanted to tell him Papa would definitely kick his ass for real.

There was no furniture to catch my attention inside the house. The unsealed wood floor was crafted of a very smooth, shiny wood. The pieces of wood were purposely not fitted closely together - leaving openings of about a centimeter that allowed fresh air to enter, making the house feel cool in the hot weather. I stared down at the curious openings, "Papa, can a thief poke a knife through these holes?" I worriedly asked, pointing at a particularly large gap.

"Danger comes in through the door, not the floor," Papa assured me. "You see those wooden hooks?" he asked, pointing at two big wooden hooks on the inside doorframe. I nodded. "And that big wooden bar?" I nodded again. "At night your grandfather put this bar across the door on the hooks, so no one could open the door from the outside. He also put those metal bars over there across the windows so no one could come in that way either."

"How about ghosts? Papa, ghosts can come in through the holes in the floor or through the windows!"

"Ghosts are just a silly fairy tale. There are no ghosts," he replied, as he walked away.

I followed him and protested, "There are too ghosts, Papa. *Yey* (Grandmother) Kong, Papa's stepmother, told me that banana trees are a ghost's favorite way to get in the house and that is why there are no banana trees near the windows."

"*Yey* Kong is silly. You are too young to think about all these things. Forget about ghosts. Come, we will go to the gravesite of your first grandma," Papa said, and I knew the conversation about ghosts was over. He took my hand and led me to the front garden. I said no more, but I knew I was right. There was a reason why my grandfather planted banana trees everywhere on the property, from the front yard to the back, but he did not plant them by the windows. There was a reason many people made banana offerings to appease the spirits. There was a reason *Yey* Kong made a *kauntong* – a bowl made of banana leaves and filled with rice - and other delicacies as an offering to the spirits. No matter how silly Papa thought ghosts were, I knew they existed. I knew they traveled through the banana leaves and got in the house. What I didn't know with all the wisdom of my five years, was the truth of his statement that real danger comes in the door and it won't be ghosts.

The smelly man was waiting for Papa downstairs. He smiled and bowed his head to show respect to Papa, "Here is the shovel, *Lok*(Sir)."

"We are leaving now. Do you stay here at night?" Papa asked, instead of thanking him.

"No, I go home." The man stood by the stairs and waited for us to leave.

The Duty of the Oldest Son

Papa grunted, took the shovel and walked toward the garden. As I followed Papa into my grandfather's garden, the overpowering scent of jasmine and gardenia filled my nose. Although overgrown, all his favorite flowers, such as golden needle, bird of paradise, and hibiscus seemed to be welcoming us. I wanted to stay and play in the garden but Papa took my hand and, holding it very tightly in his to keep me from lagging behind, he quickly led me through the garden. "You need to walk quickly, *Kaun*. We need to get back home before it is dark," he said, tightening his grip. As we stepped outside of the property, Papa stopped and pointed at the lake, "This is the lake where the boat people trade fresh fish and vegetables to the villagers. They are Vietnamese. They make a living catching fresh fish to sell at the market. The Vietnamese catch the fish and the Cambodians ferment and dry them," he continued, still walking so quickly I could barely keep up. This day the lake was quiet, no trading, only residents coming to the lake to take baths and carry water back to their homes for cooking.

As he talked of the local people, he was interrupted by cling, cling, cling, coming from behind us. As we turned, a boy of about ten years old approached, riding a very old bike. "Get out of my way, cling, cling, cling," he called out as he approached us. He did not have a horn on his bike, but was imitating the sound of the horn. Papa pulled me to the side of the path to get out of the way of the bike.

"You are naked," I shouted at the boy. He turned back to me and stuck out his tongue. He rode noisily down the path until he disappeared. "He stuck out his tongue at me, Papa," I angrily said to Papa.

"Life in the village is different from the city," he said calmly as he led me through the village. My steps quickened to keep up with his long strides. All along the way Papa waved to villagers he knew, exchanging greetings without stopping.

I could feel the sweat running down my back and into my pants. "I'm tired. My legs are sore," I whined, lagging back.

"We are almost there, *Kaun*. You can walk just a little bit farther. Come." I reluctantly took his hand and continued. When I thought I couldn't take another step, Papa stopped and pointed at a low mound. "Here it is. This is your grandmother's grave. Stay here while I dig her up." This statement amazed me and I could not imagine what he was doing. Dig up my first grandma?

I stood still for a moment and forgot all about being tired as Papa began digging. With each shovel of soil, my mind filled with ghosts and the holes in the floor that I was sure every ghost could squeeze through while I slept. After many shovels of soil, Papa bent down and picked up something from the ground. "What is that?" I asked, peering around his legs.

"Your grandma's skull," he answered, brushing the soil from the rounded object. He picked up another stick-like object and said, "And this is one of her leg bones." I stared, amazed and a little frightened as Papa continued, "Your grandma died way before you were born. When she died, it was the tradition that bodies were buried. Ten years later, we are to dig up the bones and honor the remains. I am the oldest, so it is my duty to take care of her."

I quietly watched while Papa collected all her bones, washed them with water from a nearby well, then again with coconut juice that he had carried with him in a leather bag. He then perfumed the bones with a special eau de toilette and put them back in a leather bag which we then took to the monks to be kept in the village temple.

This journey to his paternal village was an important journey for me. Even though I was very young, Papa felt it was necessary for me to understand the duties of the eldest child to his deceased parents. He wanted me to know what the gravesite and the bones looked like and not to be afraid. I have carried this memory of his duty and devotion with me all my life.

~THREE~

A SMART AND BRAVE GIRL

After moving to the house at 182 Samdech Ponn Street, when I was about six, Papa accepted a new position as General Manager of a private pharmaceutical plant. This well-known company was, at that time, owned by his friend, S.E. Phlek, Pheun, who also served the Cambodian government as a Minister of Interior.

I grew up as an only child. Because I almost never played with other children, I was socially inept with peers. I would become annoyed if they were playing with my toys or if they were dressed poorly or were dirty. I would quietly sneak behind the adults' backs and pinch the younger kids whose parents came to visit. Only my *Mak* knew I was the troublemaker. My threatening glare at the child would stop him from tattling on me. It wasn't just the kids. I didn't like many people at that time, particularly some of my older relatives. Because of some peculiar family circumstances that I only understood when I was older, I had the feeling that no one in the family liked me except my *Mak*, Papa and Cousin Phach. As a result, I would try to create trouble for those people by tattling to my Papa on everyone who was not nice to me.

Mak took me everywhere she went. She tickled my chest every time I came close to her or she saw me naked. I sucked my thumb when I heard her talk about me to her friends. My Papa told his friends that I was a bright girl and courageous. I felt so loved.

Pinching

My first school experience was at a private French pre-school. I learned quickly and soon was speaking French at home with everybody. Papa was so proud of me. My teacher said I was intelligent and qualified me to go to the French Elementary School, Petit Lycée Descartes, despite lots of trouble pinching all boys at school who annoyed me.

Pinching was my primary weapon. At four years old, I was mad at a pedicab driver who yelled at me so I pinched his penis. *Mak* had asked me to take the riel (Cambodian paper currency) to pay the pedicab man. Instead of paying him in full riel, I tore it in half to make it fifty cents. I used to see adults tear riel in half, so I did too. Seeing me do this, naturally he complained loudly and demanded the rest of his money. Well, his penis was visible through a fold in his culottes so I pinched it. Then he screeched and took off without taking the money. My strategy had worked. I then brought the money back to *Mak*. This story was told many times by everyone in the family.

However, when the pre-school year ended, I was put in a Cambodian public school instead of the private French school. What made Papa change his mind after he had said that I was 'a smart and brave girl'? I never heard a reason.

I Want from her 'Just the Bone'

Sutharot Elementary school was a girls' school run by Princess Kanitha Raksmei Sophorn, the aunt of Prince Sihanook. My Grandaunty Houn, wife of Nhiek, Soung, a dental surgeon, was the school principal. Since she was very strict, and especially since there were no boys in school, my Papa felt confident that I would have the structure needed to grow up as an appropriate young Cambodian woman.

My Papa believed he could best influence me to be proper by disciplining me while I was still young. He believed that keeping me away from boys from a very young age would prevent me from wanting to date when I grew older! Generally speaking, he sheltered me in many ways to ensure that I would not damage the family reputation as a young woman. He believed in the old saying: 'Bend the bamboo when it is still a baby!' Innocently, I didn't understand how I could be compared to a young bamboo, and how I would be bent.

When my Grandaunty talked to me, I only looked at her mole-so big, round and strong, sitting on her upper lip. 'A mole indicates a strict person,' I was told. But *Mak* had a mole on her lip, too and she was kind and she loved me, so I hoped Grandaunty would love me like *Mak*. I was placed in kindergarten with a teacher named Sokhon. On the first day of school, I heard Grandaunty tell her, "I want from her (me) just the bone."

I had no idea what this meant, but it certainly didn't sound good. I stepped back and got ready to run away, "That mole woman is going to take my bone?"

But Grandaunty ordered me to stay and told me, "She is a good teacher and you will learn a lot."

Sokhon smiled at me and assigned a seat with a gentle voice to comfort me. 'I want from her just the bone' didn't translate well, but it meant 'do what it takes to make sure she learns and succeeds'. I didn't understand this until I was older and thought about it.

As my elementary schooling went through the years, one thing I never learned in class, and it frightened me to death, was to memorize the multiplication tables. I was good in everything else except mathematics. I hated it. Every morning, before class started, we all stood up together and recited the multiplication tables. I never could finish with everyone else. When the other students finished, I was called to the blackboard to recite by myself the tables 2 to 9. Every morning, my fingertips were beaten with a bamboo stick because I could not remember them. I was put in a corner in front of the other students for an hour. I received this punishment until my teacher got tired of me; I still didn't know the tables. My opinion was, "My bamboo is not meant to be bent in this way."

Stupid Mole – Stupid Teacher

Another teacher, Maly, also had a mole on her face that worried me, a light brown one that sat on her cheek. I wanted to impress her and my classmates to prove that I was a good student, despite my "issues" with multiplication, so I raised my hand high to be called on when I knew the answer. But, my teacher ignored my raised hand and called on me only when my hand was down under the table. I did not understand her tactics; therefore, I thought she was really stupid to not know who to call on. One day, when she did not call on me, I whispered to my classmate, "She is really stupid, and she has a stupid mole."

My friend raised her hand. "*Neak Krou* (Female teacher)! She called you stupid!" She pointed her finger at me - straight into my face. I was embarrassed in front of the class, but I was also mad at the girl who told on me.

"Why do you call me stupid?" My teacher asked, standing over me. I had no answer. Her face became red and her eyelids began to blink fast. I knew she was angry. I looked down at my shoes with shame. "You will go to your grandaunt."

I went to see Grandaunty, for counseling and punishment. When I met her in her office, she did not seem angry but she told me she would let my father choose the punishment. When I got home Papa wasn't there, therefore I hoped he wouldn't be told.

Faked Stomach Ache

It seemed like hours before Papa returned. The thought of the beating is sometimes worse than the beating. I stayed hidden in my room and tried to behave, hoping to escape punishment from my Papa.

The time arrived. I heard a heavy step and a familiar voice called my name, "Vichearaaaa! Where are you?" My door was flung open. As I came out, he ordered me to sit down on the floor. Immediately, a bamboo switch about a foot long was whipping my legs, arms and back. I begged him to stop hitting me. I cried and tried to grab the bamboo, but there was no mercy. "You don't study at school. You learn nothing at school!"

Suddenly the switch was taken away by *Mak*. "Stop beating her! What is going on? You beat her like she was an animal. You have no pity."

"I was told she was not good in math at school; she insulted the teacher," Papa shouted and pointed his finger at me.

"Not true!" I defended myself.

"Stop talking back," Papa was looking for the stick to beat me again but *Mak* hid it behind her back.

"What did you do?" *Mak* tried to save me.

"I called her stupid because when I raised my hand she wouldn't call on me."

"Be patient!" She yelled at Papa. "And learn to listen to your child. You hurt your own child with no reason. It hurts me when you hurt her."

"Bend the bamboo when it is still a baby."

"Stupid! You bend too hard, the bamboo will crack."

That evening, Papa decided to teach me the multiplication tables after dinner to keep up my grades. I was so frightened and intimidated by his loud voice that I could not answer his questions quickly enough. He lost patience with me and kicked my chair angrily until I fell off. The next evening after dinner, I pretended to have a stomach ache.

"You can't teach her by yelling at her," *Mak* said very decisively to Papa. "She won't learn anything that way. Can't you see she has a stomach ache because she is afraid of you?" *Mak* knew how to handle Papa.

"Go to bed, Vicheara," said *Mak*. "Make sure you wash your feet and clean your teeth first. Remember our Khmer culture: the happiness is in the feet at night, on the face in the morning, and body at noon. I will be there in just a minute to take care of the stomach ache." *Mak* hugged me before letting me go. Slowly, I walked away with both hands across my tummy. After I disappeared from my parents' sight, I jumped on the bed and laughed. After that, no more beatings from Papa when it came to my school work. I was satisfied with my faked tummy ache. It saved my life. Years later when I was trapped in KR Hell, I remembered this day.

~FOUR~

ORPHAN

Papa remodeled the first floor of our house and turned it into four small rental apartments. One apartment was rented to a Vietnamese family with four kids. I was very happy to have them as playmates. I learned to speak Vietnamese as I played with the children and interacted with the family. I remember *Mak* collected the rent money and kept it for grocery shopping. Here we employed two female servants, Kmin and Mout, one to cook and another one to do the laundry and clean the house. Mout, my favorite maid, was a widow with two boys; she was honest and hardworking. Every night, after she finished all her chores, she told me ghost stories and fairy tales until I fell asleep. She never disappointed me when I asked her to cook spaghetti, my favorite food.

One day there was exciting news. After saving enough money, *Mak* planned to go on a trip with me. She came up to the dining table, where I was eating a bowl of soup. "How would you like to go to Hong Kong, *Kaun?*" *Mak* asked, as she brought me the dress that I should wear after breakfast.

"Where is Hong Kong?" I asked.

"It's in China and we have to fly there, so we have to go have our picture taken for our passport. We will have so much fun."

"I will be alone for a while," Papa said, poking his chopsticks into his soup and pretending to look sad.

Mak laughed, "I will taste real Chinese food. Life is too short and I want to see Hong Kong. However, I want to take care of this tumor before I go. I can't take the pain much longer. Thor said it was a simple operation. I trust him." Thor was my father's nephew, newly graduated as an M.D. from a French medical school.

The Smell of the Flowers Filled the Room

The night before my *Mak's* surgery, Papa took me to the hospital to see her. As he opened the door to her room, the lovely aroma of flowers greeted us. *Mak* was sitting up in the bed with flowers all around her. Smiling, she opened her arms to me as I ran to her bedside and she hugged me. "Papa said you are having an operation, *Mak*. I am scared for you," I said, holding on to her tightly.

"Don't worry *Kaun*. It's nothing. Thor will take good care of me. You will see; I will be home tomorrow. Then we will go to Hong Kong." She hugged me again, let me go and reached for Papa. *Mak* looked at Papa and said, "*Baung*, I told the nurses I have a stuffy nose."

"Don't be concerned. I am sure Thor knows what he's doing," Papa leaned to her and kissed on her forehead.

The next day I was playing in my room by myself. I was in front of the mirror singing an Indian song and wrapping a small silk scarf around my neck and shoulders in different ways to see how I would look. The words of the song became sad and tears welled in my eyes. I decided to pretend I was an actor in a movie. I could imitate Indian songs very well because *Mak* often took me to see the Indian movies. As I played, I heard voices coming from the living room. I didn't know who was visiting but I got the feeling that something was wrong. I was worried that something had happened to *Mak*, but I was too scared to find out for sure so I continued to sing into the mirror, playing with my scarf.

"What are you doing?" Grandaunt Hieng brusquely asked from the doorway. I was startled, but I didn't move.

"I'm singing," I answered, not turning around. She was the youngest sister of my grandpa, Papa's father, and was visiting us that time. Grandaunt Hieng was then about seventy years old. She did not like to talk much and rarely laughed or smiled at anybody. She was a short, skinny old lady, bent over with osteoporosis which made her looked even shorter. She thought it necessary to lecture and criticize me every time she came across me in the house. I respected her to her face and tried to forgive her, but I called her "the old witch" behind her back. She seemed to be perpetually disgusted with everybody, especially me.

"Why are you singing?" she hissed under her breath. I continued to sing softly, ignoring her. I didn't want to hear anything she had to say to me. I kept my mind on the words of the song. If she had anything bad to tell me about *Mak*, I didn't want to hear it. "You are an imbecile. You don't care about your *Mak*'s condition," she said, annoyed, and left me to my illusions.

I closed the door as soon as she walked away and went back to the mirror. Later that night, Papa came home very sad. I didn't want to ask him anything. I didn't want to know. I stayed away from him that evening, and he kept his distance from me.

Faint Scent of Flowers

The next day I was quiet on the car ride to the hospital to see *Mak*. Papa said nothing to me and I was afraid to say anything to him. This time, the hospital room smelled of medicine and sickness with a very faint scent of flowers. I put my hand over my nose and walked to the bed. *Mak* looked as if she were asleep. I stood looking to see if she would open her eyes. I put my hand on hers and whispered softly, "*Mak*, it's me, Vicheara, wake up," but she didn't open her eyes. I squeezed her hand and put my face close to hers. I could hear her shallow breathing. I whispered again, "'*Mak*, it's me, Vicheara, talk to me!" Again there was no response. I didn't understand why she wouldn't answer me. I just knew it wasn't right. I didn't cry or show any emotion; I was too afraid. I turned and looked at Papa. He showed no emotion either but I could feel his fear. I said nothing on the drive home; questions were not necessary.

When we got home I said, "Papa, is *Mak* dead?"

"No *Kaun*, she is fine, she was sleeping, don't worry, go to bed!" was all he offered, comforting me the only way he knew how.

Both *Lok Yey*, and Grandaunt Hieng were betel chewers. Betel plant is an evergreen and perennial creeper, with heart-shaped leaves. The leaves are edible and have a peppery taste, sometimes bitter. Betel leaves are mostly consumed in Southeast Asia to treat bad breath. They put the betel leaves with a little bit of sliced areca nut into a little bronze mortar and crushed it with a pestle until it became a paste, which is mixed with tobacco and chewed. Their lips and mouth became red from the juice. As they chewed, they spit the red juice out into a small bronze pot. It was a common habit in Cambodia at that time.

When I was in my bedroom putting away my clothes, through the open door I could hear *Lok Yey* and Grandaunt Hieng talking in the living room as they crushed betel leaves. "My daughter has been killed by her own nephew," *Lok Yey* said. "She believed in her nephew, Dr. Thor, an M.D. graduated from Paris, hah!" I could sense her frustration from the force she was applying to the mortar with the pestle, tuk, tuk, tuk.

I knew they were talking about my *Mak* and I now needed to know what was going on so I slipped out of my room and listened at the door. "He did not mean to hurt her," muttered Grandaunt through a mouthful of betel. "A nurse told me he was so angry with himself for using the wrong dosage of anesthesia that he banged his head on the wall, and ran out of the hospital," She spat noisily into the pot.

"Due to the wrong dosage, my daughter falls asleep forever? He is a doctor from Paris, how could that happen?" *Lok Yey* sighed, "My daughter trusted him. Now ....?" Her voice was shaky as she began to weep.

"Now, I think her time is coming and her work will have to be finished by somebody else," Grandaunt said, finishing *Lok Yey's* thought.

A week later, *Mak* was brought home from the hospital. My Cousin Phach and her family came to live with us so they could provide loving care to my *Mak* since Phach's husband was a nurse. Often, I stayed by *Mak's* bed praying for her. I missed her; I felt sorry to see her in this condition. Every time she was fed rice soup, I stayed next to her bed just looking at her, full of compassion and sorrow. *Mak* could neither speak nor move purposefully; she could only cry out in a strange voice and weep. I felt she was trying to tell us about the pain she had and to tell us something else but she could not speak. Months and months went by, her body became very thin and she had sores on her back, legs and hips.

Keep Hoping my *Mak* would Recover

Papa never wanted to come close to her. He never helped with her care. He came home very late every night after work, thus I rarely saw him at night, only at lunchtime. *Lok Yey* told me, "He must have been with mistresses." My house was so empty and unhappy because everyone was sad and worried about my *Mak*. I used to share a bedroom with my parents because I was scared of ghosts. In my parents' room, there were two beds. One was for me and another one for my parents. I liked to have my own bed but I often fell asleep between my parents in their bed. Since *Mak* was now in another room, I shared the room with Papa, but now Papa came home very late at night. I had to go to bed by myself, lonely and afraid of ghosts.

Once I awoke in the middle of the night and saw a flashlight shining on my vagina. I realized it was my cousins, Un and Doeun, who had come into my bedroom. I heard them laugh and then they touched me. When I moved, the flashlight was turned off and my cousins ran out of the room. I wanted to kick them and cry out for my mother, but *Mak*, ill as she was, couldn't help me and Papa was never home to keep me safe. I had to live with it. As I was still a child, I fell back to sleep. In the morning, I pretended nothing had happened because I was too embarrassed to tell anyone about the incident. I hid it from my papa as I was afraid my cousins would get into terrible trouble because of me. All I could say to Phach was that I didn't like my cousins and didn't want them to live with me. I couldn't explain, couldn't tell the secret to Phach, not even when she said, "You don't like anybody. Nothing new." I couldn't pinch them or shout at them or they would have slapped me in the face or worse.

We did not know what would happen to *Mak* but we kept hoping she would recover one day. Because we were Buddhist, we believed in prayer and karma. We believed that prayers could help to release bad karma and help the patient survive. Every night, monks were invited to give prayers for *Mak*. Because we prayed every night, I learned the Buddhist Bible very well and I also learned more from my *Lok Yey*. One night when the monks did not show up, I wanted to try to give a prayer for my *Mak* near her bed. As she heard my voice, my *Mak* turned her head and looked at me. I didn't know why but I got goose bumps and was frightened. Then I ran away and bumped into my grandmother. I told her about my fear but she encouraged me to not be scared of my own mother.

I often would offer to help grind the betel leaves for *Lok Yey*. I loved being around her. I also would watch when she altered clothes. She taught me the Buddhist Bible and told me fairy tales. She advised me to be obedient, to love my parents and be a good girl. She taught me to believe in God. She taught me that the mother is the goddess. I still remember *Lok Yey* reminding me about a story of a God who told people that, before they offered food to the monks in the temple, they should first feed the goddess at home - the mother. She also taught me the five principles of Buddhism: do not steal, do not lie, do not drink, do not cheat, and do not kill animals. She made me believe in good karma and bad karma. With her, I learned to believe in forgiveness, patience, and compassion. Every night, *Lok Yey* and I cried together and prayed for my *Mak's* recovery.

The One who Dies will Save the Life of the Other One

In Cambodia, as in many other hot climates, many workers return home for the midday meal and follow it with a nap before they return to work. One day in April of 1960, during mid-day naptime, there were many cannon shots to alert all the citizens in Cambodia that something significant had happened. Papa woke up to listen to the radio and told us, "King Suramarit died; he has been sick many years."

I was worried that the noise had scared my *Mak* and ran to her bed to comfort her, "*Mak*! You will be fine; don't be scared." *Mak* opened her eyes and looked up at the ceiling.

Some days later, Papa came early to pick me up personally from school. I was very happy since I got to go home early without riding with my Grandaunt Houn. Papa's face was sad and his eyes red as if he had been crying. "What's wrong Papa?" I asked.

My Papa's voice quivered, "*Mak*'s dead."

I was stunned and confused. How could this be? I had convinced myself that since the King and my mother had both been sick at the same time and the King had died, that my *Mak* was supposed to be safe. My prayers had not been answered; I didn't know what to think. I was eight and I just heard that my mother was gone. What did this mean to me? I was unsure. I was afraid to ask Papa because he was so sad. Was I supposed to cry? Why were there no tears in my eyes? I had two parents, now I had one. Who was going to love me the way my *Mak* did? Who was going to look after me? Hundreds of questions rolled around my mind about what would happen next in my own life. I felt something had paralyzed my heart, but could not identify what it was.

When we arrived home, I saw white pennant-shaped flags, called 'white crocodile flags' outside the house, indicating that my *Mak* had really died. I ran to upstairs to see her. I stood at the bedside where her body was covered with a white sheet. I wanted to see her face for the last time, but I was scared. I still did not cry; I was stunned by the sudden loss of my mother. I just saw her this morning and said goodbye to her like I did every morning before going to school. Just a few hours after I left the house, she was gone. She did not wait until I came back home to say "Hi" again.

I felt like hundreds of eyes were staring at me wondering how I felt about her. Maybe they also felt pity for me? Next to me, my Cousin Phach was sobbing; her eyes were red and swollen. I still could not cry. I felt lost in the crowd. Suddenly, someone grabbed my arm and ordered me to bow to my *Mak*, asking for forgiveness for whatever bad things I had done to her. I was told to pray for her to be in Heaven with God, accordingly to Cambodian culture. Someone told me I would have to shave my head to show respect to *Mak*'s spirit since I was the first and only child in the family. In our culture, if there was a male child, he was expected to shave his head and be a monk for a day or so to show respect and forward good karma to the deceased parent. Since I was the only child in the family, it fell to me to shave my head, no matter that I was a girl. Being a girl, I could not be a monk anyway so I didn't understand why I had to shave my head.

Later, I was given a new white *sampot* with a simple white blouse. This is the attire for funerals in our culture. White symbolizes purity and cleanliness. No makeup or fragrance is to be worn during the funeral.

Unbelievably, some of Papa's step-brothers and step-sisters laughed at me, and said, "Hey, *Kaun aut mehr* (Orphan)! Hey, Baldy! Your life will now be miserable!" The mean names made me angry, sad and embarrassed but when they said my life would be miserable, it devastated me. As a child I couldn't come up with the words to make them understand my feelings. I knew his step-brothers and step-sisters never liked Papa. Their relationship was ugly and unfortunate for everyone, especially me. They resented the fact that Papa had a better life than they did and that they were dependent on him. They told me that my Papa was very mean to them and never liked their mother, Papa's stepmother. So, all the mean things they said and did to me were to show their anger with my father. They did not just hate Papa, they hated *Mak* too. They were jealous that Papa married a girl who had a better life than they did. They bad-mouthed my *Mak* every chance they got. All the hate and anger that started from the bad relationship between Papa and his stepmother contaminated every family member on my father's side. This problem was never resolved.

They said they hoped my Papa would be remarried soon so I wouldn't be special to him anymore. Some nice friends who cared about me felt compassion for me. They said it would have been better to lose the father than the mother. In their belief, the widower will be under the *sampot* of the new wife after getting remarried; but widowed women will never choose a new husband over their own children. This was a miserable and frightening time for me.

Losing *Mak* wasn't a Dream

My *Lok Yey* told me that keeping the body for three days represented the three Buddhist concepts of *Buddha*, *Dharma* (the teachings of Buddha), and *Sangha* (the brotherhood of monks). I heard but I really didn't understand. Cousin Phach told me that was why we burned three incense sticks next to the body. *Sangha* Monks were invited to give a blessing every morning and night.

During the funeral, I ran around playing hide and seek with the other children. I watched people busy in the house cooking and serving food. We had a lot of friends and family members who came to help us with food and keep us company. As we were running around and playing, all of a sudden, one girl began to cry and ran downstairs to my Auntie Leng, my Papa's sister. This was the second time in my childhood that I had seen my Auntie Leng. Suddenly, she appeared at the door of the room. "Why did you slap my granddaughter?" she hissed at me as she grabbed my arm, stopping me from running away. She held my arm tightly and slapped me hard across the face.

"You are a rotten spoiled brat. I will find someone to marry your father so you can be punished for your behavior," she continued, pointed her finger at my forehead as if she were putting a curse on me. This unfair accusation made me mad. As I tried to wiggle free of her grasp, she continued, "I will find a woman to marry your father who will beat you to teach you how to behave and not let you get away with your tricks. *Kdouy mehr mee kaun aut mehr*! You no longer have a mother to protect you. Your life is in my hands now. You will pay back what your mother did to us."

Even today, I cannot understand how an adult could have said this to a grieving child. At eight years old, I was embarrassed and frightened. Her horrible threat astonished even her granddaughter who stopped crying and watched this spectacle with an open mouth.

"What did my *Mak* do to you?" was all I could say. Then I spat at her and wriggled free of her grip. I dashed into my room and locked the door. Safely inside, I screamed, "Auntie, you are an ugly bitch, a horrible wicked bitch. I will tell my Papa on you!"

I huddled behind the door thinking I might have driven her away with my childish threat but, I was so wrong. Even louder than before, like a thunderstorm shaking the house, she stomped her feet and screamed, "You talk back to me? I am going to kill you so you can be with your mother!"

These last words pierced my heart. I found myself truly crying. I called *Mak* to come back to protect me. The realization that she was really gone came flooding in on me. I really had lost my *Mak*. It wasn't a dream. I wasn't going to wake up in bed between her and Papa and have her arms to comfort me. I sobbed very loudly.

"*Chao* (Granddaughter)! Do not cry. Your tears will hurt your *Mak*'s spirit and she won't be able to go to Heaven," my *Lok* Yey's gentle voice came softly through the door. "Dry your tears; your Papa needs you downstairs. He wants you to be in a picture with him next to your *Mak*'s casket."

"Is Auntie still waiting to kill me?" I asked.

"No, she's not here. Do not be afraid of her, she won't kill you; she was just mad at you for slapping her granddaughter."

"But I didn't slap her and Auntie wouldn't listen to me. She said horrible things to me and she wants me to join *Mak* in Heaven," I insisted.

"Don't worry, she is bitter, but she won't hurt you. She is full of words, nothing more. Open the door, she is gone," *Lok Yey* coaxed.

Slowly I opened the door and looked around to ensure that I was safe. I took my Grandmother's hand and went to sit by Papa who was waiting for me next to *Mak*'s casket. I huddled close to him, still looking around for my Auntie. When I saw her glaring at me from the other door, I was sure she was going to follow through on her promise to kill me. My mind was racing with fear and emotion, and I wasn't sure what I should do. She seemed to read my mind and raised her hand and scowled threateningly at me to let me know that if I told my father I would be in worse trouble. I never told and she never forgave me, not even when I desperately needed her help years later.

The Funeral

Three days and three nights quickly passed. At 2:00 PM on the fourth day, we moved *Mak*'s body for cremation at the Prolom temple, which was located near the Royal Palace. Many people and cars joined the funeral procession. My *Lok Yey* did not participate in the mourning ceremony; neither did she come to the temple, perhaps it was too difficult for her to bear the emotion.

I was told to wear the white outfit and hold a silver container filled with popped rice and small bills of currency tied with white thread. I was only eight but I knew that later my *Mak*'s body would be cremated and she would be gone forever. My heart was aching; I was frightened and bewildered. All my relatives were dressed in white *sampots* and white blouses with white scarves over their heads. There was one lady who was always devoted to my *Mak* and sacrificed to care for her, who also dressed in white, like my relatives. She held a bamboo basket containing candles, incense, cookware, silverware and food. These offerings were to be cremated with my *Mak*'s casket so that she would have everything she needed in the spirit life.

My Papa dressed in a white *sampot* called *chang kben*. Back in the Khmer Empire, women and men, regardless of social class, all wore *sampot chang kben*. During the reign of King Ang Doung and Prince Sihanook, *sampot chang kben* was used only for traditional occasions like weddings, funerals and when nobles entered the Royal Palace at the New Year to give blessings to the King. *Chang kben* is a piece of cloth about nine feet long and eighteen inches wide. Unlike daily *sampots*, *sampot chang kben* was rolled into a knot in the front with one end stretched away from the body and pulled between the legs to tie up on the back of the waist - held in place by a belt. Men used leather belts; women used 18K gold belts. The color of *sampot chang kben* varied from one occasion to another. For funerals, only white and black were used. For weddings, the color was whatever the groom and bride liked. However, on a special occasion like entering the Royal Palace to give blessings to the king, the color of *sampot chang kben* would be dependent on the day of the week.

My *Mak*'s coffin was placed on the car by four pallbearers – Phach's husband and three male cousins. All our relatives and guests walked behind the car while traditional Cambodian funeral music played loudly. I rode in a pedicab with an old lady I did not know. Her head was also shaved. I was told to pray as I threw the paper money and popped rice to the right side, then the left side of the road. Children followed me to pick up the money. Like the offerings in the bamboo basket, the money is to help the deceased in the afterlife. We also give money to the monks who will pray for the soul of the departed. I stopped throwing money as I heard the kids fighting over it and they quickly lost interest in following me.

The funeral procession walked to the Pralom temple, located a good distance from our house. When we arrived at the temple, I distributed the rest of the money to my little cousins, and prayed for *Mak* to go to Heaven. Phach, distraught with grief, took the basket containing all the foodstuffs from the devoted lady and put it in front of the casket. Before the cremation started, about ten monks came to surround *Mak*'s coffin for the last time and gave a blessing before pushing it into the crematorium. The coffin was opened to see *Mak* for the last time. Actually, we could not see her face because her body had been wrapped in a shroud from head to toe, based on our culture.

Now my tears flowed like a river. I sobbed and wailed to bring her back, "*Mak*! Wake up as soon as you can. I do not want you to get burned."

"Auntie, you are going away from me. I never can see you anymore!" Phach knelt down crying. Everybody cried from missing *Mak* so badly. But tears wouldn't stop the process. When the time came, the coffin was pushed inside and the gate was closed; we all dropped to our knees with sorrow and pain. My Papa was crying and looked at me with tears, as he shook his head to express his grief. Everyone cried and fell down on the floor. But soon, all the guests and distant relatives started to leave us, one after another.

We went back home with only a picture of *Mak*. We returned to the temple around five that evening to accept her ashes and carry them home in a silver urn. We came back home very sad. No one talked very much. My dearest *Mak*'s bed had been removed, and was replaced with the urn. We lit a candle next to it and invited the monks to give prayers every night during the seven-day mourning period. According to Buddhist principles, it is on the seventh day that the soul comes back and tries to go back into the body. We asked the monks to pray so that *Mak*'s soul would realize that she cannot come back because her body was gone and she was dead.

Mak's Ashes and her Picture

The seven-day funeral ceremony is very important in Cambodian culture. Papa organized this ceremony at our home. I helped to make gift boxes for the monks who were asked to pray for *Mak*'s spirit. Each box contained golden cloth for the monk's robe, sugar, a can of condensed milk, one tin of cocoa and one of tea, a box of Paracetamol (Tylenol), one container of Tiger balm, a can of fruit like Logan or jackfruit, candles and incense.

This time it was only my *Mak*'s ashes and her picture that a small family group carried to the Prayouvong temple, which was located near the Monument of Independence. The urn holding *Mak*'s ashes was to be permanently kept in a private cement stupa that was built during her illness. When we arrived, the monks prayed for *Mak*, then walked around the stupa seven times before depositing her ashes inside. Then, the stupa's door was permanently sealed. My *Mak*'s name was incised on the door with the dates of her birth and death. We brought home only her picture; she was gone for real and forever. Her photo was hung on the wall with a little shelf underneath. Cousin Phach filled up a container with rice to hold incense sticks and put it on the shelf. I was asked to light the incense every night in remembrance of *Mak*.

Our trip to Hong Kong never happened. I still had her passport, but it was worthless now. I was now an orphan girl.

~FIVE~

"LIKE FATHER, LIKE DAUGHTER"

It was just three months after *Mak's* death that my Papa shocked me with an announcement that turned my life upside down again. It was during the daily siesta; I was in his room, grooming his mustache with a tweezers.

"I need a housewife to take care of you and the house." These words surprised me but what he said next shocked me, "I have made a decision to get remarried."

"No!"

"What is wrong with you? You don't want someone to take care of you?"

"No!"

"I am lonely. I miss your *Mak*."

I threw the tweezers on his chest and ran out of the room to Grandma's bedroom. I found her napping and woke her, "*Lok Yey!*" I shook her body. "Wake up! Stop Papa thinking about getting a new wife," I cried.

"What has happened, *Chao?*" She removed the handkerchief from her face and opened up one eye slowly.

"Papa says he will get remarried." I sat on the bed next to her. *Lok Yey* needed me to help her get up. "Stop crying and talk. I cannot understand you." She shook my shoulder and patted my head, "Your Papa should wait for a year or so out of respect for his deceased wife."

I wrapped my arms around her and cried, "I am scared of a stepmother, *Lok Yey*. She will torture me." I remembered well what my Auntie Leng and her brothers had said at *Mak's* funeral.

Lok Yey began to cry with me, "If he gets remarried, I would have to leave you."

"No, *Lok* Yey! I am scared. Please stay to protect me!"

"Really, *Tiev* (Uncle in law in Chinese) will be remarried?" A soft voice asked, astonishment evident in the words.

"Mean Teacher - Bad Student"

We both looked up at Phach who just walked in to her room. She brought a bouquet of lotus for *Lok Yey*. "I heard you say *Tiev* will get remarried?" We both nodded our heads. "I won't stay with *Tiev* anymore if he gets remarried. I have been away from my house for a long time to come here and care for you and your mother. Now it is time for us to return to our own home." She wiped her tears with the back of her hand, "I love you so much, but also feel very sorry for you. I don't know what to do."

28

Lok Yey put her legs on the floor. She warned me, "There are big changes coming in your life and I encourage you to try to cope with a stepmother. Your Papa will change how he treats you just to please his new wife. Kim Houn (Papa's name) is short-tempered. You should watch how you behave."

At this point I was already scared to death of getting beaten by my Papa because of his impatience and short temper. A stepmother, who would hate me as Auntie had threatened, would make my life much worse. My grandmother's words confirmed my fears and made me worried and sad. "I am going to destroy the bamboo stick," I told them with the naivety of my eight years. They both laughed and shook their heads. "I will do it," I told them, sure that the problem would be solved.

They both laughed sadly again. "That won't stop the beatings. He will find a different stick," my cousin said.

"Mean teacher, Bad student," *Lok Yey* said.

"What do you mean? Who is the teacher, who is the student?" I stopped crying.

"Kim Houn is the teacher, you are the student," *Lok Yey* explained and smiled sadly again. "He is too tough with you. He disciplines you with beatings."

Phach pointed her finger at my head, "You think you can avoid punishment by hiding the stick? If you get caught, it will result in worse trouble." Phach sighed in frustration. "Beatings and the stick will scare you but won't change your heart. Such discipline will only give you new ideas about how to rebel against your Papa. This is what we mean."

I left *Lok Yey's* room, peeked into Papa's and found him asleep with his face to the wall. On tiptoe, I took the bamboo stick from its spot between the wall and wardrobe, quickly left the room with the stick hidden behind my back and ran back to Grandama's room, "*Lok Yey!* Please hide this for me and, if you can, break it!" She just shook her head at my stubbornness.

Next day, during the siesta again, I went to talk to Papa once more, "Will you stop loving me after you are remarried? Please don't get remarried, Papa. Everyone says that the stepmother never loves the stepchild. They say that you will always believe the stepmother over your own child."

"Don't be foolish. She will take care of you. You will be the apple of my eye forever. I am strong. I won't let her or anyone come between us." He caressed my hair and closed his eyes. I was also mad at him because I would lose my grandma and my cousin, but I wisely left that alone for the moment. I was about to leave when he said, "I will take you to get a permanent wave. Would you like that?"

"*Chah* (Yes)! I want it, Papa! I hate my shaved head. Everybody makes fun of my short hair."

"I will also ask your future stepmother to look for a pair of diamond earrings for you," he told me with a smile, "and we will order some dresses from your *Mak's* tailor."

"Really?" I was thrilled. I began to think having a stepmother might not bother me so much if I had curly hair, new dresses and diamond earrings. But, the warnings and advice of my grandmother and others were still ringing in my mind and all the gifts in the world couldn't take them away.

I am not a Cauliflower Head Girl

A lot of whispered speculation went around the house after Papa announced his marriage date. I was listening to a conversation between *Lok Yey* and Grandaunt Hieng. "The woman is a Chinese-Cambodian lady. They were introduced by one of his friends," *Lok Yey* said.

"*Chah*, her name is Chinese. I think her name is Siv Phek or Si Prek, not sure which," Grandaunt shook her head to disapprove of Papa's marriage. "She is twelve years younger than Kim Houn. She is tall for a Cambodian lady, skinny, and mature, in her forties," she continued.

Cousin Phach appeared in the room and sat with us. "Has your Papa taken you to meet her yet?" She asked me softly.

"*Chah*, I have met her once. She is quiet but she giggles a lot. She has a red mole on her right cheek and big, round, scary eyes. She looks like Dracula. I don't like her." I scratched my head. "But she has well shaped eyebrows."

"I feel sorry for you. I hope the stepmother will treat you right," Phach murmured.

"She will probably make lots of dresses for me," I said optimistically. "And Papa gave me a pair of diamond earrings, new dresses and also...."

"A permanent!" My cousin finished my sentence and we laughed. Then she grew serious, "But remember, your Papa doesn't want to hear any more whining and complaining. That is why he has given you these things. By the way, what does your Papa want you to call her?"

"*Eeh*!" I looked at Phach. "He says *Eeh* is an aunt in Chinese."

"You must try to get along with her," Phach patted my head, "Your *Eeh* ! Your new stepmother!"

I stayed quiet but I had already formed my opinion of stepmother. She was self-employed as a seamstress and was very thrifty, but I thought she was stingy. I remember her making a quilt using many scraps of cloth that another person would have discarded. When I looked at her, I felt anger because, in my childish logic, she was the cause of my *Mak*'s death. I blamed her for staying single waiting for my *Mak* to die, so she could marry my Papa.

Picture of Papa's wedding: from left to right: Papa, Stepmother and *Ah Char* (the priest)

The wedding ceremony approached. All our relatives and Papa's friends attended except my cousin Phach and *Lok Yey*, as they were offended that Papa had married so soon after my mother's death without observing a respectful mourning period.

I was happy at the wedding until my father's younger half-brothers made fun of my curly hair. "Hey, Cauliflower Head! Miss Negro with a cauliflower head," one of my *Pous* taunted. "How come you are born before Papa's marriage?"

I was mortified and stomped my foot, yelling, "I am not a Cauliflower Head. This is not my name and don't call me Miss Negro." They laughed harder at my reaction. Why were they saying this? It made no sense. I was neither a Cauliflower nor a Negro. Regardless, these words stayed in my head. I knew I was being mocked but I didn't know why. Later, I realized that my dark skin and short, curly hair, neither prized in Cambodian traditional culture, were the causes of their taunts.

Don't Put a Curse on Me!

A day before my stepmother moved in, Phach and *Lok Yey* moved out and my paternal grandparents Suy and his wife, Kong, my Papa's stepmother, moved in with their youngest son, Sunthary who was about my age. It was a sad and scary day for me. I called my grandpa *Lok Tah*. He never seemed to like me, my *Mak* or my Papa at all. Grandpa used to yell at me and call me a brat. He would say,

"A mean person like your Papa deserves a daughter like you. I hope you will be miserable with your stepmother."

"*Lok Tah*! Don't put a curse on me! Why do you hate me so much? I didn't do anything to you," I sassed him and ran off as quickly as I could before he grabbed his baton to swat me. I knew by talking back to him in this manner, he would hate me more, but I did it anyway.

When he heard my Papa punish me, *Lok Tah* instead of stopping him, encouraged him to spank me more and harder. He had a habit of making animal-like huffing sounds in his throat. These sounds, along with his constant criticism of me for being spoiled and pampered, contributed to my negative feelings about him. He would go on and on about how, if I had lived during the civil war, I would not have survived because I was too spoiled and stupid. He would then wish I had lived in that time so I would know how to behave differently. It was almost like a curse he was putting on me. He would say, "You have never been poor, you don't respect your elders, you don't understand poverty and suffering. You need to suffer to know what it was like and to have more sympathy for those that went through it." Some of Grandfather's words were prophetic but not all.

Picture of *Lok Tah* **in formal jacket called** *Av Kot*

Bamboo Walls and the Gold Coins

When *Lok Tah* told me I was a spoiled brat, I would wonder what I had done for him to dislike me so much. Had I done something as a small child for him to hate me? On good days, when he forgot about hating me, I made an effort to get close to him, chatting with him to entertain him. Attached to his room there was a little balcony and two columns that supported another balcony on the upper floor. He had a hammock there which he enjoyed and forbade me to touch. Consequently, of course, I swung in it all the time when he wasn't looking. One day, I watched as he slowly walked to his hammock. In a few minutes, he went back into his room and came out with his pipe and his religious book of *Theravada* Buddhist Scripture. Looking over his reading glasses, he noticed I was there, "Do you want to hear about how the Thai military played a trick to attack Lovek in 1594?"

I slowly backed away. "No, I do not want to," I said and, under my breath, I added, "Meany *Lok Tah*, what does that story have to do with anything?"

Grandpa shook out his pipe and put tobacco in it. Despite my negative response, he continued, "*Banteay* Lovek was not an easy place to conquer because the Cambodian King had planted bamboo around the city as a protective wall. As bamboo grew, it became very thick and compact and kept the invaders out. But the clever Thais threw gold coins into the bamboo bushes. Cambodian peasants discovered the gold coins and, in their search for more coins, they cut the bamboo until the protective wall was destroyed. Once the entire bamboo barrier was destroyed, it became easy to conquer the capital."

I took a step toward him. I covered my nose due to the tobacco smoke and asked, "Why are you telling me this story? I did not play a trick like the Thais."

"You wanted to trick me by playing in my hammock when I was inside. You didn't think I saw you, but I did. You are a brat." I still did not understand why my behavior had reminded him about those in 1594. Maybe it was because he disliked me as much as he disliked the Thais.

The Family Issues

It was very confusing but Papa shared a story with me that helped me understand some of the family issues. He told me, "When I moved to live on my own in Phnom Penh, my stepmother, your *Yey Kong*, expected me to support all of her children when they came to the city to be educated. Because I did not accept her command, my Papa, your *Lok Tah*, was angry with me and resented me. In my mind, I believed *Yey* Kong was the main cause of the problem, because she was jealous and greedy." I listened and nodded my head. "Another reason for the problems concerned my stepsister, Sithoeur, the fifth child, who was sent to live with me in Phnom Penh. Sithoeur was pretty and the favorite daughter in the family. She was the first daughter sent to the city for higher education. Your grandparents hoped that she would have a bright future like me. However, once she lived with our family, she never stopped complaining to your grandparents about me and your mother. She was never satisfied with the way she was treated at our house, as she expected more and more. She refused to help your cousin Phach around the house. She did not like to help babysit you. She said only a servant should be asked to do such things. She was jealous of Phach as she believed Phach was my favorite. Finally, I sent her home. This made your grandparents furious with me and your mother. In your grandparents' minds, your mother was the cause of Sithoeur leaving."

"Papa, please explain to *Lok Tah* about Auntie." I held his hand to beg him, "Maybe then they won't hate me."

"No, there is no point; they are not going to listen to me." I glanced at his feet and noticed he was rubbing them together nervously. "Because of all these issues, I became disrespectful to *Yey* Kong. I was angry at my Papa for marrying a stupid peasant woman."

"But Papa, why do they live here with us if they don't like us?"

"Because it is my responsibility to care for them in their old age; I am the eldest son."

Trying to control the situation, Papa told me to stay away from his parents and particularly from his stepmother. During this time, I was so confused and very lonely. First, my mother died, then *Lok Yey* and Cousin Phach left me, then my Papa got remarried, and now my Papa would punish me if he saw me be friendly with his stepmother. It was difficult. However, I still slipped away to visit *Yey* Kong every day to make friends with her but always before my Papa came back home at around 5 PM. She was not bad, as my Papa said, but she was nothing like Phach and *Lok Yey*, although she was also a betel chewer.

When I came downstairs to chat with *Yey* Kong, *Lok Tah* would chase me out of the house, because he believed that I also caused the trouble with his daughter, even though I had been a toddler when she had lived with us. I didn't even remember her. "Don't live in the past. Forget about it. I want to be close to you," I pleaded with him. "Don't say 'like father, like daughter'. I don't want to hear it anymore."

However, Grandpa, self-centered and stubborn as he was, never forgot and forgave. He kept mumbling as I passed by, "Like father, like daughter," just to irritate me.

Since I couldn't win with him, I tried to defend myself to my step-grandma, *Yey* Kong. One afternoon, when I found her sitting alone in the front yard under the jackfruit tree, I hurried over in hopes of a conversation. Usually, when I tried to trick her into a conversation, she laughed, spitting red saliva from chewing betel and areca nuts on me. Not this time. "Why does everyone hate Papa?" My question made her blush; I didn't know if it was from anger or shame.

"Your Papa is a screamer just like his grandfather, your great-grandfather Puth. You don't know that your great-grandfather was very abusive, like your Papa. He abused all the servants, called slaves at that time, who came to live under his roof. His voice could be heard about a hundred kilometers away." This was the first time I had heard such a thing and I was shocked; that was certainly very different from Papa's reasons for the discord.

"Liar," I said quickly, without thinking, but always ready to defend my father.

Yey Kong raised her hand, intending to strike me, but she stopped. "Your Papa also abused everybody in the family. He abused my daughter and my oldest son. Va got beaten very hard in front of your cousin Phach. He hates your Papa."

"But I heard he skipped school and didn't tell Papa the truth. I heard everyone knew he did it and they even made a joke about it, and said, *'Il est en vacance* – he is on vacation.' So his nickname was first *'vacance'* then it was shortened to 'Va' and now everyone calls him that." Her silence encouraged me to keep pushing her more. "Isn't it true?" Knowing I had outsmarted her, I kept pushing her, "How about me? Why do people in the family dislike me?"

"Because you always cried and told your Papa on people to get them into trouble. Your Papa always got even with whoever made you cry," she angrily said.

"I remember they were mean to me first. Every time they met me, they yelled and blamed me and wanted to hit me behind my Papa's back. I told Papa because I was scared. But, now I am a grown-up person. I'm nine years old! I want to be liked."

"Nine years old? You think you are old enough?"

"*Chah!*" I stuck out my tongue at her.

"You mistreat Sunthary very badly."

"Wrong."

"Everyone knows who you are. You make Sunthary cry all the time."

"Wrong!! We get along very well. We play together. But, he is just a crybaby and runs to you when ...." I paused, "I do not know what is wrong with him."

We stopped talking, as the conversation was getting testy. My grandparents still had their youngest son with them; he was my age. He was skinny and shorter than me at that time. My little *Pou* Sunthary was quiet and timid. He cried when he was mad; he cried when he was scared; he cried when he was sad. I used to tease him to make him cry more when I played with him. He was a mama's boy, but I grew to love him dearly.

Land of Gold – Broken Bamboo Wall

Grandpa's story of the bamboo walls and the gold coins of the Thai invaders was true. What I learned from history, like Grandpa, was the feeling of regret for my country and anger toward Thailand and Vietnam. We learned Cambodia had repeatedly been invaded by her neighbors. History showed us evidence that the Khmers were enslaved by the Thais. Obviously, I could see the successive Khmer capitals of *Angkor* (Holy city) and *Banteay* Longvek were subjected to terrible devastation. In these periods of devastation, the great sages and scholars were taken prisoner and sent to serve in the invaders' country. It was so painful to see all this tragedy that happened to my country.

I did not know how to analyze history at that time as I was young, but as I grew older, it seemed to me that the Khmer rulers were overly concerned with their superiority and pride. Once their pride was injured and their superiority in doubt, they ran for military assistance from foreign countries, usually neighboring Vietnam and Thailand, and got themselves into trouble. My teacher reminded the students: "We, the Khmer, originated from the *Sovanna Phum*, meaning the Golden Territory. In Chinese, it was called Founan. In Khmer legend, it was called *Nokor Kok Thlok* which reminds us that the land was rich in natural resources and gold. Many people were involved with gold trading. However, by the thirteenth century, the *Sovanna Phum* was conquered by Thailand. Foreign invasions of the Khmer territory were possible because Khmer leaders were stubbornly convinced of their own superiority, and failed to realize that the country was headed for disaster. Our historical lands shrunk because of incursions from Thailand and Vietnam."

This was the final elementary school history lesson, but I didn't pay much attention as I believed history to be the past and not relevant. Nothing could happen to our land again since we had learned the lesson. How wrong could someone be?

PART II

CAMBODIA UNDER THE REIGN OF PRINCE NORODOM SIHANOUK

Who is Prince Norodom Sihanouk?

We, Khmer people called him *Samdech* Sihanook. He is a son of King Suaramarit and Queen Sisowat KossaMak. After his father died in 1960, *Samdech* Sihanouk won a general election as *"Samdech Pra Mouk Raut"*, head of state of Cambodia. During this time, the Vietnam War was growing in Cambodia's neighbor to the east. The Prince's policies were to promote Cambodia's security and neutrality. Perhaps he should have built another Bamboo Wall, but one where no gold coins could be thrown inside by Thais or Vietnamese. Perhaps he knew the history of his ancestors too well, or perhaps he had not learned that lesson. However, in 1965, he agreed with communist China to allow the Viet Cong (North Vietnamese communists) to station soldiers in bases inside Cambodia. He then allowed the Chinese to resupply them, using Cambodia's Sihanouk Ville port.

Publicly, *Samdech* Sihanouk supported Maoist Marxism, and called the victory of communism in all of SE Asia a foregone conclusion. However, in 1966-67, *Samdech* Sihanouk's actions in Cambodia put him at odds with China, which at this time was at the height of its Cultural Revolution. His relationship with China collapsed and he was left with the North Vietnamese in Cambodia and the American armies at his door. Mao's influence was growing steadily in Cambodia among the poor and oppressed peasant classes. Cambodia's dark days were beginning.

~SIX~

PAPA'S DISCIPLINE

Under the reign of *Samdech* Sihanouk, Papa was elected to the Cambodian Congress for a two year term in 1963. Papa now wore a pin on the right side of his *Av Kot*, a Khmer traditional white jacket, to denote his new status. Our lifestyle changed; we were now classified as upper class, a distinction made by his position and growing wealth. Social status was very important at this time. Social interaction was dominated by close attention to class status. Indeed, a speaker must always be conscious of the social class of the person spoken to and address them accordingly.

Papa dressed in Khmer traditional jacket called *Av Kot*

Social status in Cambodia during *Samdech* Sihanouk's reign was classified as lower class, upper class and noble class. Lower classes were the people who were uneducated, such as farmers, laborers, blue-collar workers, servants, etc. as well as poorly paid public servants. Many of these people lived in the provinces.

People were considered upper class if they were highly educated such as doctors, pharmacists, and PhD's, or held a high rank in the military service, government, or business. Noble class was reserved for the royal family, royal relatives and those from old and very wealthy families. There were also many subtle distinctions in each of the classes. Wealth was an important distinction and Papa had become wealthy from his pharmaceutical business.

Papa's office was next to the Royal Palace in Phnom Penh. It was in a place called *Rot Sophear* (the National Assembly). He worked for *Samdech* Sihanouk and every day he dressed in a formal suit to meet with Generals and Prime ministers. He was a tall and imposing man; combining an air of authority, a booming voice and a bad temper. And yet, he had a soft heart, which yearned to help the people. Because of these traits, people either loved or hated him.

One Hundred Thieves

There is a Khmer adage, 'Raising a daughter is like raising one hundred thieves.' Papa would repeat this adage to me when he disapproved of something I did or did not do. Usually he was hitting me with a stick at the same time. When I entered puberty at twelve, Papa became more strict than usual. He was kind and indulgent to me most of the time but he also believed that sparing the rod would spoil the child and he disciplined me very harshly. He wanted to raise me as a traditional Cambodian woman and persuade me, with the discipline of the bamboo switch, to reject western influences. He believed if he did this, he could keep me away from boys and away from doing rebellious and embarrassing deeds. Traditional Cambodians did not allow their girls to go out at night, to go to parties or to accept the visits of male friends. Avoidance of humiliation in Cambodian culture was the first priority in social life. Shamed girls found it very hard to marry well and would be ostracized by their social class. The bending of the bamboo became more rigid as I grew older.

"Vicheara," came the booming voice from the living room. I began to tremble, not so much from fear as from anger. When he used this tone of voice, I knew I had done something he disapproved of and that he would greet me with bamboo switch in hand. Not again, I thought as I reluctantly made my way to the living room where he was standing as I expected. He seemed so big when he was in this mood. I slowly sat on the floor in the middle of the room. The beating was inevitable. My anger at him grew with each of his bellowed words.

"Remember this, raising a girl is like raising one hundred thieves," Papa screamed at me as the switch lashed across my back. I gritted my teeth as the next lash and the next found their marks. It stung and I could feel the warmth of the welts begin to rise beneath my thin blouse. "You will remember these words when you have children."

"No, I won't," I said under my breath but kept silent. I was being beaten just for telling him I had been chased by a group of guys, so, next time he would hear nothing from me. I was becoming angrier and angrier with each accusation. I played humble as the next verbal tirade began. I knew the louder he screamed, the more brutal would be the next barrage of lashes.

"Neighbors keep their eyes on the family who has a daughter," he roared. "They spread gossip that can cause humiliation to the girl's parents."

"I am more humiliated than you as everyone can hear you scream," I thought.

"Once that happens it is hard to undo the damage. Do you think of that before you do rebellious things?"

I did not answer but I wanted to scream back at him, 'Because you have damaged my reputation first with this screaming."

"You will not do this to our family. You will think before you act. You will think of the consequences." Now he had worked himself into a fury. Angry tears filled my eyes as the switch whistled through the air and assaulted my already throbbing back and arms. What he said went in one ear and out the other as my mind went to ways to get back at him. I wanted to punish him as he was punishing me.

"Parents must protect their daughters for the value of the family. We have to make sure our daughters don't sleep around, get pregnant before marriage, or choose a husband on their own. You think you can do as you please? You think you are smart enough to make the right decisions? You think you are smarter than me and you don't have to do as I order you? The stick will show you who is smarter."

I was sure all the neighbors, for many blocks, heard every word he said, he was so loud. Why did he have to scream? I wasn't deaf, just defiant. The last onslaught of lashes seemed less vicious or maybe I was numb with anger. I knew if I showed anger, the beating would continue, so I lowered my head and looked down at my folded hands, feigning humility. His lectures became a daily routine.

"A Woman is a Rose, a Man is a Bumblebee"

Papa hollered at me through the window one day when I was in the garden. Usually, I found it difficult to pay attention to what he said when he screamed it at me, but this time I couldn't help it, he was purposely embarrassing me. The neighbors could hear every word. I went into the house as quickly as I could to stop him from hollering anything else out the window. "Why do you embarrass me so much?" I asked when I entered the living room.

"To make you ashamed so you stop misbehaving."

I wanted to argue with him, to tell him if he loved me he wouldn't embarrass me like that. I wanted to tell him he was embarrassing himself as well, and that he was the one who was encouraging the hundred thieves by yelling out the window, but I knew I had better keep my mouth shut before he looked for the switch or worse, the leather strap.

"Where are your culottes?" He stood up in the middle of the living room.

I went to my room and came out rapidly with culottes in hand. Papa took them to the kitchen and burned then on the electric stove. I was furious and told myself I would get another pair and be sure he never saw them. Stepmother ran to the stove and grabbed the burning fabric and threw it on the concrete floor, "Are you crazy? You will burn down the house."

"Only prostitutes wear culottes. Are you a daughter of a high class family or not?" Papa shouted at me.

"*Chah!*" I responded, looking at my burned culottes. Who told him? It must be that old bitch - my stepmother. "But you didn't have to burn them," I said calmly.

"When you show all your meat, men think you invite them to taste it for free. After they enjoy it, they will laugh at you and go on to a new girl. Remember this proverb, 'A woman is a rose, a man is a bumblebee'."

Oh, *Mon Dieu* (My Lord)! He has too many stupid adages, it never ends. We go from the thieves to the rose, then to the bumblebee. I wanted to argue with him but, looking at the bamboo stick, I knew I should keep quiet. Frustration got the better part of good sense and I said, "I know the bumblebee flies from one flower to another, but what has that got to do with me?"

"Men are like bumblebees. They go from woman to woman like the bumblebee goes from flower to flower. Men cheat on their wives. I don't want you to be cheated by men. I want you to think about what you do. Men don't care about your feelings; to them you are just another flower. This is acceptable in our culture, so you, as the flower, must protect yourself. If you do not, your reputation will be lost. When your reputation is lost, you cannot get it back again. You not only embarrass and humiliate yourself; you also ruin the reputation of your entire family. I will not let you do that. Protect your flower," he ordered.

Hearing this made me resentful. It was not fair to allow husbands to have many mistresses, while women had to stay devoted to their husband and responsible for his welfare until death. I had an opinion but I couldn't say it out loud. I knew the bamboo switch was not far away.

"All men are the same. That is how it is in our culture. You will protect your flower from the bumblebees," his voice began to rise again, so I thought it better to let him believe he won.

"*Chah*, Papa," I answered and went to my room.

"Did you hear me?"

"*Chah!*"

In the end, all Papa's preaching and beatings had exactly the opposite effect he wanted. Rather than admiring and following the Cambodian culture, I admired western culture. I disliked Cambodian culture that restricted only the girls. It was so unfair that in the old tradition girls were not allowed to go to school since parents were afraid they would make connections with boys. Some parents believed that once the girls knew how to write, they would start to write love letters to boyfriends. My Cousin Phach was a good example of what happened to women. She barely knew how to write in Cambodian. As she grew up, she was very upset with Papa because he did not allow her to go to school like his stepbrothers and sisters. As a result of not being educated, Phach was naïve, afraid and passive.

I particularly disliked the concept that laughing aloud by men was fine, but unacceptable for women. Girls were to laugh gently with one hand covering their mouth. They were to walk gracefully and silently. If girls acted like men, they would be called monsters, and bring no luck to the family.

I Was just Medium Wild

My father announced his decision about my continued education after I finished elementary school, "I have talked with your Grandaunty Houn about finding a good college for you. You will attend Preah Norodom College."

I was out of elementary school. I felt like I was a person now, like I had just been released from prison. College (high school in the U.S.) would change my life. Never again would I have to sit by my Grandaunty like a stick and obey her rules. However, I was already becoming arrogant because of my father's rank in society as a member of Congress, so I was sure I deserved the best.

Preah Norodom was a top ranked College in Phnom Penh for girls only; most of the professors were women. Most of the high class and royal families sent their daughters to this College because the professors were wives of wealthy husbands, the curriculum had higher standards compared to other schools in the city, and the school discipline was supposed to be very strict. There were also some bad rumors about girls in this school. Did Papa know about it? Perhaps not. I knew but I certainly wasn't going to tell him.

One of my male cousins, Leat, step-brother of Dr. Thor, questioned Papa's choice of Preah Norodom College. "Do you believe you can keep Vicheara away from boys? Is that your main concern?"

"I do the best I can," he responded.

Hearing this was exciting but also scary as I wanted to be wild but just, maybe, medium wild. I laughed as though he was making a joke and continued to listen, "Those girls aren't ashamed of teasing men." He laughed and I laughed with him but Papa was silent.

"You are happy to hear it, heh?" Cousin Leat asked me.

"No." I stopped laughing.

"Cover up your mouth when you are laughing. Don't make a sound like a thunderstorm. This is not the way you were raised," Papa scolded me. He didn't know the way he embarrassed me in front of this young man would make me more resentful and rebellious.

Leat continued to worry Papa, "Look at Vicheara! The way she dresses and acts. She is westernized. Don't you see it? I hate to tell you this. Girls in this school jump over the fence to meet guys and go to the theatre together instead of staying in class. They skip classes. They are wild, crazy like female horses. Do you know the Capitol Theatre behind the College or the Lux Theatre at the corner? These two places are where the girls meet their boyfriends."

Papa said nothing; I worried for a while that he would find another school but he didn't.

Indeed, all girls in the College showed good behavior in front of the female teachers, but behind their backs, some behaved very poorly, used bad words, and teased male professors. Not that there were many male professors working in this College, only two among forty to fifty female professors. No male teacher lasted more than three months teaching any class and I could understand why. We made one of new male teachers cry and resign and he never wanted to show his face again. I heard one girl in my class use a sexual term to intimidate a male professor during class. Next recess he was gone.

"Drop by Drop will Fill the *Bampong*" and "Don't Tell the Fountain that you won't Drink its Water"

We discovered the best time to get away with something was during the sewing period while the Vietnamese teacher, *Kò* Yeo, was focused on assisting students who were serious and came to her desk asking questions. Once the desk became crowded, *Kò* Yeo didn't notice the disappearance of other students. In those moments, some girls pretended to go to the restroom and never came back, others jumped out the window and then climbed up the fence to go on a date in the movie theatre or go to the market - exactly as cousin Leat had warned Papa. But, I was not a crazy female horse. Never!

I watched the girls going off on these adventures, but I felt that I could not. I did not want to betray Papa's trust. I took the sewing class seriously because my stepmother, with whom I had a very difficult relationship, was an accomplished seamstress and I wanted to be as good as she was or better. I wanted to learn as much as I could from my teacher but every time I asked for her opinion on what I had done, she would change my design and ask me to redo it.

The proverb, "Drop by drop will fill the *bampong* (bamboo container used to collect palm juice)" encouraged me to be patient with her. However, each time she disparaged my design and asked me to redo it, I got more and more discouraged and became careless about learning. I would never have the patience to wait until my *bampong* was filled up. I began to dislike the class and decided I would do exactly what the other girls did during the sewing period. "I don't care. I don't want to learn sewing anyway and I will never need it," I mumbled to myself in frustration. A response from behind me came in French, "*Ne pas dire que fontaine je ne boirai pas ton eau* – Do not tell the fountain that you won't drink its water." I turned around and smiled at my friend. She then said "Remember this adage; you may need this sewing skill in the future." How was I to know her words were prophetic?

Satisfying and Hilarious Revenge

In Cambodia, men and women wear long skirts called *sarongs* at home. A woman's *sarong* is called *"sarong batik"*, and is made with beautifully colored prints of flowers or sometimes animals. Men usually wear a sarong printed in small squares of different colors, but sometimes men wore *sarong batik* as well. My Papa usually wore a silk *sarong*; this was common for his status. A *sarong* is wrapped around the body and tied at the waist.

Because my cousin Or wore a *sarong*, it was easy for me to tease him. One day, I extended my leg underneath the dining table so my toes could reach his *sarong*. I gripped it tightly between my toes waiting for him to get up. As I wished, he got up, carrying a bowl of soup in both hands. My hold on his *sarong* caused it to drop off in front of my parents. He was the only one who knew why it had happened. After everybody left the table, he warned me to not do it again; otherwise he will be walking naked in front of me. "I won't be scared to look at it if you want me to see it," I said, sticking my tongue out at him.

It was harder to do mean things to my stepmother. The only thing I could do to assuage my anger was to unlock and look at everything in her bedroom when I found her misplaced keys. I went through her closet and sprayed her perfume; I ate the delicious desserts she hid in the fridge; I opened up her jewelry box. Sometimes when I was very angry at her, I poured out her perfume into my bottle and filled hers up with water. She never noticed the difference or if she did, she wouldn't give me the satisfaction of knowing it bothered her.

~SEVEN~

VISITING ANGKOR WAT

One weekend in April 1965, before the Cambodian New Year, Papa surprised us with the news that he was going to take us to visit Angkor Wat. I was so happy; I had been waiting so long to see this famous ancient temple. We rose early for the drive to Siem Reap province.

The Story of Battambang Province

It was interesting to hear this story again while driving to Siem Reap. I had heard it over and over since my childhood, but, this time Papa explained in more detail. "Battambang province has a strong agricultural economy and produces tremendous amounts of rice. It also produces many fruits and vegetables. It is a rich province. Many ancient temples used to be in this area, some still exist, but many others have almost completely disappeared. Centuries ago, this province was invaded by Siam, causing much loss of life and forcing the Khmer people to lose their property. The Thais forced them to abandon Khmer culture, clothing, speaking, and writing. It wasn't until the end of World War II that Battambang province was returned to Cambodia by the French Government. Before leaving, the Thais grabbed everything of value from Battambang."

This interested me and I intently listened, but I was also thinking about a special mango that I had heard of, "I cannot wait to eat *Svay ktis* at Battambang. What does it look like, Papa?"

"Silly girl. Why do you want to eat it when you don't know what it is?"

"I know it's a mango that looks green outside but is crispy and juicy on the inside. It is medium sweet with a flavor of coconut milk."

"It doesn't sound good to me. I don't want it."

At the very last minute, Papa changed the route we would take, "I will go to Siem Reap by crossing the *Tonlé Sap*. I am hungry for crispy prawn cakes."

Papa drove to *Prek (lake)* Kdam Ferry, in Kompong Loung District, of Kandal province. As we waited for the ferry boat to cross the *Tonlé Sap*, Papa bought us deep-fried, crispy prawn cakes. They are a specialty of the *Prek* Kdam area. Dipped in a sauce made with lemon, salt, and pepper, they are crunchy and delicious but can be treacherous because the shells are not removed.

He poked *Eeh*, "Hey, sit like a monk, do you want a prawn cake?" She slapped away his hand. "I know why you don't want any," Papa poked her again. "You have false teeth and you can't chew them."

"Stop poking me, it hurts," she snapped, becoming angry.

"Ouch, the prawn bit my tongue." Papa laughed and handed me the rest of the prawn cakes.

Le Grand Hotel

Mid afternoon, Papa pulled the car into the driveway of the biggest hotel in Siem Reap province. "We are staying at the Le Grand Hotel. This is the most luxurious hotel in Siem Reap and we will be treated like royalty. I know you like French food, which is why I brought you to this hotel. Also, it's close to the main gate of Angkor Wat."

I saw a three story, elegant building, by far the tallest and grandest building in the heart of Siem Reap. Many bellmen were waiting to welcome the guests; before Papa could even turn off the engine, they opened our car doors and began unloading our luggage. They then led us to the lobby to check in. I turned around to look at the large, immaculately landscaped garden in front of the hotel with its colorful flowers and green trees manicured into many shapes. It was breathtaking. Walking into the lobby of the hotel, we were instantly cooled and our sweat-soaked clothes dried by the air-conditioning. Papa was right. Now I felt like I was in the Royal Palace. Papa stood up straight with a great smile, posing like a king. "You don't look like a King at all." I teased him.

After Papa had checked in, a bellman led us down a long, photograph-lined corridor. The photographs were of Apsara dancers and the famous Angkor Wat temples. Western style pots were filled with fresh flowers and lush tropical plants stood on the floor. You could see the French influence in the décor everywhere you looked. As I was about to insert the key to my own room, Papa called me, "Don't unpack yet, just freshen up and we will go see the market first."

In the small nearby market, wicker crafts, hand-woven cotton scarves, and *sampots* of pure silk were all piled up on the shelves. Large and small Khmer carvings of Buddha and of Apsara dancers were available in both stone and wood. There was so much variety in Khmer handicrafts; I couldn't decide which one to pick. In the big market, they sold dried fish and prawns, as well as fruit and vegetables. Siem Reap was the place to be if you were in the mood to taste exotic tropical fruit such as durian, mangoosteen, rambootan and lychee. There were many vendors selling street food – all kinds of cakes and sweets but we returned to the hotel for dinner. Many young women about my age called out to us to buy their products but I paid little attention to them as I thought most street food was dirty and disgusting. I barely looked at these young street vendors and if I had given them any thought, which I didn't, I would have felt we lived in different worlds. Years later, the next time I saw Angkor Wat, I would remember this day and those young street vendors.

Everything Looked Unfamiliar except Watercress

At dinner we were seated by the window giving us a view of the swimming pool, where bikini-clad girls strolled around holding glasses of wine or chatted with their lovers. Children laughed and squealed as they splashed in the pool. In the middle of our table sat a silver tray in classic Khmer style, holding a little red candle. Everything seemed so elegant and even romantic. Papa was looking at the menu, turning the pages slowly, searching the wine selection. *Eeh* sat like a statue, staring first at me, then the people around her.

"Do you want me to order for you?" Papa asked her.

"There are too many selections and I don't know what these things are," she replied as she continued to look at the other patrons.

"I will order *Blanquette de veau*. It is a famous French dish of veal and vegetables. "How about you?" he asked me, while I was turning pages one after another looking for something I recognized. I looked up and saw a waiter in his crisp white uniform staring down at me, waiting for my response. The room seemed to go silent as all eyes turned to me. I was beginning to feel as uncomfortable as Stepmother did, but I was not going to admit it. I would appear more knowledgeable. I closed the menu, put my hands on my lap, looked up at the waiter and triumphantly announced, "I'll have the watercress!" Silence. I cringed as I saw puzzled looks on nearby faces.

"You will need meat to go with that," Papa tried to help me.

"No, I love watercress," I insisted and looked back at the hovering waiter and repeated, "I'll have the watercress." The waiter looked at me quizzically and reluctantly wrote down our order, repeating it as he wrote, "One glass of red wine, two orders of *Blanquette de veau*, and," he paused, "one order of watercress." I tilted my chin high, and turned my head back to my table, dismissing him.

When the dishes were served and a plate of plain watercress with vinegar, pepper and salt was set in front of me, I did my best to hide my disappointment. "Are you sure you want just watercress?" Papa asked again. I looked up to see if the waiter had left, unfortunately, he was still there, staring at me.

"*Chah*. I am fine. This is exactly what I wanted. I have been craving watercress all day," I smiled at him. I wanted the waiter to know I was not stupid and I had ordered exactly what I wanted. I ate all my watercress. My pride had made a real fool of me.

Pyramid

In the morning, Papa drove us to Angkor Wat. I was thrilled to finally see the most famous temple in Cambodia. Along the street, large flowering *romdoul* trees provided both shade and fragrance. *Romdoul* is an exotic Asian fragrance that legend says will make you fall in love with Angkor Wat so you will never want to leave. The fragrance of the *romdoul* flower lingers even after it is dried. I felt the spirit of the ancient Khmer Angkorians all around us urging us to treasure Angkor Wat.

Papa parked and we walked into the main entrance where a very skinny and short tour guide started his work by slowly speaking in Cambodian mixed with French. "As everyone knows, the meaning of Siem Reap is 'a defeat of Siam or Thais' and everyone knows why we named it that," he began.

"*Chah*, everyone knows that by heart," I impatiently agreed.

He continued, "This name refers to a victory of the Khmer Empire over the Thai army of Ayutthaya in the seventh century. Angkor Wat was built by a Cambodian King, Suryavarman II, as his tomb in the twelfth century. The main entrance faces west," the guide turned to the west, "to the setting sun, the symbol of death, whereas temples like Angkor Thom, Bantey Srey, and others have their main entrance to the east," the guide turned to the east, "where the sun rises. In those days, the Khmer Empire worshipped Hindu gods." I opened my eyes wide with surprise. Now that was news to me.

The guide wiped his face with a small pink handkerchief. I smirked at him wondering why a man would use a pink handkerchief. He caught my look and volunteered, "My girlfriend gave it to me." He continued, "Many of the bas reliefs in Angkor Wat show the Hindu gods Shiva and Vishnu."

We all walked to the next gallery. I walked in front of him, as I was impatient with the slow pace of his presentation. I noticed the carvings of Apsara dancers on the walls and stopped for a closer view. "They are beautifully carved. You will notice that they are all bare-breasted and wearing heavy jewelry," the tour guide said. "That was common among all classes from the peasant to the royal family, even the queen."

"Their costumes look similar to Thai's," I commented.

"Originally, it was believed that classical Khmer dance and costumes had been influenced by Thai classical dance. Ultimately, it was found to be the other way around. Classical Thai dancing descended from Khmer dance of the Angkor period after Ayuthaya sacked *Angkor* and adopted its traditions," the man explained. "They also worshipped '*Linga*' – the male reproductive organ and '*Yoni*' – the female reproductive organ."

He took a break to allow us to burn candles and wish for prosperity, happiness, health and great fortune at the *linga* and *yoni* sculptures.

"Papa, what do you wish for?"

"I wish you would stop being so stubborn and mouthy."

"Do you want to know what I wish for?"

"No." Papa glared at me.

"I wish you would stop being so stubborn and mouthy," I sassed him, but then I laughed and whispered in his ear, "Papa, these are just pieces of stone. Why would anyone worship a piece of stone?"

"I don't know. I just ..." He didn't finish as he noticed the guide watching us. The tour guide also showed us a bas-relief of daily life with women trading in the market and another of the war with Thailand during King Suryavarman II's reign. It was explained that the Khmer Empire had gone through many invasions by the Thais before *Angkor* was abandoned in the jungle.

"You see," the man pointed at the headless Buddhas, "All of the heads of the Buddhas were stolen by Siam during the defeat of *Angkor*." He swatted at a fly trying to sit on his nose. "However, some of them were returned and kept in the French museum during the colonial period."

Papa teased him, "There's another fly on your nose. It must be a female fly." Papa made people around him laugh.

"Are we done now? I want to climb up the pyramid."

"You can go." Papa gave me permission to leave.

Pyramid at Angkor Wat

When I got to the pyramid, I looked up at the many steps leading to the phallic shaped temple at the top with its yawning, inviting door. The steps were small and so narrow I could fit only half my foot on each and there were no handrails. Half-way up, I looked down and became frightened at the steepness of the steps. My heart began wildly beating and I was thinking of going back down when I saw Papa watching me. Somehow, knowing he was watching me gave me the strength to continue climbing. When I reached the top, I breathlessly looked around and gasped at the magnificence spread out below me. I had a panoramic view of the entire Siem Reap province. A proud, godlike, transcendental feeling filled me as I looked over the land. When I looked down I saw Papa looking up at me. I waved, letting him know I had made it. I was so filled with awe that I was reluctant to descend. I looked down the steps and had a dizzy feeling of tipping and tumbling, bouncing and sliding down every single step uncontrollably. I looked around and noticed everyone crawling down backwards like turtles and decided this was probably a good idea. Stepmother and Papa were waiting for me when I finally put my feet on the ground. I decided not to climb any more pyramids.

Famous Traditional Dances

I bought a bamboo flute as a souvenir of Siem Reap from a persistent young child who followed me around and begged me to buy it. The thing that surprised me the most at Angkor Wat was that the village boys and girls could urge us to buy their goods in many languages – French, English, and Russian. We stopped and watched another group of Cambodian folk dancers. It was a *Robam* (dance performance) *Kap* (kill) *Krabei* (Buffalo) *Pheok* (drink) *Sra* (liquor). The whole meaning was a Buffalo Sacrifice Dance which was performed during the New Year. I did not like to watch this dance as it looked violent to me when the dancers were pretending to kill the buffalo and drink alcohol. They used some kind of buffalo horn covered with a cloth to represent the buffalo itself during the performance. This folk dance originated from the hill tribe people of Ratanakiri province in northeastern Cambodia. The dancers were all males dressed in tribal outfits. Drums were played very loudly as they "killed the buffalo" and symbolically drank its blood mixed with liquor.

"Uh! It is cruel. I don't like it," I stepped out from the crowd.

By then, my parents were tired and wanted to go back and take a rest at the hotel. We decided to visit Angkor Thom the next morning. I couldn't wait to see the next temple. I prayed Papa would not miss Bantey Srey, but he did, which made me crazy. "We are born here, we can come back next trip anytime. Your country never runs away." These were his words as he got in the car, after deciding not to visit what we had missed. What a pain!

I missed Angkor Wat and wished to go back to visit Bantey Srey. However, there is a superstition in Cambodia that if one plans to visit Angkor Wat, you will never make it; the visit has to be spontaneous. I brought home my bamboo flute, a wicker purse and *romdoul* flowers.

I was feeling sorry for myself since Papa didn't visit Bantey Srey, but I realized how unimportant such events were when we pulled up at our house and were met by a tearful Cousin Phach. Fear gripped my heart and I ran to hug her also ask what was wrong. In a choked and trembling voice, with tears streaming down her cheeks, she told us, *"Lok Yey* is dead."

Her voice was just like Papa's when he came to pick me up at school to tell me my mother had died. Memories flooded my heart. My beloved Grandma Sem was gone. She had loved me and protected me. She had been my rock when *Mak* left me. Now she was gone too? I felt a physical pain in my heart; how could it be that I continued to lose the people I loved the most?

"When, how, and where?" Papa and I asked at the same time. Grandma Sem had been diagnosed with mouth cancer earlier in the year, probably caused by years of betel chewing. She had gone back to her natal village after the diagnosis.

"A few days ago in the village; she wished to die there."

"Oh Papa, we have not visited *Lok Yey* for a long time!?"

"Yes, I have been busy." That was his excuse but Papa and Grandma had been estranged ever since his marriage so soon after my *Mak*'s death.

To pay our respect to *Lok Yey*, my beloved grandma and Papa's former mother-in-law, we went to see her grave later in Kratié province.

~EIGHT~

RENEGADE BAMBOO

Papa was re-elected to the Cambodian Congress for a second two-year term in around 1965. He also continued in his job in the pharmaceutical plant, SOKEPH. Later, he was promoted to President/ Director General of this well-known company. He owned the company later when his friend, S.E. Phlek, Phoeun, retired. However, I never heard that from him because he kept his business secret as he tried to protect his assets from *Eeh*. He also believed that if I knew how wealthy he was, I might develop a superior attitude. However, my attitude was already a problem for him. I was a bamboo that had not bent in the direction he wanted.

Westernized

I was very independent, fashionable, westernized, rebellious, and stubborn and that made Papa very frustrated as it was completely opposite of the way he wanted me to be. I disagreed with him about everything. It looked like I listened to him, but behind his back I did anything I wanted to that I knew I could get away with. I had a good heart inside but could act very rude and cold outside, just like Papa. I had a lot of pride and was prejudiced, just like Papa. I was very emotional and short-tempered like Papa. When I became angry, I behaved badly. I lost respect for anybody who made me mad and I held grudges. I never forgot a slight. I had no idea what the universe was getting ready to teach me.

After graduating from secondary school with good grades, I hoped to continue my education with medical school in Paris. However, the idea of sending me to Paris was unthinkable to Papa. I was very unhappy that he did not agree with me and I tried in many ways to convince him to allow me to go to France. I could not tell him the truth – how much I wanted to get away from him and step-mother. However, Papa was way smarter than I imagined.

"You will do stupid things when you are away from me. I know you. I have enough frustration because of you right now. When you are away from me it will like the old adage: while the cat's away, the mouse will play."

"Like what, Papa?"

"Don't you know that a lot of children turn wild when their parents send them to Paris? Girls, instead of concentrating on their education, learn to be westernized and act like prostitutes. It is very shameful!"

"Papa, I won't be that kind of girl, I promise you."

"OK, show me from now on that you listen to me. Attend pharmacy school at the University of Phnom Penh for the first year program and I will send you to Paris the following year."

There was nothing I could do so I bit my lip to silence myself. I forced myself to do what he expected, even though I hated chemistry. Studying chemistry was just like sticking my finger in boiling water. I entered the pre-pharmacy program in the pharmacy school at the University of Phnom Penh as Papa arranged. Papa knew I was unhappy with his decision and he softened my disappointment by buying me a car a couple of months later.

It Is not a Fake Stomachache this Time

While I was seventeen years old and in pharmacy school, I had a high temperature and a lot of pain low on the right side of my belly. I felt weak and was in such great pain that I couldn't walk straight.

Immediately, Papa took me to the Aurore Clinic owned by my cousin Thor, where I was diagnosed with appendicitis that would require immediate surgery. Papa stayed with me until we were at the door of the operating room; I went in alone with no idea of what to expect.

"You are brave! You are brave and smart…..you will be fine….."A man in the room comforted me just as Papa had when I was young. I waved at Papa and then I was asleep. When I woke up, I found myself alone in a very small room. I was so thirsty, in pain with a catheter and a tube through my nose. An IV line was in my left hand. To get someone's attention, I decided to throw a sack of ice at the door. Suddenly, the door was opened and I saw the smile of my cousin Peach, a daughter of my first uncle Than, on my mom's side. She gave me an ice cube instead of water.

"Where is Papa?" I asked.

"He just stepped out of the room before you woke up."

"How about *Eeh*?"

"Never saw her."

Three days later, I was recovered enough to go home. During those three days, Papa stopped by only one time to visit me and he didn't stay long. He gave me a strange feeling. Why did he act like that? What could *Eeh* have said about me now? Did he no longer love me because of her? Papa picked me up from the hospital. In the car, I reminded him that the doctor had said to eat only light food, like mashed potatoes and spaghetti, for a couple of weeks until my recovery was complete.

"Tell her (*Eeh*) to make for you."

"It is best to have you tell her for me." He nodded his head.

At my first lunch at home, I was looking forward to the new menu and expected my stepmother would follow the doctor's instructions. Unfortunately, the smell of food was familiar to me; I could tell it was greasy deep fried fish as usual and sweet and sour soup. Where are the potatoes and spaghetti? She had nothing else to offer and there was no explanation. Maybe Papa never told her?

At the table, she was oddly quiet, as was Papa. What a mess this was. I wondered if I was the cause. As I pulled out my chair, she forestalled any comments from me by started in on me, "Walk like a normal person. Stop spoiling yourself. You want a lot of pity from people."

I wanted to ask why she didn't follow the doctor's recommendation but I dealt with her criticism first. "Don't you know I have an incision? I feel tight and it hurts," I tried to explain my condition, hoping she would be concerned for me.

"It doesn't hurt that much. You create the pain."

"No, it really hurts." I said.

Cousin Or didn't ask me anything. Papa didn't say a word. Everyone seemed distracted and I was obviously the least of their worries. What was going on? I stayed home for another week before I went back to school. Friends at school were more concerned about my surgery than my family.

Papa is a Bumblebee Himself

One evening soon after my surgery, I had a remarkable conversation with *Eeh* after dinnertime without the presence of Or. I was very surprised to hear her say, "Vicheara, I heard a rumor from one of your Papa's staff saying that he has a mistress. He has had her for a long time. She knows he has a wife, but I never knew about her."

I was taken aback and didn't know what to say. Was this the cause of all the silence and coldness in the house?

"Where does she live?" I asked, trying to keep her talking but not really knowing where to go with the information that my Papa was cheating on her.

"She lives in the north of the city, with her father who is very poor. I was told your Papa sent his clothes to represent him during their wedding."

At that time in Cambodia, many high class men had mistresses. They would have a commitment ceremony which was not a legal marriage but which satisfied the woman's family.

"What do you mean?"

"I mean your Papa was not physically there during his wedding ceremony. He only came for the honeymoon."

"How can Papa do that?"

"It is common with high class people to avoid the loss of their reputations."

"I am mad at Papa; he shouldn't cheat on you like that. Papa is a bumblebee himself!!"

"I was told that your Papa wanted to marry this woman for children since I could not get pregnant."

"Really?" It was big news to me that my Papa wanted more children. I felt a cold spot in my chest.

"I have never been happy with your Papa. He never gives me extra money, just enough for the food."

"It does not seem to me you need it because Papa buys everything. Look at all the food in storage, the household supplies and much more - from small things to big things, including clothing and fabric." I tried to defend my Papa but my mind was whirling.

"I should be in charge of his accounts. I am his wife. I never know how much money he has, including his income. I feel he uses me to babysit you and everybody else, like your grandparents." She blew her nose and wiped her tears with a napkin, "I've never felt that he loves me as a wife." I waited for her to continue. "Do you remember a young woman who came here crying, and reporting to your Papa that her house had burned down?"

"Oh! She was young and pretty, came in with an old man."

"The old man is her father. She is the mistress."

"No wonder Papa rushed them out of the house quickly without giving them a chance to explain anything; he was afraid you would discover his true face," I said.

"I am angry with your father. He should not do this to me." Then she said, "I want to see you happy with a man you love." I trusted my instinct and kept quiet; she was not on my side. "Do you have a boyfriend?" She pushed me to confide in her. "Your Papa is bad when he is mad. He shouldn't stop you from loving a man, because you are old enough to get married. I feel sorry for you."

She got up and walked to her room and I went to mine, to study and to think about this conversation. What did this information mean for my life? I felt weird with this confidence from her.

I Choose a Husband on my Own

I had a first date with one of my classmates, Leang. He was the oldest son of a business family; unfortunately, not the rich family that my Papa was planning for me. His parents originated from Kompong Cham. His father was an entrepreneur; not a famous or wealthy man. He was self-employed, but he made enough money to support his family. My father would classify him as lower class, because he was neither employed by the government nor a professional. In our society, at that time, his son was a completely inappropriate suitor for me.

Leang was the eldest son with six siblings, three boys and three girls. Both younger girls were very mouthy and spoiled. Leang was a little taller than I was, with soft brown eyes and full lips, very kissable lips, I thought every time I saw him. He was slender but strong, and had beautiful soft hair. He was not an exceptionally good-looking man but it was his personality I was attracted to, not his looks. He was gentle and kind. He was a great listener, and he made me feel like the most important person in the world.

Their house was two stories but not big like our house. There were no servants, only one adopted girl who worked as a servant. My boyfriend's father was a handsome man, strong, opinionated, skillful, dominant and smart. His mother was small and skinny, talkative and sweet but a nag. She spoke very slowly and could be very sneaky and tricky.

I met my boyfriend every single day; we sat next to each other in the classroom as well as outside when we studied in-group. We went out a lot to restaurants for lunch when we did not have class. Over time, we fell in love. He wanted to marry me but I knew that it would be a big problem. My Papa not only wouldn't think the family was acceptable but wouldn't agree because he wanted me to graduate first. I told Leang, "Papa had taught me to have the man come to Papa first, asking for the marriage through the parents." I leaned on his chest to allow his kiss on my hair.

"I won't give up; I will challenge your Papa and show my honesty, loyalty and my true love for you. And I will ask my parents for permission for us to marry."

Everybody in the pharmacy program called us "Male and Female Pigeon." This meant "Love Story" in Cambodian culture. Since the school was small, it didn't take long before "Male and Female Pigeon" was heard by Papa because all the pharmacy professors knew my Papa, as he was a president of a famous pharmaceutical company.

I will Disown You

When we went out to have meals together, we took my car since my boyfriend rode a motorcycle. We crossed paths with Papa all the time but for quite a while we were fortunate that he did not pay attention to my car. That all ended the day we were caught by Papa when we were walking along the market street looking for shoes. I saw Papa's car first, driving toward me. Immediately, I pushed my boyfriend away and dashed into the shoe store. I felt miserable hiding there, pretending like I was looking for shoes. My boyfriend innocently followed me and asked, "Why did you push me away?"

"I saw Papa. He must have seen us before I escaped into the store."

"Uh! We are in trouble."

"Just wait and see if he beats me when I get home."

"*Aun*, let me know right away if he does so. I will elope you if he does not want me to marry you."

"I am so worried now," I confessed.

"Do not worry before it happens!" he comforted me. "Would he come to cause us trouble in the middle of the market? I don't think so."

"He would if he could; he would not wait for the next day."

"He may follow us to the University, then?" Leang asked.

"If he does, I will be very embarrassed in front of hundreds and hundreds of students in the same area."

Papa did not come to school but, when I came home after school, he was there in the living room. "Come here, Vi..chea...ra!!" I knew I was in big trouble. "Who was that with you at the market? I heard a rumor that you had a boyfriend, was it him?"

"He's just my friend."

He raised the leather strap and lashed me with it. "You will stop this 'friendship' with him. Don't you know you disobeyed my rule? Don't you know that I will be humiliated if someone sees you or hears you have a boyfriend? I do not want to see it happen in our family." I could see red marks on my arms and my legs and knew I had others on my back from the strap. I felt my face get hot with fear.

"If I see you with him again, I will disown you."

I remember hearing these words and how they scared me. What should I do if my boyfriend wouldn't give me up? I would never want to be kicked out of my father's house.

"I love you a lot, *Kaun*, but I will disown you if you do not obey my rules. I am taking away your car. Our chauffeur will take you to school. Go back to your room, wash your face and make up your mind before it is too late."

I did as he told me and then went out to set up the table for lunchtime. Before he left for work, I heard him knock on the door of my bedroom. As I opened the door, I saw a bill of 300 riels handed to me. "Spend this money and stop thinking about something stupid," he said.

I was happy with the money. I was rich today. Papa thought the money he gave me would change my mind about my boyfriend but that was not going to happen. I loved him, and he loved me. We would just have to be more careful. That afternoon during break time, we went to a quiet place on the sixth floor balcony of the pharmacy school. Leang held me tightly and whispered in my ear, "This is my suggestion. We should stop going together for a while until everything calms down."

I felt his warm kiss on my forehead and his lips were like a magic wand turning me into Cinderella dancing with a prince. These warm kisses dissolved all the physical pain and the fear. I could hear his heart beating with passion and true love for me. His warm hand caressed my cheek and arm and I felt secure that he wouldn't turn into a bumblebee flying from one flower to another and wouldn't turn me to a rotten flower like Papa warned me.

"Papa has taken away my car," I whispered.

"It is OK. It doesn't take away my love for you. In fact, it makes me love you more. Let's study harder for our future," he said to me, taking out the book for us to study together.

Papa came to pick me up every day after school at 6:00 PM, so I wouldn't be able to go anywhere with my boyfriend. We had to be cautious so we would not be caught again. For a couple of months, everything went smoothly; my Papa thought that I had given up my boyfriend. He once again let me drive my car to school. By this time, my boyfriend had his own car and we used his car when we wanted to go out for lunch. Our relationship was growing deeper all the time. My boyfriend bought clothes for me; we shared everything together, like husband and wife, but we were never physically intimate.

~NINE~

BREAK THE ICE

Papa came home early one day and went straight to his room. As he came out of his room, he called me and I could tell he was furious. I was shivering with fear, what did I do wrong now? What has my stepmother told him about me this time?

"I want you to get an education, not to have a boyfriend." I stood up like a stick in the middle of the living room waiting for the axe to fall. His voice could be heard clearly from upstairs to downstairs, from inside to outside. He obviously didn't remember Yey Kong's insistence that we keep our secrets in the family. He was so clearly out of control that I was terrified. My feet became paralyzed, my head was congested, my hands were freezing, my heart was pounding like a drum, and my eyes were soaked with tears. I knew from the tone of his voice that I was in serious trouble and I looked around me to find someone who could protect me. He called me again; I walked slowly to him.

"Sit down," he demanded, with the leather strap in his hand. I sat down on the floor and begged him to forgive me and listen to me. Without listening to any explanation, he began to hit me almost hard enough to kill me. My feet got hit and became numb because he hit me so hard in the same place over and over. Both my hands got hit because I used them to protect my feet. I felt miserable and terrified. "That is it!! Are you pregnant?" he demanded.

"No, I listened to you, Papa; I did not have sex with him. He loves me and wants to marry me!' I cried.

"A man is a piece of gold, a woman is a piece of white cloth." As he finished this sentence, he began to cry and hit me again. I knew that was because he felt he had lost his pride, respect and dignity. "I am so humiliated right now because of you. His parents will not respect me because of your behavior. I will have to beg his parents to allow him to marry you. I reminded you all the time that men are just like a piece of gold. You, a girl, are like a piece of white cloth. When gold is soiled, it is temporary; when white cloth is soiled, it is permanent. I told you a million times to concentrate on education first. Later, after graduation, you will have more than enough men to choose for a husband. If you cannot get one, it won't hurt you to stay alone. I do not want you to be betrayed by any man." He did not stop hitting me. "A man is like a butterfly; flies from one flower to another. Men betray women. A man will not chase you after he gets what he wants. This is mankind. I raised you to be strong with men."

I had heard it a million times. I was tired of being hurt with his beatings. My body became numb everywhere but then I became stubborn in front of him because of the pain. "Papa! Hurt me more and more and kill me if you want to. I am ready!" Then I asked one question. "Papa, how can you beat me so hard all the time? Am I your own daughter? If I am not your own daughter, please give me back to my bio-parents."

He stopped hitting me as I urged him to kill me, but then he went to his room and came out again with a leather-bound stick. I did not know where he got it. Before he hit me again, he ordered *Eeh*, "Go tell *Yey* Kong and *Yey* Hieng (Papa called Grandaunt Hieng) to come here!"

Amazingly, before she walked away, she tried to grab the stick from his hand, "You are crazy. It is too late to discipline her. She is a grown woman."

"You are my own blood." He shouted at me, as he raised the stick. I remembered the pain of being hit with this stick. This kind of stick was used to beat criminals. I tried to move away from him before he hit me again. I begged him to stop hitting me because my arms, fingers, and legs were swollen now. However he did not listen to me, he just hit me again and again. He called *Eeh* to come back in. I tried to get behind her but she sat on the floor about a foot from me with her back against the wall. She asked him, "You want to beat her to death for what?"

My Papa said, "I am humiliated, my pride, my pride!!"

Instead of helping me, *Eeh* knew how to push the button to make him even angrier. She said, "This is the result of protecting her from this, that and anything! This is the result of you spoiling her. Everybody laughs at you for spoiling her. Who are you keeping your daughter for, the prince?"

Papa, of course, didn't want to hear that anyone blamed him, especially about me. He lost his temper quickly when he got blamed. He hit me again and said angrily, "I do not know her boyfriend's parents, or what they do for a living. What is his family background? Now, I have to talk to them and beg them to marry you! It is not the future I planned for you. I hate his parents and will never ask them to talk to me for any reason."

Thank God, my Grandaunt and *Yey* Kong now both appeared at the door of the living room with worry written on their faces. There is no stop sign, I thought, please come inside and rescue me.

"If you continue to hit her, it won't solve the problem. She is your daughter." Grandaunt shouted first.

"You are acting like an animal. You beat her like she is an animal. This is not right," *Yey* Kong shouted at him next.

"I will prove to all of you now that I never spoil her." His voice was loud and fierce like soldier shouting on the battlefield.

"If a *sarong* got ripped, would you want to repair or wreck it?" Grandaunt shouted over Papa's voice.

"Leave us alone!" Papa yelled, but he stopped hitting me and then reached into his belt and put a gun on the table. I wept in misery both from the beating and from the terror of wondering why he had a gun. Had he been going to kill me?

Eeh then said something I never expected, "You have spoiled her for so long. You gave everything to her, why can't you give her the man she wants?" My father didn't answer but left the room.

"Your Papa is very stubborn, poor Vicheara! Said *Yey* Kong as she and Grandaunt left together.

Unexpected Visit

Thank God, my favorite Cousin Phach showed up at that time with her family to visit my parents. I was so sad for her to hear I was in such a bad situation. Papa was furious with me, and did not want to see me anymore. He told my cousin to take me away from him for the weekend.

"Pack up your clothes. Your Papa wants me to talk to you," Phach said.

We both cried. We decided to leave as soon as possible since my Papa was not talking to anybody. On the way to my cousin's house, her husband was teasing me about my childhood to distract me from my misery. Phach laughed and agreed with him saying, "You were a cranky baby. Your parents left you with me both days and nights. You were a strange baby, you'd wake up and enjoy playing with the light bulb at night, sleep all day. You cried almost every time I put you in the crib." We all laughed.

"Oh! Cousin, I am so sorry to hear I kept you awake. When I have a good job, I will take care of you. I still remember the pink blouse with a ruffle in the front that you sewed for me when I was little. Everything you gave me was made exactly the way I wanted it. How come I have lost all my favorite people, *Mak*, my servant Mout, *Lok Yey*, then you? Why do all the people who love me leave me?"

I enjoyed my time at my cousin's home without being worried about the stepmother who was so critical but never gave me any useful advice. My cousin cooked my favorite foods and spoiled me as usual. All I did was play, eat and sleep for two days and three nights, like living in paradise despite the bruises and welts from the brutal beating. Time to go home was all too soon. "I hope everything will be all right for you at home with your Papa!" My cousin said.

"I am not happy to go back home. I am scared of Papa, unhappy with *Eeh*. I am too lonely."

"You are his daughter, he will never kill you, just treat you badly because he wants to raise you in the way he expects!"

On arrival, my Cousin Phach and her family stayed for a while talking with *Eeh* and then left. I came to sit next to my stepmother to find out about Papa. "He left home the same time you did. I do not know where he went. He was so upset about you having a boyfriend! I do not know why he wants to keep you single so long. I think you are ready to be a wife at your age!"

We stayed in silence watching all my dogs chasing each other around us. My Papa did not show up for another three days and three nights.

The Defeat of Papa

I doubted my Papa would listen to anybody but himself. However, there was one person he might listen to - my cousin Thor. He was tougher than Papa and he could make Papa listen to him. Perhaps this was a way to defeat Papa. As soon as I could, I went to meet his wife at home and begged her to help me with this problem. I do not know how much time her husband spent on my Papa to calm him down, but the result was great afterwards. When I returned to find out what had happened, she told me, "After a long unsuccessful talk with your Papa, my husband asked him only one question."

Tightly, I grabbed her hands, "What did he say?"

She laughed and then became serious, "He asked your father if he wants to keep you for himself?" I released her hands as I felt like this question was way out of line. I didn't like it. I hesitated to ask her more, but she said, "Your Papa could not answer it. It means he has to agree to let you have a husband."

Now I was worried how Papa would react to this kind of question? Would he take out his anger on me since he had been chided by Cousin Thor? Papa came back home later, still angry. He was still opposed to my relationship. He told me not to get close to my boyfriend until his parents came to the house, asking Papa's permission for me to marry him.

My job now was to forward Papa's words to my boyfriend immediately. I wanted his mother hear it and work on Papa. 'Don't wait for the rain to fall', is a Khmer adage I finally found appropriate. It was not long before my boyfriend's mother showed up at our house to begin the conversation about an engagement. Papa was aggravated by her unexpected presence, and I was scared to death. She didn't know how tough my Papa was; maybe she thought it would be easy for her to meet him and everything would go smoothly like water going between the rocks. I thought it would be more like going over a waterfall in a small boat.

After the first unsuccessful meeting, Leang's mother came back again in two weeks; she cleverly came during the mid-day nap time, the only time Papa couldn't escape from her. Then she came every week to visit Papa, asking the same question, permission to set up an engagement for both of us. Papa tried to find excuses to not come down to see her as often as he could, leaving the unpleasant messenger responsibility to *Eeh*. Getting tired of her duty, she quickly gave up.

Papa continued to look for excuses just to protect his pride. He didn't like that Leang's mother approached him so directly; he said it showed she had no class. He felt she was insincere and saccharine; a phony. He didn't feel it was safe for me to join her family because Leang had many brothers and sisters, and I would wind up responsible for all of them, as Papa had been for all his step-siblings. Most importantly, of course, Papa looked at her family as lower class. Papa refused her request many times but her persistence finally broke the ice.

It was in November of 1973, when he finally approved that we could become engaged. I was twenty two years old. In Cambodia, engagement involves a very big ceremony similar to a wedding ceremony. This was what my Papa wanted;

however, there was still a dark shadow in his mind that made him worry about me. He didn't trust my boyfriend's family. He still firmly expressed his feelings that, "Your mother-in- law does not love you for real. I feel she is not honest to you or to me. She will sweet talk to buy your love but once you trust her, she will bleed you dry. Keep in mind, I know how to read people. Your mother-in-law wants her son to marry you only for my money because you are my only child. I will never let her know how rich I am. I never let your stepmother know anything about my money either." I didn't care what he said and wouldn't believe what Papa said about Leang's mother.

Prolonged my Wedding for Three Years

Nothing my prospective mother-in-law did to please Papa was appreciated by him, including the gifts I received from her. Papa told me to put away my diamond engagement ring. He didn't value it as he was not happy about the family I was marrying into and he thought the diamond was too small for his daughter. My Papa wouldn't even look at my fiancé, much less talk to him. He would leave home when Leang came to visit me. This problem continued to grow every day.

One day Papa told me to tell my fiancé to keep away from me until the wedding date was set. He also said, "I allow your fiancé to meet you when only you have something to study together. I will allow you to get married three years after the engagement." This was his message to the world he was not happy with my fiancé and his family. His indirect disapproval of my fiancé had put me in a tough situation. I needed to please them both; I needed to listen to Papa and also wanted to keep my relationship with Leang alive.

In addition to the sad situation, I also received more sad news from Cousin Phach that, after many years of marriage, she and her husband were splitting up. She and her younger children were leaving Phnom Penh to live in Battambang province. She told me she would begin her own small business selling food in the market to support her children. Her two oldest sons were left in Phnom Penh to pursue their studies since she believed that the schools in the city were better and the boys would have better opportunities. She separated from her husband as he was cheating on her with another nurse. It had been a sad engagement party without my favorite cousin's presence, and now it was even sadder when they left me. All my favorite people left me; first my *Mak*, then my *Lok Yey*, now my favorite Cousin Phach had not only left my house, she had left the city.

~TEN~

WEAKNESS OF PAPA

Eeh had been diagnosed with hyperthyroidism by my cousin Thor. He prescribed an injection of streptomycin every day. Her eyes were round and stuck out so far they looked like they would fall out of her head. Her skin was very dehydrated and scaly. She started to gain a lot of weight due to the medication. In addition to western medicine, she also took Cambodian traditional medicine that was made from a whole roasted monkey. This traditional medicine was believed to help with the hot flashes caused by hyperthyroidism. She became easily panicked and angry. She kicked my favorite dog when I was not around and insulted him like she insulted me. She was difficult when relatively healthy; when sick, she was especially miserable.

She liked to spend time alone in her room every afternoon after my Papa left the house. As a younger child, I'd sometimes quietly sneak in just to see what she was doing. Most of the time, I found her using a very small magnifying glass to look at diamonds because she was a diamond trader. She got diamonds from her mom and distributed some to her partners to sell; both of her partners were Papa's cousins, Phon and Nimm. They both were very nice and friendly to me and Papa. I called both of them *Keo* (in Cambodian this means Aunt on the Papa's side, while in the West they are considered my second cousins). Occasionally *Eeh* would misplace a diamond and then be very sad and upset. When it happened, she always came up to me begging me to find them for her. This was a good time for me to get close to her. I believed helping her when she needed me would build up a good relationship with her. I hoped she would show her appreciation by letting me eat the good food rather than hiding it, and stop talking bad about me.

Getting Pregnant Outside of the Marriage

In 1974, our servant Kilen was discovered to be pregnant; she claimed the father was the custodian for a karate club next to our house. She said they met every night. As she slept downstairs by herself, her story was plausible. In our culture, we disapprove of women of any social class getting pregnant outside of marriage. When this situation happens, we believed it would bring bad luck to the house. However, the servant was already pregnant and there was nothing we could do about that. My Papa didn't want to keep her at our house but *Eeh* disagreed with him. She said 'we should be kind to Kilen because she was a hard worker'.

The nine months quickly passed and, because she was mainly my servant, I was the one who was responsible to take her to the maternity hospital. Luckily, the hospital was owned by my dear friend, so the care was free. My parents did not seem to care too much about her until she gave birth to a baby boy. We gave him the name "Chamroeun" meaning prosperity. After she came back home, I was again responsible for the baby, taking him to get a shot, to the hospital when he was sick, and buying medicine when he got a fever.

The relationship between *Eeh* and the servant changed drastically when the baby arrived home. Eeh sewed baby clothes for him. She took Chamroeun everywhere and showed him off to everyone. In the beginning, Papa never touched the baby because he was born with no father, and the baby of the servant.

My grandparents complained a lot and said we should not keep the baby and the servant in the house, because an illegitimate child would bring bad luck to the family. I agreed with them.

Because their complaints fell on deaf ears, my grandparents then suspected that the baby must be Papa's. That rumor began to creep around the family.

"Kilen got pregnant with Papa? This baby is my stepbrother?" I asked myself. No way, it didn't happen like this.

Well! Month after month, the baby grew; soon he was crawling around the house. The house used to be quiet, now we had one new little creature. The car used to have only three people, now we had four. Chamroeun sat on *Eeh*'s lap in the front seat, with his face turned to me. I was not happy with this turn of events. Later, both my parents began to call Chamroeun "*Kaun*". This was very upsetting to me. I was not sure if Chamroeun was going to be my legal stepbrother, as my grandparents predicted. I became even more disappointed when I heard *Eeh* say that Chamroeun will be her own son, and will bear my Papa's last name. This announcement made me furious.

I talked to Papa about Chamroeun. "Will you accept this stupid dirty creature to be your son?"

"Do not be stupid. I have you only," he said.

"Papa, I saw you holding him and playing with him. You enjoyed him."

"You are stupid!"

Papa lied to me. Soon, every time he came home from work, he asked for Chamroeun. He put Chamroeun on his lap. He, *Eeh* and the baby went visiting without me. Papa talked to me less than before.

Do not Trust People Who wouldn't Steal Food

One day shortly thereafter, my stepmother appeared worried and was very quiet. There was something wrong with her; I asked her, "Are you ill?"

"I lost a package of one hundred precious stones, diamonds and rubies. I can't understand how it disappeared."

I volunteered to help her, but still we could not find them. "Have you asked Kilen? You better do it and hear what she has to say," I suggested.

"Are you crazy? What makes you think she stole it? She wouldn't do such a thing to me and, besides that, she is too dumb."

"Have you heard the proverb, 'Do not trust people who wouldn't steal food when they are hungry'?" There was no answer; instead she gave me an ugly look.

"How can you naively believe that Kilen never goes outside of the house, or is unfamiliar with the city? This may have been true in the beginning when she was alone and new to the city but, right now, she has a child, and a boyfriend. In fact, the boyfriend now lives nearby. He might have suggested that she do something so they could afford to leave and live on their own. They meet each other at night." I could imagine how mad she was when I next told her, "Kilen has asked me where the pawnshop is."

"When?"

"Not very long ago; when did you lose the bag?"

"A week ago."

"Kilen asked me a couple days ago. I was surprised that she was looking for a pawnshop. I don't even know where one is."

"What did you tell her?"

"I said I didn't know. In any case, let me investigate and see what I can find out about the stones." I could tell from her face that it would be a nightmare for her to kick Kilen out of the house and lose the baby if I could prove Kilen took the stones.

I slipped into Kilen's room and went through it to see what I could find. I spent about ten minutes going through all her belongings and I finally found the package that my stepmother described to me. I opened it up and counted all the stones. They were all in there. I brought them to my stepmother, but instead of thanking me, she asked, "Did you put the package in her clothes to set her up? I don't believe Kilen is a thief."

I laughed and told Papa about it. I never heard about any punishment of Kilen. In spite of being suspicious of her, my stepmother continued to treat her well and pamper the baby. I was a fool to help her find the stones because, no matter what, *Eeh* wanted the baby and would never kick Kilen out. In fact, she was afraid Kilen would take away the baby from her. In Cambodian society, if my father made the boy his legal heir then my stepmother's position in the family would be protected and the boy would be responsible for her welfare for the rest of her life. The baby was her social security.

My Ring was Stolen

Now it was my turn to suffer the loss of jewelry. It was a diamond ring that had been my *Mak*'s and was given to me by Papa after her death. I cried and ran to Papa. "My precious ring has been stolen."

"What did you say? The diamond ring with the ruby in the middle?" He asked me.

"It must be *Eeh* or maybe Kilen." I sobbed. "I remember *Eeh* stared at this ring every time I wore it; and, remember Papa, she is a jewelry seller. We have two thieves at home now."

Papa took a deep breath and looked away with disappointment. Amazingly, he then confessed, "Another diamond ring of your mother's disappeared from a safe box that I kept in the wardrobe. I have planned to give it to you when you marry but …"

"Papa, we can protect ourselves from thieves coming from outside, but cannot be safe when the thieves are living with us."

"*Kaun*, it is humiliating. Keep this in the family. Material things can be replaced, but the family relations are more important."

The whole situation was crazy. *Eeh* was jealous of me and hated me because Papa was not open with her about his business affairs, and would not share all his money with her. She felt abused so she abused me. She could not have children and knew I would inherit from Papa and then her future would be in doubt, so she was determined to replace me with the servant's child and convince Papa that I was an immoral slut so he would disinherit me. The servant knew a good thing when she saw it and connived with stepmother to create a good future for her child. No matter what she did, she would be protected by *Eeh*. Papa knew things weren't right but he refused to investigate to avoid the conflict in the family. What power did *Eeh* have over him? Could it have been about his mistress? Was there something else she knew and held over his head?

PART III

OVERTHROW OF PRINCE SIHANOOK

Preview: The war between Vietnam and the US was raging and communist rebels were active all over Southeast Asia.

In March 1970, *Samdech* Sihanook, or *Samdech Pra Mouk Raud* of the state of Cambodia was officially deposed and General Lon, Nol was designated as the President of the Khmer Republic. In Phnom Penh, many educated Khmers accepted the change and welcomed Lon, Nol as a hero of the Cambodia State. However, in the villages, they still believed in *Samdech* as God Father.

The pro-western coup resulted in *Samdech* forming a government-in-exile in Peking and in the declaration of Cambodia as a Republic. At that time, he announced his support of the Cambodian Communist Khmer Rouge rebels under General Pol Pot in their efforts to overthrow Lon, Nol. As a result of *Samdech's* support, the KR rapidly increased because Cambodian peasants, very naïve and devoted to the God Father, believed that if they fought with the KR they could return *Samdech* to power. Many unsophisticated country people literally worshiped *Samdech*. As history tells us, *Samdech* did regain his title as Head of State with the support of the communists but he was just a figurehead because Pol Pot, in fact, had all the power. This deal with the devil led to the catastrophe in Cambodia in the late seventies.

~ELEVEN~

LIVER WITH LIQUOR

Papa was elected around 1968 as a member of Constitutional Council of Cambodia working under Lon, Nol, and the President of the Khmer Republic. There he worked side by side with his friend, S.E. Phlek, Pheun, who was also a member of Constitutional Council. Other colleagues were: Yem, Sambo; Seun, San; Chhan, Sokhom; and Ung, Hiem (Governor).

Papa usually didn't share much information about anything political with us, unless his worries were extreme. Everyone in the extended family regarded Papa as the family expert on politics.

One evening at dinner, in 1974, after hearing about the continued success of the KR in the provinces, I asked if the country could fall to the KR. Papa explained, "It is very complicated and you won't understand it politically. I cannot explain all the details but *Samdech* is not allowed to come back to Cambodia. He thought it was smart to declare Cambodia neutral but secretly, he visited Peking in 1969 and held the hands of the Viet Cong." Papa shook his head.

A chill ran up my spine. "Viet Cong, Communist Vietnamese from North Vietnam?" I straightened up and shivered.

"But, nothing is going to happen to our country," assured Papa. "A coup was much easier to accomplish when he was not in the country; and it was not just General Lon Nol alone who is strong enough to overthrow *Samdech*. There is another strong person, his cousin – Prince Sisowath Sirik Matak. He and Lon, Nol have planned this coup for a long time."

"Uh! He betrayed *Samdech* for power. It just like in Khmer history, the royal family has betrayed each other to gain power in the past."

"Yes and no. You are right but *Samdech* wouldn't listen to anybody. He is arrogant and stubborn and has brought this upon himself."

"Not new. In history, all the Khmer kings were stubborn and arrogant. They never learned from the past." I picked up my dog that was looking up at me and wagging his tail.

"Almost all the provinces in Cambodia are now occupied by KR troops. I have been ordered by Lon, Nol, to have a meeting with the KR leaders to bring peace to the people of Cambodia. The meeting will be here at our house."

Conversation about the KR had become common at the dinner table, but this shocking statement from Papa got everyone's attention. "I have heard that they eat uncooked human liver with liquor after killing their captives," Papa continued, as if he was talking about the weather. This bizarre announcement scared all of us and our chopsticks stopped in mid-air. Calmly Papa added, "Their eyes turn red after eating the human liver."

"Papa! Why .... and you said 'nothing is going to hap....'" I didn't finish my sentence as Papa raised his hand to silence me. Everybody looked at each other with fear and confusion. I forgot to breathe for a while due to this strange and dangerous decision.

"Not good. Inviting them to our house is to show them where to find us. They will kill us easily," Stepmother warned him.

"No, it won't happen. We will negotiate with them and create a coalition. I will have the dinner catered from a fine restaurant. Don't be frightened! I have taken this risk to help the country find peace as I believe what Prime Minister Lon, Nol has told me." Papa wiped his mouth with his napkin.

I was so uninformed about politics that I did not understand who was being captured and killed or why. I did not fully understand who the KR were but I knew they were very dangerous. I know this sounds impossible for a university student but I lived a very sheltered life. I was angry with Papa for accepting this dangerous mission and also worried that the KR would recognize our faces later and murder us. Papa told us to stay calm; he had a plan. Here again, the same promise firmly assured us, "Nothing is going to happen to our country."

Dangerous Negotiator

Some weeks later in November 1974, around 5 PM, a group of ten KR leaders and members came to our house. They were all dressed in black with red cotton *kramas* around their necks. I peeked at them through the door when the waiter that Papa had hired opened it to pick up the food trays. Their eyes were red because they had been eating uncooked human liver; my Papa's claim was accurate! They all sat at the long mahogany dining table as they had dinner and talked with my Papa and the other government leaders he had invited.

I was afraid of them but believed that the KR rebels wouldn't dare to do something bad to us in the heart of the city. *Eeh* was angry with Papa for this risky mission and told me she thought it was stupid. The meeting lasted about two hours, including dinner. After they left, my Papa came in with a smile. He told us he was confident that our country would find peace. He said he would report to Prime Minister Lon, Nol that the KR had accepted reconciliation with the new government of Lon, Nol, and they looked forward to having a meeting with Prime Minister.

I trusted Papa. Later, I heard him talking on the phone to Dr. Thor, "Everything will be fine as long as I am here. Nothing is going to happen." His left hand held the phone close to his ear while his right hand tapped the desk.

Papa was not the only official who believed in reconciliation with KR. His associate ministers S.E.Phlek, Pheun and Yem, Sambo also believed. Papa believed that meeting with the KR in a respectful way would stop them from attacking the country. However, Papa could not have been completely confident because he also discussed with Cousin Thor a plan of going to France in January 1975, to meet my Auntie Leng, and also to open an account in a French bank.

"Why do you want to do this, Papa?"

"I suggested to Thor that we deposit the money in a French bank because I am worried that our country may become socialist or communist and that individual accounts may be taken by the government. I met with the KR leaders to bring peace to our country because fighting, killing and bombing will destroy the country and our people. I hope we can work together in peace but I also must protect my assets."

"How do you know that Cambodia will become commu.....?" I was terrified to say this word, "communist". I thought that Papa was right. I heard earlier that the American army had withdrawn from Cambodia's border as a sign that the KR could occupy the country.

Soon after this, my girlfriend from the University, Savy, told me that KR troops had invaded nearby areas. Savy was the oldest daughter of Dr. Mey, a business partner of my Cousin Thor at the Aurore Clinic. Because of his good friendship with both my cousin Thor and Papa, Savy and I became best friends. We could hear the bombing from the pharmacy school all day long, and see the smoke. At night, we could see fires burning. All of our pharmacy friends were concerned about these attacks and urged each other to find ways to leave the country as soon as possible. Most students just had to go with the flow because they didn't have the financial resources to leave the country.

We talked about communism and how tough the daily life would be if Cambodia turned communist. We never thought about nor discussed concerns such as starvation and mass executions. We thought the war would stop when the KR troops reached the city of Phnom Penh because Cambodia would then become communist/socialist. We were completely ignorant of the radical political agenda of the KR and saw them as another political party.

My Friends Evacuated

A couple of months later, Savy was very sad about leaving all her friends and her parents as she was being sent out of the country for her safety. I told Papa that she was being sent to France and asked if I could also go. He refused again. "I am working on it and you have to stay calm and trust me." As usual, he got angry with my request.

"Papa, let me go to France. What are you uncertain about? Savy told me her father forced her to go due to the insecurity in Cambodia. Her father doesn't feel safe in our country, Papa." I tried to convince him to wake up from the dream of saving Cambodia with nonviolence.

"I am not like her father. Do not bring this up to me again," he shouted.

"Remember, you are not a hero, Papa?" I shouted too and followed him as he started to walk away from me.

"I love my country. I will die and live as a hero."

"Papa, if you die, I want your name on the big wall. Don't be used by someone because they are scared to do something themselves. You are being used now and they will have their name on the walls. You are so naïve. I don't say you aren't smart, but you are kidding yourself."

"You don't know any better than me, shut up!" He disappeared in the room. I couldn't do anything to overcome his stubbornness. I would have to live with it.

I went to the airport to see my friend off. Savy cried a lot with her boyfriend. I cried with her too but mostly because of my anger with Papa. I heard her boyfriend assure her he would join her very soon. During the same time, Cousin Thor sent his two children to France to live with Auntie Leng. I continue to bargain with Papa and nag him to send me to Paris. He still refused. "I am still thinking about it."

"This is the only answer you have for me?"

"I am working with Thor to deposit money in the French bank first before sending you out to France." I knew it was just an excuse.

"Your friend S.E.Phlek, Pheun also sent his kids to France. When will you decide to send me out?"

"I am thinking about it." This was the same answer I had received before.

"Do you know, Papa, Grandaunty Houn sent her children to Paris?"

Then, another cousin did the same because they couldn't trust the political situation. Papa still kept telling me that he was working on sending me. "When? I do not see any sign of you letting me go," I cried. Papa did not respond. I couldn't understand his thinking.

As the KR successfully moved forward toward the city, bombings became commonplace, happening unpredictably everywhere, in the banks, the central market, the airport. Many people were killed and injured. Ambulances sped through the streets every day and the hospitals filled with injured people. People from the countryside fled into the center of Phnom Penh. We couldn't tell them from the KR troops as they all wore black outfits. We couldn't identify who was KR, or who was an innocent citizen because they were all Cambodian. My Papa hired one of the KR delegates who had been at the dinner at our house. Papa wanted to improve his life and encourage him to be a good person using the non-violence strategy. His name was Sambath. In Cambodian this means heritage. Sambath was employed as a security guard at Papa's pharmaceutical plant.

~TWELVE~

MY TRADITIONAL WEDDING

I looked at Papa open-mouthed and startled, when he called me from my room. "I have set the wedding date." I was frozen to the spot. Had I correctly heard him? What had happened to change his mind? I never expected this to happen so soon. I was expecting to have to wait the three years he had originally insisted upon after the engagement.

"Sit down, I want to talk to you." He said firmly, nodding at the seat next to him. The tone of his voice sent chills down my spine. I nervously looked around the room and walked to the recliner instead. "You have humiliated me more than I can tolerate. I am now forced to let you marry this nobody! Is it what you want?"

In spite of his obvious disappointment, hearing him give his permission for me to marry Leang gave me uncontrollable butterflies. I sat still without saying a word, my mind reeling. Although he allowed our engagement amid disapproval and protests, I never really believed the marriage would actually take place. I couldn't believe my ears. Had he actually said YES??! My mind instantly went to the traditional wedding costume, the color and style I would wear to impress my friends. I began to tremble with excitement, but my excitement was mixed with the fear that he might still beat me. I tried to control the trembling so Papa wouldn't notice, but I couldn't. Fortunately, Papa was so absorbed in his anger; he did not notice me. I looked around to see if *Eeh* was somewhere listening to our conversation. Fortunately, she was not there to add fuel to the fire.

Papa got up. He walked to his desk located next to the chair I was sitting in. There was no escape if he decided to beat me. He just continued his tirade, his voice rising with each word. "I don't want you to marry at all right now, least of all to this insignificant fool. I must consent to this marriage to save my reputation."

This last statement shocked me from my jubilation. My excitement and fear dissolved into sadness and disappointment. I looked down, ashamed, scratching the arm of the couch searching for something to replace my discomfort.

"The date of the wedding will be January 1st. We don't have much time left, but at least we have more than a month to prepare for this. Due to political situation now, I decided to postpone my trip to France with Thor," Papa said, pulling a cigarette from the box and opening one drawer after another looking for matches. When it was obvious he was more interested in finding a light for his cigarette than beating me, my excitement returned.

January 1st was not far away. My thoughts returned to the wedding plans. My wedding outfit, how I would look; how I would behave, who would be invited.

The unlit cigarette bouncing between his lips, Papa continued, "There will be no Western music, only the traditional music, both at home and at the restaurant. This is what I like." He returned to his search for matches, "I want to see what gifts that phony soon-to-be mother-in-law of yours will give you. I want to see if I am right; I bet she won't honor me appropriately because her son dated you without my permission." His irritation increased as each drawer was found void of matches and was slammed in frustration. He was rifling through the papers on his desk when *Eeh* walked into the room.

"What is all the noise about?" She turned from Papa and saw me sitting in the chair like a little puppy. She openly scowled at me.

"I am allowing her to get married. The date will be January 1st. Help her to find good diamonds for her ring and pendant," he curtly ordered.

Instead of complying, she coughed that annoying cough she passed off as a laugh and said, "After the wedding you will live with your husband's family. In your mother-in-law's house you won't be treated like a spoiled brat. She will put you to work. You will be just one more mouth to feed." She looked at me with a satisfied smile and coughed again.

I tried to pretend she didn't bother me but she wasn't fooled. She purposely walked up to me, and coughed again, just to annoy me. I was sure she knew she disgusted me, but she was now in control and she knew it. Papa had given her that control when he gave her the money to select a diamond for me. She would lie to Papa about the price and the quality. I could feel how desperately hungry for money she was, and cleverly sought ways to glean every penny she could from Papa. Offering her even a small amount of money would make her dance like a rabbit on the moon.

"Keep your stupid opinions to yourself," Papa said lighting his cigarette with matches he finally located in his jacket pocket. Inhaling deeply, he turned back to me, "You will live with me after the wedding."

I lowered my head and looked at my hands. I had no say in the matter.

Eeh's defeated, whining voice prodded Papa, "Give me the money then. I will find the diamonds for her. You will be sorry if you let her stay here."

The conversation was over. I left for my room, her insults following me down the hall. I hated it, but I now had to be nice to her. I had to feign respect I could not feel. I could not show how upset I was or show her any sort of animosity.

Stepmother's Attack

The wedding announcement made *Eeh* grow even more angry and jealous of me. I overheard a conversation between her and Kilen in the living room. As I approached, I could hear her saying, "Your mistress will get married very soon, so you will no longer serve her. Do not respect her and her husband."

I was upset by her words but I did not believe Kilen would do this to me. However, I was wrong and Kilen's behavior to me changed; she ignored me; she did not serve me as she did before. She talked to me without respect. She didn't come up to my room to gather my clothes as before, nor did she clean my room. To buy her service, I had to give her money every day. I paid her to keep her mouth shut and to gather information from my stepmother. As time went on, the relationship between three of us got worse. Papa was not aware of this problem, because I never knew how he would react to disturbing news.

One day, in the early morning, after I closed the door of my room and before I reached the stairs, I heard someone behind me. Before I even knew who it was, I felt my hair pulled hard. I recognized *Eeh*'s voice when she insulted me with, "*Mee samphung* (Whore)! I hate you. I want you to get out of my house."

I was so surprised that I shouted back, "I hate you too."

In response to my insult, she kicked me in the legs. Now, I got into a physical fight with her, in front of Kilen. I could feel how much anger she had held within herself for so long. I could sense how much hate she held in her heart. If she could have killed me right then, she would have. She grabbed me by my hair and pulled. I resisted her attack by using one of my hands to try to keep her from me, the other to pry her hand from my hair. "It hurts!" I shouted at her. "Leave me alone, I need to go to school before I'm late for my exam."

She would not listen to me, and slapped my face very hard. Again, I was surprised when she did this to me; I still could not understand what had set her off.

My servant was nearby and I said to her, "See how badly she treats me."

Kilen looked at me then, turned her face away, ignoring it.

Eeh kept calling me "*Mee samphung,*" without letting go of my hair. I could not hold my patience anymore. I kicked at her, backwards, one kick after another, faster and harder until her hands released my hair. I turned around and saw her *sarong* falling off and her dentures dropping on the floor. What would she do first - kick me back, pick up her *sarong,* or retrieve her dentures? What a surprise, she must have lost her mind due to the anger; instead of taking care of her nakedness, she was scrambling for her teeth. I would have laughed, if I was not in so much pain! As soon as she picked up her teeth, she tried arranging her *sarong.* Her hands were shaking like a vibrating machine. One hand was pulling up her *sarong,* another putting her dentures back in her mouth. She was also crying.

"Why?" I thought angrily. "*Mon Dieu!* What brought this on?"

She was crying, and only now did I notice what a mess her mouth was. I never had paid attention to her teeth before, but since she was right in front of me, mouth open, I now had no choice. I thought that nothing could be bigger and longer than her teeth. She really looked like a smiling horse. My goodness, I said to myself as I watched her trying to tidy up her *sarong,* she is really ugly. Then she was about to jump on me once more, but her *sarong* fell for a second time. Angrily she glared at me, her eyes never left me. She stared at me like I was her prey and she was a wild animal or something. I knew this time she wouldn't leave me alive, if I waited until her *sarong* was fixed. I ran to the stairs and got out of the house as quickly as I could. I could hear her voice; she was still calling me names from inside the house. I could also hear her say something like, "I will tell your father to abandon you and you will never receive an inheritance."

Tell Papa? What is she going to tell him? I was the victim of her attack. To be smart, I decided to tell Papa before she could. I was so mad at her; I was crying in the car. Life was just not fair for me. My face still had a red mark from the slap. It hurt me physically and emotionally. There was an hour left before the exam started and I would have plenty of time to talk to Papa. Fortunately, his car was still at his office. As my Papa saw me in tears with a red mark on my face, he rushed to ask me what was wrong. After listening to the problem, I was surprised that he took my side. I stopped crying for a while because I could not believe my eyes and ears that for once he did not criticize and chastise me. I begged him, "Papa, please do not kick me out of the house. She's the one who purposely started the problems." He cried with me and said quietly, "You are my daughter. I will never choose her before you. Calm down. Concentrate on the exam."

That night, when Papa got back home, and before he walked into his bedroom to meet *Eeh*, I stared at Papa to make sure he would keep his promise to me. He nodded at me and told me to go to my room. I waited patiently in my room; in about ten minutes, I heard footsteps in front of my room and the sound of my stepmother crying. I opened the door and my Papa approached me and told me sadly, "She has decided to leave me tonight because I told her not to ever touch you again, *Kaun*."

I was so happy that my Papa decided to keep me rather than kick me out, but on the other hand, my conscience was telling me that I was the cause of their separation. I felt guilty seeing my Papa separated from her. I came close to him and said, "Papa, I got involved in this problem too. I will stop her and ask her for forgiveness."

My Papa replied, "Just let it go. She told me if I chose you, she would have to leave. Then she did. She will come back, I guess."

Next day, our house was very quiet. However, I was surprised that the family, especially *Lok Tah* was not worried about my stepmother leaving; instead they asked me quietly what Papa did to straighten things out.

"Papa chose me and *Eeh* left the house!" I responded with confidence, chin up with a smile. I didn't let him see how worried I was that *Eeh* might return. She had tried to kill me and might succeed the next time because she believed I caused her problem.

"She is a witch. Why would she want your Papa to abandon you?" *Lok Tah* hissed through his teeth.

"*Chah*, she is not a regular witch; she is evil," I agreed.

My *Pou* Sunthary just laughed after I told him that I kicked my stepmother and her skirt dropped on the floor. Only my cousin Or, the favorite of my stepmother, said something I did not appreciate at that time, "You are too small to fight with the mountain."

I looked at his face to understand his meaning. He was sincere. "Yes, I understand what you mean. She has more power than I do."

I felt a lot of happiness, freedom, and peace in the house after she left. However, my Papa did not show up at lunchtime, nor dinnertime and he came back home very late at night. Where has he been? Was he staying with his mistress? About a week later, my Papa came back home and *Eeh* was with him. I felt the trouble come back. She did not greet anybody; she went straight to her room and lay on the bed. Papa called me and suggested that I go see her and apologize.

I rationalized, "I hate doing things that are unfair but I have to do it for my Papa." I thought for a while to regain my strength before I talked to her. I sat down on the floor near her bed and said, "*Eeh*, please forgive me for the day I did wrong to you. I will not do it again." She did not say a word; I guess she still hated me and it was not her plan to see me in the house. After a long silence, I started to talk to her again, "Please forgive me, and please love me as your daughter and I will love you as my *Mak*."

Again, she did not reply to me. I was so humiliated. I got up and left the room. My Papa, who waited for me outside, was worried about the lack of results. Afterwards, he encouraged me with a loving voice, "You did everything that you were supposed to do for yourself and for me. People will see from now on who is wrong and who is right."

The relationship between us got worse every day. She talked to me only when I asked a question; otherwise, she ignored me and gave me a bad look just like she would like to kill me. Life for me was unpredictable, just like the Cambodian saying, "Sunshine in the morning, rain in the afternoon or vice versa." I shed many tears from the deep pain of a bitter relationship with my stepmother.

Hide the Love for Children

Leang and I both flunked the third year pharmacy exam on the first session. It was not happy news to my Papa, "I told you if you get involved with love, you will lose your concentration on your studies. Here, this is the proof."

I told him, "Papa, I still have one more chance to study for the second session. I will study harder to pass the exam." For this reason, my fiancé was allowed to come to my house so we could study together every day. We passed the exam and while he was happy with my success, I asked Papa again if he would now send me to Paris to continue my studies.

"No! My plan is to have you stay with me and take care of my company after I retire. I have plenty of money to support you and even your children. If you left, I would miss you. I have nobody to replace you."

"Don't you love me? Don't you care about me? All others parents love their children; they give them what they want for their future. Why can't you?"

"Those parents are stupid. I am different. If you want something very bad, I won't give it to you."

I was so mad at him. Why would he give me anything I wanted except to go to Paris? Little did I know what enormous and tragic consequences his decision would have for my life?

Was it the Khmer adage "Never let the children know that you love them, otherwise, they will be greedy and lazy" that was guiding his behavior? It was no surprise that I was so confused about his love toward me; most of the time I felt he did not love me. Sometimes he said he had no money; sometimes he said he had lots of money. He said he loved me but he beat me miserably if he was angry with me. He insulted me anywhere, anytime when he was upset with me. When he was angry, he screamed loudly so everybody heard my problems. He did not want to raise me in a westernized way, but he allowed me to have friendships with lots of foreigners. He bought me French magazines; he took me to see French movies, and bought lots of French music. He was happy when I sang a French song for him. He told everybody he wouldn't spoil me, but he gave me everything I wanted. I was really confused with Papa.

"Education is Good for Life!"

One day he took me for a ride around the city. We had a good talk and from that time I knew how much he cared for and loved me. I learned a lot and understood more what he wanted from me. His words, "I show you my love by pushing you hard to study. I love you but I won't give you everything you want; only what you need."

"Yes, I know that," I said, but I was really confused as to what he thought I needed.

However his next words clarified my confusion. "You must stay here to finish your Pharmacy degree; then you can go to Paris to get a doctorate in Pharmacy. No matter what happens, you can't lose. If you cannot get a doctorate in Pharmacy, you can still come back home and work as a pharmacist in our pharmaceutical plant. Right now, you are still in the middle of nowhere. Get as much education as you can now; education is good for life; no one can steal it from you."

I was surprised that he then revealed the truth about his wealth. "Recently, I bought two more houses, one for you, and more land for investment. I have ten properties so far and will look around to buy more. I never let your stepmother knows about this; I can see she is not honest with me."

I thought, "Wow, exciting! I am dying to see it happen soon because I won't need to see *Eeh* anymore!"

Then he told me his biggest secret. "I have money saved in 'black accounts' that only my secretary (my cousin Suy, Pech) and I know about."

I did not tell him my secret – that Suy, Pech had already blabbed about the accounts to me. Since Papa was being so forthcoming, I decided to ask him about the new BMW that had been sitting in the garage for quite a while and that he didn't want to talk about. I remembered that he angrily told Stepmother that this car was not his and belonged to Phlek, Pheun. Taking the advantage of this moment, I decided to find out the truth. "Is the BMW your car or your friend's?"

"Mine; I bought it with money I won in the lottery."

Hmm…I thought, Suy, Pech was right! She told me secretly that Papa won a lottery. I now realized that Papa did not want me to associate with her because he was afraid she would tell his secrets. His fears were justified. "Why don't you drive it?"

"Because I told her (*Eeh*) it was my friend's car. I don't want her to know about my finances. She keeps asking me about money, and if she knew all my secrets she would spend all my money, leaving nothing to you. I want to keep it for you."

"It sounds reasonable. I believe you, Papa!"

Papa continued, "I am doing big business but I need to hire a person I can trust to help handle it. That person is S.E. Phlek, Pheun's nephew. His name is Chhorn. I just sent him money to start a business in Bangkok."

"Maybe he took your money and went to play."

"I will travel to Bangkok soon to make sure all is well. We will grow orchids."

I did not know enough to ask any intelligent questions about the orchid business, but then Papa told me that he also owned a travel agency. "What is its name?"

"Hanouman Travel Agency."

"Wow, I am rich."

"Do not tell any of this to your stepmother"

"OK." I quietly listened to him and I felt I loved my Papa more. I was surprised that he could hide everything so well for so long.

Resentful

The day before the wedding, I was in my bedroom, excitedly going over in my mind what tomorrow would be like, how I would look, what would happen. The door opened and *Eeh* came in without knocking. She threw a little bag in front of me. "Here," she said, and stood waiting for me to open the bag. I untied the ribbon at the top of the little bag. I took out a diamond pendant and a ring. I was sure she was standing there to see the look on my face. The diamonds were very small and had no luster. Diamonds were supposed to sparkle and twinkle when the light hit them. These diamonds, if they even were diamonds, did none of that. I knew she had done exactly as I suspected she would. She found the lowest quality diamonds to show her dislike for me as well as pocket as much money as she could.

"Why are they so small, *Eeh*? Why aren't they sparkling?" I asked.

"They are good diamonds." I was sure she just wanted to see me miserable with disappointment.

Much as I would have liked to have, I couldn't hide my feelings. I put them on and looked in the mirror. They looked as if they had come from a peddler on the street. I held my hand up to show her my wrist. *"Eeh,* where is the bracelet? You forgot the bracelet." I shook the little bag thinking it was still in the bottom. "It's not here. When will I get the diamond bracelet?"

"You will have to ask your Papa for more money. I barely had enough for what you've got." she said maliciously and left me staring into the mirror, defeated. She got exactly what she had come for, to see me miserable. I wanted to tell Papa about the bracelet and the poor quality of the diamonds, but my conscience stopped me. Papa was allowing the wedding against his better judgment and I was too ashamed to complain.

The Singing Birds Replaced

Cambodian weddings can traditionally last three days, however, because of the terrible political situation, Papa compressed the festivities from three days to one.

Early the next morning, I stood at my window and looked out at the commotion on the street. Papa had a large tent built in front of the house. It was made of bamboo poles with a fabric cover. Each bamboo pole was decorated with coconut leaves hanging from the edges of the cover. This structure blocked traffic on both sides of the street in front of the house. The tent was to receive guests and provide a shady place to eat during the wedding ceremony, which would last all day. The garage was also decorated with coconut leaves and set up as a room for the groom to change clothes. The groom was not allowed to be alone with the bride until the wedding ended. The furniture in the living room had been moved to *Lok Tah's* living room. The floor was blanketed with the finest quality Persian rugs on which the guests would sit and the room was decorated in classic Persian décor, in shades of red and gold.

I was still in disbelief. Was I really getting married today? Could my dream really be coming true? I heard the sounds of the distant guns and bombs. They seemed to be closer than usual and this frightened me. My mind vacillated between my happiness and my fear. I looked out onto the street and, amid the sounds of the bombing, the morning seemed eerily empty. Usually as the sun rose, the street came alive and was bustling with traffic. By this time the birds were singing and flying around chasing each other; bakers selling French bread would pass by loudly calling out their wares; Chinese merchants would call from the front gate selling donuts and cakes for us to have with morning coffee. Why were all these familiar sounds and activities not happening this morning?

The sun was shrouded in heavy dark clouds. Not the dark clouds like those before a monsoon rain; these were different. They hung ominously still in the air. The singing birds had been replaced by the sound of guns and bombs. In the past, attacks usually lasted one night and were over by morning. We got used to the routine. They had never been serious attacks, and were over by morning, but this morning was different and frightening.

By seven, the woman whom I hired to dress me and do my makeup had still not shown up. Anxiously, I walked back and forth in the room anticipating the events of the day. I kept checking my watch wondering if she would show up at all.

Unexpectedly, Papa came to see me, not to give me his blessings, or even to see how I was doing, just to deliver news. "Everything is messed up. *Ah Char* (the priest) came in late because he had trouble getting here. He wants to leave early to take care of his family; he is anxious," Papa said worriedly. "I have to keep the ceremony going no matter what. I do not know how many guests will show up today. I expected many to be here by now. Only a few have arrived so far. Maybe all of them are having trouble getting here." He walked back to the living room, leaving me very sad and disappointed in my room.

He scared me. What happens if the KR takes over the city today during the wedding? Will they want to kill us? What would I do? As I asked myself these questions, Monith and Poch, my cousins who were to be my attendants arrived smiling and happily chattering, "Sorry, we would have been here sooner but we woke up late."

"You are here now. Hurry up. Don't talk too much," I said seriously, still affected by Papa's behavior. However, the girls didn't seem to be worried about anything; instead they were giggling and teasing me as if nothing mattered but my wedding. I began to relax and laugh with them. I wondered if other people living in the city were as oblivious to the KR chaos.

I looked at my watch again, worried about the dresser who was bringing the wedding costumes. As I sat down in front of the vanity, I looked into the mirror desperately trying to will her to arrive. I closed my eyes sending a silent prayer. When I opened my eyes, a skinny lady in her late thirties, dressed in *sampot hol*, and a yellow lace blouse, appeared in the mirror behind me.

"There was no pedicab. The streets are a mess. There is chaos everywhere," she said, noisily dropping a very large suitcase on the floor beside her. As she stretched, arching her back, she dropped two smaller shoulder bags beside the bigger suitcase. Wiping sweat from her face with her silk scarf, she ran her fingers through her disheveled hair and continued. "I'm sorry, in all the confusion; I forgot to comb my hair." I was so relieved she had arrived; I didn't care what she looked like. She was here and we could get on with the preparations.

"No matter, you're here now. I am happy you made it," I said giving her a spontaneous hug. "I was so scared you wouldn't get here at all."

Behind her was a young woman about my age. I assumed they were mother and daughter. "People in my neighborhood are in a panic. They are rushing everywhere trying to find a safe place. The roads are crowded with everyone not knowing where to go. I heard the attacks are now not far from the city," she continued, her hands skillfully working on my hair.

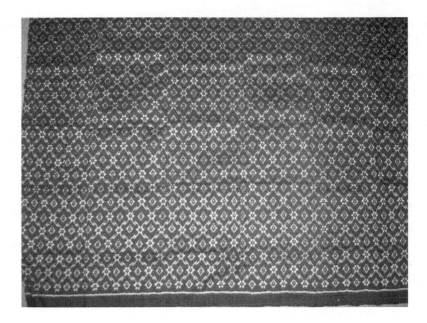

Sampot hol, a Khmer traditional silk woven skirt

The Competing Sounds of Gongs and Bombs

The older woman opened the large suitcase and hurriedly removed the wedding costumes. There was also a beautifully embroidered scarf. She laid them out on the floor to make it easier for me to see them. "What color do you want?" Unlike the western customs, Cambodian wedding dresses are almost always rented. They are traditional *sampots,* very elaborately decorated. Without waiting for my answer, she picked up the red *sampot chang kben.* She continued to talk of her worries about the KR attacks. This was not what I thought my wedding day would be like. It was supposed to be happy and the talk should have been about the wedding and the life Leang and I would share; our plans and dreams for the future, not about war and bombs. Instead of praying for a happy marriage and healthy children, I prayed nothing bad would happen and that my wedding would take place without incident. This was supposed to be my day. But I was eclipsed by the KR and the threat to the city. I felt so very small and trivial.

Her talk went on for the hour or so it took for her to finish my hair, my makeup and the fitting of the wedding costume. She told me she was a widow, the bread winner in her home, taking care of her elderly parents and her two children. She also did the beautiful embroidery work on her own traditional shawl – a skill she had learned from her mother. Her daughter was also skilled and experienced.

She helped my two bridesmaids get dressed in their *sampots chang kben*, the same color as mine. I was then adorned with masses of traditional jewelry.

I walked to the full length mirror and stared at myself. I didn't recognize myself immediately. I was beautiful. Would Leang be pleased when he saw me? When she was finished dressing me, the mother hurried to the garage to dress the groom. I began to hear different voices in the living room which told me more guests had arrived. I was sure they were talking of nothing but the KR and how this would affect my wedding. I asked my bridesmaids to check the living room to see how many guests were. They came back excited and giggling.

"Are you nervous?" asked Monith.

"Terribly."

"There are lots of important people out there. You should see. Everyone is here," Monith grabbed my hands.

"Be prepared to walk out with me when you hear the gong. The groom looks so handsome in his wedding outfit. You make a striking couple," said the dresser as she hurried back into the room.

"Oh! Are you finished dressing him already?" I asked, a little shocked, as my costumer was back so quickly.

"It is not difficult to dress the groom, unlike the bride. He doesn't need that," she said, pointing at the jewelry, "or that, or that." She continued pointing to everything in the room. We all laughed at the thought of Leang wearing any of it. Then we heard the gong beat loudly; it seemed to be competing with the sounds of the bombs and guns. I heard a soft voice directing that the gong be beat a second time - my signal to leave the room. When the gong stopped, the silence was replaced with the sound of gunfire in the distance, like many fireworks going off simultaneously.

I left the room, followed by the two bridesmaids. Their giggling voices teased me from behind, "One, two, three, climb the tree and you fall down."

"Sh... Enough." I whispered

As I entered the living room the heady aroma of fresh fruit mingled with the scent of jasmine and roses filled my nostrils and I forgot my fear of the bombs and laughed with my cousins. This is the way a wedding supposed to be. For a moment I was happy. Still laughing, I looked up and found myself in the middle of the crowded room and suddenly became terrified. Not of the bombs this time but of the hundreds and hundreds of eyes staring at me. I was both elated and scared.

The crowd of people sitting everywhere on the lush carpet in the living room was overwhelming and I wanted to turn and run back to the room. I was surprised; everyone seemed to be here. I didn't hear any voices; I may have forgotten to breathe. I felt warm and frozen at the same time. I could only look straight ahead of me and could only hear the person in front of me asking me to kneel. It was the *Ah Char*, a gentleman in his fifties, dark skinned, with silver hair. He also wore *sampot chang kben* and a white traditional Khmer jacket. When I could look around, I saw

Leang standing behind the *Ah Char*. My heart began to fly; he looked so handsome dressed in red *sampot chang kben* with a traditional gold Khmer jacket.

The groom's party was waiting to enter the house and tradition demanded that first the bride would kneel and wash his feet. In the old days, the groom's family would have walked all the way from his house to mine, but Leang and his entourage came by car and only walked the last 100 feet. When they arrived, there were formal introductions and the *Ah Char* asked my Papa for permission to enter the house. We then accepted the bridegroom's gifts to symbolize the agreement for the marriage. The groom's wedding party began with the *Ah Char* followed by a flower girl and boy. Next, came Leang and two friends, followed two people carrying areca nut flowers on stemmed silver trays. The next two bearers carried trays bringing new clothes for the bride, to symbolize a new beginning for her. The rest of the processions were bearers of food.

The first trays carried two complete roasted piglets to symbolize the wealth of the family. The train of people carrying food was like a colorful Chinese dragon waving its way down the street. One hundred dishes were presented as the groom's dowry to the bride. All the gifts were arranged in baskets decorated with roses on the handles. I don't know why Papa chose one hundred, but there had to be one hundred gifts in the dowry, and, later, one hundred tables of ten at the restaurant for the reception. I then knelt to wash Leang's feet. Well, not really – modern brides did not physically wash the groom's feet as in the old ways. Instead I knelt and patted his feet with water floating with jasmine flowers and scented with cologne. "King Leang" his friend teased, nudging him gently in the side with his elbow.

Leang nudged back, "Kneel to the King!" They all laughed. I couldn't help it; I had to suppress a laugh, too. Then, Leang saw Papa appear behind me and corrected himself, standing straight as a flag pole and looking very nervous. He looked so handsome; was he thinking the same about me? We exchanged a secret smile and I knew I didn't displease him. I'd found my angel. His honest brown eyes that told me he would never break his word. I loved the way he looked at me, I could see through to his soul. His voice was like soft music calming my heart. I loved everything about him. I smiled at him again and he returned the smile before he followed me inside.

In front of us, Papa sat beside my new mother-in-law. He did not look happy. Leang and I sat down in front of them. We bowed deeply to offer respect and thanks for allowing us to be married. My eyes met Papa's and, for a moment, we looked deeply into each other's eyes. I saw what I interpreted to be despair and disappointment and I tried to look away. How could he not see how much I loved Leang and why could he not be happy for me?

I looked around the room; I felt someone was missing - of course, Stepmother. I couldn't see her anywhere. Had she refused to attend my wedding? I looked around again and through the open door to the dining room. I saw *Lok Tah* and

Yey Kong, sitting quietly, like statues, not talking, not smiling. They showed no emotion. I wanted them to be happy. It was my wedding. Everyone was supposed to be happy. Papa looked annoyed. His demeanor made me feel even more uncomfortable. I wondered what was on his mind. Was it the wedding gifts my mother-in-law offered him? Had they not met his expectations? Was he upset that *Eeh* had refused to attend? Was he worried about the bombing, or maybe it was just my mother-in-law's incessant chatter that made him uncomfortable. After greeting family and relatives on both sides, my fiancé offered me a diamond wedding ring and, in return, I offered him a band of gold.

The absence of my stepmother worried me a little, but the absence of Cousin Phach made me feel like a piece of the puzzle was missing. A couple of days before my wedding day, she came in to see me and brought me a red blanket for a wedding gift. I loved it; red was my favorite color. She told me she was afraid to attend my wedding because my papa was mad at her due to a dispute between her and my stepmother over money. Papa's unhappiness and the absence of Stepmother and Phach replaced the worries of the KR attack and the bombs. As I worried about this, I noticed Papa talking to the *Ah Char* asking him to shorten the ceremony as much as he could, meaning it was not necessary to prolong speeches.

Guests Chatted about the KR Invasion

Despite the fact that the *Ah Char* had said he wanted to go home early, rather than starting the ceremony, he spent his time talking, to anyone who would listen, about his experiences the night before. "I heard shooting not far away from where I live. I couldn't sleep all night worrying about the gunfire and the political situation. I don't know where else I can go. What is President Lon Nol going to do to protect us?" He took a deep breath, "I almost didn't make it today. Oh! I pray nothing worse happens to the people."

Papa seemed calm. Only I could understand that Papa was not happy but he tried to pretend nothing was happening. Now, when I look back, I realize how surreal it all was. Guests chatted to each other about the KR invasion in the city. They now occupied the region between the city and Pochen Tong airport. The airport had become a hot zone. Airline schedules were temporarily cancelled; no one could leave due to the bombings. However, it still did not bother me much as I felt that Papa would have known first if something bad was going to happen. Prime Minister Lon, Nol would not let us die.

Traditional live music accompanied the ceremony and competed with the sound of the bombs. Soon it was time to have breakfast and I returned to my bedroom to prepare for the next phase of the ceremony. Papa had ordered ground pork porridge mixed with scallops, mushrooms, fish balls, and shredded ginger. The porridge was served with Chinese donuts. The aroma of ginger and fried garlic made me hungry. I sat in my room waiting for someone to bring me a bowl, but it seemed as if I were invisible when the food arrived. Everyone was taking care of themselves and totally forgot about me. I finally got up and found one of my bridesmaids.

"Where have you been? I am starving. Bring me a bowl of porridge," I demanded.

"You are on a diet so you can look sexy on your wedding night," she had grabbed a Chinese donut for herself. "The groom is not hungry; he is nervous and cannot eat. Why are you so hungry?" she asked, her mouth stuffed with donuts, so she was barely audible.

"I am different, I am hungry. I need food."

They brought me a dish but before I could finish eating I was urged to go back to the room. "Hurry up, you need to change," said my dresser, holding the *sampot charabab* (a tapestry woven with silver and gold thread) in her hand. "I also need to dress the groom, so hurry," she added. After she finished with me, she rushed to the garage to take care of Leang.

My Dream Comes True

One by one, friends and relatives came to check on me in the bedroom. I felt special. Is this how a queen or a movie star feels? I was elated. This was how I dreamed it would be. I was the center of attention. I enjoyed every second of this attention.

Haircuts

The next part of the ceremony was the ritual haircuts. As I left my room to join Leang, once again summoned by the beating of a gong, I kept my eyes on the floor and peeked at the crowd through my eyelashes. The room was filled with brightly dressed women smiling radiantly at me. It seemed as if each woman was putting herself in my place, remembering her own wedding or thinking of her wedding yet to come. It was as if the memory or anticipation had erased the fear and threat of the attack, if only for a moment. The ceremonial music continued to play and the man who had been singing was offered a pair of golden scissors. In his other hand was put a golden comb. He began dancing around us, accompanied by a woman singer who also began dancing. The woman was holding a silver challis in which to put the locks of hair. They gracefully danced and sang around both of us. I shyly looked at my new husband from the corner of my eyes. His eyes met mine the same way and we smiled. I could smell his familiar cologne and I wanted to be in his arms. I felt my heart nearly leaping from my chest. I couldn't believe we were finally married.

Leang turned away, looking straight ahead, pretending the exchange never happened. After dancing around us a couple of times, the man cut a tiny piece of hair from each of our heads and put them into the challis. The *Ah Char* was the next to do the same. Then in pairs, and in order of importance, the rest of the wedding party followed suit, each cutting a minute amount of hair to put in the silver challis. Cutting the hair of the groom and bride symbolized cutting off all the prior bad luck associated with the body. It was believed that this would bring a successful life and harmony into the relationship. Originally, it was a real haircut. However, for my wedding it was only symbolic. Papa chose cousin Princess Sisowath Saman Met to accompany him for the ceremonies since Stepmother refused to attend. The cutting ceremony lasted about a half hour. Again the gong was hit to announce our return to our rooms.

Blessing Ceremony by the Monks

We paused for the noon meal. At 1:00 PM, a man beat a bronze plate to call the bride and groom for the blessing ceremony by the monks. Now, we both were dressed in *sampot charabab*. Traditional music, played by a group of five men, accompanied the blessing ceremony. The bronze plate was hit again to announce the end of the blessing, so the groom and bride could once again return to their own rooms.

Preah Thong Neang Neak – Gathering Ceremony

At 3:00 PM, the music played to announce the Gathering Ceremony. A woman, accompanied by dancers, sang in front of my bedroom door to alert me to be ready to return to the ceremony. I wore a long scarf, beautifully hand embroidered with sequins, wrapped around my chest and draped over my shoulder leaving the other shoulder bare. I was to bow first to honor my father, then my mother, then all my ancestors. Tears welled in my eyes as I thought about my mother; she was not here to see me. My father was here but he was not happy for me. He is here to save his reputation. He is not here for me, only for himself. Are my ancestors here with me now? Would any of them care? None of my relatives are here for me. Stepmother hates me so much that she refuses to attend. If *Mak* were still alive, Papa would be happier and the song would be meaningful to me. If my Cousin Phach was here, she would hug me and laugh with me to make my day blissful. As I waited, these thoughts made the gong sound so hollow and meaningless. I blinked back my tears of disenchantment and waited for someone to walk me out. I could not have felt worse than I did at that moment; I felt wretched and lonesome.

I was scared to go out again. What if Papa was not there for me? His actions were unpredictable. What if he decided he didn't want to see me because I disappointed him so much? The song coming from the room was romantic and should be filling my heart with joy and happy expectations, but the song failed to deliver its message. Papa's unhappiness was breaking my heart. Though the room was filled with people, I felt very lonely and sad. Would all of Papa's predictions about my new mother-in-law come true? Why did my stepmother hate me so much she could not attend my wedding?

As the song finished, the bronze plate was hit again and the curtain opened. I forced myself to smile at Leng, the wife of Cousin Thor, who came in to accompany me. She took my hand and walked me through the curtain and into the main room to sit next to Leang. The bridesmaids sat behind us with the two men who accompanied Leang. We sat back on the thick red Persian rug with our elbows on the floor. This was a fun part of the wedding, when the bride and groom competed to see who had the highest shoulder. It was a traditional belief that the highest shoulder indicated who would "wear the pants" in the family. Everyone expected the groom's shoulder to be higher than the bride's. I was encouraged to sit up straight to ensure that my shoulder was higher than his. Relatives on both sides stuffed pillows under our elbows. I was pushed to lean on my husband. This was a moment I would remember all my life. His arms enveloped me; I felt loved and protected. All my fears disappeared.

The sound of the bombs, the worries about *Eeh* and Papa, the uncertainty of my mother-in-law and my new relatives, everything disappeared, except for that wonderful feeling of being loved and protected. The rest of the room seemed to disappear as I listened to the rhythm of his heartbeat, the rise and fall of his chest seemed as if he were breathing for both of us. His warm breath on my neck caressed me with promises of what was to come. I wanted this love, this bliss, this euphoria, this feeling that everything would be perfect, and nothing could harm us or come between us, to last forever. I looked up at his face and smiled. His eyes were filled with softness and desire.

Bay Khon Chang Dai or **Tying the Wrists ceremony**

The next phase was the longest phase and would last more than an hour. It started out with *"Bay Khon Chang Dai* -Tying the Wrists" ceremony. We both sat on the Persian carpet as family and friends were invited to give us a blessing by tying red cotton thread around our wrists. Parents, friends and relatives tied red thread around our wrists and then wet our hands with scented water. When Papa came to tie my wrist, I thought of my *Mak* and how much I missed her and wished she could have been there to give me her blessing. I felt my eyes well up again and I couldn't help it, the tears spilled down my cheeks. I heard a voice from behind me reminding me that it was bad luck to cry during your wedding. I looked apprehensively around for Papa; nevertheless, he had quickly disappeared after tying my wrist. I hoped his sudden departure and my tears were not an omen of unhappiness for our future.

I was relieved when he came back for the next and last session of the wedding. It was a *"Bangvel Po Pil* – the Rotation of Seven Times" session. Only married couples participated as a symbol of bringing a strong relationship to the new bridal couple. The married couples sat around the groom and bride as a gong was loudly beaten to acknowledge and witness the wishes for success, well-being, and long-lasting love to the new married couple. The *Ah Char* lit three candles, each held in an ornately decorated silver holder. The candles were passed among the crowd sitting with the bride and groom. Whoever received the candle would wave their hand over the flame to symbolize brushing away evil. With the sound of the gong and Papa's reappearance, I felt my strength returning. It seemed that the up and down feelings of love and happiness vs. disappointment and sadness hung on what Papa did and how he stayed for each ceremony. If only he could better hide his disappointment from me. If only he could pretend to be happy for me and Leang.

Phkar Slar Tossing

This ceremony was followed by the *Phkar* (flower) *Slar* (areca nut) tossing. We used the flowers from the areca nut tree for this ceremony. The *Ah Char* laid the flowers on a silver tray and the guests picked them up and threw them at the newly married couple to wish happiness for them. During this flower tossing, the *Ah Char* officially announced that we were husband and wife. He advised us that a husband has to be honest, loyal and faithful to his wife. The husband has to love and take care of the wife forever, to provide for the family and, as much as he can, to make his wife happy. A husband has to protect his wife, speak nicely to her and treat her with love and respect, even when angry. A husband should not beat his wife even when he loses his temper.

The wife is expected to do the same for the husband: to provide love, caring, loyalty, and honesty, to forgive and forget. Treat the husband with respect and compassion. Do not ask the husband for more than he can afford and spend money wisely. He then blessed all of us and gongs were again loudly beaten to announce the end of the ceremony and to acknowledge our marriage.

The words husband and wife made me shiver with excitement. But then, I was stabbed again with worry and my mind raced, "Am I really the wife of this man who Papa so disapproves?" I knew in Papa's eyes I should not be a wife to Leang, and that he felt Leang was not good enough to be my husband. I knew *Eeh* would look for any reason to cause problems. Living in Papa's house was not going to be easy. Both Papa and *Eeh* were unhappy with our marriage; each for their own reasons.

I did not know how long the music had lasted as I was lost in my own world. I was brought back to reality when someone from behind tapped me on the shoulder telling me the music was over and it was time to get up. A laughing voice shouted, "Get up faster than your husband and you will be the boss in your home." How could I get up fast? My legs were numb from sitting for hours on the floor. Suddenly someone grabbed me from behind and quickly lifted me up before Leang had a chance to move. I lost my balance and fell over Leang. My husband caught me and helped me to regain my balance. He then turned me around so my back was to him. He was told to hold on the hem of my garment to follow me to the room for the honey moon just like *Preah Thong* followed *Neang Neak* to the ocean for a honeymoon, according to the Cambodian legend.

I looked over my shoulder sending my love for him that burned in my breast like an eternal flame. Our eyes met and sprays of love flew to him as I gazed into his eyes. Could he feel it too? I wanted to devour him and keep him inside me always. I felt we were only two people that existed in the world.

Photographers, teenagers and young women surrounded my husband and me. They teased us as we fed bananas and grapes to each other. My husband gathered me in his arms and kissed me on the neck. "We are finally married," he said in a trembling voice, holding my face in his hands to look in my eyes. My heart soared at the mere sound of his voice. Such joy! He satiated me as the waters of his love filled me up to overflowing. Acreca nut flowers fluttered down upon us, wishing us a happy honeymoon.

I relaxed in his hands and wanted to tell him that my soul was overflowing with my love for him, take my heart - it is his. Without him I have no use for it. I was constantly amazed by the delight I felt when we were together. I wanted to know if he felt the same magical connection. I also wanted to warn him to please be strong and well-prepared for what was sure to come if we lived in Papa's house. His steadfast gaze and his kiss on my forehead reassured me he would be a strong man and everything would work out for us. Tears of happiness began to form at the corners of my eyes. I blinked them back to give me strength and to prove to him I also would be strong by not allowing tears during the wedding.

"Don't worry about your Papa and your *Eeh*," he caressed my lips, "I promise I will melt their hearts. I am more worried about the shelling now." These words brought me back to the reality outside our wedding ceremonies. As all the guests left for the reception, the sounds of the shelling continued unabated.

The War Moves Closer

After the daylong ceremony, there was a lavish reception at "La Lune" restaurant. Papa invited more than a thousand people from the Prime Minister of Cambodia to acquaintances. They all came except the Prime Minister, Lon, Nol. Not surprisingly, he did not attend due to security concerns. The bombs had gotten louder as the day progressed indicating that the attack was coming closer. Despite this, Papa did not appear very worried. Because he had been so distant for the previous few days and so preoccupied during the wedding, I had assumed that he was not happy with me, my husband and his family. It didn't occur to me that his behavior might have nothing to do with me and the wedding and everything to do with the approach of the KR. This was typical of Papa; I never really knew what he was thinking unless he was angry.

I was happy we could make it through the wedding and the reception. We kept praying everything would be all right and that we would be safe, especially at the reception because no one had any idea where the next bomb would hit. Papa asked that the food be served early so we could finish early. It was sad since there was no dancing and everyone hurriedly ate and rushed to get back home. The next bomb very well could have hit the restaurant.

When we arrived back home, we went downstairs to bow at my grandparents' feet. Each advised us, "Love each other, take care of each other, and listen to each other for a healthy relationship. I pray for your relationship to last for eternity. Remember, we do not marry for a divorce."

At midnight, we bowed at our parents' feet asking for blessings and forgiveness and also asking for permission to go on a honeymoon. A calm Papa firmly told my husband, "I do not believe in divorce. My daughter is my heart and I want you to love my daughter as I love her. Be a good husband to her." We were about to bow to *Eeh*, however, she coldly told us she was not my biological mother and it was not necessary. Typical.

My Honeymoon

We entered my room exhausted but exhilarated. Without even looking at each other, we flopped diagonally on the bed and breathed deeply. The pink sheet was covered with the jasmine flowers. We filled our lungs with the intoxicating scents. Leang found my hand and gently squeezed it. "*Aun*, we made it. We challenged Papa, and we made it," my husband whispered.

My tears fell with happiness for the moment and for my new husband. All the arguments, all the protests, all the stubbornness had led to this moment. "I never thought Papa would ever allow us to be together in this room." I turned my head to hide my tears, even though they were tears of joy.

"True love will melt his tough heart. When he sees how happy were are and how well I treat you; when he understands how we were meant to be together, he will come around," my husband said, caressing my back. He flipped me over so he could rub my feet with his. "You are crying." He wiped my tears and kissed me on the neck and forehead. "Do not cry, *Aun*. We are not going to stay with Papa any longer than we have to. Your stepmother will give us more trouble than we want. We won't have children until I get my pharmacy degree and then we can move to our own place. We both have only one year to go."

He continued to caress me. His fingers ran down to my face and stopped at my mouth. I parted my lips in response to him. He continued across my upper lip back and forth. His finger was soon replaced by his soft lips. This was the first kiss of our married life - a real kiss, a passionate kiss, a kiss that I didn't have to break off for fear of breaking Papa's rules. We lay still for a moment.

"I will take off your clothes," he playfully said, as his mouth tugged at the strap on my shoulder. One hand found the zipper and slowly pulled it down while the other searched for other obstacles in his path. His kisses became more demanding. He released the hook on the back of my bra. I turned back to him and kissed him again. I removed his formal jacket and threw it on the floor. I unbuttoned his shirt and unfastened his belt. He impatiently removed his own shirt and pants.

"We need to take a shower first," he said, lifting me up and caring me to the shower. "*Aun*, I love you," his trembling voice whispered in my ear, nearly drowned out by the sounds of the bombs in the distance.

And so, our married life began amid conflict and turmoil on every level. We found joy in each other but misery and uncertainty all around us – in the house and in the ever more precarious political situation.

Ignored

Papa made it obvious, daily, that he was not happy with my choice for a husband. Papa purposely intimidated him and Leang's fear of being disliked by my Papa intensified. They avoided each other; Papa had lunch before we did and rarely came home for dinner. *Eeh* openly made fun of Leang to Papa and treated him as if he were a stupid man, someone beneath her. I was not surprised, since she didn't like me, it would only follow she wouldn't like my husband either, no matter who I chose. When Papa stayed home, Leang did not leave our bedroom.

As Papa ignored my husband, he also ignored me. Every day when he came back home from work, the first person he looked for was my servant's child. Once I heard *Eeh* say this child would inherit from Papa and bear his last name, I became more jealous of him.

Despite all the warnings I received from Papa that my husband's family was only after his money, to me it seemed like they were more loving and caring than my own family. They received me like a princess. I found my two little sisters-in-law, Lony and Vanny, to be cute and talkative. I loved both of them as they always came to talk to me, and asked me many of questions. Sometimes they asked me for something that they wanted and their parents would not buy them, so I bought it for them. The older sisters, Maum and Srey, were quiet and shy. Maum was already married and had a little boy about a year old. However, the three boys were immature and continually talked back to their parents. Whenever I visited, I never saw them smile as they were always fighting with someone in the family, usually with their mother who always lectured them.

"Time will tell," Papa often predicted when he talked about my in-laws. As time went by, it appeared to me that Papa's prediction that they would "bleed you dry" might be coming true. Later on, I caught my husband hiding money under the mattress. He told me his brother needed money and he would give it to him. He said he didn't want to tell me because he was afraid that I wouldn't let him have the money. I believed him but from then on I was careful with money and gasoline because all the boys had problems with money. I learned the two little girls were really no different. They used me to acquire the things they wanted.

My mother-in-law was always curious about Papa's money. She was willing to believe the worst about anyone and accepted the gossip that Kilen's baby was Papa's son because he was so attached to the baby. She was not just curious about Papa's business; she insulted Papa, calling him 'selfish' for not letting us go to Paris.

I overheard, as I am sure I was supposed to, 'If Leang had married the daughter of Dr. Mey, and my son would be safe in Paris'.

So that was another reason Leang's parents had been eager for the marriage – the possibility that we would be sent safely out of the country.

~THIRTEEN~

THINGS WILL BE UPSIDE DOWN

Some days after my wedding, I was looking for Papa to once again ask about going to France, when I overheard his phone conversation with Cousin Thor.

"When do you plan to go to France again? I want to convert my money into dollars and set up an account in France. Will it be possible?" I also heard him tell my cousin, "As long as I stay, nothing is going to happen to our country." He looked up the ceiling and took a deep breath. I felt something must be worrying Papa. "I think we can go together in February. Will it be possible? I think the airport will be safe then." He then nodded his head to agree with the voice in the phone. "Well, still, to be on the safe side, we have to prepare for serious unrest."

Worriedly, I asked him, "What is wrong Papa?" He raised his hand to quiet me and continued to talk with Thor, "It is not a bad idea to stock up on dried fish in case a civil war does happen." Papa turned to me again and mouthed, "I am talking to Thor."

"What does he say?" I pulled gently on his shirt.

"Nothing; you wouldn't understand."

"Papa, tell me. It must be about the KR, the civil war, food..." Then I shouted at him, "I am not a child, Papa. This conversation is very important to me too."

"I plan to send both of you to France. But I cannot do this until I set up a bank account in France. I am working on it, just trust me. We are safe for the moment." This plan pacified and excited me.

Ban's Prediction

Outside of the city, the KR bombings became more frequent and daily life was more perilous. Daily, routine things such as grocery shopping or going to work became more and more dangerous. I was very frightened for our future. I decided, at the beginning of February, to pay a visit to Ban, a relative I knew was a psychic. I believed Ban could see what would happen to Cambodia in the future and I desperately wanted to know.

"Tell your Papa to leave the country before April. It will be *kralap chak* (Things will be upside down). That was all he said.

"What do you mean? Tell me more details."

He smiled, "Your papa will understand."

"Your smile confuses me."

"He always smiles when he talks to people," his wife spoke for him.

I left him filled with worry; I hoped Papa could explain more. I still believed we were leaving soon so I didn't think we would be involved in this "upside down" word. If it happened in April, we would be safe in France, but I told Papa anyway and he just said "Ban is foolish."

Papa must be wrong or maybe he did not want to scare me. I noticed my cousin Or, a police inspector who wore a police uniform for work, carried a spare outfit of civilian clothes in case the KR invaded the city. When I asked him about the clothes, he said, "The situation is getting tough and dangerous now. I will change my police uniform to civilian clothes rapidly if KR gains power so they won't kill me."

"What is happening?" I followed him, as he started to leave.

"I cannot disclose anything I know to you," he said gently and hurried down the stairs.

"Things will be upside down?" I called after him but he was gone before he could hear me. After that day, he rarely came to visit us any more due to the attacks. He was called to permanently guard the police station and the civilian employees.

During this time, inflation was extreme since the country was in such disarray and there was no certainty about the political situation from day to day. People could no longer survive on their salaries as business people took this opportunity to raise their prices. Stepmother used to spend 50 riels for grocery shopping each day and this could amply feed us; now she spent 100 riels and got less food than before. Gas prices tremendously increased. Farmers left their land because of the bombing and the KR invasion. They fled into the city for safety, living in the marketplace, in front of the cinema, or wherever they could find places to stay. They begged to feed their families. Electricity was often cut off, leaving the city in the dark. We used candles and oil lamps to light the house. Everyone was worried and wondered how they would survive the economic crisis and if the government could control the rampant inflation.

Loud Cries for Change

The people lost faith in the government as the economy continued to worsen. It didn't take long before anti-government whispers became loud cries for change, radical change. We began to hear many people advocate for communism or socialism. They believed socialism or communism would mean the end of the social class structure and would bring a redistribution of wealth. People would be all the same, dress the same, drive the same cars, and eat the same amount of food. It would be utopia. Worse, some teachers, professors, students, doctors, and state employees began to disappear, leaving their worried families behind. We all knew that the men had joined the KR because they believed that when the "Things will be upside down" happened, they and their family would be safe since they had aligned with the guerillas.

In early March, Papa finally decided it was time to leave the country, but we had waited too long. The airport had become very dangerous due to KR bombings. Subsequently, he told me, "Prepare a small bag and be ready to leave on a helicopter from the American Embassy when I get the word."

"Is it true? Are you sure you want to leave your Papa?" Grandaunt Hieng asked me.

"Yes, I am sure. Papa will follow us soon."

"You are the apple of his eye. How could you leave him?"

I felt guilty hearing this and went to talk to Papa right away, "I cannot go without you."

He said, "I cannot leave without my father, your grandpa. I don't mind leaving *Yey* Kong since she is not my biological mother and I am not responsible for her, but I won't leave without my father."

"Then, I won't go without you either. My husband can go alone."

I was also worried about my dogs. They depended on me. There would be no one to look after them after we left, whereas Papa could take care of himself, but Papa insisted. "You will go when I tell you," he ordered.

There was a pro KR demonstration by college students of Lycée Preah Yukanthor, now called Lycée of 18 Mars. It lasted more than a day and the situation got very violent. To resolve the problem, Thach, Chea and Kao, Song Kim, - both Lon, Nol's subordinates, went out to talk to the students. It was an example of how badly government officials had misjudged the severity of the situation because they were assassinated in the classroom. We did not know the exact details but I heard that someone who was connected with the KR shot them.

In early April, Papa sadly announced, "Prime Minister Lon, Nol has gone into exile and the American Embassy was closed before any helicopter arrangements could be made."

"Papa! Papa! You waited too long. You had listened to your friend Phlek, Pheun too many times. You always have to have his advice before you do anything. You made a bad decision, Papa!" I could do nothing but be angry with my father.

NEW YEAR'S DAY, APRIL 1975

The holiday lasted for three days, from April 14-16. *Chaul Chnam Thmey* – the Cambodian New Year signals the end of the harvest season, before the rainy season begins. The first day of the New Year is called '*Moha Sangkran*', the second day is '*Wanabat*', and the third is '*Tngai Leung Sak*'.

Grandaunt Hieng explained the meaning of the three days of New Year's celebration. "On *Moha Sangkran*, people dress in new clothes and bring food to the monks. In return, the monks forward all those goodies to your ancestors through prayer. The monks will give you holy water to bring home and use to wash your face the next morning." Grandaunt stopped to spit the betel juice. "On the second day of the celebration, the *Wanabat,* people make a contribution to the poor, servants, and low income families. Is that right, Kim Houn?" she looked at Papa.

"Don't you remember? I just gave you money!" he replied.

Grandaunt laughed. "How about the third day, what will we do?"

"I dressed in *sampot chang kben* to go to the Royal Palace with my wife on *Tngai Leung Sak.* Do you remember? State employees who lived in Phnom Penh were invited to bring wishes of longevity, good luck, happiness and prosperity to the King. Also, people go to the temple to clean the statues of Buddha in the temple. At home, members of each family will give baths to their parents and elders," he said. "You know all that too. Why ask me?"

Papa and *Eeh* dressed in *Sampot chang kben* to go to the Royal Palace

"I am old. My memories are not good anymore. It takes someone else to bring back all these memories."

"I forgot to give you a bath. Do you want one?" Papa teased her.

"Foolish." Grandaunt didn't get the joke.

"Where is Leang?" Papa asked me about my husband.

"He went to visit his parents."

"Don't you go anywhere; it's too dangerous, OK?"

"That won't stop people who want to play games and go out for parties all night."

"True, but let them enjoy themselves before the KR invasion."

"Why do you say that, Pa?"

"Those people don't know the danger that is coming. Don't you hear the shelling getting worse?"

I had a growing sense of apprehension as I looked out the windows. The street was empty, noiseless, and eerie. I knew people were afraid of the attacks so they sought safety inside. To fill the emptiness, I flipped on the radio, but even the traditional Khmer music "*Rom Vong*" didn't make me feel better. "Papa, I forgot to tell you what I heard today. The rumors said the KR will expel all the people to the jungle, and then raze the houses to the ground, and will kill anyone left in the city. Will it be true?"

Papa was quiet. This only made me more frightened, but I rationalized that it was just hysterical rumors and that the worst was probably over and things would begin to return to normal.

"What are we going to do to celebrate the New Year, Papa?"

"We still have to bring food to the temple where we put your *Mak*'s ashes. At least we will do something," he said.

"At least?" I repeated after him. "Do you think this is the last time we do this for *Mak*?"

No response. Instead he said, "What she's cooking?" pointing his finger at *Eeh*.

"Chicken curry and roasted duck filled with lots of stuff like clear noodles, and ground pork mixed with dried banana flowers," I responded.

"Good enough," Papa said.

Papa and I brought food to the temple and invited the monks to give a blessing for *Mak*'s spirit at her stupa. We moved hastily, no time to socialize with the monks. They sent us home with a blessing for a safe trip. I looked at them and silently wished the same to them. Papa focused intently on driving and there was no conversation on the way home. Maybe he was as frightened as I was, by the gunfire in the distance. The city looked miserable and when the noises of war stopped, the silence was ominous.

Traditional Games

Next to my house, young women and men were playing a traditional game called "*Bos Angkunh - Throwing Angkunh.*" *Angkunh* is the name of a fruit seed which is brown and round like the kneecap. Two groups – one of boys and one of girls are needed. Three *angkunhs* are placed on the ground as targets. Each group throws their own *angkunh* to hit the targets. The side that hits all three targets wins. The winner can then knock the knees of the losers with the *angkunh*. This is the fun part as the losers run away and try to hide from the winners. All around us, people were home with their families although this was a traditional night for large parties. Were they also worried about the danger coming? Maybe they wanted to forget their worries just as I did. Playing a game with the family would help all of us calm down. Seeing Papa silently pacing back and forth, I tried to change the atmosphere, "Papa, let's play "*Khla Khlok.*" Papa smiled; it seemed he needed a distraction too.

"How much money do you have?" he teased me.

"Sunthary! Do you want to play?" I kicked him on the back and chased him around to pull off his *sarong*. He liked being chased by me. *Pou* Sunthary was a goof. He would pull his *sarong* up to the top of his head when walking around the house. He left only his face uncovered, otherwise he couldn't see, nor breathe. He was as lazy and spoiled an ass as I had ever seen in my life.

"OK. I will play. I want all your money," he laughed.

At the same time my husband came back home from visiting his parents. He checked out his pockets, "Hmm...I lost money with this game when I played at my parents' house."

Papa shook the die in a closed bowl. We wagered on the object that we believed would be on the upper surface of the die when the bowl was opened.

"Are you done?" Papa warned us to stop messing around before he opened the bow cover.

"I win!" I was so happy to get Papa's money. I lost the money as the game went on and soon my pocket was empty and I had to beg Papa, "Can you give my money back, Papa?

"Here, one riel back to you only," he laughed. We all did; we didn't know this would be the last carefree moment we would share for a long, long time. We all went to bed after the game as Papa had to work the next day, April 17, 1975, the day life, as we knew it, ended.

~FOURTEEN~

WE WILL BE REUNITED

The laughter, the games, the family time vanished overnight. Nothing was left, we didn't remember yesterday; we were worried about today. Yesterday we lived in a house and still had hope for the future; today, we were leaving our house, full of terror. The KR had invaded and we were ordered to leave Phnom Penh. The slamming of the car door echoed the hopeless emptiness in my heart. As I turned on the ignition and pushed the gas pedal, I cried inside with sorrow and fear. Tears threatened to blur my vision. I refused to look in the rear view mirror, knowing if I did I would still see my house and my dogs and I wouldn't be able to control the rising fear. I had to stay strong for Papa and my grandparents. I could feel their fear or was it my own? I couldn't tell. It all melded into one. As we drove out of the gate, fear hung like a thick fog in the car. Pain stabbed at my heart as I turned a corner and I knew I no longer had the choice to look back one more time. It was gone.

Horrible Scene

Once we got on the main road, Monivong Blvd., the scene became surreal. I was petrified by the noise – vehicles of every kind, but mostly people. People were screaming, shouting and crying. Gunfire and explosions were heard from near and far. It looked like a scene from a movie, but this was not a movie. It was real. What was happening to Phnom Penh, to us, was real. The onslaught of fear gripping the city tightened its chokehold with the sound of each bullet fired.

Thousands of people of all ages were forced from their homes, hospitals, offices and businesses and expelled from the city. We were all told to join the vast river of people moving out of the city but never were we told where we were going. Some, who did not have cars, towed bamboo carts attached to the back seat of a bicycle where small children sat surrounded by bags of food, clothes and pots. Other men carried their children on their back while the wives shouldered bags of food and other valuables. Others towed a bed where their kids and their parents sat.

The sights and sounds were overwhelming but I had to keep my eyes on Papa's car so our family would stay together. A quarter mile away from our house, Papa changed his mind and gave us a signal to follow his car. He quickly moved out of the stream of traffic and shot down a side street. My husband said, "Your Papa is going toward my parent's house." He had no sooner said this than the sound of bullets hitting the side of the car made me scream with terror. We were not supposed to go off the appointed route and the black clad KR showed that they were happy to kill us.

"Hit the gas, *Aun*, before they shoot at us again," my husband urged.

I hit the gas and careened after Papa's car. By some miracle there were no KR on that deserted street and no one followed us as we moved quickly through the neighborhood to my husband's family home with no more incidents. My in-laws, their children and some extended family members had waited until the last minute hoping Leang would make his way to them.

My in-laws had emptied out their food storage and put it in the truck, as well as clothing and equipment suitable for a rough life in the countryside. It appeared to me that they knew more about what was going on with the KR than Papa, because my father-in-law had taken everything he thought might be useful. I felt sorry for my parents who did not have anything with them because Papa wanted to keep his car clean. Papa, as did I, regretted this decision again and again. I heard my mother-in-law tell Papa, "Don't worry about food. I have plenty that will feed all of us for the three days."

However, she whispered in my ear, "You will have to learn a new way to live. Do not show people you are a city girl or you will be killed. The KR are murdering all the educated people, all the government workers, and the wealthy class. You must look and act like a peasant to keep yourself safe, your father, too."

I told Papa exactly what my mother-in-law had said. Papa was silent. I expected him to refute what she said, as he usually did, but he did not, not this time. He kept silent. Papa had seen for himself how his employee, Sambath, turned away from him; he knew that the phones were cut off; Lon, Nol was exiled; his friend Yem, Sambo was exiled; the government had disappeared and the KR did not appear see him as an exception. Where were all the colleagues he invited to have dinner at the house? None were here to rescue us. We were to be expelled to an unknown destination just like all the other city residents. What would the KR do next? Our fate was as unknown as our destination.

"The KR is threatening to kill everybody, Papa," I said, as I approached him from behind. He was quiet and did not turn around. I continued, "*Pou Ban* was right. He predicted Cambodia was going to be upside down. Remember his words, Papa?" Papa did not respond and walked toward my father-in-law who was busy tying bundles to the roof of the car.

I wanted to tell Papa the two dreams I had the night before but I was afraid to say them aloud. I was afraid if I voiced them they would be prophetic. "Where we should go?" Papa asked, as he approached my father-in-law.

"Just follow me. Make sure we stay close together," he replied and continued loading the truck which was full of food, clothes, axes, a shovel, and rope. Anything that wasn't nailed down was strapped on one way or another. When nothing else could be added, all the family crowded into the cars and the truck and we joined a caravan on the main road.

The traffic moved slowly and made many stops as the road was swollen with people, cars, bicycles, motorbikes, and merchants with trailers. I saw women giving birth along the side of the road. Babies were crying because the moms could not stop to breastfeed. There was no milk, no water, neither food nor medicine. No stores were open. Everyone was at risk. Cambodian currency was thrown away on the road; I didn't understand why. I was about to stop to collect it but my instinct asked why the other people did not pick it up before me? As we moved farther out of the city, we did find places along the road that would take Cambodian currency for food and water but at vastly inflated prices. I wondered who was doing this. What sense did it make?

It won't Benefit us If we Keep You

On the side of the road, elders who became weak from hunger and dehydration in the summer heat lay on pieces of clothing used as sheets. We were forced by a small group of armed and brutal soldiers to keep moving forward without looking back. Loudspeakers on the KR military trucks repeatedly ordered us to move out of the capital of Phnom Penh. Young soldiers who were marching in line in the opposite direction looked very angry. We were told they believed we were capitalists who were poisoned by riches and a comfortable life in the city while they were living in the forest sacrificing their sweat and blood to save the country from the Americans. It was now time for their revenge and they would transform their hatred into devastating action. They would teach us how to value that which we created with our own hands, and the sweat of our brows.

The soldiers warned us not to speak and intimidated us with their guns. They said, "You will be *vay chol* (slaughtered) if you do not do as we say." They threatened us by repeatedly shouting, "It won't benefit us if we keep you, and we won't lose anything if you are eliminated. All you wealthy people took advantage of poor people."

A very small soldier of about eleven, holding a gun nearly as large as he, screamed at us in a voice that had not yet reached puberty, "You are all our enemies! All of you lived in luxury, now it is your turn to understand poverty. I will make you live as miserably as we did. You should be *vay chol* because you are worthless. You made us work very hard in the jungle to rescue you. Who will rescue you now?" I knew the little parrot knew nothing except what he was taught to say but it was still very frustrating not to be able to defend ourselves.

Vay Chol! *Angkar* doesn't Want to Waste a Bullet to Kill You!

"*Vay chol* on the back of the neck with axes," these words were repeated over and over. I could not believe my ears. How could they even contemplate the execution of such a huge number of people? It was terrifying when we were treated like enemies, and had no voice.

"The choice to live or die is in our mouths," *Pou* Sunthary warned. He meant that we should keep our mouths shut and not let them know who we were or anything about us.

We soon realized that the KR had lied to us. There were no Americans hidden in the city. Their real enemy was "us", Cambodian urbanites. How could this happen to the city? How could hundreds of thousands of people be expelled from the city with only a few hours notice and no government support? We did not know that the government people, those not already murdered, were in the same boat as were.

The frustration and the uncertainty of the political situation had worn us out. We agreed to stop at the University of Law, a couple of kilometers from the Kbal Thnal Bridge.

"We don't have plates. How can we eat?" *Eeh* said to Papa.

"We can use our hands temporarily until we return home," Leang replied.

A man who had been listening to our conversation, offered, "There is a warehouse about a half mile from here; I just got green beans and a plate from there; but the people are like animals fighting over food. Just be careful."

"Go check out the warehouse. See what you can find but be careful," Father-in-law ordered Leang, who left immediately with his brother.

The area around the university had been quiet, clean and well maintained, but now it was a refugee camp. Garbage was spilled over the ground and the smell of urine was very strong. Fear and hysteria ruled the refugees and it was every man for himself. No one showed deference to Papa and this truly did turn his world upside down. Papa paced as he did when frustrated and spoke aloud about the bad behavior. My mother-in-law approached me and whispered, "There is no upper class anymore. Tell your Papa to change," then she turned around to look for *Eeh*. "Tell her to get out of the car and help. She is not a mistress here." Coincidentally, at that moment, *Eeh* got out of the car but not to help or participate just to relieve herself.

I watched people going into every house, looting anything they could carry. They broke glass doors and windows, grabbed what they could and then discarded what they didn't need. It looked like chaos, but it also looked to me like a good idea. We were stupid for not taking anything with us. We were lied to; now we would have to fight for the things we need. I needed to look for clothes or anything I could find to help my family. Good and bad, morality and immorality suddenly seemed irrelevant. We needed to survive.

"I am going to go across the street and look for clothes and plates, maybe even food." I told Papa." He was nonresponsive. The house across the street belonged to a cousin Lu, Ban Hap. I was confident I would find many of the things we needed. However, I was not the first person to pick this house. The entire front glass door was broken in; all the kitchen drawers were empty and lay on the floor. The closets and the food storage had been emptied. Only a pair of placemats remained unclaimed at the corner of the kitchen, waiting for me. I grabbed them.

This I could use to make a shirt if I need to, who knows? I left my cousin's house and hurried back to tell Papa that, "Ban Hap's house has been looted, Papa! Everything is gone. Do you think that is happening to our house?" Papa looked saddened. I stopped worrying Papa when I saw Leang and his brother returning from the warehouse with a pile of aluminum plates and green beans that he had wrapped in his shirt.

"Gosh, people are not human anymore. They fought like animals for the food," Leang explained the situation at the warehouse. "KR soldiers chased us out and shot in the air to intimidate us."

We camped there over night. The next morning, around 6 AM, a young soldier walked by and ordered us to move, "Go! Go! Leave this place immediately." He never gave us a direction or a destination, just to leave. We had to obey without complaint.

"Impossible. Is he out of mind or what?" I quietly said to my husband and turned to Papa. "This is our second day; one more day and we will be allowed to go back home, right, Papa?" I anxiously asked.

"You're right. I think the communist president will do something about it," Papa encouraged us.

Around 9:00 AM, the KR loudspeakers mounted on trucks asked for all state employees, educated and professional people to come forward to help rebuild the country. My father-in-law was surprised and disgusted with this announcement, "*Kdouy mehr vear*! You kick us out of the house, now you ask us to go back! Rebuild the country? What kind of system is it?"

As the trucks continued to broadcast the message and we saw some in the crowd moving toward the soldiers, father-in-law said, "Should we volunteer?" He then urged Papa to raise his hand, "You will be needed first as a government employee."

I pulled Papa's shirt to stop him, "Papa, don't do it yet."

"It's all right, we will be allowed to go back home now," Papa was about to raise his hand but fortunately, my father-in-law's brother, Hack, had the foresight to prevent him.

"Don't fall into their trap. This is the way they will eliminate the professional and educated people first."

"Really?" Papa wondered.

"You better stay incognito," Hack said.

This announcement by the KR was just as Hack suspected – evil trickery; an inhumane betrayal befitting such a ruthless and merciless agenda. Tragically, many of the naïve raised their hands and placed themselves at the mercy of their enemy – an enemy without mercy.

Prachea Chun Thmey! Prachea Chun Chah

At noon, we arrived at Bassac River, where we were supposed to cross. There was no bridge; we would have to abandon the cars. Despite all their preparation, my in-laws had to leave nearly everything at the riverside. Each person took only what they could carry - mostly food and clothes. Papa didn't have much to leave behind except the car that he had been so concerned about keeping clean.

"What will we do with the car, Papa?" I asked but there was no answer.

"We will use the tires to make sandals," my father-in-law said and ordered Leang, "Go find the clippers in my car. Hurry up!!"

Papa just looked at my father-in-law working on the tires. He made no move to help; he seemed stunned and confused. Each of us got a pair of sandals as the boat arrived.

"Where are we going?" Papa asked.

"I'll go first. I'll go find my friend, Sreng, who lives in a nearby village on the other side of the river." My father-in law walked to the boat, "Everyone wait for me here."

"Why should we go there?" Papa asked, as he followed him to the small boat.

"This village is close in case we are allowed to return home, or if we can't return home, it will be easier to escape by boat to Vietnam."

Papa walked back and both of us sadly looked at our car. "You didn't want to get the car dirty, now it has bullet holes and no tires," I waited for his answer, but Papa stayed quiet.

Then he seemed to come out of his daze and asked, "Why didn't he ruin his own car?"

"Papa, please don't make any trouble here."

"He used my tires to make sandals for everyone. At least I got a pair from my own tires," Papa said sarcastically. "This is what I mean," he said, looking at me. "I do everything for you; they bleed you dry." I understood very well what he meant, but this was not the time to reopen those old grievances. I kept my mouth shut.

"Now, he wants to go to Vietnam by boat. The idea of going straight to Vietnam isn't a solution, because I did not bring any gold with me to pay the boat people, and I don't think your in-law's family can afford to pay for us. Your father-in-law said it would cost at least one milligram of gold per person, and for all of us it ...." Papa stopped. I looked at him wondering why he stopped.

The boat was approaching and it was very small. Papa began to complain and draw attention to himself. "Papa....don't..." I wanted to say more, but it never came out. Everything was mixed up in my mind and I couldn't resolve any of it. Everything had happened too fast. First, I left my beloved home and my dear dogs, which was so painful. Now we had to leave the cars. If we happen to return home, our cars would be gone, would my dogs be dead? Maybe they found a way to escape the KR?

"The boat can take only.... four people.... in one... trip," father-in-law said breathlessly. I looked back at my car for the last time before I walked to the boat.

My husband pulled me by my hand, "*Aun*, our life is more important than our car."

Leaving the car seemed so final. Fear enveloped all of us. We were ordered to cross the *Tonlé* Bassac (Bassac River) in the tiny boat abandoning all that we could not carry. We didn't know what we were crossing for or crossing to. The nightmare increased with every order, every step, and every clumsy stumble as we moved on. There was no going back, there was no escape, there was only moving forward, but forward to what? I just wanted to go home. I silently cried for my losses, and for the powerlessness of our circumstances.

The water smelled fishy and looked murky, reflecting our situation. It disgusted me. The warm summer wind made me sticky with sweat. Will I have to bathe in this river to clean my body, this smelly and murky water? I asked myself. Disgusted as I was, my answer was, I will drink the murky water; drink the smelly and dirty water like everyone else.

Finally, after many trips across the river, our family group arrived at a small village - Prek Chi Heung. It had taken days to travel only a few miles because of the masses of people. We hoped to stay at the house of my father-in-law's friend, Sreng. Since the vast majority of people had no place to stay and were waiting for the orders of the KR, we knew we were lucky to know someone but we didn't feel lucky. The village had a variety of simple houses; Sreng's seemed larger and more prosperous than the others nearby. It was on stilts with a thatched roof. There was a covered balcony along one long side and a separate, very simple kitchen in the rear. A lean-to along one wall sheltered a large bamboo bed used for afternoon siestas in the open air. The farm animals lived under the house, some tethered to the stilts.

As I neared the house, I smelled something repulsive. "What a horrible smell," I gasped and held my breath, but I couldn't hold it forever so I covered my nose with my hand.

"It's manure," Leang said, taking my hand from my nose.

"Manure?" I asked, returning my hand to my nose.

My little *Pou* Sunthary cut me off, "Shut up, don't talk so loud, don't you know we are in a danger zone now? When are you going to wake up?"

"It's cow shit. You also smell grass and probably chicken shit. It's the smell of a farm. I think you had better get used to it," whispered Leang, his hand covering his mouth so no one would hear.

Sreng came around the corner of the house to greet us. He was very thin and coughed like a person with TB, but he was friendly and pleasant. He told us that we, the *Prachea Chun Thmey* (New People or Refugees) could temporarily stay with him, the *Prachea Chun Chas* (Old People), until *Angkar* (The KR Leadership) decided where to place us.

"How will we get food?" Papa asked, raising an eyebrow at Sreng.

"You must claim your meal ration at the *Angkar* leader's house," responded Sreng in a gentle voice, pointing at the house next to his and he cleared his throat. Then, he counted the number of people in my family. "You have eight adults and one child. Do you have a small bag?" he asked, turning to Kilen.

"*Chah*," Kilen answered, looking at *Eeh* who then threw a little bag to her.

"Follow me." Sreng said to Kilen and they left.

We greeted a woman I was sure was Sieng's wife, a woman about fifty wearing big, long gold earrings, in the old traditional style. She was a betel chewer, super skinny, and appeared unhealthy and slow. She was hesitant to talk to me, and I sensed she was suspicious of us and leery about having us around. Silently, I looked at her, taking a deep breath without knowing what to say. She looked around for watchful eyes before walking toward me and saying in a low voice, "I am worried for all of you, especially you and your father." She looked into my eyes saying, "You stand out from the other people in this group. *Angkar* targets people like the both of you."

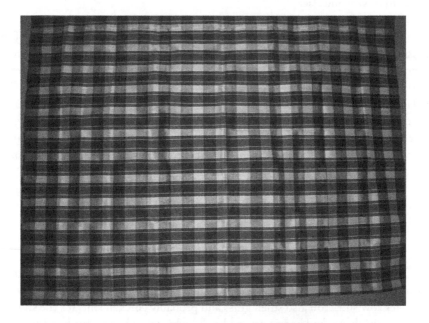

Picture of man's silk *sarong*

This really scared me. She also said to let Papa know that wearing a silk *sarong* in the village was a red flag and very dangerous. She cautioned us that talking too much in front of her house would attract *Angkar*'s attention. Later, it appeared that my mother-in-law had missed no opportunity to spread gossip when Sieng's wife also told me to not let anyone know how I felt about my servant and her child and to stay in Kilen's good graces so she would not report us as bourgeois. Now, our lives were truly upside down. Before we had power over the servant; now Kilen had our lives in her hands whether she knew it or not. It seemed that we were under threat everywhere.

I suggested to Papa that he should send Kilen back to her maternal village, but he said, "She doesn't want to go. She left the village a long time ago and she wouldn't know anyone there anymore."

When I told *Pou* Sunthary and my husband what Sreng's wife said about Kilen, they both agreed and told me to be very careful around her.

"You are right; I will be as nice as I can to her," I agreed.

"And *Ah* Koy is always on her lap; it makes me sick," said *Pou* Sunthary.

"*Ah* Koy?" I looked at my *Pou* in surprise because adding '*Ah*' to a name is an insult. While I was still very disturbed about the baby's place in the family, he was just a baby and this seemed petty.

"Yes, Chamroeun, your stepmother's fake son. I nicknamed him Koy. Call him *Ah* Koy," he grinned, "he is even starting to look like your stepmother."

Kilen came back looking very unhappy. "What did you get, Kilen?" I asked in as friendly a tone as I could.

"Just sweet potatoes. One kilogram of potatoes per person, per day," she answered, frowning.

"What?" just potatoes for the whole meal?" Kilen ignored my question.

"Shut up," Leang reminded me.

Kilen dumped the potatoes from the bag onto the bamboo bed in the lean-to and walked away. I looked at Leang and *Pou* Sunthary.

"You see, this is the "upside down" thing. She is no longer your friend, nor is she your servant anymore," *Pou* Sunthary said, aggravated by her attitude.

We all were assigned a spot to sleep. We were not welcome inside the house even though it seemed quite large. Papa, *Eeh*, Kilen and her son stayed upstairs on the balcony. My husband and I, Grandaunt Hieng, grandparents and my little *Pou* stayed downstairs in the lean-to where the farmers stored wood. As was common, there was a large daytime bed under the lean-to for guests or to relax in the heat of the day. Wood was burned at night to chase away the mosquitoes. All of us slept together on the one bed with no headboard, mattress or pillows. We slept directly on the wood. They did let us borrow a mosquito net. We used the bed as a table during the day.

Alternative Approach

As the days went by, all the worries wore me out because I was very hungry. I also knew Papa and the others were hungry. Seeing the mature banana clusters hanging from the trees in the yard made me even hungrier. I said to myself, "I wish I could steal some but there is no way. Stealing is bad karma but worse, if I get caught, I would have given *Angkar* a good reason to execute me. I need to find a way of approaching these people to ask for a few bananas."

Earlier I heard the locals complaining about various ailments and knew they would appreciate any medicine. Medicine was one of the few things I had taken from my house and had hidden in my bag. I began to formulate a plan to get bananas. First, I approached Sreng's wife showing her the B complex ampoules that I had hidden in my clothes. As soon as she saw the western medicines, I had her full attention, "This is what we need," she whispered, "How many do you have?"

I started to negotiate with her. I whispered back, "How many bananas will you give me for three ampoules?"

She smiled and looked around to make sure we were alone, "I will give you one bunch."

"No, I want a cluster."

"I cannot. These are apple bananas, the best fruit. I cannot pick them for you either. They all belong to *Angkar*," and she showed me a bamboo basket covered with a rice sack.

"I have couple of bunches of bananas in the basket. I can trade one bunch and save the rest for my family."

I nodded my head, "It's a deal."

I happily shared the delicious fruit with all the family. My business became more successful when later Sreng's neighbor came looking for me. I negotiated for the delicious bananas every day. With the bananas and the food rations, we hung on. Word got around and the local folks began to trust me. I secretly gave them injections of vitamins every day. As soon as they felt better, they became my friends. Instead of watching us, they were watching out for us.

Three Days or Three Years?

"It's been way more than three days since we left home, Pa, we still have not heard anything new at all."

"Just wait for another week, we might return home," Papa responded. Another week went by, and still no sign of returning home. "Maybe in three weeks we will return home. The KR said three days but maybe they meant three weeks or three months," Papa suggested.

"Or three years?" I asked, despondent and hungry.

Papa said, "That won't happen. I am sure of it."

I turned around and told my grandparents, "We will return home in a week." They were comforted by my assurance. It was all I had to offer.

I woke up with panic one morning because my period was a week late. I discussed this with my husband and we suspected I might be pregnant. My husband and I agreed that we shouldn't have a baby during this horrible time. I was very frightened about this. I had heard that drinking very dry alcohol would abort a fetus. I decided to sneak out of the house during the evening to look for alcohol to trade. I was surprised to meet *Pou* Va's family about a block away from Sreng's house. We had no idea he was in the same village He was my father's younger step-brother who got beaten by Papa for skipping school. To this time he still hated Papa. I shared my pregnancy fears with his wife and learned that she was in the same predicament, "Then we are in trouble together."

Nowhere could I find any alcohol. I just had to live with it. I went back to the cabin and told Papa about *Pou* Va, and, that he and his young family were hungry. "I do not know who can help who at this time, and we need to rescue ourselves first," answered Papa.

Sweet Potatoes are our Meals

Since our food had quickly run out and we were hungry, the sweet potatoes that we used to eat for dessert at home were now used to replace meals. Making a fire in primitive conditions was a skill I couldn't master at first and the smoke burned my eyes as I made multiple attempts. I looked around and saw Sreng's wife staring at me, wondering what I was doing. I was so nervous about not being able to cook and Stepmother was completely useless. Fortunately, Sreng's wife told me to use her kitchen as she was just finished cooking and the fire was still hot. From that time, I could use her kitchen to cook the sweet potatoes. My fingers got burned from touching the hot potatoes; my tongue was burned from eating them. My husband and *Pou* Sunthary had little sympathy when I showed them my fingers and my tongue.

"Cut your fingernails shorter and cut your hair. There is no more Françoise Hardy (a famous French singer whose look I had emulated) in this village. The KR will identify you if you do not change your appearance," my husband said in a manner that I took seriously.

I became irritated with another villager who always stood with her hands on her hips as she watched me cooking. It did not help when she criticized, "You do not know how to make a fire. You do not know how to cook. Be careful, I am worried for you. Remember *Angkar* said: Keeping you won't benefit us, losing you won't hurt us." This warning registered but I found it hard to believe that they would kill human beings who did nothing wrong. Could I have been more wrong?

Sugar Cane

For a week, we had nothing to eat but the sweet potatoes and dried corn. Our tummies suffered from such small amounts of unusual food every day. The dream of having a full meal was all I could think about. However, the fear of being executed had a way of keeping us silent; masking our feelings, pretending nothing bothered us. Every day, every minute, we secretly wished for a bit of real food or something good to add to the corn and sweet potatoes. The problem of clean water was as serious. For days we had no clean water to drink, much less clean water to bath in. There was plenty of water – the murky Bassac River was nearby but we knew the water would make us sick. I knew we should boil it but that precaution would draw the attention we were trying to avoid. The "Old People" had been drinking from the Mekong all their lives and we needed to blend in.

One afternoon the answer to our dream of sweet, clean water arrived. A pouring rain pounded the ground, along with sending a cool breeze to chase away the smell of the manure. I rushed to put out every container to catch the rain. Thunder and lightning roared at each other, challenging the sound of the raindrops pounding the roof. I had never imagined how loud the thunderstorms were as I waited it out sitting on the bamboo bed in the open air. You could not imagine how scared I was seeing the lightning strike from the sky, while I was in the unprotected bed under the overhang. My grandparents who rested next to me had to get up to stand next to the house wall as the rain soaked their bedding. *Pou* held his clothing bag against his chest to prevent it from getting soaked. My husband kept himself busy making a fire to chase away the mosquitoes who were not deterred at all by the downpour.

During the pouring rain, I noticed Kilen washing her clothes in the bonanza of clean water and then she walked off purposefully towards the fields. Sreng's wife came over to me and said, "Follow her. There is a field of sugar cane a short distance from our house. All the good canes have already been harvested, only the young ones that the farmers did not want remain. You can go collect them if you want. *Angkar* won't punish you!" She urged me to go to the field and gave me the directions.

I put on one of my husband's long sleeved shirts, rolled my pants up to the knees, wrapped my *krama* around my head, and followed Kilen to the field. I acted like I was born on the farm. I knew many KR soldiers sat on the balcony of Sreng's neighbor's house and I didn't want to draw attention to myself. As I moved away from the village, my sandals became heavy with mud and it became very difficult to walk. I couldn't keep up with Kilen because either my feet got stuck in the mud or I slipped and fell. I stopped and cleaned off my sandals frequently. Finally, I just took them off and carried them. Walking in the heavy rain, I looked and felt like a homeless, hopeless person. My *krama* became soaked, my loose clothes grew heavy with rain, and I struggled to stay on my feet in the slippery mud. I wanted to give up but when I thought about my hungry family, I was motivated to keep going and move faster. My Papa and grandparents were waiting for me, depending on me to bring something extra to ease their hunger. I had to be strong and not be afraid of anything.

The field was huge, about one thousand square meters. Sugarcane can grow very high and has leaves similar to corn. Sreng's wife was right that all the good canes had been picked; the young ones that were still small and very green, or maybe not as sweet as the old ones, stayed unpicked. When I arrived at the field,

I did not care about either young or old, I was dying to get many canes but I did not know how to cut them without a big knife.

I watched Kilen kick them down one after another and then wrap about five big pieces up with her *krama*, balance them on her head and leave without looking at me. She walked in the rain with no problem. It seemed easy. I did as I had seen her do but I became exhausted after kicking down only three pieces of sugar cane. I decided to bring home these three, but they kept falling off of my head. I then, decided to drop one and deal only with the two on my head but I had to hold them with both hands on the way home. I soon dropped another.

It was hard to walk as the ground was slick. I was regretting all the hard work I had done for only one stem of sugarcane to bring home but at least I could bring home something to impress my husband and Papa. After walking for a while, my head started to hurt me and my legs became heavy in the muddy ground. I stopped and broke the sugar cane in two small pieces so I could carry one in each hand. It seemed to take forever to get back home with only two small pieces of sugarcane. My worried husband was waiting for me and laughed when he saw two small pieces in my hand.

Be Careful with a Twelve Year Old Kid

A few days after the rainstorm, I decided to go with my in-laws to bathe in the Bassac River (the Bassac River is the bifurcation of Tonlé Sap and Tonlé Mekong). We came across a twelve year old KR soldier, the son of Sreng's neighbor. He took a bath with all of us, me, my mother-in-law, Leang's sisters and Grandaunt Hieng. I foolishly approached him and asked, "When we will be allowed to go home, *Samak Mit pbone* (Comrade Little Brother)?"

It was a mistake to underestimate this young boy. He was furious with this question. Instead of answering my question, he lashed out at me, "It would be better if you were *vay chol.*"

I was stunned with his reaction.

"You lived a life of luxury in the city while I and my companions fought for freedom and justice for you."

How could a twelve year old have fought for us? When did that happen? If I could have kicked his ass or drowned him, I would have. He was just a moronic kid but he held the gun. "We, *Angkar,* don't want to waste a bullet to kill you. It is best to kill you with an axe. Don't ever expect to return home. You will work on the farm and learn to value labor."

Even though he was just twelve, he had the power and I shrunk from him. He intimidated me. He quickly finished his bath and left without looking back at us. After he left, Srey, my younger sister-in-law, who was also horrified by him, told me, "*Baung* (Sister), don't even bother talking to that stupid kid. He is impolite, cold, and stupid; but he does have the power to report you and if he did, you could be killed. It is better not to say anything until all of this passes."

"You are so right; I shouldn't have talked to him." Shaken, I went back to my bath and looked out across the river. I saw something floating about twenty feet away. I thought it was a log but after blinking my eyes a few times, I screamed, "There's a dead body floating in the water."

My older sister-in-law, Maum, looked where I was pointing and we screamed together and scrambled to get out of the water. We stood on the shore and watched as the body floated by. It was swollen and the skin was dark. We couldn't see the face nor tell if it was a villager or a refugee.

"That body must has been killed and dumped in the water a couple days ago. Can you smell it?" Maum asked everyone.

"No!" I said.

"I smell it," she said.

"Don't look at it," I told her.

"It looks like the stomach has been cut open and filled with grass."

"Enough! Don't tell me anymore." I covered up my face with my *krama*. "Why would someone do such a thing? What does it mean?"

"Who knows?"

"Enough. Let's go home and forget we even saw that," mother-in-law interrupted. Let's go home and forget we even saw that," mother-in-law interrupted. I closed my eyes and turned to leave. I wanted to vomit thinking of what I had just seen and thinking I had just bathed in that water and that I would have to drink it when the rainwater was used up.

On the way back to Sreng's house, I met Sreng and told him that the child of his neighbor had insulted and frightened me.

"Be careful of the young kids. They are more harmful than the adults," he warned me.

"He has no morality, no respect for others."

"These young kids were taught to have no humanity. If there is no humanity, there will be no morality. Be careful. Stay away from all of them. I have to respect and obey their rules too. Before, his father was poorer than me and had no power. Now he is the *Angkar* leader, he has the power. Everything is upside down."

In the minds of the KR, we were their enemy. They blamed us for American involvement in Cambodia. I tried to reason out the statement that they rescued us. Rescued us from what? Rescuing means protecting us and keeping us safe, but their mantra "keeping you won't benefit us, destroying you won't hurt us" did not match up to any meaning of rescue I had ever heard. I had many things I wanted to say to these ignorant and abusive morons but I knew that speaking my mind wouldn't help me. I knew I would have to avoid them as much as possible. I doubted that we were going to return anytime soon to the city.

Three Tons of Rice per Hectare

There was much activity around the house both day and night. The house next door was inhabited by a family poorer than Sreng's, but the man of the house was chosen to be a leader by *Angkar*, so he was superior in authority and rank. No one else in the village was allowed to own a radio. Lots of black uniforms with colorful cotton *kramas* went in and out for meetings at this house. When we did hear the radio, nothing was said about us or our return home. All we heard were KR songs and lousy speeches about their victory:

"We are building socialism without a model. We do not wish to copy anyone; we shall use the experience gained in the course of the liberation struggle. There are no schools, faculties or universities in the traditional sense, although they did exist in our country prior to liberation, because we wish to do away with all vestiges of the past. There is no money, no commerce, as the state takes care of provisioning all its citizens. The cities have been resettled as this is the way things had to be. We evacuated the cities; we resettled the inhabitants in the rural areas where the living conditions could be provided for this segment of the population of new Cambodia. The countryside should be the focus of attention in our revolution, and the people will decide the fate of the cities. New people are expected to produce three tons of rice per hectare."

"Communist *Kdouy mher vear*, we are not machines!" Papa mumbled.

There was also the concept of the "year zero." Society was beginning anew with the KR takeover. The past no longer existed. Modernity was evil. They would create a new pure society built upon agricultural labor. People were told to *lot dom* (straighten up); that they were the instruments *"Opakar"* of the ruling body known as *Angkar*. These words were repeated over and over until my father muttered, "They are barbarians. God will kill them. I hope Americans will come to rescue us very soon. *Kdouy mehr vear*, building socialism without a model, my ass!" Papa was angry.

Along the road in front of the house, more "New People" who had no decisive direction yet, kept moving forward. I recognized families of two of my pharmacy professors, Dr. Ong, Boran, professor of Botany, and Chhay, Han Chheng, professor of Chemistry. If any of them met my eyes, they just shook their heads indicating that they did not know what was going on with their lives and that they were as frightened as we were. We all were hiding our real identities so we never let on that we recognized anyone.

Every morning, Sreng got up early and left for "the farm". He never told me where the farm was or what he was doing. His wife kept silent in the house. "Where does Sreng go?" I asked his wife.

"To do something, somewhere. We need to look busy and productive, not lazy. We make sure that the house is quiet so *Angkar* believes we are out in the farm. That is the way they want it! "You, too!" She pointed her finger at me. "If you do not go out in the fields, make sure you hide yourself somewhere. Do not walk around like a queen in the house."

"Where am I supposed to hide while I live out here in the open? We sleep and eat in the same place."

"Walk to the fields where you can sleep and rest where no one will see you. Come back home when the sun is down. Be smart."

So my *Pou* Sunthary, my husband, and I left each day as if we had some place to go, pretending we were busy, just to empty out the house. The neighbor, the big guy who served the *Angkar*, sat there all day and night smoking and listening to the radio and talking with other black-shirted crows.

Human Liver with Liquor

A few weeks after arriving in the village, I heard the rumor that the famous singer, Sin Si Samout, was murdered in a village about a mile away. My question was the same as others: why would they kill a singer? He had not done anything wrong. Nobody had a response. Later, we heard that the KR ordered him to sing two songs and dig a grave for himself before finishing him off. I still did not believe that this could happen to him; maybe it was just a rumor. But, it still frightened me. I felt pain and fear for him. If it were me or a member of my family, what would I do?

It got very dark outside around 8 PM and very quiet because no one was allowed to leave the house or hang out talking. As it was so quiet, it was also easy to hear footsteps and voices. I heard someone passing in front of our place begging for mercy. In the morning, the "Old People" told us what happened to anyone who was escorted this way by the KR soldiers. They escorted the "New People" to a place where they killed them with an axe or a shovel blow to the neck. To help us escape punishment or worse from *Angkar*, the "Old People" warned us to keep our mouths, our ears and our eyes closed, "You hear nothing, you see nothing and you ask nothing."

The next night, there was a strange meeting at the leader's house. About six men dressed all in black, with *kramas* around their necks, came in and sat on the floor of the balcony. The light of the petroleum lamp made it easy to see their faces. Each one of them rolled a cigarette from the dried tobacco the leader's wife was slicing while breastfeeding her baby about five feet from them. It was silent for a while. I could hear only the squeaking of the scissors as she cut the tobacco leaves into thin strips. Then the rumble of male voices broke the silence, followed by loud laughter. They shared a few pieces of meat and drank from small glasses. I couldn't stand to watch these people eating and drinking while we were all starved. I dropped the mosquito net and we all tried to sleep.

The next morning, Sreng's wife signaled for me to follow her. "Do you know what happened last night?" she whispered.

"*Chah*, six men came in, had a good meal and drank liquor."

"Their good meal was a human liver."

"What? You're kidding!" I instinctively put my hands over my ears. I was shocked. "Whose liver was it?"

"They keep that a secret. Nobody knows. But, his wife told me."

"How did they kill them?"

"I don't know that either. But, be careful. I care about your family."

An icy hand of fear gripped my throat as I instantly remembered where I had first heard that the KR ate their enemies' livers. Just the previous year, Papa had invited the KR leaders to a negotiating dinner at our house. He had warned us that they were dangerous men and that they were rumored to eat the livers of their victims and wash it down with liquor. That had frightened me but I had been somewhat skeptical because it seemed preposterous. Now, I saw with my own eyes that this nightmare scenario was a reality. Should I tell Papa that he was right about it? Yes, because it would make him more cautious.

Isolating the New People

Three weeks later, *Angkar* relocated us. They moved us to stay along the small lake, which was three hundred meters away from Sreng's house. We had to build our own shelter. Sreng kindly helped my father-in-law build a bamboo cabin and he covered the roof with palm leaves with the help of all the women in the family. Sreng provided an axe and a large knife and demonstrated the skills necessary to cut and shred the bamboo to make string. No nails or electric saws were available. It was built like in primitive times. In three days, with a lot of help from my husband, his brothers and Sreng, my father-in-law's cabin was completely finished. The cabin was simple with just two rooms. The main room was nearly filled with a communal bed made from bamboo that had to accommodate the whole family; the smaller room was just for cooking.

When their cabin was completely finished, the next task was to build another one for Papa's family. I heard my father-in-law complain that if it were for only Papa he wouldn't care what happened, but he would do it anyway out of compassion for my grandparents. I started to notice that my husband's family became more open about their dislike and disrespect for Papa. From this time, I became more protective of my Papa. I told myself I would die for him. Papa had no skills to build a bamboo cabin as my father-in-law did so he did little but watch and help with the cooking while my father-in-law and my husband were working cutting the bamboo, carrying the stalks from the forest and building the cabin.

My father-in-law began to criticize my Papa behind his back. "Your Papa is a lazy person, worthless." I was not happy to hear this.

Lazy? Papa was not lazy. He was just frustrated with the changes. He was a city man. All he had ever done was work with papers and pens at a desk. When it came to farm work, father-in-law would have to accept Papa as a student. Different from my Papa, father-in-law was used to manual labor on a farm as he was born in a lower class family. Beside the class differences, there was a big age difference. Older men, like Papa, are just like old bamboo that can never be bent. I saw Papa try very hard to work around father-in-law, to help him as much as he could. However, this quality of help didn't seem enough for my father-in-law. He expected more and more from Papa; unfortunately, he didn't have it to give. I wished father-in-law had the same understanding as I, so, he could stop talking bad about Papa. Father-in-law was not concerned about Papa's life like Sreng's wife. He was mad at Papa for a different reason; sooner or later we would find out.

Finally, our bamboo cabin was built. Papa's family stayed there with my grandparents and Grandaunt Hieng. This house had no furniture or household goods. The only dish was an aluminum plate that had been the cover of some kind of casserole that we picked up from a warehouse along the road; we got a spoon from the same place. My husband and I and my *Pou* stayed in a small house between them next to a tamarind tree. The villagers built it to relax in the shade during the heat of the day. In front of the cabins, the small lake stretched to the end of the village. The water was very dirty and had a yellow tinge, but we had to use it for cooking and drinking, bathing and washing clothes. We let the water sit overnight to make the impurities settle, poured off the clearer water, then boiled it. Every morning, I wished I had a toothbrush and toothpaste; I couldn't believe that I had forgotten my toothbrush. I so wanted to properly clean my teeth. Using my *krama* to clean my teeth wasn't the same.

Papa only washed his face with dirty water and dried it with his *krama*, instead of a clean soft towel. He thought changing from the silk sarong to cotton one would help him blend in better, but I still saw the same person, and he still stood out in the village. He was bigger and taller than most villagers and his soft, light skin and well-cut silver hair made me worry. However, it seemed he had an angel looking after him because the KR seemed to ignore him. It seemed like Papa had a job, not an office job, but the job to report to father-in-law four or five times a day if he received any good news from Sreng. Even though he received the same negative report every day, Papa still hoped this regime was nearly over. He believed this was a war against humanity and that the world would take notice and someone would come to our rescue. This was our hope, our dream. We believed that God would send someone to rescue us from this pure evil.

One time he came home with news that *Samdech* Sihanook was in Peking with his wife.

"I cannot believe he won't do anything to rescue us," Father-in-law said angrily.

"No, Sihanook supported Pol Pot to regain his power. He doesn't give a shit about us," Sreng said.

"Why did Pol Pot devastate his own country? Why won't America step in to help us?" Mother-in-law got involved with the conversation.

"Pol Pot is a power hungry man. He sold his country and his soul to China for power. Look at Vietnam," Sreng said.

"How do you know for sure?" Papa asked.

"It was said on the radio," Sreng responded.

"It happened to Vietnam, too?" I asked him.

"*Bat*, Vietnam collapsed too, just a week after Cambodia, but their people remained in the cities. There was no execution, no starvation like us." Sreng said.

"For centuries, Cambodia has faced the same problems. The Khmer Kings ran for help from either Thailand or Vietnam, because of power hungry rulers. We had lost land, culture, and people. Now it happens again, but this time Pol Pot ran for help from China. Sihanook ran for help from Pol Pot. It is all about the hunger for power," father-in-law said.

"Keep this to yourself. I don't want you to discuss this matter with anybody around you. Don't trust anyone, at this time. They are thinking about themselves and could cause you *vay chol*," Sreng warned. He then shared this advice with us: "To be safe, learn to not ask questions, talk, or complain. Plant a blind and deaf tree. Learn and practice the farmer's life style fast before you get noticed."

I got so frustrated with all of this but I had no way to escape. "Did you hear that, Papa?"

He nodded his head and said, "I pray the Americans don't ignore us. They will come to protect us very soon."

"Papa, don't talk too loud." I warned him again.

We finally realized our leader Sihanook had betrayed his own country. He allowed the KR to destroy his patriots to get revenge on Lon, Nol. We never heard anything on the radio to give us hope of returning home; instead we heard the music of *Angkar* singing about their victory. We started hearing more about Pol Pot; Khiev, Samphan; and Ieng Sary who were the leaders of KR. What frightened us most was that we kept hearing warnings from the soldiers such as:

"Laziness and faked illness will cause you to be *vay chol*."

"*Angkar* uses both our hands to achieve the victory and sweat to build up our country."

"We do not need foreign help. Foreigners are enemies."

"Those who do not follow or agree with our doctrine and principles and are against us will be killed with the back of the axe. We do not need to waste a single bullet to kill the enemies."

Dried Corn and One Spoon of Salt

Every day we were called by *Angkar* to pick up the food rations. We were allotted only one can of yellow dried corn per adult, and half of a can for children up to twelve years old. We were given one spoon of salt per person. Everyone got digestive problems after eating the corn.

In spite of this situation, my mother-in-law somehow found enough food to feed her whole family. She used her sewing skills to do alterations for *Angkar* and "Old People" and was paid with dried food, vegetables, fresh fish, and sometimes rice. They cooked rice with corn to fill up our hungry bellies. However, my Papa's family had only corn and salt. Once in a while, I was able to give them bananas or rice from a little trading I did with the "Old People." With the medicines, I could barter with them to get some things I needed. My Papa had Kilen steal rice from the farm at night for additional nutrition.

The food rations from *Angkar* were not consistently distributed. Sometimes, Kilen came back with an empty bag due to transportation delays. Despite our struggle during this time, I still lived in hope that one day the regime would change and we would go back home. My patience gave me strength to live and get up in the morning and look for any possible food to feed my family to fight starvation and malnutrition.

Lok Tah complained all the time about being hungry. Every time he saw me, he asked the same question, "Why do all of you starve the elderly to death? I am hungry. Don't you have compassion for us?"

I tried to get him to understand that it was not us who starved them, it was *Angkar*. We were all starving. My explanation was not heard by Grandpa, he still believed that we did it to them. Before we were forced out of the city, Grandpa had always had a big appetite; at eighty nine years old, he still could walk fast without a cane. He was physically strong and healthy; a big man, like Papa, but his mind was not good. He used to have four healthy meals a day, now he got one scoop of corn mixed with a few grains of rice twice a day. He used to snack on fruit; now he had only one spoon of salt to replace everything he had before this dreadful time.

Stepmother really Wanted to Kill me

One day I walked into my Papa's cabin to boil a potion for my *Yey* Kong who was sick in bed. I remember I was sitting down on the ground blowing through the bamboo to make a fire when I was pushed very hard from behind. The bamboo blower dropped from my hand; my knees hit the ground, but, luckily, I was able to prevent my body from falling into the fire. As I regained my balance, I used my right hand to push someone from my back. I knew immediately from the woman's voice hissing, "Go to Hell!" that it was my stepmother.

"Help me!" I shrieked to anyone who might hear.

"Kim Houn! She tried to kill her!" My grandparents could not get up fast enough to rescue me since they were weak from starvation, but they screamed loudly for help.

Quickly, my Papa appeared and ran toward me. He pulled *Eeh* away from me asking, "What are you doing to her? Why?"

Eeh yelled, "Get out of my sight, *Kdouy mehr vear.*" She wanted to jump on me again but Papa got in front of her and pushed her away. When I got up and turned to look at her, all I could see were her eyes - round, big and bulging. As she got skinner, her eyeballs became more and more noticeable. She was very ugly inside and out. She never stopped hating me. Why? My Papa just shook his head and took me outside. I wanted to lean on my Papa's chest and pour out my feelings. I wanted to tell him what I felt about his choice of marrying this woman, this fool, a witch or whatever she was.

Papa tried to persuade me to not get mad at her. "She is very sick. She is crazy and her life won't last much longer. *Kaun*, I see everything. Right now just try to cooperate with me by keeping your mouth shut, be patient until we return home. I will get rid of her." Hearing this, I started to cry and felt very sorry for my family. I understood from that time that my life was not safe around her.

The True Hell was only Beginning

My *Yey* Kong had been suffering with bladder infections for a long time before the government fell, and now she became very sick. We had no way to help her since *Angkar* had eliminated everything including hospitals, doctors, and medicine, we just had to watch her suffering and pray. One night, I heard *Yey* crying with pain until morning. She passed away at 7 AM. We were very sad to lose her, but we were thankful that she was not suffering so horribly any longer. We wrapped her up in her blanket and carried her to the forest. We buried her in a good place, not far away from our shelter around 10:00 AM. When we came back home, my Papa woke my grandpa. Instead of getting up, he asked my papa, "Is she gone?"

Desolately, Papa said, "*Bat*, Pa."

Grandpa's head fell off the cushion without saying another word. My Papa screamed with panic, "Pa, Pa, don't go," and wept with rage and sorrow as he held his dead father. "I don't know how to protect you," he wept into his *krama*.

I was stunned by the sudden loss of both my grandparents in the same morning.

My Papa said, "It is good for them to go so they can ease our burden. Now we have to worry about the rest of us."

We had to go back to the same place where we buried *Yey* to put *Lok Tah* next to her. We had enough pain for one day. I couldn't believe it happened. My grandparents had wished many times they could die rather than starve. All I could think about was Grandpa asking me if I had anything for him to eat. He was hungry and confused and he died in misery. But the true Hell was only beginning.

Relocated the "New People"

More than two months had passed. I found out I was not pregnant. It was just poor nutrition, the emotions and the life style changes had caused my period to stop. This news made me happy as I did not wish to see a baby suffering with all of us. It was hard enough to see Kilen's son crying and hungry.

Early one morning, Sreng came hurrying up the road with an announcement. "There were big boats waiting at the river for all of you. *Angkar* will transport you to a different place by boat," he said.

"Are you sure?" *Neak* (Leang's mother) asked, as she was boiling water to soften the corn.

"*Bat*, this is what I have been told," he said, but he was not smiling nor acting like this was good news.

"Are we going back home? Please tell me the truth," my father-in-law smiled with hope. "We are going home by boat. This is good news. Everything we heard before has come true."

"Maybe. But, I doubt it. I heard you will be transported to the provinces to do farm labor," Sreng lowered his voice when he delivered this dark bit of gossip.

"No, it is not true. We will go back home," Papa assured us, his voice rising with excitement. He walked around with his hands crossed behind him. He felt vindicated. "We have the chance to return home. I was sure Lon, Nol or America would do something to help us. It is so stupid to rebuild the country this way."

"Oh, Papa, how about *Lok Tah* and *Yey*? I am very sad they could not wait a little longer to return home with us."

I followed him to his cabin, but stopped at the entrance door when I saw *Eeh* glaring at me.

"No more discussion. Pack your stuff and let's leave this nightmare," my father-in-law loudly ordered.

Another of the villagers then arrived at the house and told us with a smile that ten ships were ready to bring us back home. We were so happy. We hugged each other; we laughed and said goodbye to nearby "Old People". Some looked at us with jealousy. One of the ladies who used to trade with me gave me a couple of bananas. She said, "Do not forget me, at least send us a letter when you arrive home."

However, there was one lady, Saroeun, whose husband was a soldier in the KR, who said, "Dear, good luck, I hope everything will be fine for you and God help you. I am worried for the next trip. Where are you going to be sent?"

I turned and asked, "Papa, did you hear what she said? Why did she say that?"

My Papa said, "That lady knows nothing."

She then pulled me aside and said, "Ra" (she chose to call me this instead of Vicheara), "Do not leave this village with the other people. I will adopt you. If you leave, you will die. Don't you know that *Angkar* always relocates people, and then kills them? The next place will be the death zone."

I had known this woman since the time I entered this village. She had been very sick with no medical care and was bedridden. I gave her calcium syrup that I had hidden from *Angkar*, and B complex vitamin injections. With these medicines, she started to get better every day and since that time, she and I were fast friends. Every time I visited her house she gave me dried fish, fermented fish and potatoes and told me to share the food with Papa. She also warned me that my mother-in-law was not honest with me. This message echoed the warnings that Papa gave me. Since I had begun to believe the warnings about my in-laws, I was afraid that she was right again now.

I became so frustrated and anxious. I was very afraid to leave but I could not live without Papa. My reaction to her was, "I will play the lottery now. If I win, I will live. If I lose, I will die. We are born once, and die once."

She cried and said again, "Don't go…. Don't go, Ra, you will die."

"How come you are so sure about my future trip?" I walked away as quick as I could with my few possessions in a bag upon my head. I told myself that any woman married to a KR soldier couldn't be trusted.

Are we Going to be Home Very Soon?

It was mid-July and raining. It was difficult to walk to the boat in the heavy mud, but our hearts were light since we were finally going home. We did not care what we brought with us; we just wanted to see our sweet home. Sreng and his wife followed us until we got on the boat. They wished us good luck; Sreng waved and smiled but his wife stayed quiet. She looked concerned like usual, and barely smiled. The boat was overloaded; we all had to stand to fit on the deck, but Papa said, "We are going to be back home very soon, do not worry about this." We did not complain nor ask questions even though we wanted to know where in the Phnom Penh bay area the boat would drop us off.

On the day we left the village, *Pou* Sunthary carried Grandaunt Hieng on his back all the way to the boat over the rough muddy ground. I didn't know what made him decide to talk; he had been quiet so long after the death of his parents (my grandparents). As he got close to me, he murmured, "It is a blessing that my parents passed away before this trip, otherwise, they would have been a big burden. Your father doesn't care about the elderly. Without me, she would have left alone in the bamboo cabin." He eased Grandaunt from his back to let her sit in between our feet. He looked down at her and she just silently lifted up her chin like a lost child. I knew she was very frightened to be alone now. "I don't know if I should stay with the family or go off on my own now that my parents are gone."

"*Pou* Sunthary! Why would you say such a thing? You are our family and you have lived with us for years," I whispered softly.

"I lived with my parents, not with your father. I don't think your father will keep me as his half-brother anymore. I just don't have the feeling that he will."

He looked down to check Grandaunt who asked for water. Before we could answer her, the sharp voice of a black clad KR interrupted our conversation, "Move! Move! Faster!"

I felt guilty for not paying much attention to his feelings or to the changes in his behavior. I could understand his depression and insecurity, but I couldn't do anything about it at that moment.

As the boat moved off, the people were quiet and listened to their own hearts beating. An hour later, we saw the Royal Palace of Phnom Penh and stood silently waiting for the ship to make for the shore.

"We are almost there," Papa smiled with confidence.

I smiled back, but was still very worried about the warnings I had received in the village. I hoped I was wrong. "The boat should have turned toward shore by now, Papa." I whispered.

But there was no sign of the boat moving in the direction we expected. Instead, it was still in the middle of *Tonlé* Sap Lake and continuing downstream, we knew not where. Soon we realized that there was no sign of stopping at the city at all. Papa's face changed as he realized what was happening. All of us were quiet with

123

despair and disappointment. Papa looked at Phnom Penh without saying a word; he might be forgetting to breathe as sadness replaced his hope.

For the whole day we stood on the boat with no food, no shade, and nothing to drink. We shivered in the early morning rain and then cooked under the midday sun. I looked down at my grandaunt who had quickly become weak from dehydration. Stepmother was so weak that she sat down between Papa's legs with *Ah* Koy sleeping on her lap. Grandaunt Hieng looked up, asking me, "Are we home yet?" Sunthary's answer was full of rage, frustration, sadness and terror, "NO!!!"

In the pitch darkness around 10 PM, we could feel the boat start to change direction and move slowly to the shore. We hadn't seen any lights for a long time. The engine was turned off and the silence was complete. Then the KR announced over a bullhorn that this was where we could spend the night; we were to get off the boat. Everybody stayed quiet; it was dark and we were all apprehensive as to where we were and what lay beyond the boat. Tired, frightened, hungry and thirsty, people obeyed without questioning. No one said much, just quickly gathered their loved ones and their belongings and began getting off the boat. *Pou* Sunthary put Grandaunt on his back and carefully walked the narrow board that connected the boat to the shore. About twenty feet onto the shore, he let her slide off his back to the ground; she lay motionless. The misery of the trip had taken its toll on her.

"I don't think she will live much longer. She is very weak." *Pou* Sunthary sighed. "Your father doesn't care about her anymore," he complained. "Your step mother cares only about *Ah* Koy. Grandaunt is a stranger now."

"Papa lost his mind when the boat didn't stop at Phnom Penh. It is not him anymore, don't you see? Only my father-in-law has remained strong," I tried to explain my father's behavior.

Everyone was physically, emotionally and mentally exhausted. Nobody paid much attention to anyone but their own family and finding a place for them to safely rest. We were ordered to start walking down a road. The full moon had been peeping in and out from behind clouds all evening. With the moon behind the clouds, we struggled blindly into the darkness. When looking on either side of the road, it seemed as if the land was moving. When the moon came from behind the clouds, everyone gasped. The full moon was reflected on water.

"Shit, it is flooded on both sides of the road!" my father-in-law exclaimed.

Off in the distance, it looked as if houses were floating on the water. Where were we? No one had any idea and the KR wasn't volunteering any information. Men and women, children and the elderly filled the road, bumping into each other as we were herded down the narrow road. Those who still had the energy carried the family belongings, the infants and the sleeping children. Others carried their elderly parents on their backs. Whispered questions filled the night, where are we? Is this our final destination? We had nobody to provide answers. We were overwhelmed. What were we to believe? Was all this really happening or was it a nightmare from which we would soon awaken? Had we all died and this was Hell?

It was dark; no electricity, no light, no candle. Again the bullhorn blared and we were told, "You may rest somewhere here, but get off the road."

Somewhere? Where? Everything but the road was flooded. As we got closer to the houses, it became apparent that the town was empty. "Use those small boats." The soldier pointed at the small narrow boats pulled up on the road.

"Are we going to live here?" I asked Leang.

"Nobody knows and the soldier didn't say. He refused to answer any questions. So…" He walked toward the boats.

"It is Kampong Thom province. This was a marketplace before the flood. Fuck the soldiers expecting us to stay in flooded houses," father-in-law whispered to us.

As in many Cambodian villages, these houses were built on stilts for ventilation and to provide cover for animals. This town had been flooded by the river and abandoned. I remembered that *Pou* Phan's family had left for Kampong Thom. But they weren't here; where were they? In the dark, in the water, carrying our children and our infirm, we made our way to the empty houses. We had no way to make a fire to boil water so we drank the river water. We knew it would probably make us sick but we had no choice. We lay on the floor with the spiders and tried to sleep. Everywhere, children wailed with hunger.

Different School, Different School Supplies

In the morning, gunshots awoke us and the KR announced over the loudspeaker that we were all, more than a hundred people, to get into military trucks that were waiting on the road. As we carried our belongings to the trucks, the soldiers with impassive faces abrasively used knives to poke through the sacks searching for anything forbidden like radio, camera, watches, perhaps weapons and knives. Papa and I had watches but we hid them somewhere else.

"All of you will have to pass the test. Graduation will be for those who can prove themselves with hard work on the farm. We do not use our minds; we use both hands like our ancestors. You have slept on soft mattresses, had air conditioning; drove cars. Now we will make you sleep on the ground as we did, in the mud; you will work in the rain. The farm will be your paper, cows and buffalos your pencils," they announced over a loud speaker.

My father-in-law was disgusted with these statements. He said in a low voice with his face turned to Papa and me, "If I had a gun, I would shoot this idiot right between the eyes. The longer I look at this idiot crow, the more I want to blow his brains out. Why can't we kill them now? There are just a few of them and we are more than one hundred." *Neak* quickly intervened and tried to restrain him from talking anymore; my Papa just shook his head without saying a word. How about my stepmother? Nothing new, with her fake son on her hip, she angrily stared at me. I wondered why she didn't get tired of staring at me. With all the misery we had to endure, how could she still be carrying around old anger and grudges?

I didn't care about her anymore. I was more worried about how to bring all my belongings without being caught by the soldiers. I hid the rest of my medicines, cosmetics and my jewelry in a pair of tight pants underneath an outer pair of loose pants. All these things made me look fat but I got by the soldiers without being caught.

Just like on the boat, we were packed in the trucks like sticks, standing straight back to back or belly to belly. Only Grandaunt sat down in between *Pou* and I and we ensured nobody felt on her. I looked around me, everyone was quiet; we had nothing to talk about. We were beginning to understand that we were dead men walking. The trucks started and everybody was quiet. They drove very fast on the small national road, it felt like about 100 km per hour, with no stops anywhere for the restroom or anything else. We were jolted and jostled as the truck swayed with every bump in the road.

"Ah, we now passing Pursat province," Papa murmured. "So, your father-in-law was wrong for saying we were at Kompong Thom last night. Actually, it was Kampong Chhnang."

"Whatever. Who cares?" I didn't want to hear anything else, true or false. What worried me was what was ahead, how much worse that could be and how long we could survive. Where were we going?

As we passed small villages, the children of the village and the "Old People" clapped their hands and smiled at us. It was peculiar. We certainly had nothing to be happy about. We traveled for a day, again no food, no water, no stop for rest or relief. We were told we were away from Battambang province, but we still didn't know where we were when our truck finally pulled over in a village. The truck behind us kept going despite the cries of passengers whose families were now separated. It appeared that the trucks were each going to a different village; we then realized that we were lucky to have all gotten on the same truck. As we struggled down, we met the new faces of "Old People" who stared at us with pity and worry.

My Childhood Fears Come True

Five trucks eventually stopped at this village. However, those people who were dropped off later had been assigned to the other side of the road. We were immediately told not to cross the road. No reason – just don't. The driver ordered us to choose any available house. Our hope of returning home was no longer discussed.

"Hurry, walk faster so we can get a house close to the road," my father-in-law rushed us. He was in front, walking fast, carrying the heavy sacks. As he wished, we found a large cabin near the road. "Just relax for tonight, I will repair the bamboo bed tomorrow," said father-in-law, as we dropped our bundles with relief and *Pou* Sunthary gently eased Grandaunt to the ground.

This house was located about three hundred feet away from the road. People who walked slower behind us had to go farther until they found an available place to live.

"Where is Papa going to stay?" I asked Leang.

"Your papa's family can stay there, next to us," father-in-law answered for Leang. He, then, pointed at a small hut next to a bamboo patch.

There was something about that bamboo patch that horrified me as soon as I saw it; I didn't know why but it filled me with dread. My childhood fear of ghosts rushed back. I knew it was irrational but when I looked at that bamboo patch I knew that malignant spirits were waiting there to steal the lives of my family. My father had told me to fear only real people who would come in the doors if they wished to harm us. We were now surrounded by them – KR murderers with their black uniforms and desire for revenge. Ghosts and murderers – the stuff of childish nightmares was now my reality.

As a steady stream of people moved up the road, Leang and I walked out to see who we might know. Surprisingly, I again met *Pou* Va, and his family, who had been on a different boat and dropped off by a later truck. *Pou* Va's attitude was much changed since I had seen him last. "Oh Vicheara, I am glad we are in the same village and on the same side of the road. How is *Baung* (my Papa)? How are my parents?"

"They died a month ago at Prek Chi Heung village."

He was shocked. "My parents died?"

My head bobbed. I then asked, "Do you still hate my Papa?"

"Oh, no, I don't. We all live in Hell. I have no time to think about the past anymore."

We were interrupted by his wife who pushed him to keep moving. We walked with them until he finally found a good-sized house some ways up the road. There were no soldiers around and many of the village houses were deserted. I didn't know why; it was very curious. I told him that Papa's family, all six, were in a tiny bamboo hut.

"You can stay with us if you want to. Live and die together," *Pou* Va told Leang and me.

"We will. Let me help my family first," Leang replied.

"Is *Baung* (Papa) here?" *Pou* Va asked since he changed his behavior toward Papa.

"Yes, everybody else is here. What is the name of this village?" I asked him

"I don't know. We will find out soon enough. I don't care about the name, but I do care what *Angkar* is going to do with us," *Pou* Va replied.

"Don't worry about feeding us, we will only stay with you at night, we will eat at my parents' house," Leang said to Va.

"You can live with us, and eat whatever we can afford. Live and die together. We are not going to return home. We will be forced to live here until we die."

We had no answer. Leang, *Pou* Sunthary and I stayed with *Pou* Va's family. A second family with four children was also moved in by *Angkar* later that day. There were two large rooms, they had one, and we had one.

PART IV

FORCED LABOR CAMP

Many aspects of the Khmer culture that were highly valued by educated and sophisticated Cambodians were eliminated by the Pol Pot regime. This was particularly true of the behaviors that acknowledged the distinctions between social classes but also included religion and many traditions that had been observed for centuries such as greeting others with steepled hands and a bow. Behaviors such as a slow walk, sitting with crossed legs, hands on the hips, and a graceful attitude were all the target of *Angkar* to look for the upper and noble classes. All of this was called "*Sakadek Phoun* regime (Capitalism)".

The new rules of Angkar were:

We, "New People or *Prachea Chun Thmey*" and "Old People or *Prachea Chun Chas*" couldn't walk around the village; cross the street; chat with neighbors in the alley; or walk from house to house without a reason.

We needed a permission slip to go from one place to another, from one village to another.

We weren't permitted to cross the street at any time unless we had a permission slip from the KR leader or had an acceptable reason.

We couldn't pick any vegetables or coconuts; or drink sugar without permission.

Sex outside of marriage (*Sellator* rule) was a cause for *vay chol*." The rules were different for KR soldiers - they would only be demoted and punished with a work assignment. They would be watched and then returned to duty when their probation (*Kaursang*) ended.

If you were caught stealing, you could be executed.

Food was doled out at the whim of the leaders.

~FIFTEEN~

TURNED INTO ZOMBIES

The first thing the next morning, we heard a man's voice with an unfamiliar accent shouting, "*Krok! Krok* — Get up! Get up! It is time to get up. You have to be in the fields soon. You have to work for the revolution."

I rolled over on the hard wood floor and felt an ache in every part of my body, "The sun isn't even up yet. We have to go to work already?"

"*Aun!* you have to get up and be ready to leave as quickly as you can. You will wake up as you are walking," said my young husband. "Be sure to bring your *krama* and your plate."

There was no water to wash our face. No toothpaste, nor toothbrush, nothing to prepare us for the morning and certainly no food. Our lives were about to change dramatically. I continued to complain, "I am still tired and my body hurts from sleeping on the hard wood floor."

Leang didn't hear the last sentence because he was already outside with *Pou* Sunthary. I slowly walked to join them, wrapping my *krama* around my head. I knew I had to adapt, but I hadn't totally accepted my role as a peasant. "I want to brush my teeth," I yawned, when I had caught up to them, "I can't believe I forgot to bring my toothbrush."

"It is not important anymore, you will find many things are not important anymore," *Pou* Sunthary said in a low voice, as we waited to be told where to go by the soldiers.

My husband pulled my *krama* and rubbed my teeth. I pushed him away, "Don't do this for me. I don't want to attract *Angkar*'s attention."

All the young men and women were ordered to one side of the road, the young kids from six to twelve on the other side. The elderly and the very young were not called. A tall soldier dressed in black with a green *krama* around his neck interrogated us one by one.

I was asked, "What is your name?"

"Vicheara." He wrote down my name and incorrectly spelled it as Vira. He voiced each letter like a child first learning his letters. He shook his pen, pretending he was running out of ink, but he couldn't hide his ignorance from me. I said nothing, pretending not to notice. "What did you do for a living before the revolution?"

"Merchant." Here again, he couldn't spell it.

"What?" he asked me again, "What did you sell?"

"Charcoal, petroleum."

He didn't write it down, but used his pencil to tap on the paper. I assumed that he had no idea how to spell those words either.

"What grade did you finish in school?" he looked at me.

I lied, "Ninth grade."

"What did your father do for a living?" This question was very dangerous. I knew I would have to lie.

"Charcoal seller," I said. I had been taught not to lie and that it was against Buddhist principles, but I was comfortable with my lie; lying to these crows was necessary to save my life.

"Next." He called my husband.

"What did you tell him?" Leang whispered, as he walked past me.

"Hide your identity," I whispered. He nodded his head. I turned to Sunthary and told him the same thing, "Hide your identity."

After each person was interrogated, the soldier ordered both groups of men and women to follow him. All the children were led away by "Old People." They were quiet like the adults, as they sensed something was very wrong. They were tired, hungry and scared, but had to do as they were told. It wasn't the same as being ordered to do something by their parents and they knew it. There was no room for argument.

"*Mit Yeung*! follow me. We go to the labor camp. You need to be *lot dom*," the soldier said with a sarcastic smile. We walked single file on the national road unsure and anxious of what the work would be and where we were to live.

Your New Home, Your New Office for *lot dom*

After about a mile, the fields on our left became deeply flooded. In the distance, a long structure became visible on the right side. As we neared, we could see it was rectangular, about fourteen feet wide, fifty feet long and ten feet high. Fresh green bamboo poles supported a roof of palm leaves. There were no walls, no beds, no toilet and no floor. It was built to hold maybe fifty people but we greatly exceeded fifty. The gravel would be our bed and our floor. Where were the toilets? We had learned over the past months that most farmers in the villages never had one. The bush would be the place where we would relieve ourselves if we actually ate enough to need to; wild leaves were our toilet paper. We understood that the murky water in the flooded fields would be our only option for drinking, and bathing. It was either this murky, disgusting water or die of thirst.

The soldier announced, "*Mit Yeung*, this is the place where you will rest." He pointed at the long structure. Everybody looked at it. "This is your new home," then he turned to the other side of the road and pointed to the wide expanse of flooded field. "There is your office where you will practice your canal digging skills." He laughed aloud as everybody turned to look at the muddy expanse and then at each other. "Your certificate will be your sweat. The harder you work, the bigger your certificate." He then clapped his hands and ordered us into the water, "Faster, Faster! *Baun chegn polikam Samrok* – Use your energy to work harder! We must build a canal wall!"

"Parrot!" said Leang. "They all just repeat the same nonsense."

"No, they are crows with no hearts; they will slaughter us if we do not obey," said Sunthary. "Build a canal in the deep water? These crows are evil and also ignorant!"

"I never heard of such thing in my life. Where does the canal begin and end, and for what purpose?" Leang complained and then said in resignation as he rolled up his sleeves, "Just do what the evil crow says to keep safe."

Building the Canal

I put my hand on my forehead to shade my eyes from the sun. I looked around to see if there were any clues about the scope of the job or how long we would have to be here to finish this nonsensical canal? The flooded area was very large and it would take many months to do as they asked. Slowly and sadly, I went down and carefully stepped in the water. I felt the car tire sandals that my father-in-law made get stuck in the mud. As I tried to pull my foot from the mud, the sandal string broke, I lost my balance and slid bottom first into the water up to my waist. The water was cooler than I thought, even under the hot sun. As I struggled to my feet and climbed the bank, I felt a light wind blowing on my wet pants and knew I now smelled just like the fishy, murky water.

Soldiers and some "Old People" got in the water; they demonstrated how to fill a wicker basket with mud, carry it to the edge of the field and dump it to form the wall of the canal. The *pakee*, a wicker basket in a shape of a shell, would then be thrown back to the "New People" to refill. Their motion stirred up the mud in water, generating waves that made me think of the time I was playing the ocean with my cousins chasing a balloon. I closed my eyes as that good memory played in my mind. This place had no fun, no laughter, and no balloon to play with. My cousins were now somewhere else, living the nightmare as I was. My brain told me to go; my feet refused to move. I was standing still on the edge watching a few pieces of broken glass reflecting the sunlight like little fireflies. I stared at them wondering what else could be underneath the water. Cow shit or more glass stuck in the mud waiting for me to step on it and cut my feet? "I am so scared. I don't know how to do this, how do they expect me to get in that horrible water?" I said to myself.

I knew my poor hands would have to touch this mud; I looked at women, the "New People", miserably fighting with the heavy *pakee*, carrying it on their shoulders. Soon my shoulders would have to carry those *pakee*, full of mud, from one place to another. I turned around to look at the long cabin on the other side again, could I escape from this place? Maybe this is just a nightmare? My thoughts reeled.

"Hurry up, *Aun*, what are you waiting for? You cannot escape," Leang called to me, as if reading my mind.

I rolled my wet pants above my knees, and slowly walked into the murky water. I was filled with fear and despair as the fishy smell assaulted my nose. I put my hand over my nose, but my hand smelled just as fishy. I tried to cover my nose with my sleeve; then I smelled my own body odor. Deodorant was now a thing of the past. Walking in the mud was not easy, especially with broken sandals. The mud stuck to my sandals like magnets. This mud had added more weight to my car tire sandals. I could barely lift my feet and walk, as the water was getting deeper with each step until finally reaching my knees. I spent half my time scraping the mud from my sandals, the other half wanting to scream, cry and run from this horrible place. I finally took off the sandals and left them on the side of the road. The mud now stuck to my naked feet that were now bleeding from stepping on sharp things in the water.

"Here is the *pakee*. I will put a little bit of mud in it and you carry it," Leang said and threw it in front of me. I jumped as the smelly, muddy water splashed in my face. I stopped and cleaned my face with my *krama*. There was more murky water and mud on my *krama* and then on my blouse. I did my best to brush off the mud but the more I tried, the muddier I got. I was frustrated and about to cry. I looked up; it was Leang who splashed the murky water on me on purpose. I got upset at him, but he said, "*Aun*, you have to get dirty so you can live. Life is more important than the mud on your face. There are no more face creams, lotions, or cleansing creams. Your life has changed. You know the word of *Angkar*: they are going to eliminate the regime of *Sakadek Phoum*. Stop acting like you have never done this before. You have to fit in and be one of them. Watch everyone else and do what they do or you will stand out and they will kill you."

Elimination

I had never done physical labor. And I had no idea – none - how hard it was to work in water up to my knees, carrying a *pakee* of mud. I quickly became exhausted and my muscles began to shake. Soon, my face, shirt and pants were all wet and covered with mud. The cold water and wet clothes made me shiver even though the sun was hot. I kept feeling things on my legs, but when I looked there was nothing but weeds. I felt as if my skin was crawling and kept checking. Just as I was getting used to the feeling, I saw black things stuck to my legs. Thinking they were weeds, I tried to pull them off but they stretched like rubber bands and wiggled. I screamed and ran, looking for Leang.

"What is on my legs? Take them off," I screeched frantically.

"Hold still," my husband ordered, "they are just leeches."

"Uh... Do leeches look like that, *Baung*?" I asked, with my eyes closed.

"Make sure they don't get into your pants or they could crawl into your body and then you will die," said my husband. I quickly checked my pants, terrified that I would die from these creepy sticky creatures.

"Hurry, *Baung*, get them off me and kill them," I cried, shivering with fear.

"Hold still."

"Won't they come back to suck my blood again?" I asked him.

"Do what I told you to protect yourself. They won't kill you by just sucking blood from your leg."

My husband found some string and I tied my pants tightly around my knees. As I straightened up, one of the soldiers asked me if I had discovered the leeches. "*Chah*, I am scared," I said, hoping for sympathy.

He looked at me coldly, "Being killed by an axe will be much more painful than a few leeches on your skin. Did you ever hear of people being killed by leeches?" I knew I wouldn't draw attention to myself again, no matter what.

After the soldier moved on, *Pou* Sunthary looked at me and laughed, "You have never been scared of your husband's leech, have you?"

I was insulted but tried not to be angry with him. My husband checked my face to see if I was mad at *Pou* Sunthary. I guess he thought it didn't bother me because he then laughed with my *Pou*. Was it the last laugh I ever shared with Leang and *Pou*?

~SIXTEEN~

THE PRISON WITHOUT WALLS

At 11:00 AM, we were told to stop working and claim our food ration. We sat in a line on the gravel under the hot sun in our wet and muddy clothes, eating our meal like animals. Months in the village had taught us all to carry our own plates with us and a spoon if we could find one. Leang, Sunthary and I had no spoons. We were told to use our hands to eat, like our ancestors. *Pou* Sunthary and my husband sat in a line for men and I sat with the women. I covered my head with an abandoned palm leaf hat I found on the road. I couldn't complain; it was more than most had and I was learning to value anything I had.

He will Eat When he is Hungry

I sat flat on the ground with my sandals under me to protect my bottom from touching the hot gravel. All my clothes were soaked with the murky water and smelled like fish. I remembered when I was a child that I had covered my nose when walking past a man I met at Grandpa's house because he smelled fishy. Now I smelled just like him. I was disgusted.

We were waiting for the 'rice soup' to be handed out. As I waited, mental pictures of the 'rice porridge' served at my wedding played in my mind and tortured my empty stomach. The memory of the aromas of fired garlic, spicy ginger, shrimp, meat balls, scallops, onion and cilantro made my mouth water. I now regretted not eating a lot of the delicious porridge that day because I was more concerned about showing off a tiny waist in my wedding dress. Now, as I waited for the nasty, watery gruel that *Angkar* called rice soup, there was no tantalizing aroma of fried garlic, instead heavy smoke from the wood fires threatened to choke me. All the smells around me were revolting – the food, the people, the murky, fishy water, the open fields where hundreds relieved themselves. But, after a while, these smells became normal and then I hardly noticed them as my priorities became filling my stomach, working hard, and escaping the notice of *Angkar*.

Rather than traditional Cambodian music accompanying my meal, I listened to the insults of the cook, "You have been spoiled; now we give you a taste of a new rice soup. Just see how long can you survive on what we have eaten all our lives. Live or die," she was smirking and chewing tobacco at the same time, her eyes darting back and forth over the "New People" like a hawk seeking prey, "we don't care. We will punish you for being spoiled too long ----*Lot dom! Lot dom!* (Straighten up! Straighten up!)" That old woman finally came out of the kitchen carrying a big heavy aluminum pot in both hands. Following her was a teenager. Both were dressed in the KR uniform of a black *sampot*, a long sleeved black blouse, and a *krama* wrapped around the head. They both wore sandals made of car tires.

Neither of them looked very friendly. The old lady gave us one scoop of rice soup. This girl gave us one small spoon of large grained rock salt.

Next to me was a woman in her early twenties. She was trying to take care of her son who was about two. He was with her because she had no one to leave him with at the village. She grew increasingly agitated as he refused to eat the rice soup. I tried to entertain him with smiles and funny faces so he would swallow the soup but he still refused. He smiled back and then ran after his mother when she got up to walk back to the shed where we all slept. He began to wail as he tried to catch up with her and she turned and shouted, "Go back and sit, I will be back." The toddler didn't seem to understand his mother because he kept running after her crying. I couldn't blame the child for refusing to eat the food. Watery rice soup with nothing but salt wasn't enough to satisfy anyone, not even a small child. She turned and came back with her son still running behind her, crying even louder.

"He is hungry for real food," she explained. "He will eat when he's hungry enough."

Her words, 'He will eat when he's hungry' stayed with me. All of us were going to eat what *Angkar* gave us because we were hungry. If I were as rich, as I was before, I would take this child and his mother and sit at a nice table at La Lune and buy them a big delicious meal. My thoughts went to the lavish catered dinner Papa had provided in our home for the KR delegates as he and other ministers tried to negotiate peace for Cambodia. What did he get for his money? This! Captured, starved and at hard labor in the fields. Papa didn't know he was feeding those who would murder and enslave his family.

As I watched, the young mother began crying with her son, who kept refusing to eat. She held his head with one hand to stop him turning his face away from the bowl and, with the other hand, she brought the bowl close to his mouth, saying "Eat." She kept pushing the bowl between his lips. The child choked and coughed, refusing to swallow the soup. I looked away from this misery.

The salt looked like a little grayish piece of rock. It sank, adding its salty flavor to the soup. One of my fellow "New People", a lady, appeared in front of me, offering me an aluminum spoon. Anything I received now was an invaluable gift that I appreciated. It amazed me that at this time some people still kept a good and generous heart. We now had one spoon between three of us. I showed it to Leang and *Pou* Sunthary who were watching from the men's line. I thanked her, although the spoon was not shiny, clean and fancy, like our silverware that sat on the mahogany dining table at home. It was small, dirty and broken. We would have tossed it out long ago.

"Don't be picky. Just use it rather than using your fingers," she whispered as I smiled at her.

Now, how to clean this spoon? All I had was my stinky wet pants to rub off the dirt. I scooped up the rice soup and met Leang's eyes before putting it in my mouth. I bit down on a hard piece of salt, making a sound similar to eating the crispy Chow Mein noodles at a Chinese restaurant. However, my tummy immediately rejected the fishy gruel and the few mouthfuls of soup splashed on the ground next to the toddler who was sitting next to me. He looked at me. I looked at him. We were in the same boat. You refused your unfamiliar food; my tummy refuses my unfamiliar food. I felt many eyes looking at me; if I could get all my food back from the ground, I would.

My retching got the cook's attention. She asked me, "What is wrong? Do you want me to replace it?" Hesitant to say *"Chah"* loudly, I just nodded my head, looking in her eyes asking for pity and forgivingness. She came out with the same amount of soup, but this time, only the broth, no rice. "This is what's left that soldiers didn't eat. I was going to throw it out." I had to slowly swallow the watery leavings and try not to think about crispy Chow Mein anymore. My tummy started to roll and get ready to push this new food out again, but I kept swallowing, pushing down, and swallowing until it settled down.

After the poor meal was completely finished, *Pou* Sunthary approached and whispered to me, "I felt nothing after finishing the meal. Learn to eat what we have or you will die or be killed. You know *Angkar* watches us like a hawk. *Angkar* has many eyes like the pineapple skin."

There was no equality in food rations between the "Old People" and "New People." We got only very small rations of food while the "Old People" ate rice with meat. They didn't need to be punished the way we were punished, or be treated like enemies because they were farmers, poor people, and good people. The "Old People" worked less, ate better and supervised our work.

"How the Hell can we live with one scoop of rice soup and one spoon of salt? I finished my food in one second and didn't even fill up my tummy," my husband said, and he and *Pou* shook their heads.

"We are their enemies and prisoners. They plan to slowly kill us," Sunthary answered.

I could hear the KR laughing and joking in the open-air kitchen. We were then allowed to rest in the shelter for a short while and then it was back to the *pakees* and the mud until darkness approached.

We Slept Directly on the Bare Ground

Day time…

We all slept directly on the bare ground. I remembered complaining to Papa that my mattress was either too thin or too thick or too heavy or too hot or too old or it hurt my back or I just didn't feel comfortable. Papa kept changing it until I found a very comfortable one. Now, I found myself wishing for at least a big rice sack to use as a sheet and a little piece of rock for a pillow. Looking around me, there were no rocks, nothing but bushes, yellow grasses, and trees. On the other side of our "new home" was the road with the flooded field next to it.

Everyone tried to rest on the gravel. I could hear nothing, but unfamiliar animal calls. I had no idea what these animals looked like. Leang, lying down next to me, said, "That's a *kook*."

"You name it as it sounds? What's the real name?"

"I don't know, *Aun*," he closed his eyes, trying to fall asleep.

"How about the noise that sounds like starting an engine. What kind of animal is that?"

"Woodpecker."

"What he is doing now?"

"Pecking the--- t—r---e---e," his words faded as he fell asleep.

"Pecking what?" Leang started to snore. I sat next to him watching black crows flying around, dropping to the ground where I had vomited. Like the KR crows, they couldn't care less about us who cry for food. What did Papa have for dinner today? Is he hungry like me?

Night time...

After more hours in the mud and water, we were fed the same watery soup for supper and then returned to the shelter. Nocturnal animals howled from the trees, warning us they were there to take our spirits away. Crickets were singing like they wanted to put us to sleep. Once in a while, I woke and clung to my husband because the yelping of foxes frightened me. I woke up many times during the night to chase away mosquitoes. The thin *krama* that I tried to cover myself wasn't enough to keep them away. *Pou* Sunthary, who slept next to me, swatted at the mosquitoes that incessantly bothered his ears, "Damn mosquitoes, they either sing in my ears or bite me."

My husband fell into a deep sleep, softly snoring. Once in a while, he changed position, but he didn't wake up. As he stretched out his legs, he kicked the head of our neighbor who was alternately snoring, or talking in his sleep, "No, don't do that," the man ground his teeth and kept mumbling with strange sounds that I couldn't understand.

Too much was going around me and I could not sleep. I tried to sleep in a sitting position as it was more comfortable. Before I closed my eyes again, I noticed the shadow of a woman, big and strong, waving her hand at me. It was the same lady who gave me the spoon that morning. She whispered, "Ra, I want to give you a blanket."

Happy, like receiving a gift from God, I crawled to her place, about two feet from mine.

"Please don't feel offended; this blanket was used for cows. I traded my *sarong* for these blankets. We are all in the same boat now; I believe if I do something good for someone, good karma will return to me and my family."

"Amazing! The cows had blankets for protection? We, the "New People", are treated lower than the cows?" I asked as I held the blanket.

"Don't talk now. Go to sleep to restore your energy for tomorrow." She went back to sleep. Under the moonlight, I could see the blanket was nothing like my beloved red blanket, that Phach gave me for a wedding gift. This blanket looked grey with two darker stripes on each end. I was very thankful for it though because it protected me from the biting mosquitoes, at least.

Raining ......

We suffered enough each day with the incredibly hard work and the brutal treatment. Now we also had to suffer with the rain, a monsoon that punished us by not leaving us anywhere dry to sleep. The monsoon brought terrifying thunder and lightning accompanied by heavy downpours. It scared me to death as I huddled in the shelter without walls. Why didn't it rain only during the daytime, so, it would cool everything off and be dry at night? I watched a stream of water coming from the road running near my feet. Soon, it soaked the sleeping area so that everyone was sleeping in a pool of water. We all scrambled for a higher place to sleep or sit but there was nowhere dry. Frustrated, Leang got out of the rest area and ran to the middle of the road, as if enjoying the rain. I understood him; it was not pleasure but frustration and anger at how powerless we were.

"Come on, let's go back to sleep in the water. It won't melt us. If we cannot work tomorrow, it will be a big problem," said a man about five feet away from me; he didn't bother getting up. But, I could not sleep in a pond. I kept looking for a better place where the stream of water was not so strong and found one next to a pole. I called Leang and Sunthary to sit around the pole. We slept sitting crossed legged, our backs were leaning on each other, like a tripod.

Our Honeymoon had Become a Murky Moon

We had now been many days in the fields. I stared at my husband who looked so different from the man I had married. His blue shirt had faded in the scorching sun. It was torn and covered in mud. His brown shorts had been his father's pants and were cut to make a pair of shorts. Both pockets were turned inside out as he got tired of putting them back after his wet, muddy hands reached for tobacco. Then, when the tobacco was gone, there was no reason to put his pockets back and so he left them out, looking like floppy, puppy dog ears. His lips were dark, dried and cracked from smoking and dehydration. His eyes were sunken and tired from sleeping on the gravel floor. The skin on his face looked rough from continually burning and peeling under the relentless sun. He was physically a wreck, not the handsome man I married. But when he looked at me, I could still see the warmth in his heart and how much he loved me. No amount of mud or sun could take that from him. Physically, we never sat very far from each other but we dared not show any sign of affection. *Angkar's* rule was that no one was allowed to show any emotion toward another person especially romantic emotion.

Our eyes met. He smiled at me, but not the smile I had seen on our wedding day; this smile was racked with pain, fear, disappointment and anger; only I could understand him because we were one. His teeth were yellowish and stained from lack of brushing and the tobacco. We had been many days in the water hauling mud; I wondered how bad I looked. I knew how bad I smelled. I knew how bad I felt.

Pou Sunthary was quiet. He sat on the ground with his head in his hands. He raised his face and looked up at the sky. His eyes met mine and we exchanged a bitter smile. How our life had changed.

Papa's Place

Since I missed my father so much, I took a chance and I lied to a soldier, "*Samak Mit*, can you give me a permission slip to see my *Pouk* (Father)? He is very sick." I used the peasant word *Pouk* to refer to my Papa because we were always careful to try to blend into the peasant culture. "New People" also called all peasant men older than themselves *Pouk* as a general sign of respect since we knew they had the power of life and death over us.

This was a good excuse to release me from work and go see Papa. The permission slip allowed me to return no later than dinnertime. I left at lunchtime carrying my rice soup ration in a container that I picked up from the street. It was aluminum can for baby formula. If I could have flown, I would have. Papa would be proud of me bringing him food. Going to see Papa was more exciting than going to France; I walked as fast as I could. I tried to run but felt I was running backwards because I was running against the wind and I was weak from overwork and starvation rations. After about ten steps, I ran out of breath. My excitement over seeing Papa motivated me to keep going as fast as I was able. I didn't know how long had I been walking, but I made it and searched for Papa. My heart was pounding with excitement. I found what I was sure was the big cabin where I had last seen him. I was sure that was where Papa was safe. He would be there, and must be very busy. He would be surprised to see me.

The cabin was divided into two large rooms. The main supports were wood and the walls and roof were covered with palm leaves. It had only a dirt floor and again sat next to a bamboo patch. The first room had two doorways. The first, on the alley side, was blocked by a large communal bed on which one entire family: a man named Sok, his wife, and his five children slept. The second entrance had no door and faced the porch. The second room was inhabited by a Vietnamese mother and three girls, and a Cambodian family of three, grandmother, mother and a daughter. These three people were Sok's relatives.

Papa's family lived in an open area on the outside of the house covered by a palm leaf roof. At one corner, there was a big bamboo bush that gave him a tiny bit of privacy from the alley. Papa's place had only a communal bed that was used for the entire family: Kilen, her son, *Eeh*, Grandaunt, and Papa. I overheard my father-in-law say he had extended the roof off the side of the cabin and helped Papa build the bed. Near the front entrance were three rocks arranged in a triangle so Papa could make a cooking fire in between them.

As I looked around for Papa, I saw only my Grandaunt Hieng who lay on the bamboo bed with Kilen's son. As soon as she saw me, she tried to get up and grabbed my hand. She was so skinny and weak, not even able to speak. I had to bend over to hear her say, "Do not leave me alone, I want to go with you."

I helped her to sit up and told her, "You wouldn't be allowed to come with me to where I work but I won't forget you when we were liberated."

"I want to go to Bangkok when we are liberated." Bangkok? She must be hallucinating.

"Please take me with you," she barely had the strength to finish her sentence, "I am very hungry." She then whispered in my ear, "Kim Houn is mean; he will not feed me, only one spoon of rice soup."

"We are all hungry. We don't have much to eat either. *Angkar* is starving us," I told her but I do not think she heard me.

One Can of Rice and One Spoon of Salt per Person per Day

I looked at Koy. He did not say a word, just stared at me. Koy was not the toddler that I used to see sitting on *Eeh*'s lap. He had grown taller but was very, very skinny. I wondered how his face could resemble Stepmother, but it did. He was physically weak; he couldn't even get off the bed. Poor child! I smiled at him with affection and pity; he gave me a little smile back but it was unhealthy and defeated. He then, pointed to the pot saying, "There!" I followed his direction. I opened up the pot's lid, but it was empty. I looked up and I saw Papa coming from the forest. He smiled when he saw me. He also was skinner than before, but he still looked better than Grandaunt Hieng.

"I carried her to the forest," I knew he was talking about *Eeh* since I did not see her around. "There is no real restroom. All of us have to go poop there in the bush and use leaves to clean up," he said.

We walked back to the forest, where he left *Eeh*. I was shocked when I saw her; she had changed so drastically. She now looked like a cadaver. She had shaved her hair to get rid of lice and her eyes were even bigger than before, maybe due to her sickness. However, her goiter was gone.

"What happened to her goiter? Did she get healed from her sickness?" I asked Papa, surprised. *Eeh* could not hold her head up straight because she was so weak from starvation.

"Not really, she won't last long." Papa had to carry her back to the cabin. It was clear her days were numbered.

"Papa, I want you to stay healthy and God will always be with you to protect you from sickness and starvation," I could not hold back my tears.

"I am a strong man, *Kaun*. I will return home with you," he assured me with a smile and hugged me. He turned his face away, pretending he was looking for something but I saw him wiping his eyes. It shocked me, and I tried to encourage him, "Papa, be strong, and be active." Papa hid his face in his *krama*.

"How does *Angkar* feed you?" Without letting him answer, I asked my next question, "What does he feed you?"

"Stupid *Angkar*, that *Kdouy mehr vear Angkar*, gives us one can (16oz) of rice and one spoon of salt per person per day. The children are allowed only a half can."

"It is better than the dried corn we received at Prek Chi Heung then; but it is still not fair to starve us. They want to slowly kill us Papa."

"We will soon return home. The food distribution doesn't bother me. It won't last long. Someone will step up and destroy this regime."

"Do you still believe this, Papa?" I brushed dirt from his shirt, "I want to make sure you take good care of yourself and live from day to day."

Papa changed the subject, "I have a Chinese friend who stays in the abandoned cabin over there." He pointed. "He showed me wild herbs that are good for food."

"What do these herbs looks like?"

"They're easy to find. They grow everywhere along the side of the road. When you come again, pick some for me. It is not good for me to walk around because I get noticed by *Angkar*," Papa showed me the wild herbs.

"Oh, I know this. I have seen a lot growing along the road. What do you do every day? Do the *Angkar* ever come looking for you?"

He nodded his head, "I remain still under the blanket. They saw me. They thought I was sick so they left me alone."

I cracked up. "You are smart, Papa. I should learn from you."

"Actually, Praub is my best friend. He won't hurt me," Papa assured me.

"Who is he?"

"He is a young man in his thirties. He comes to chat in the morning. He brings me a full hand of tobacco. He is one of the "Old People.""

"Old People, Papa! Don't trust anybody."

"No, he hates this regime as much as I do. He remembered me from when I came here with Phlek, Pheun to campaign. This district, *Preah Netr Preah*, shares a border with Siem Reap province."

"*Preah Netr Preah?* So that is where we are. Huh…Papa it is very dangerous if he remember seeing you. Does he know who were you working for?"

"No, I won't tell him and you are wrong. He wishes someone would destroy this stupid regime. Anyway, different topic, did you know this village is in the malaria zone?"

As soon as I heard the word malaria, I didn't want to hear anything else he was going to tell me. I was in shock. Malaria! I knew how malaria attacked people and what the symptoms were. I had learned that in pharmacy school. I became very frightened for Papa. What could I do to prevent him from getting malaria? I was lost in thought when suddenly, a new word he said scared me again.

"What did you just say, Papa?" I asked.

"I said people in this village believe in animism."

I nodded my head. "*Chah*, we walk on eggshells with these ideas. We need to learn what to do and not to do to keep us safe. We also need to respect their beliefs."

"You are right, *Kaun*. They believe trees, stones, nocturnal birds and mountains all have spirits. They will not cut down trees without asking their permission. They don't allow people to carry bamboo with the cut end facing the village because they think the tree's spirit will then take people's life sooner than they should. You cannot curse anybody because the spirit will do what you say. Do you know about the nocturnal bird?"

"*Chah*, they say it is a bad bird. When he screams on someone's roof, it is telling them that someone in that house will die soon. They should curse the bird and chase it away. I remember when *Mak* was very sick and a week before she passed away, a nocturnal bird screamed on our roof every night."

"Why don't these birds scream on the roofs of the KR every night and then the spirits will kill the KR because we curse them every day."

Our conversation was interrupted by Koy's calling for Papa, "*Lok Tah*, I'm hungry."

"We don't have anything to give you. Stop crying."

This only made the little boy cry more, but it was more of a whimper as he was very weak. I looked at Stepmother who was lying down next to Grandaunt. Her eyes were closed halfway.

"I saved this rice soup from work for all of you. It looks much better than what you have at home," I told Papa. He transferred the rice soup to the Le Creucet pot and covered it.

"I have to go back to work now, Papa."

Seeing my family in this condition broke my heart. I hoped they would stay strong; it was so difficult to leave, but I had to go back to work or risk the wrath of *Angkar*. After I left Papa, I stopped at my in-laws to show them respect. They all looked healthy. None of them had lost weight like Papa's family. My mother-in-law kept herself busy in her back yard that was near the lake. She planted banana trees, peppers and mustards; she was so smart in getting all these seeds from her neighbors. "*Neak*," I called my mother-in-law.

"Oh, did Leang come with you?" She gave me a friendly smile, sticking out her tongue to push back her denture that was falling out.

"No!"

She continued planting the little banana trees. I had nothing more to say and started to walk away when she surprised me by saying, "I have sewn a pair of loose silk pants for you. Don't forget to take them with you. Also I have made you a brown blouse with two pockets. Make sure you hide your identity to avoid attention by working hard."

"*Chah*." I went inside the house where Maum, handed me the blouse and pants.

"How is your work, *Baung?*" she asked me politely.

"It's a nightmare. I don't know how long I can do it."

"*Kdouy mehr vear*, they use us to replace buffalo," she said, angry at *Angkar*.

"Right, you are lucky to stay home with the baby."

"If you had a baby, you could stay home like me too"

"You are right, but I'd rather see myself starve. Seeing my baby cry for food would hurt me more. I have seen one at the fields and it breaks my heart." I grabbed my stuff and left the house.

Bamboo Patch!

I went back and forth to visit Papa every five days. One day when I visited, I found *Eeh* dead on the bamboo bed with glazed eyes. Next to her, Grandaunt had become very weak. She could no longer talk. Papa lost Stepmother. Soon he would be alone with Koy and Kilen.

Bamboo patch, please be nice to my family. Please don't make my superstitions become true. I cannot lose my father.

Day after day, week after week, we did the same work and were allowed to stop only for meals. One day, I was attacked by a strange shivering and strong stomach cramps. I felt so cold inside, but hot on the outside. The shivering became more intense around 4 PM. We had no medicines, no doctors, and no hospitals. I shivered in my husband's arms at night without treatment. "W..h..y a..m... I ... fee....ling so co..ld? H..ug.. me clo..ser, I am shive..ring." I asked him through my chattering teeth.

"Your body is very warm, honey! Why are you shivering? I have nothing to cover you."

He took off his shirt; my *Pou* Sunthary also gave me his shirt and *krama* in place of a blanket. The gray cow blanket had been stolen long ago.

"I am still very cold and colder on the inside of my tummy. What is it?"

My husband went to see one of the soldiers in the eating area to tell him about my sickness. He followed my husband to our sleeping area. "You have malaria; I do not have any medicine. I can send you home," he said, looking at me coldly.

"She cannot walk right now," my husband answered for me.

"Just wait until the shivering period is over."

"How long is that?"

"Usually about a half hour."

My husband hugged me tighter trying to warm my body. It was about a half hour until the shivering was gone, but my head hurt, my body was very hot and I felt dehydrated.

"I need something to drink!"

"Wait! I will go get warm water from the eating area." A few minutes later, my husband came back with a bowl of rice soup.

"*Aun!* The cook gave me this." I didn't look, as the smell was familiar to me. I knew there was no special food for sick people.

"No! I am thirsty only. I can't eat anything, my tongue has no taste."

My husband drained out the rice leaving only the broth and fed me with the spoon. The group leader showed up in our sleeping area and told me, "You are to go home tomorrow. We do not keep sick people here, our food rations are limited to people who can work for the revolution."

"Can you give me a permission slip to take my wife home? She is very weak and has a high temperature."

"The permission slip is good for going and coming back only. It is not to go around crossing the road from one place to another. You," he pointed to my husband, "will have to come back right away or you will be in trouble if we have to go find you."

The next morning, Leang went to the cooking area to claim my food ration. He then held me up and we slowly left my *Pou* Sunthary and the work area.

You have to Have Hope!

At that time, my husband's family house was across the alley from my Papa's, about fifty feet away. When I was sent home sick, I stayed with my husband's family, lying on a bamboo bed next to an open window. My mother-in-law treated me by boiling herbs to relieve the headache and high fever. I stayed in bed sick for a long time, suffering and shivering with a high fever. I became very weak, lost my appetite and waited for death to come. I was dreaming about delicious food when I felt something touch my mouth. I opened my eyes and saw a pink capsule held in a man's hand. It was my Papa; he smiled at me and told me in a compassionate voice, "*Kaun*, I just got this for you. You will be cured because I am here for you. You have to live and go back home with me!! You have to have HOPE!!" Then, he quickly left my in-law's house.

Immediately, my mother-in-law came in asking me. "What has your Papa given you?" I showed her the medicine. She said, "Your Papa doesn't love you. He doesn't know how to take care of you."

I paid no attention to her; instead, I swallowed the pill and tried hard to stand up to look out the window to see my Papa to assure myself he was okay. "I love you Papa, I will sacrifice my life for you," I said in my heart. I felt my Papa and I were the same spirit that lived together and would die together.

I began to recover as soon as I took the little pink pill and, as I grew stronger, I watched the activity outside my window. My in-law's house was about the biggest house in this village. They were very lucky to have a house that could fit all of their children. Because there were so many of them, they did not have to share their space with another family. My in-law's house was more peaceful than Papa's. I often heard him screaming at Koy, and, then, the child's cries. He had nothing to say to the toddler other than, "Stop crying, I have no food for you."

It was heartbreaking to hear little Koy who had no understanding of the nightmare we were living. Like the other children, he depended on adults to provide him food and he couldn't understand that we had nothing to give him.

Tried to be Even

The river was right behind my in-law's house and Papa crossed the alley several times a day as he went to the river to get water or to take a bath. I got up and watched him, first through the front door and then the back, carrying the water bucket. I felt much better when seeing him without him knowing he was being watched because I could better gauge his health without him pretending. He planted peppers by the wall; my in-laws also planted peppers and vegetables like mustard greens, lettuce, and eggplant as well as banana trees. I did not know how they got those seeds or where they got them. All of their vegetables grew big and healthy, whereas Papa's peppers stayed small regardless of how vigilantly Papa tended them.

I felt a lot better after taking just one of the pink pills. Soon, I regained enough strength to get up and walk by myself. I found out from my Papa that my Grandaunt passed away after the death of *Eeh*.

It soon became clear to me that my in-laws had real problems with Papa and I could not count on them to help him or anyone in his family. At the beginning of our marriage, my crazy stepmother would not socialize with my mother-in-law and this was very insulting. Papa's behavior when he was trying to break up my relationship before I was married and then his behavior towards my husband when we were first married, further alienated my in-laws. Thus, I should not have been too surprised when the tables were turned that they got even with Papa. The fact that Papa did not have anything to contribute and he had no skills to help himself in this new rural life caused my mother-in-law to look at Papa as nothing but unnecessary baggage to her. She was the rich one now and it looked like she was going to treat him exactly as he had treated her. She looked down on him. He was worthless to her.

My father-in-law, on the other hand, did not like Papa since he was forced to do slave labor in the forest while, for reasons none of us could understand, Papa stayed home and was not assigned to a work group. However, once in a while, my father-in-law did bring my Papa a bowl of soup made from baby banana trees and fish that my father-in-law caught with an old fish net given to him by one of his neighbors. I was so happy to see Papa get something good from my in-laws because he was starving.

Learned by Watching

During my recovery, my husband was sent home with malaria. He was worse than I was. He was not even able to talk or eat anything. My Papa secretly gave me a pink pill for my husband. He did so to prove the selfishness of my mother-in-law. He knew she also had the malaria medicine, but for some reason she did not offer it to me when I was sick. He was right. After I gave the pill to my husband, my mother-in-law gave him her medicine. Why she didn't give her son her medicine immediately? I couldn't understand her.

Angkar checked on us every day to ensure that we were not pretending to be sick. They had the power to cut off our food rations or to kill us if we were not productive or feigning sickness. I don't know how long we had been sick since we did not have a calendar available. All we knew was that it was day when the sun was up and night was when the sun was down.

One morning, I sat on the bed inside the house watching my father-in-law giving my husband a haircut. I carefully watched him without missing any steps. I thought, this man has a lot of talent; he is flexible and a hard worker, I am impressed. I wish Papa could adapt the way my father-in-law has. Poor Papa, he could not do anything right now. He had no helpful skills, and he wasn't willing to learn any. Suddenly, I heard father-in-law screaming, "Leang! Leang! *Kaun*, what is wrong with you?"

This scream caused *Neak* to abandon her work in her garden and run to the men. I heard her scream, "*Kaun*, my darling! Don't die without me!"

"I am fine. Don't yell!" I heard Leang reassure them. Leang leaned on his father as he guided him inside the house. "I am fine. I just fell off the chair," Leang said, out of breath from walking the few steps from outside to the bed. He looked so weak; his lips were so pale. Slowly, he took my hand, "I am fine, *Aun*. I fainted from sitting too long, but I didn't tell *Neak* the truth. I said I fell. Please don't tell her. I am afraid she will have a heart attack worrying about me."

My husband and I recovered in about a month or so and we knew we had to go back to work again so our food rations would improve.

"What happened to *Pou* Sunthary? Is he okay?" I questioned my husband, "Did you see him before you came home sick?"

"He was sick too, but he refused to come back home with me. He said nobody wanted him. He feels his life is worth nothing since his parents died. He is probably okay since we haven't heard any bad news about him," my husband said positively, "but we can ask our friends and neighbors when they come home."

I changed the subject, "I forgot to tell you. *Neak* asked for the diamond rings and bracelet that she gave me as a wedding gift. She kept all the jewelry I have. She said she was going to sew me a bag to hide the jewelry. Can you ask her for me if she has done this?"

"I will."

Bad Karma

My Papa had become closer to me since the death of my stepmother. However, he still lived with Kilen and her little boy. I kept seeing my Papa's face smiling at me when he gave me one of the pink capsules to treat the malaria. I did not ask where he got it, but, he let me know later, after I recovered, that he got fifteen capsules by trading his Omega watch with a soldier. I was grateful and told him to remember that I still was hiding my Omega watch, and that when I felt better, I would trade it for more capsules in case we need them later.

"Their favorite watch is 'Citizen'. He will give me twenty five capsules if I have one."

"Didn't you tell him that the Omega is more expensive?"

"You know, the morons have a small brain. I am lucky he took it. But, I could tell he was not all that happy."

I went back and forth to visit my Papa. That caused Kilen to become jealous of me. Papa shared the only bed with her and Koy. I did not feel comfortable seeing this. My in-laws suspected that they had a relationship. I could not confirm their suspicions because Kilen usually was not with Papa when I was there.

"What is happening with Kilen?" I asked Papa.

"I don't care about her," he responded without looking at me, but his hand kept scratching the stain on the bamboo bed. "I keep her around because she provides me with firewood. I cannot go to the forest by myself."

One day, as I walked to Papa's place, I saw Kilen throw the rice pot at my Papa's head and shout loudly, "*Angkar*, take him away and finish him off. He was a Minister, a high-class person."

Kilen didn't look like a real human to me; she shaved her head, like Stepmother. She wore her blouse, her *sarong*, and who knew what else. Her round face, big, round eyes, small mouth and thin lips made her look like a demon. From her expression, I could tell if she had the power, she would kill my Papa, burn him down into ashes. What did Papa do to her? I was so mad at her, but held my tongue because she held the power.

I expected Papa to punish her for her disrespectful attitude. Yet, Papa stayed calm and smiled at me as I approached. "Why did she treat you like you were her husband?"

Papa said, "Let her go to Hell. She is crazy. She wants me to choose between you and her, and I told her I would always choose my daughter." Fortunately, no one showed up to take my Papa away or 'finish him off'.

About a month after Stepmother died, Koy became very sick. This was the only time that Kilen spoke with me, begging me to find medicine to treat her son's sickness. She took off her 24 K necklace and offered it to me to locate antibiotics for her son. "Please help me."

In compassion for this innocent child, I decided to sneak around the village asking for the medicine to treat his diarrhea although it was very dangerous for me to do so. Koy cried relentlessly from pain. He repeatedly asked for his mother, "Yeng", as he couldn't pronounce Kilen. He tried to swallow his saliva, so he could talk more, but could not.

It took me awhile to be able to find someone who had the right antibiotic and was willing to exchange for the necklace. But, by then, he was very, very sick as well as starved. As night fell, Papa tried to get him to fall asleep since his mother was busy talking to the neighbor next to us, paying no attention to her sick son. I sat next to the toddler watching him. Before I could give him the last pill, he took his last breath and passed away with his eyes and mouth open. His last word was his mother's name, "Yeng".

"Kilen, he is gone," Papa called her. She ran to the bed, "*Kaun*, what is wrong?" But his life was over before she could give him a last kiss. His body was kept overnight with Papa and he was buried in the forest next day. Kilen, the demon, disappeared from our cabin without a word. She probably felt guilty for mistreating Papa.

Bleed me Dry was just the Beginning

One day, my husband called me to follow him to his parents' house. At the doorway, he pulled a brown silk bag out of his pocket. I realized that it must be my jewelry bag that his mother made it for me. Immediately, I opened it up to verify if all the jewelry I had given her was still there but it was not. "Where is my wedding ring and bracelet?"

"I'll keep it for you, do not worry about it; it will be dangerous for you to have it if you get caught by the group leader," *Neak* responded from inside of the house. This did not make me happy. I looked at my husband to see if he agreed.

He kept silent. I felt he did not agree with her either, but he had no say in the matter. I had now become quite suspicious of my mother-in-law's motives. I was beginning to see who she really was, but she didn't know who I was. Since she thought she had outsmarted me where the jewelry was concerned, she continued to push me, little by little, trying to convince me that I should stay away from my beloved father. She tried hard to make Papa look so bad. Many times, when I chatted with her, she suggested that I abandon him. She would say things like, "If you stay with him, you will die because he cannot provide for you." She also criticized his weakness and lack of ability to work on the farm as they did. I explained to her that was the very reason that he needed me - to take care of him and love him more than ever.

After all of this happened to me, I decided to live permanently with Papa even though I knew I would eat better if I stayed with her family. At that time, my husband had been sent to work in the fields far away from home; we never knew when he would be back.

Just his Bag Returned

"What has happened to *Pou* Sunthary? I haven't heard from him in about a month. Have you?" I asked Papa, when I saw Sok's son was home with his family.

"He…." Papa looked at me but seemed reluctant to go on.

I pointed my finger at Sok's son, "He went to dig the canal with us too, now he is home. I think the canal work is over. I expect *Pou* Sunthary will return home soon."

"The last thing I heard was from Sok's son, who reported that Sunthary was very sick and had been sent to the revolutionary hospital.

"Did he say where the hospital is located?"

"He told me, but I don't remember. I believed him because Sunthary's clothes were sent home with Sok's son, too." Papa showed me his bag of clothes.

"Oh, Papa, if they sent his clothes home he must have died. When did you receive this bag?" I went through his bag. I recognized *Pou*'s shirt, his shorts and a photo of his girlfriend.

"If *Angkar* didn't give him medicine, he probably died from malaria, but I still hope he is alive and will return soon," Papa worried, but didn't respond to the question.

I knew the revolutionary hospital was just a dirty little farmhouse with a dirt floor. There were no medical professionals, no physicians, and no proper care system. Herbal medicine that I called Rabbit Shit pills was the common revolutionary medicine used to treat multiple sickness symptoms: diarrhea, fever, malaria, headache, even tummy aches. These pills were made of sugar palm and the residue of rice grinding. It was rolled into a ball the size of small rabbit dropping. Worthless as this sound, patients were lucky to even get these weird pills. Teenagers who were children of the KR soldiers, or untrained "Old People" were the only ones who worked in this health care system. I had been sent to that care system once. The young "caretakers" gave me an injection of coconut juice in the buttocks. They insisted they do it; if I refused, I might be killed. Since I had learned in pharmacy school that coconut juice, isotonic, could be tolerated by our body system if used appropriately, I let them inject it - intra-muscular only. I was actually hoping I would die from receiving this injection, but I did not. From my experience with the KR health care system, I had a picture of how *Pou* Sunthary had been treated. I was angry to hear about his misfortune, but I could do nothing to protect him.

Days passed by in misery as we starved. Then one day we were informed by someone who came home from the revolutionary hospital that *Pou* Sunthary had been miserably sick and passed away. Even though this confirmed our fears, we were still shocked and sorrowful.

"How did he die?" I asked.

"I saw he was very swollen, could not get up or eat anything. He could talk very little and his last words were to tell you 'Goodbye and not to expect him anymore'. He lived by his will alone. He was in a coma for a couple days at the end. It was miserable to see him."

We all took a deep breath with the sorrow of his leaving. "Well, it's better this way; he can rest now instead of working so hard in the canal. He is lucky," Papa said, with a sad smile.

"But he died miserably before he could see us," I disagreed with him. "He shouldn't have lost hope too soon." I laid his bag on my lap. Death had become commonplace but the loss of my little uncle hurt my heart.

Bathing in the River

Late that day after our meager meal, Papa sat quietly on the bamboo bed, facing the bamboo patch as if watching for something, and frequently scratching his head.

"I haven't taken a bath for months," he said, when I took a close look at his head and told him I thought he had lice. "Why bother? We have no soap, no shampoo, nothing to wash ourselves with."

"Hai, Hai! Papa, you must take a bath. You must have lice. I think I have lice too. Why don't you go to the river?"

"Because I do not want to leave my place. People around us just wait for me to step away so they can steal anything possible." Then he nodded toward the neighbor who lived next to us.

"Papa, we have nothing for them to steal."

"They could steal our wood underneath the bed. They could steal our rice. Do you know that their children steal?" He pointed at the Vietnamese kids, "It is easier for them to steal my wood than go to the forest to find their own."

"Okay, go take a bath in the river right now. I will wait in the cabin until you come back," I assured him with a smile.

He walked to the riverbank that was located behind our neighbor's house instead of behind my in-laws'. He wasn't gone very long.

"Um.., how did you take a bath so quickly?" I wondered.

"I just wet the *krama* and washed my body," he said, looking annoyed to stop me from asking him again. Papa was the same as ever - STUBBORN.

"Papa, I want to wash your pants. You've had them on for almost two years."

"No, *Kaun*, it is worthless as we don't have any laundry soap. I will throw them away when we return home," he said, laughing.

"No soap because you don't want to get the car dirty, remember?" I teased him.

"If I had allowed you to bring the laundry soap, it would be gone by now anyway."

Kilen came back to stay with Papa for a few days and was sent to work in a different place. However, she still came back and forth to visit my Papa when I was not around. Some months later, she was sent to work far away. The last time I saw her, she came in very sick with a swollen body like a little elephant. She walked very slowly with a bamboo stick to support her. As soon as she saw me with Papa, she left; then she disappeared forever. The three main causes of death for the new people in the villages were diarrhea, malaria and execution.

The Only Regret

Because our place was not a real house, just a lean-to on the outside of the cabin, we could be seen easily by anyone just by walking by. Luckily, one side was screened with bamboo bushes. Every morning, I would see Papa sitting quietly on the bamboo bed scratching a little piece of bamboo for no reason. I guessed he was thinking, disappointed about everything. Papa had been a big and strong man; a healthy person in his sixties when we were expelled from the city. Papa was a man who was never silly or frivolous; he was used to being in charge and making the rules. At home, we had a very difficult relationship because of his abusive discipline, his bad temper, and his intimidating voice disciplining me in front of others.

However, now he was not the same person he used to be. The only thing that had not changed was that he still behaved like he was an authority figure; for this, or some other reason, he did not have to work like the other elders. Also Papa was smart in dealing with people. He easily made friends with everybody; as a result he was liked, never was reported. He was fortunate to receive tobacco for cigarettes from his friends all the time. During the two years we had lived in this place, I never saw anybody bother him for any reason.

Papa physically changed a lot in two years. He became very skinny in his grey, formal pants, the only ones he brought with him. These pants later became shorts with the waist tied up with a piece of string. His light green, clean, crisp short-sleeved shirt was now smelly and greasy with two years' worth of dirt and sweat stains holding it together. His hair was silver and cut short. His eyes had also become silver. They looked unhealthy, dehydrated, and white. They were filled with sadness and disappointment. Papa often told me when he saw me, "We will be fine, and we will be liberated very soon!! I hope this regime won't last much longer!!"

"I know that, but we still have to fight against starvation and sickness while we are here," I said to motivate Papa to move more. One time when I sat by him as he looked at his swollen feet, I let my despair get the better of me and I lashed out at him, "You are responsible for our miserable life because you did not make the decision to leave the country in time."

I blamed him with this mean statement impulsively. I loved him but I had plenty of time to think as I worked very hard in the forced labor fields. Maybe I was still immature or maybe I was just exhausted and deadened by the horrible crimes inflicted by this cruel regime. My words were to blame him for the wrong decisions that caused the death of everybody in the family.

Hearing my blame, he did not say a word to defend himself. He was not mad at me either. I wanted him to admit that it was his mistake that we did not leave the country when we could - before all this horror happened. He should have known better than anybody else since he worked with the politicians and government. Instead, he responded slowly, his eyes filled with sadness and regret mixed with love, "The only thing I will regret for the rest of my life is to not being able to establish your life in the way I wanted." Then he quietly looked down and shook his head. I turned and sat next to him silently. He turned his back to me and grabbed his *krama* to wipe his tears.

I hugged him around his bony shoulders, "Papa, I am sorry. I don't mean to hurt you. I love you and I am always here for you. I love you even more since you decided to choose me over Kilen." The smelly, greasy shirt should have disgusted me, but I learned to like it. This smell was the real odor of my beloved father. I hoped this smell would last until we returned home.

Memory of Eating Watercress

My husband and I rarely lived together; he only was allowed to come home once in a while and I was assigned to work units near the village. He worked very hard in the fields, acted and behaved as they expected so the KR would leave him alone. I tried very hard to cope with life on the farm, imitating their language, their behaviors, and their accents. Everything in me had to change completely in order to live. I knew that I could do nothing that wasn't noticed by everyone in the village. My goal was to keep Papa alive. I would do anything to keep him healthy and responded to his needs as much as I could. Usually, the best I could do was to provide him with herbal tonics and firewood. Thus, at the work camp, at noon during lunchtime, I did not rest like others. I went to the forest to cut the little baby bamboo branches and brought them home for Papa to cook potions to treat his swollen feet. I did not know how to forage for wild food and could not find anything else besides bamboo branches.

We were horribly starved, with barely enough food to stay alive and we fantasized about food all the time. "I am hungry for fish. Imagine us having a fish dish right now...." Papa swallowed saliva, "Yum, yum...," he lifted the pot, "the pot is empty, no fish." He turned to a little sack and untied it, "We have only a half can (16oz.) of rice for both of us. It would be enough if we had vegetables to add to it. But, we don't have any."

Just at that moment, his Chinese friend next door came in and brought us a handful of wild greens. Smiling widely, he said, "Hey, *Kong* (Grandfather in Chinese), an 'old fellow' just paid me with these vegetables after I repaired his watch. I will share some with you." Papa gratefully took the greens from his friend and thanked him.

"What do you call this?" I asked as I picked up the leaves and smelled them, "Weird smell." The greens reminded me of the watercress I ate at the Le Grand Hotel, when we were on our family trip to Angkor Wat.

"I don't know, but the "Old People" eat it," *Kong* answered, taking off his reading glasses before leaving us to our feast.

"Hey, *Kong*, do you need more tobacco?" Papa called after him.

"I have enough for now," he answered and disappeared behind the bamboo patch.

"Where do you get the tobacco? You have something to trade with?" I questioned Papa.

"No, I know one woman who has been widow for a long time. She lives alone and gives me tobacco because she pities me. Sometimes she brings me a bowl of delicious soup with fish and vegetables. You know the adage, "Do good things for people, you will receive good things in return."

"Is she "Old People" or "New" like us?"

"Old."

"Don't trust anybody, Papa!!"

"She hates this regime too."

He washed the greens, "I know this vegetable. It grows in the water, but I can't think of the name."

"I dream about eating watercress, Papa. Remember at the Le Grand hotel when we visited Angkor Wat, I ate watercress with butter?" He laughed with that memory. "I imagine eating fish with this vegetable. Salt is the desert I ate at the Le Grand Hotel." He laughed again.

"I saw your father-in-law carrying a big fish net yesterday. He must catch a lot of fish," said Papa as he slowly ate the greens, savoring each piece as if it were a precious delicacy.

"I don't know, Papa. If we had a fish net, I wouldn't know how to use it anyway. Why bother to think about it."

Papa started to make a fire; I washed the pot and put a quarter can of rice in it. I filled it with water to the top of the pot.

"Papa, I am going to take a bath; the rice soup will be ready when I come back." Having wild vegetables motivated Papa. He got up and worked faster than he had in days.

As I walked by my in-law's house to the lake, mother-in-law caught me, "When you come back from the lake, make sure you stop by and get a bowl of soup for your father."

"*Chah.*"

Hearing my mother-in-law wanting to give Papa a bowl of soup sounded too good to be true, a miracle, a blessing. I felt as if a million lights were shining on me. I rushed to finish my bath before she changed her mind. I wondered what kind of soup she would give us. As I stepped in the house, I saw she was in the kitchen and hadn't noticed me. She was filling a bowl; it must be the bowl for me. Then I saw her take something out of the bowl. What was she doing? I heard her daughter telling her, "Put in more broth." Without seeing me behind her, my mother-in-law put more banana tree slices in the bowl, and she used a spoon to smash something in the bowl. Her daughter noticed me first and said, "*Baung* is here."

Neak gave me the bowl, "Your father-in-law didn't catch many fish but at least you have a taste of it." I took it and hurried to leave," *Aur koun, Neak.*"

As soon as he saw me, Papa came to help. Taking the bowl from my hand, he asked, "What is it?"

"I got a bowl of soup from mother-in-law. She made it with fish and baby banana tree."

Papa smelled it again, "Yum, smells so good....yum, yum."

I decided to not tell Papa about what *Neak* had done to the soup - smashing a tiny bit of fish in the bottom of the bowl so that it would not float on top of the soup, making it look like she had given us a lot of fish. I was angry that she had removed another piece of fish from the bowl. It was there but she changed her mind and took it back. This was a common behavior with her so I had learned to immediately take anything she offered me before she changed her mind.

"Good, we are rich. Pretend like we are eating at the restaurant." As long as Papa was happy, I would be happy. When the rice soup was ready, Papa used the ladle to serve the rice soup - one scoop for him and one for me until it was gone. "We are lucky today. We eat rice soup with banana tree soup but how about tomorrow?"

"I don't know Papa. We will be hungry again tomorrow. We live one day at a time." We had an equal amount of rice soup and we survived for another day.

He was Always There for me

Since I was now allowed to sleep at home and not at the camp, Papa always waited for me outside the cabin so we could have dinner together. I brought home the rice soup and a small spoon of salt from work to share with Papa in addition to the food rations from the village. Also, I brought some of the plants growing along the road to eat with rice soup, pretending like we were eating watercress, fish and dessert.

I was very scared at night to go to the latrine alone, so I called for Papa to come with me. I was still scared of ghosts the same as when I was a child. I was still his little girl and he treated me as if I were the most special part of his heart. I could feel it. What I called the latrine was a hole in the ground with two pieces of wood covering it. To cover our nakedness when sitting, we wrapped ourselves with a *krama* if we were lucky enough to have one. We used leaves as toilet paper.

All the medicines I had hidden in my pants were long gone. Now I traded cosmetics. Cosmetics were valuable to the village girls who were hungry for beauty. Girls are the same wherever you go even in a poor farming village.

"Who doesn't want to smell good, and look pretty?" I commented to Papa.

"It is a sign of the fall of the KR regime." Papa wiped his forehead. "People want to live normal lives."

"I wish." Without looking at him, I kept going through my cosmetics hidden in a bag.

"This is my favorite perfume." I showed him the bottle of perfume from Paris, "I want to keep it but it is worth more in trade for food. I will give it up just for you, Papa. I am happy when you have food."

Then I let him smell it. "It smells like jasmine. Keep it, *Kaun*," he raised his eyebrows.

"Your life is more important, Papa! And the girl who wants this perfume will come here very soon."

"What will you ask from her?"

"She will give me what she can afford. She will steal food from her parents for this perfume, I am sure."

"Ask her for *prahok* (Khmer Anchovy)", Papa said. "I am hungry for *prahok*."

"Sh....I hear someone coming." I got up. The girl came in, sat down on my bamboo bed and took something wrapped in banana leaves from her pocket.

156

"Is that a *prahok?*" I whispered.

"I stole it from my parents. Unfortunately, we don't have much left. If I took all of them, my parents will question me and I will be in trouble." She was out of breath.

I showed her the perfume. She was excited and immediately wrapped it in her *krama*. As she was about to leave, she turned to me asking, "Do you have makeup?" I showed her a Lancôme fond de teint and powder. She smiled. "Keep it all for me. I will look for more food to trade with you." She left. We both were happy. She had the perfume; we had the food. It was a huge blessing.

After we got the *prahok*, Papa dreamed about peppers. He got up from the bamboo bed to check his one and only pepper plant that never grew much in two years. He complained to the plant, "My poor pepper, for two years I have faithfully watered you, you never give me a pepper. I need only one for now, for my *prahok*." He walked back to inside saying, "It must be a male pepper. I want to take a bath first, clean my body, so I can enjoy my magic meal later." He quickly left with his *krama* in hand, excited about the impending feast.

I teased him, "Every time you have new food, you want to take a bath. Make sure you take a real bath not just a wash with your *krama*."

I was so proud that I was able to feed Papa today. I wasn't even thinking about tomorrow. If there were no food tomorrow, we could only hope the next day or the next following day we would have food. We survived from day to day. When he came back from the lake, we started our meal with the watery rice soup. Amazingly, Papa showed me a handful of hot peppers.

"Where did you get them?"

"From your mother-in-law."

"Aha! So, when you need a pepper, you take a bath at the river behind her house. I understand you now. Did you ask her for the peppers?"

"Why should I?"

"I heard her complain her peppers were picked by people who came to take a bath at the lake." I said, smiling at my clever Papa.

"I don't know why her peppers grow big and bear lots of fruit and mine give me nothing."

"You just said yours is a male pepper." We laughed. I loved to laugh with my Papa. The twinkle in his eye had returned, if only for today.

"If your mother-in-law knew we have *prahok* today, she would be here at the door, asking for some."

"We can give her some, but we don't have to, because she has enough food for her family. We have none. She feels no obligation to share with us, why should we feel an obligation to share our small amount with her?"

I kept trading my cosmetics to the same girl until my bag was empty. Now we looked for possible ways to trade our remaining clothes – particularly *sarong batik*. *Sarong batik* was very much in demand by the old people. They could barely afford *sarong batik* before the KR regime; now it was their time to take advantage of the new people. We needed food, they wanted *sarongs*. However, not many of us brought many *sarongs* with us. Papa had bought more than dozen *sarongs* for both of us, but we only took a few when we left. I kept trading them for whatever the old people offered us as food in return. Papa had a silk *sarong* which was more valuable than *sarong batik*, but we wanted to keep it for last.

~SEVENTEEN~

THE FOREST HAS MANY EARS

Living in the "Prison Without Walls", we quickly learned our freedom, peace, and happiness were taken away. We lived every second with the threat of torture and death. We were limited in where we could go and what we could say. Any complaints against the KR or how we were treated could get us killed. Young kids and teenage soldiers were sent to spy on us. They would hide in the bamboo patch, behind the banana trees, under the bed, or outside the house, listening to conversations in the night.

Realizing what a liability the bamboo patch next to our place was, I became irate. "I'm going to cut down the banana trees, Papa," I said, very angry and frustrated. "If I cut them down, the *chlop* (spies) won't be able to hide in them."

"What banana trees?" asked Papa, confused since there were none close to the cabin.

"There," I angrily pointed at the bamboo. "When I look at the bamboo, I see the banana trees that *Yey Kong* said allowed the ghosts to come into the house. When I was a child, I also feared they could come in through the holes in the floor. Now we have no floor and no walls, no door to keep us safe. All my fears have come true. There are ghosts and murderers now for real, for real."

"You are being silly again."

"Papa, don't you know *Chlop* have become both of them?"

"Yeas, you are right. But, cutting down the bamboo would cost you your life. It isn't worth it. Besides, if the bamboo patch was gone, they would find another way to spy on us. We just have to be careful what we say. Keep your voice down if you have to complain," Papa said, trying to calm me down.

"Papa, I don't know what makes me say banana instead of bamboo. You know, I had a premonition when I first saw this bamboo patch." I blinked to force back tears, "We have been robbed of our freedom, our right to free speech. It's not fair. We have been robbed of everything. Papa, how long can this last?" I said softly, looking around to make sure there were no soldier ears listening before I continued. "Those murderous black crows eat our flesh and our brains, and drink our blood while we are still alive and we are helpless to do anything about it. When will this all end? Will we all die in this horrible place Papa?" I said in frustration and anger.

"Keep your voice down, *Kaun*, or you will be reported to *Angkar* and they will come for you. Just do as they say and pray we are rescued soon," Papa comforted me.

159

"Coo, Coo, Hoo, Hoo, Hoo." Nocturnal birds and river animals, seemed to be taunting me as I lay awake wondering how we could escape from this living Hell. I envied the night creatures. They could go anywhere they wanted without threat of punishment. They seemed to know this and flaunted their freedom with each heckle in the darkness.

"Owooo, Owooo." The howling of foxes far in the forest terrified me. I knew they were digging up a body that had been buried early. Cambodians believed that if you heard a nocturnal animal, it was sent from the devil to claim a soul.

"Crack, Crack." The cries of the foxes were interrupted by the snapping of branches and rustling of leaves. Spies were hopping from one place to another like grasshoppers, as they tried to catch one of us in an incriminating conversation. Silent tears ran down my cheeks as I fell asleep, praying for freedom. Maybe I would feel freedom in my dreams, if not in my waking life.

The Old People Awaken!

The daily rice ration became smaller and smaller. At first, we were given a can of rice for each person per day. Later it became a half a can per person, then a half a can per two people, then one quarter per person, and then none. We were going to die unless I could think of a solution. I decided to look for the wild greens that *Kong* had given us. At least I hoped it was the same. I had seen a spot where it grew wild along the side of the road; it looked like watercress. I boiled in water with salt. I put the cooked leaves on each of our plates and served it to Papa as if I were serving a gourmet meal at Grand Hotel in Siem Reap. I closed my eyes and imagined I was eating fresh watercress with all the trimmings. As I was lost in my imaginary meal, my stomach rolled and spewed the grass out faster than I had ingested it. I was persistent and ate it until my stomach accepted it. The vegetable grew slower than I picked and was soon gone. I looked to the banana trees in my mother-in-law's garden.

"I'm going to ask *Neak* for a baby banana tree. She won't say no," I told Papa. He nodded but did not move. He moved very little now. His face and feet were so swollen he just lay immobile on the bamboo bed.

Neak agreed to cut the mother banana tree down for food. She gave me a quarter of what she harvested. We peeled the few top layers of hardened leaves off the tree, like shucking corn. We then sliced the interior crosswise, like slicing an onion. It had the texture of an onion and we ate it raw. We ate this for lunch and dinner. This was our meal every day for about a week.

I watched Papa deteriorate more and more each day. I had to do something. I needed to look for *prakrab*, a medicinal herb that had strange characteristics. The leaves became slack when touched and then perked up again. I mixed them with bamboo leaves as a diuretic treatment to make a potion, which I believed would relieve Papa's swollen face and feet.

"Lately, I have diarrhea," Papa complained, before he finished the last of the potion out of the aluminum plate. My frustration increased as each new problem surfaced.

"Well....., huh.... the main problem is from lack of decent food. I have to find things to trade for food. You need food to keep you stronger, Papa. However, trading with the "Old People" is harder all the time! Their supplies are running low and they worry about their neighbors spying on them, too. I think they have finally woken up. They are tired of being restricted in what they can and cannot do to look after their families. *Angkar's* rules are causing them to question the communists; they realize the KR cannot be trusted. They work hard to produce rice only to have *Angkar* take it from them. They have fishing equipment but they have to sneak around to use it. They are nearly as frustrated as we are," I ranted, as quietly as I could.

"It is still dangerous and even riskier than before. The forest has many ears. People spy on each other, good people who wouldn't otherwise be like that. Everyone has to take care of themselves in any way they can, friends turn on friends, and family turns on family. You can trust no one and no one is safe." Papa warned.

"I know Papa, everyone is starving; we are all fighting for food."

I said this because starvation, desperation and jealousy had driven the 'New People' to spy on each other and report to the KR so they would get a reward of food. Execution had become routine for minor offenses. In the first two years, *Angkar* looked for excuses to kill us; now they would kill people on a whim particularly if they were mad or drunk, or maybe they were bored and had the urge to see one of us suffer and die. We dared not even look at them for fear they would see something in our eyes they could use as an excuse to kill us.

Papa just nodded his head, "*Angkar* owns everything in the village: the land, the crops, the coconut trees and the palm trees. A man in the village told me he was the owner of the land and the palm trees before. He was the one who collected the palm sugar. But, now he collects it for *Angkar*. I am hungry for sugar palm, *Kaun!*" Papa said, his pale tongue moving slowly over cracked lips and his glazed eyes looking off into the distance as if he were sitting in a café ordering a gourmet dish. A faint smile played at the corners of his mouth.

"Sugar palm is hard to find, Papa. It would be a miracle if I could get even a small spoon," I said, with a twinge of guilt at squelching his wish. Looking at his distant eyes, I knew he wasn't hearing what he didn't want to hear. "But, I will have some for you one day, Papa. We will be happy when we are eating the sugar palm together."

I knew Papa needed this small hope. I needed this small hope. I closed my eyes and imagined the sugar palm in my mouth. I wanted to taste the sugar palm in my mind as Papa was. We both needed something to believe in, even if it were only a small amount of sugar palm. "I will find it for you. Papa," I vowed.

Sugar palm was my second priority. For now, my responsibility was to make a tea from *prakrab* and bamboo leaves, but the real problem was to encourage Papa to drink an additional potion of shredded guava bark to treat the diarrhea, perhaps due to the bitter flavor.

"Maybe the *prakrab* potion gave me diarrhea," Papa said.

"I don't know. We have no other medicine, Papa. Drink whatever we can afford," I said, very frustrated.

Fighting Over Food.

Parents fought with their children over food rations. The relationship between parents and children, husband and wives, neighbor and neighbor was becoming critical. The Vietnamese mother who screamed at her children constantly came to me one day, "My daughter is very selfish and mean to me. She got sweet potatoes and would not share them with anyone, not even with me."

When she was gone, the daughter came to me, "I am very skinny and very sick. I will die soon if I do not eat. My *Mak* wanted to take away my food. I need this food."

The mother later returned for another visit. "I am going to tell *Angkar* to eliminate her because she is evil," the mother said, sitting on the ground in front of the dying fire.

"What did she do?" I asked gently and sat on the bed on the other side of the fire.

"She called me *Kdouy mehr vear*," she cried, staring at the ground. Her hand swiftly swept the air as she caught a grasshopper in mid leap and threw it on the dying embers, "It hurts me; how can my own child hurt me like that?"

"And you want her to be killed for one little potato?" I was listening to the grasshopper crackling in the fire.

"Let her die, evil daughter." She picked the grasshopper from the fire and set it down to cool.

"Because of one small piece of potato you would have your own daughter killed? Let me ask you, if you had that small piece of potato, would you live for a hundred years?"

"I know we all are going to die of starvation, so what difference does one small piece of potato make?" she said and popped the cooled grasshopper in her mouth.

The sound of her crunching on her little snack caused bile to rise in my throat. I swallowed hard and shuddered. I still could not bring myself to eat these disgusting insects.

"*Ah Thmil Aut Sasna!* (Evil atheists!) They have caused all of this," she said, now blaming Angkar.

"We are living with *Thmil* (evil). Keep praying to God that we are rescued before we die," I said.

"Love your Papa; he loves you. He talks good about you all the time. I see you are good with him too. I believe God will bless you."

"My responsibility is to keep him alive. He is the first person in the world that I need to fight for him." Our conversation ended when she got up and I filled the aluminum plate with the potion for Papa.

When she left, I felt happy I had calmed her down and given her good advice.

Barber – My First Entrepreneur Attempt

On the day I went to my mother-in-law's house to help cut the banana trees, my father-in-law was giving someone a haircut. This interested me and I watched him cut the man's hair from beginning to end. This gave me the idea of offering to cut hair myself to earn rice to survive. It looked easy enough so why shouldn't I try my hand at haircutting.

"I talked to people to see if anyone needed a haircut," I told my father. "I would charge only two cans of rice per head.

Papa asked, "Do you know how to cut hair, *Kaun*?"

"*Chah*! I have observed my father-in-law cutting hair twice. It doesn't look hard; I know I can do it."

"Ha! Ha! I am afraid you will be asked to give back the rice when you give a bad haircut. But, you are smart and brave, as always, and I believe in you."

"Wait and see. I know I can do it."

A woman named Soon had been a hairdresser. When I suggested that I cut her hair, she said, "I will give you two cans of rice if I am satisfied with your haircut."

"Your hair is naturally curly; it will look great after I cut it and I will give you a better style," I said with more confidence that I felt. She sat down. Luckily, Papa had scissors from somewhere, I didn't ask, and I had a little piece of broken mirror I found on the way to work. My Papa covered his face and looked away pretending to be laughing at something in the other direction. It took me almost a half-day to cut her hair. She was happy with what I did and gave me two cans of rice. Success!

"Papa! She paid me with two cans of rice. See? I will cut hair and we will have food."

"You can cut my hair next time," Papa teased.

"Me, too!" Sok, Papa's friend, said cheerfully.

Milliner – My Second Entrepreneurial Attempt

Soon was the first and last customer I had so I needed a new idea. "Papa! I could not find any customers for the haircuts. Instead, I will learn to make hats for the workers who must be in the sun all day." I asked a friend to show me how to make the hats from palm leaves. I learned very quickly and made a hat for myself to advertise my business. It worked and I soon had customers. Each paid me with two cans of rice per hat.

"My business is growing, Papa. Now our sack of rice is fat." However, my business of making hats was short-lived and my sack of rice that had so been fat, now was becoming thinner and thinner.

"Do not worry, *Kaun*! We are going to be okay; I believe we are going to return home when the rice sack is empty," Papa encouraged me.

"Papa, stop talking about returning home, stop thinking about it, I want to make sure we survive from day to day with enough food right here where we are," I said in frustration. He said nothing and sadly looked away. I knew I hurt his feelings and I felt bad, but I wanted him to be realistic. I should have left him with his fantasies.

Lingerie Designer – My Next Entrepreneurial Attempt

"Papa! Don't worry. I can sew bras to earn rice...."

"Where will you get the fabric?"

"Whoever wants me to make one will have to provide her own fabric."

"How much will you charge?"

"It won't be expensive; I just need customers."

"I didn't know you could sew things like this."

"Papa! It is easy. I know how to sew. I watched *Neak* sew. She does this every day and she gets paid with everything, like fish, rice and vegetables."

"She stays home every day; she has more time to sew. You go to work. I am afraid you won't be able to finish what you start. Anyway, all the people around here are your mother-in-law's clients."

"Do not worry, not all of them like her. Most of them have started to dislike her because she is greedy."

I secretly started my business by offering the old people a free service first. I would do alterations. It worked and I usually got paid something. I made bras by hand and charged less than *Neak* did. I was also faster than she was. I got my first customer. I received fish sauce, vegetables and rice for my work. We were happy. "We are rich again, Pa!"

"Your mother-in-law will be angry if she finds out you do the same job as she does for less pay."

"What difference does that make? She is always angry about something."

One day when I visited my mother-in-law while she was sewing, she asked, "Vicheara! I saw your Papa has more rice, did you know about it? Where did he get it?"

"I earned it from sewing bras and hats."

"You are not honest with us. You care only about your Papa, how about us? You used to eat here with us, sleep here, but your mind and heart are with your Papa."

"I am all Papa has. You have each other. Papa has nobody to support him beside me. His life depends on me."

"Your Papa is lazy, always hiding in the cabin, pretending he is disabled."

"He is sick, he has swollen legs."

"It is his excuse. Tell your Papa to wake up; this is not the place where he can do what he wants. Everybody has been watching him. Anyway, why is he so fortunate? I never saw anybody try to force him to go to work. Look at your father-in-law! He works his butt off. He is skinny now, eats less and works harder."

"My Papa is skinner and has swollen legs. He eats only what I can provide for him."

"Whatever, just be careful; if they find out he is lazy or that he is a high class person, he will be *vay chol*."

"Butchered?" I shook my head. "It is not going to happen to him. I am here to protect him." She infuriated me. I walked away so I didn't have to talk to her anymore. Walking back to Papa's cabin, I dropped on the bed, facing the bamboo patch. Papa saw how unhappy I was and comforted me the only way he knew how. He always said same old thing, we will be fine and we will return home soon.

"Papa! *Neak* knew we had more rice." I kicked the hardened ground in frustration.

"Her job is to watch me, spy on me."

"Next time, I will be more careful when I bring anything home," I turned toward to Papa.

"She is a bad person," he sighed, brushing the dust from his blanket with his hand. "Be patient, this regime will end someday and we will return home. When we get home and everything is back to normal, we will decide who will remain our friends and who won't."

"If Leang were here, his mother wouldn't be so greedy and annoying. He will listen to me more than her; but, he is not around enough to discuss anything."

I used a coconut shell to scoop the water from the bucket that was sitting at the edge of the bamboo bed. I washed my feet and dried them with my *krama*. I put my feet up and sat on the bed next to Papa, thinking about my husband. We had grown apart because we had been separated for so long. But when we were together, we never fought over food even though we were both starving.

Papa may have been reading my mind. "When will Leang come visit us again?" he asked, his voice was filled with concern.

"I don't know, Papa." My eyes scanned the alley in both directions searching the shadows for any sign of my husband returning home. He had been so good to me so many times, except once when he disappointed me over two small fish. I remembered that day; he had stopped by to see me. As always, he smiled warmly, and in his soft caring voice, he asked me to come close to him. I thought he would kiss me when he was sure *Angkar* was not watching, but instead, he put a few little fish in my hand. He left to go back to work, but he returned a few minutes later saying he forgot to tell me something. "I will not leave until you have finished the fish. I brought these for you, not your Papa," he repeated firmly. I couldn't believe he was saying this to me. I was very disappointed in him. How could he leave one person and return a few minutes later a different person? He had no compassion for the father of his wife? He had to know not sharing with my Papa would break my heart. I looked at the determination in his eyes and decided to eat the fish.

Why did I do what he told me to do? Was I scared of Leang? Why didn't I protest a little more until he agreed with me? Perhaps I did as he asked because I was greedy and so hungry? Later that night as Papa lay on the bed, he said he was hungry for fish and he swallowed his saliva. I felt guilty that I had been so selfish and I had not argued with Leang enough so that he would agree I could share with Papa. If I could have brought the fish from my stomach to share with him I would have.

Stir-fry

Papa made many friends around the cabin, from the new to old People. Who did not know "Silver-Haired *Lok Tah?*" Our life had improved a little after I began to get additional rice from sewing bras, making hats from palm leaves, and altering shirts for the KR leaders. With these skills, people knew me better and allowed me to collect pieces of scrap wood left over from building houses. But this reprieve only lasted a short while and then a new rule forbade bartering for rice and we were destitute again.

Praub unexpectedly showed up at our cabin when Papa was busy boiling a potion for his swollen feet. Papa did not notice Praub's presence as he was blowing on the bamboo to make a fire. I greeted our visitor, "Come in, *Samak Mit* Praub, have a seat." I gestured for him to sit.

Papa looked up and smiled at Praub. He stopped blowing the bamboo and came to sit down on the bed next to Praub.

"I just wanted to check and see how you are doing?" Praub initiated the conversation.

"I am making a potion of *prakrab* and bamboo leaves."

"It should be good for your swollen feet," Praub said and touched Papa's feet. "Has it helped you?"

"I think they look better, "Papa said as he rubbed his feet.

There was a bit of awkward silence as we waited to hear Praub had come by. He looked around for spies and started to tell us a story. "A drunken soldier came to see me last night," he began.

"Why and who was he?" Papa asked, as Praub always spoke slowly in a low voice and through his teeth. He took him forever to tell a story.

"A drunken soldier happened to visit us last night," he said again, as Papa waited impatiently. Praub continued, "He told us that he executed a woman soldier and cut off her breasts."

I clutched my breasts and gasped! At that moment Sok, Papa's friend, walked by. Seeing we had company, he decided to join the conversation. "Do you have tobacco, Praub?" Sok asked, tapping him on his shoulder. Praub turned to Papa.

"Here, I can share with you," Papa said, handing Sok his pouch of tobacco.

"Aur koun, Baung." Sok turned to Praub, "What's new?"

"Nothing new. Just reminding them that we need to obey *Angkar's* rules very carefully as they execute people whenever they are mad. I just told Silver-Haired

Lok Tah," he was pointing at Papa, "about a drunken soldier who killed a woman like an animal. He raped her first, and then cut off her breasts before executing her. He then stir fried her breasts and ate them."

Sok's face told me that he was as astounded with this story as I was, but Papa just exhaled smoke through his nose. He acted as if nothing were out of the ordinary. Maybe he was at the point that nothing surprised him anymore.

"Why did he kill her? I cannot believe a soldier would kill another soldier," Sok asked and then he asked Papa for a light for his pipe.

Praub continued with his story, "Apparently, she slept with another soldier without *Angkar's* permission. That was her crime."

"Do you believe this soldier?" Sok asked, and exhaled the smoke through his nostrils.

"*Bat,* I believed him. It happens all the time. When they want to kill somebody, they drink to build up their courage and then go wild. Don't spread this story. If you tell people, you will be responsible," Praub warned us.

"Responsible for what?" Sok exhaled more smoke as he bent down to poke his swollen feet, "Ha! My feet are getting better, don't you think?" he laughed, seeming to forget the awful story.

"We both have swollen feet, but we need to live." Papa smiled, turned around looking for his *krama* to dry the sweat on his forehead.

"Don't tell anyone you heard the story of sty-frying the breast from me. If you are caught, *Angkar* will execute you, not me." Again, Praub spoke through his teeth as he got up.

He was leaving when Sok asked him, "Did you see any rice coming in to the warehouse today?"

"*Bat,* it was just coming in, but it will be rice with chaff," Praub responded and started to walk away.

"How much will we get today?" Sok shouted at his retreating back.

Praub stopped and turned to answer, "I am not sure, maybe a half can for three people. I saw only three sacks of rice coming in to our village and we have to split with people living on the other side of the road." He then disappeared around the corner of the hut.

"A half can for three people? *Kdouy mehr vear!* They are killing us. When we remove the chaff, it will be only a few mouthfuls each." Sok and Papa and I looked at each other; we knew we wouldn't last long on these starvations rations. We could smell death coming.

Papa cursed and asked Sok, "Do you ever see any cats or dogs running around anymore? I have not seen any." The farm animals had disappeared long ago – all eaten.

"The crows eat the dogs and cats too, you know that?"

"*Bat,* I have known this for a long time. If they can eat the human liver, they will eat anything."

As Papa said this, I thought of my beloved dogs and wondered if this had been their fate. I looked at Sok and Papa with their swollen feet and was overwhelmed with sorrow.

"It is bad enough that Khmer have always been the target for both Vietnam and Thailand as they tried to eliminate us and swallow our land. Now Pol Pot devastates his own country and eliminates his own people. Who does he want to give Cambodia to? He wants to be like Hitler. Maybe his plan is to give Cambodia to China," Papa wiped his eyes with his *krama*, after finishing his angry opinion.

"Papa, not so loud," I reminded him, trying to stop him from saying more.

"I don't care anymore. I am starved." He wiped his tears with *krama*.

"Hitler killed the Jews. Pol Pot kills his own people. No difference. Killing is killing." Frustrated, Sok got up and left.

"What are you looking for, Papa?" He was frantically searching the pocket of his shorts. He emptied the contents of both pockets onto the bed.

"What are you looking for?" I asked him again but he ignored me. I watched him for a few minutes, trying to read his mind.

"The seeds that *Kong* gave me," he finally volunteered, smiling as he carefully extinguished his cigarette on the floor, then picked it up and put it in his pocket. He then went through all the pockets of his shirt, and his little pouch of tobacco. "Here it is," he declared, holding a little folded piece of paper in one hand and the tobacco pouch in the other. He smiled widely and held the paper as if it were a beloved trophy. He quickly unfolded the paper and showed me the seeds, "These are the mustard greens seeds that *Kong* gave me," he handed them to me. "Plant them now, *Kaun*, and we won't die any time soon."

"We are rich, Pa!" I said excitedly. I immediately planted the seeds. Together, we tended the precious plants as if they were children...

No Rice Until Further Notice

In every afternoon, usually before sunset, Praub walked by every house to announce the arrival of the rice rations for all the inhabitants of the village. Since our food was supplied day by day, his voice was welcome, like an angel giving us a blessing with rice. One afternoon, Praub's voice was not heard and people soon were asking each other if they had missed his announcement. I walked to the leader's house and waited like everyone else, hour after hour, but no sign of any rice. We came back again the next evening to the same spot only to get the same silence. On the fifth day, the leader came out and announced, "We will have no rice until further notice." I wanted to cry but I couldn't. I wanted to scream at him, but I couldn't. I wanted to ask him only one question - did he make an effort to provide us anything else in place of the rice? But, I still couldn't. Fear of execution had shut my mouth. I could only ask myself, "What was I supposed to do? How would my Papa survive?"

When I returned home Papa came out of the cabin smiling at me as usual, hoping I brought home rice. "No, Papa. The leader told us he doesn't know when we will have rice." I said, not knowing how I could make this right.

"It's fine, *Kaun*." Papa encouraged us both. "We will start using our earned rice." Papa opened up the sack where we stored our six cans of rice. He smiled. "See? We can live together on this. Maybe the leader will have rice by tomorrow."

My Decision to Leave Papa to Save his Life

I was quiet and did not look at the little sack of rice. I was thinking about how I could save all the earned rice for only Papa. I lay down, pretending to fall asleep so he wouldn't ask me any more questions. I was thinking and thinking. Suddenly, my thoughts were interrupted by the sound of a group of women walking by our cabin. My neighbor asked them, "Where are you going?"

"*Angkar* wants people to volunteer to work in the fields. We are going to join the group on the road."

This was the answer I sought. I would receive rations if I was at the farm camp so I got up immediately and grabbed my *krama* and bag of clothes. Papa, who had been sitting at the corner of the bamboo bed facing our little garden, was surprised at my sudden activity and asked me, "Where are you going, *Kaun*?"

"Papa, I believe you can survive on the vegetables and the earned rice. The rice is for you. I have to go away for a few days to work in the fields; don't tell Praub that I am not here so he will give you rice for both of us. You will have enough food to eat. I promise I will visit you in a few days. You can survive with the vegetables and earned rice until I come back home."

"I will be fine with the rice you earned from doing your business, *Kaun*. I can take care of myself. Also our vegetables will grow faster to feed me." I knew Papa was sad to see me leave, but I had to do this to save his life. I didn't say goodbye and hid my face in the *krama* as I followed everyone to the labor camp. I didn't want Praub to know I was gone.

In the fields, my job was to chop sod with a shovel. Exactly why I was chopping the sod remained a mystery. I was not sure and the leaders never gave us a reason. People around me said we were preparing the land for a new rice paddy. Since I had no experience with this fieldwork, I didn't question anything and I didn't care. My only concern was not to draw attention to myself. It soon became apparent that working in this group was not a good idea as my weakness and lack of experience made me too obvious. A young woman *Angkar* leader, one of the old people, took an instant dislike to me and made me work harder than anyone else. When she thought I wasn't working hard enough, she would punish me by taking away my food ration. She would also stare at me constantly, watching my every move and then criticize my work and give me the most difficult tasks - like a big tree to chop down on my own.

"I will never be able to chop down this tree by myself," I thought. "She is trying to kill me." The axe was heavy and bigger than my skinny arm. I could barely lift it, let alone swing it enough to even make a nick in the tree. I managed one chop, two chops and that was it. My feet gave out from under me. The axe became heavier every time I lifted it. I was sure it weighed more than hundred kilograms. I was sure I would soon accidentally chop my body in half. I only worked when she was walking by; when she disappeared, I stopped and sat down on the ground.

The next day, I hid my face in my *krama* so she wouldn't recognize me. I left her group and joined another group, where my new duty was again to chop sod with a shovel. The group leader didn't care about me and paid me no attention. I could slow down my work, sit down when tired, or hide in the bushes pretending I went to urinate. No one came around to check or criticize my work.

I had been in the fields almost a week when I realized I had completely forgotten that I had promised Papa to visit him in a couple days. However, that day, my upper right eyelid was twitching frequently. I had a feeling something good would happen, based on an old Khmer superstition. What could it be? Returning home? As soon as I got off work for lunch, I walked straight to the kitchen area to claim my food ration, as usual. I looked around, nothing new today. It was the usual scoop of rice soup and salt. Exhausted from work and disappointed as always with the food, I slowly walked back to the sleeping area saying to myself, if I eat this food, I will still be hungry. If I don't eat it, I will still be hungry. Consequently, eating or not eating won't make any difference. I choose to sleep rather than eat. My body needs rest to regain energy, so I can wake up fresh and ready for the work in this afternoon, if I am still alive.

Looking at my sleeping place, I had nothing but a *krama* that I folded to make a pillow; my bag of clothes had nothing more than a blouse and a worn out *sampot hol* that *Neak* had sewn. I took out this blouse and looked at the handmade embroidery. It had been a placemat that I picked up from my cousin's house two years ago. If cousin Ban Hap knew I used his placemat for a blouse, would he feel pity for me or would he laugh at me? It fit me well since I lost a lot of weight and was very tiny. I lay down with sweat running underneath my shirt. I covered my eyes with the bag of clothes and just as I was about to doze off, I heard a woman's voice calling my name, "*Baung* Vicheara, your Papa sent you vegetables!" I smiled, recognizing the voice. It was the Vietnamese girl who lived next to Papa. I pushed aside the bag of clothes and opened my eyes. I saw a small bag of fresh greens next to my hand.

"Oh, my upper lid has been twitching all day. I cannot believe my luck receiving this bag of vegetables from Papa."

She exhaled cigarette smoke through her nostrils and took a letter from her pocket, "Here, he sends a letter too." She smiled, showing her brown teeth from smoking cigarettes for many years. She then spit on the floor before she said, "Your Papa is fine, but something else happened after you left." I looked at her, waiting for the story, while she took another drag from her cigarette. "A soldier went to your mother-in-law's, then went straight to your Papa's and looked through everything, because she must have told him your Papa had things hidden. When the soldier looked underneath your cushion, your Papa tried to grab your jewelry bag but he accidently dropped it and that caught attention of the soldier. When the soldier asked your Papa what it was, it was too late to lie because the soldier already had it in his hand. I heard your Papa tell him it was yours and the soldier took all your jewelry."

Papa's Letter

I stayed quiet, but I was very upset and frustrated. I needed my husband with me now to discuss things. Who was I to believe? On one side is my father, on the other mother-in-law. I cared about my jewelry, but they were just material things. Papa's health and the treachery of my mother-in-law worried me now. I offered to share the greens with the messenger for her trouble but she refused.

"No, it is OK. I am fine. Keep them for yourself. Your Papa gave me some," she said and left.

Nothing could make happier than hearing Papa was safe. This news was the best gift anyone could have brought me. That day, I had fresh greens with the rice soup. While eating, I read the letter:

Kaun,
These are the vegetables from your hard work. I am fine now, but my feet bother me a lot. I share meals with my Chinese friend who lives in the rice storage next to our place. I like him and promised him I will give him some money when we are liberated. I still have the six cans of rice and we will eat together when you return home. Also, Sok is very sick. He won't last long. Papa

Mon Dieu! I forgot to visit him as promised, but his letter proved that he could manage without me, I consoled myself. However, a week later, I got a second message from the same Vietnamese girl who had just come back from visiting her mom frightened me. She said, "You'd better go see your Papa, he is very sick. He is alone on the bamboo bed, shivering from a malaria attack."

Tears filled my eyes. I panicked. I blamed myself, why didn't I visit him like I promised? I asked permission to leave work right away, to take care of my Papa. I also brought my rice soup in a can hoping it would help save him. My heart wrenched with despair.

When I saw Papa, I blinked desperately, trying to hold back the flood of tears that threatened to blind me. His body was skinnier than before and his face and feet were swollen as if someone had blown them up like a balloon. Lying on the bed shivering, covered with a cow blanket, was my Papa who used to be so strong, brave and healthy, who once was a proud and noble gentleman. As I got closer to him, I could no longer hold back my tears.

"Papa, don't you go anywhere. I am here to help you. You will be better soon," I sobbed, sitting on the bed beside him.

171

There was no wood stored under the bed. The hearth was empty, telling me that Papa had not gotten up to cook anything for a long time. The proud figure that he used to be, quietly turned and stared at me, not saying a word. He did not get up when saw me, as he would have done in the past. Then he recognized me and smiled, a weak, sad smile, full of gratitude and disappointment. I understood him; I came to hug him, to protect him from sickness, "Do you have any medicine left, Pa?" He shook his head negatively. "Papa, get up, I saved rice soup from work for you."

I came closer to him to help him get up. It was like holding a skeleton covered with tissue paper. He had a high temperature. His body was horribly weak and light. He struggled to get up, making a frail attempt to hold on to me. I put a spoon of soup to his lips and he tried to swallow and fell back on the bed.

"I am thirsty," he mumbled.

I understood that he had malaria and that his body was dehydrated from the high fever. I borrowed some pieces of wood from neighbors to boil a new potion of margosa leaves for him to relieve the fever and shivering.

"Papa, get up. I have this potion for you."

He tried very hard to pull himself up and, with my help, he was able to sit. He drank the potion out of a coconut shell. "Ah, bitter... very bitter.." he complained, and then gave it back to me.

"Finish it, Papa. Drink more. It is very concentrated."

His tired head fell back on the bed. "Do you have water? My throat is dry," he whispered.

"No, finish this first and I will give you water later." I refused to give him water right away because I knew he wouldn't drink the rest of the potion if he drank the water. A couple of hours later, after the potion had taken effect, he sat up and told me the events that took place after I left him.

"I am happy you can speak a little louder. It feels to me like the fever is gone," I said as I arranged his shirt.

"When the fever is gone, I feel like a real person, healthy and happy." He buttoned his shirt, "Oops, one button is missing," he said, smiling at me.

"I will fix it later for you, Papa. Continue what you were saying," I said, as I gave him boiled water to drink.

"A soldier came to search our cabin because your mother-in-law had reported that we had hidden jewelry. This was what he told me. The soldier found your bag of jewelry underneath the cushion." Papa paused to drink more water. "I cannot believe your mother-in-law did this to me."

"It was my mistake to leave my jewelry underneath the cushion without telling you to hide it for me. I was too rushed to leave before Praub noticed me in the crowd. It is hard to believe that my mother-in-law could have sent the soldiers to our cabin. I know she is mean and dishonest, but it is hard to believe she went that far."

Later, I went to my in-law's house and *Neak* volunteered a different story without being asked. She pulled down her eyeglasses to look at me. She paused from her sewing, then cried, "Vicheara, *Kaun*, everything is gone." She wiped her nose with her *krama*. I looked over at my father-in-law who was staring at me instead of getting involved with her crying. "A soldier came to my house and found all the jewelry I had hidden and took it all, including your rings and bracelet." She cried harder, wiping her tears with her *krama*.

My father-in-law still didn't add anything to the conversation. Why he didn't say anything? Should I believe her? She was so expert in hiding stuff, so manipulative, and so good at creating a diversion; but it could be real because I was not there. The soldiers could have come searching houses looking for jewelry.

I said to myself, "Oh! That is it, then. I have lost all my jewelry on both sides. Now, I have nothing left to trade when we are desperate."

Sugar Palm, A Gift From God

A couple days later, I again became very sick with malaria. Papa and I took turns, every other day, taking care of each other. When I recovered, I got up to make a potion for my Papa; when he recovered, he made a potion for me. On my second recovery, after the shivering period was over, I felt like I was blessed with a lot of energy. I took off the blanket and got up, while Papa was still blowing on the fire next to bed. He asked, "Where are you going? I am still making the potion."

"I am going to the leader's house to ask for any amount of palm sugar they can give me."

Without looking at Papa, I covered up with my *krama* and walked to the village leader's house. Somewhere I found the strength to walk without thinking about the fever wracking my body. I didn't know how I got away with walking to the house of the big leader of the village, called Kreun, without permission slip but no one stopped me. I guess I didn't look too threatening to the many *Angkar* people who sat on the floor around *Pouk* Kreun, the leader. I respectfully bowed to all of them in the traditional Cambodian way. My body felt dehydrated, my hands were still trembling from sickness, and my head throbbed. I was cold from the fever and hot from the midday sun. Of course, I was delirious but I didn't know that.

The look on his wife's face was full of compassion, "Your face is red from the sun and you are shaking like a leaf. You must be very sick from malaria, my dear." I was surprised she recognized the symptoms. "You need palm sugar. Give me your coconut shell," she said, taking it from my trembling hands. She surprised me again when she filled it to the top with palm sugar.

This *Angkar* leader's wife was so generous. She gave me a full container of palm sugar to take home. I knew Papa would be happy when he received the sugar because it would help his swollen feet and face. I thanked her and quickly left. I was confident we would survive a little longer. For a fleeting moment, I thought that if I traded this palm sugar for gold, I would have at least two oz. of 24 K. But, our lives were more important than two oz. of gold. I was hungry for sugar too.

For a selfish moment I thought I could eat it all and keep it a secret from Papa. But, I knew I couldn't do this either.

I was so happy to get the sugar for my Papa. This was a big blessing for us. Palm sugar at this time was worth a lot and I believe it was a gift from God. A lot of people had been trying hard to get palm sugar by offering to trade gold but I got it easily and a lot more than I expected, by the generosity of the leader's wife. Now, as I returned home, I was worried that *Neak* might see me holding the coconut shell and chase me to find out what was in it. I knew if she found it was sugar, she either would be mad at me or she would ask me to share with her. I wouldn't mind sharing but Papa was the first priority in my life because he was very ill.

"*Mon Dieu!* Please do not let her see me holding the sugar." I covered as much of myself with my *krama* as I could to hide the coconut shell from the jealous eyes of my husband's family. I walked as fast I could past their house. Fortunately, no one noticed me. I was so happy and proud of myself.

Papa smiled and whispered, "Did your mother-in-law see what you had in the container?"

"Absolutely not!" I grinned.

"She would come asking for the sugar from us right away, even though she has some. She is greedy," my Papa said. He also warned me about my two little sisters-in-law, who always snuck around his cabin to spy on him.

"*Chah*, Papa, I know. They spy on me too because they were told by their mother to keep an eye on you in case you have something good to eat. It isn't just the girls, my mother-in-law spies on me too."

Papa told me that my youngest brother-in-law, Pisith, the fifth son, also watched him. "However," he said, "I like Phanara, (the fourth son). He likes to come over and talk; he asks me for tobacco. We have been talking about going back home."

"*Chah*, Papa! He is nicer than Pisith. He is still nice to me but Pisith has changed since we got here. He used to ask me for money every time I visited his house in Phnom Penh, now that I have nothing, he treats me differently."

"I know this family. I was right about them from the start! Your mother in law is very sharp, direct, and has no shame. But, let's stop talking about her now. I want to make soy sauce while I am still well enough. Tomorrow, the malaria may be back."

Papa made soy sauce from the sugar; he filled up a few small containers with soy sauce and hung them along the bar of the roof. The next day, I walked to a different house and begged for help. I got a bowl of rice noodle soup, "*Samlar Noom Banchok*" which was made with lemongrass and fish. Oh, it smells delicious; we have not had food like this food for two years. Today my Papa will be happy, I thought. I gave it all to him and watched him eat it. I was so happy to have helped him. I had demonstrated how much I loved and respected him. When I watched Papa eat, I became full as well. I had done what I could do for him, so I would not have to live with regret. I never hid food from Papa; I never fought over food rations with him. By loving and respecting him, I felt God would bless me.

A Message from God Again!

We were both sick with malaria when Papa gave me another pink capsule. He told me it was the only capsule he had left and said, "You need it more than I do; you need to stay strong because you are still young."

I knew he wanted me to live. He told me he would be okay with the herbal medicines and insisted that I take the last capsule, even though I wanted him to have it. He suggested that as soon as I felt better, I try to barter our last Omega watch with the soldier who had the malaria drugs. That night, the nocturnal bird who was the harbinger of death flew over our roof and screamed loudly. He was gone before I could curse him. I ran to hold Papa tightly and save his soul from this evil bird. That same night, I dreamed Papa and I were being chased by a monster. As I ran by the temple, there was a monk who called to me to come inside, while my Papa kept running in a different direction. When I woke up, I told Papa about the dream. He interpreted it positively and said, "The dream means you will be safe, *Kaun*. Now, remember, no matter what happens to me; do not forget to do what I say…" I waited as he paused to take a breath, because he was very weak. "When you go back home, finish your pharmacy degree first before you do anything else."

"I promise. I will do what you ask," I told him as tears welled again in my eyes at the finality of his request.

"Don't cry, *Kaun*. Remember, never forget where you come from," he whispered, his voice barely audible and choked with tears.

"Don't cry, Papa. What else do you want to tell me?"

"Find Mr. Chhorn, the nephew of my dear friend Phlek Pheun and ask him for help. I gave him lots of money to open the business in Bangkok; he won't refuse to help you."

"Where will I find him?" I asked and then noticed that Papa was feebly trying to pull the blanket up. "Are you starting a malaria attack again, Papa?" I cried.

"Yes, I feel the shivering period coming on now," he answered. With his eyes closed, he swallowed a few times, and with great difficulty continued, "He may have been in Bangkok when Cambodia fell, but I am not sure. If he was, he will still be alive and still have money."

"He might have spent all your money."

Papa didn't answer. He probably agreed with me that his money might be gone, like leaves in the wind, in the hands of this man but he said no more. I held him close to share my body heat as he was began to shiver. His teeth were chattering, "I ….am…..very.. cold…..cold…."

"Pa..Pa…be strong," I cried. He didn't answer as he was trying to fight the shivering. I got up to boil a potion. I kept giving him the potion until the shivering was over. Then his body had to fight with the fever before he recovered.

"Oh, Papa… I will look for malaria tablets as soon as I can." I gave him a massage on his head to ease his headache and put a wet *krama* on his forehead to reduce the fever. Papa fell asleep…..

Next day, Papa got up and smiled at me. The attack was over. "I think the potion you made worked very well for the malaria. What did you use?"

"Bamboo and *margosa* leaves this time. It seems to work well to ease malaria symptoms and swollen feet."

"Where did you get the *margosa?*" Papa searched his pouch for tobacco.

"I exchanged one container of soy sauce with a Vietnamese girl." I got off the bed to make another batch of the potion. While I blew on the fire, I tried to joke with him, "I am glad you can talk better now. Papa, when I cut your hair we will be liberated."

Papa chuckled, "I still have big hopes that we will return home. When we do, I will cook a special dessert for you. Oh! I am hungry for that now."

I had never in my life heard Papa chuckle like that. He seemed a different person, happy and healthy. I loved seeing him this way. Why couldn't Papa stay this way? After a short silence, he asked, "Did you know that Sok's mother died just before you came back from the labor camp? And the mother of the young girl next door is very sick. She talks to her daughter twenty hours a day trying to prepare the daughter for her death. She won't last long either."

I didn't want to discuss it; everywhere I looked was grief and death. I was emotionally overwhelmed and could not think about anyone else's misfortune.

"How about you? Papa?"

"I am strong and healthy and will go back home."

This is what I wanted to hear from him.

~EIGHTEEN~

AMERICA! COME RESCUE US!

The following day, we woke early to the sound of birds singing from the roof of our cabin. "That's odd," Papa said, "For two years, I've never heard birds singing like this - only the nocturnal birds calling for our souls." Papa was folding his blanket and smelled it, "Still smells disgusting," he quipped and turned to me with a smile. "Look at our little garden; the mustard greens have grown very fast; it's only been a week since you came back from the labor camp and they have flowers already." He got up and walked to our little garden.

I looked at our Vietnamese neighbor sitting nearby on the ground; her little sister was crouched behind her searching her hair for lice, like a little monkey. Once in a while, her little sister shouted at her, "I cannot kill lice if you don't stay still."

"It is itchy. Anyway, you are too slow to ever catch any lice," the older sister replied as she continued to scratch her head.

Next to them, Sok's wife was standing with her hands on her hips. She shook her head and smiled. "You two are always fighting over something. Be nice to each other."

Watching them made my head itchy too. We had lived without soap and shampoo for two years. I struggled to keep my hair clean and to stay away from anybody with lice. I never borrowed anyone's comb without washing it with boiling water first. I wound up with lice anyway. I looked at Sok's wife and asked her," Do you have a fine comb that I can borrow?"

She smiled and teased me," I don't think lice will stay on your head anyway." She gave me the comb.

"Do you have lice?" Papa knocked on my head with his knuckle.

"If I sleep next to you that means you have lice too. They hop from one heat to another when they get the chance," I laughed and grabbed his hand before he knocked on my head again.

Killed Twice

We were surprised to see Sok walk toward our bed; he sat down next to me. I moved away from him, "Don't come close to me when I comb my hair. Lice will fly from my head to yours."

He laughed and as he got up, he looked at Papa and asked, "Is your malaria better?"

"I am better. I think it is not my time to go yet; how about you?"

"I am still fighting with it. Today, I think I will feel all right. There is no sign of the shivering attack yet, but maybe it will come tonight or tomorrow. I have taken western medicine and herbal medicine, both from my son in-law who knows the witch doctor around here. But, I am still not quite recovered. Strange." Sok patted his hairy chest.

"What kind of herbal medicine you have been taken?"

"I don't know. They called it Rabbit Shit pills. It tasted sweet; I heard they made with honey and rice powder or something. I don't know. Whether they do any good or not, they taste good."

Papa murmured, "*Ah Thmil Aut Sasna!* They have nothing but these stupid pills from a witch doctor for medicine, when we are sick."

Sok's wife joined in, "Go to Hell you evil crows! Communism is not what they said it would be. They said we would all be the same; live the same; and eat the same. There would be no rich, or no poor. What is the same between us and *Angkar?* Nothing! They have plenty of food and share nothing. While they fill their bellies with the rich harvests of Battambang, they offer us a spoonful of rice and a pinch of salt."

Suddenly her youngest son called out, "*Mak*, come to see Pheap; she has a tummy ache." She hurried away to tend to her child.

Papa said, "I heard all the rice crop has been sent to China to pay what the KR owed Mao."

Sok nodded and looked around to make sure we were not overheard. "Who told you this?" Sok asked as he spat on the ground.

"A soldier friend, a young man I have known for a while."

"Praub?" Sok scratched his head, "Lice are bothering me. I should have my hair shaved off."

"*Bat*, Praub." Papa also lit a cigarette; they blew the smoke at each other.

"He is a good man. I like him," Sok said in between coughs.

"*Bat*, he came here a few days ago, bringing me tobacco. What he heard from his soldier friend, he shared with me."

"Did he tell you anything about returning home?"

"No, but he would like this regime to be defeated by someone stronger," Papa said, "America."

"America," Sok repeated after Papa. "They need to come in their big helicopters and shoot the crows now before we all die. I pray for the Americans to come to our rescue and give us food. Imagine, American soldiers marching into our village today. Imagine American airplanes dropping large sacks of food for all of us. We would be so happy. Do you know last week, we were not allowed to cross the international road or hang around the road at noon?"

"*Chah*, I remember it too." I volunteered to get involved in their conversation, continuing to pull the comb slowly through my short hair. "I wonder why."

Sok whispered to Papa, "*Samdech* came to visit Siem Reap province."

"Sihanouk? How do you know this?" Papa whispered back. I just looked at their eyes to make sure I heard right that *Samdech* Sihanouk came here. If he found out that we are prohibited from seeing him and that the crows have tortured us, could he do something to rescue us? These thoughts kept me smiling; maybe there was some hope we would be liberated.

To my disappointment, Sok answered, "There was no way the KR would let *Samdech* find out about our real condition – starvation, pain, and massacre. My son-in-law heard it directly from the KR leader; they made sure none of us got to see him."

"Why would we want to see him? Sihanook betrayed us; he is selfish and cruel. He kills his own people for his own gain. He is..."

"Shh......no more politic." I stopped Papa as his voice rose in anger and frustration.

"What else did Praub have to say?" Sok tried to calm Papa down.

"His brother-in-law was captured and killed twice. Praub hates this regime too."

"Twice? How can someone be killed twice?"

"He was a teacher working in Battambang province. He returned to his parents' house when the KR took over. He lived with his family for a month before his identity was discovered. A soldier came to arrest him right during their dinner; everybody in the family was frightened. That soldier was also a former teacher working in the same school as Praub's brother. The next night, his mother heard a voice asking to open the door. She was afraid and hesitated at first until she recognized her son's voice. She was thrilled that he was still alive but when she opened the door, he passed out and crumpled at her feet. His body was covered with blood and dirt. On the back of his head was a big, gaping wound. They hid him in the house while they treated his wounds. When he finally regained consciousness, he said the soldier tortured him with a knife all over his body and left him for dead in the field. He crawled back home hoping to survive. The next part is very painful."

"What is next? Is he here?" Sok asked.

"No, he was killed. The soldier came back to the house and tortured his mother. To save his mother, he decided to turn himself in. Praub never saw his brother-in-law again."

"*Ah Thmil Aut Sasna,*" Sok hissed. "How did the soldier find out he was not dead?"

"I'm not sure. Maybe it was getting late and he wanted to finish him off the next day. Maybe he was tired or needed to get drunk, but in the morning when he came back to finish him off, he found the body was gone," I speculated.

"Could be, *Kaun,*" Papa said.

"Why didn't his mother hide him?" Sok pulled out more tobacco and rolled it in a piece of paper.

"You can't hide much in a farm house. Look at the houses around here. When you walk in through the main door, you can see the whole house. Why the mother didn't send him to live in a different house? I can only imagine maybe she was still shocked from the sight of how tortured he was. I don't want to see this problem happen to my family. I won't do anything crazy to allow myself to get in any sort of trouble," I assured Papa and we stopped talking about it. Sok walked away, deep in anger at the injustice of the KR.

When My Hair gets Cut We will Return Home

I started to look for somebody who would exchange malaria medicine for our remaining Omega watch. Unfortunately, nobody had any medicine and no one wanted the watch. There were no soldiers around; they were the most likely customers. Papa said, *"Kaun,* do not worry about me, I will be okay. I want you to cut my hair when the fever passes today."

He pulled out a pair of scissors and gave them to me. "I want you to cut my hair. Remember your joke? When my hair gets cut, we will return home."

"You are confident with my skill as a barber?" I teased him.

I sat him on a piece of wood and covered his shoulder with his *krama.* Sok came by to watch the event. "Will you cut mine when you are done with your Papa? I want to return home too." We all laughed but it was bitter, disgusted laughter.

"Sok, come here, I will cut your hair. Don't bother her! She has enough to do," his wife shouted from his house.

"Uh, my boss is calling me," he laughed again and walked toward his house. They both had a haircut on the same day.

~NINETEEN~

LAST WORDS

Papa continued to suffer as I could find no one with western medicine. I watched his handsome square face blow up to the shape of the full moon. Every day his eyes seemed to sink deeper into this bloated moon face. The skin on his feet was stretched to its limit; it was shiny and looked ready to burst. His face was very pale with a yellowish tinge in his eyes. He rarely got up at all, only to relieve himself. He lay on the bed most of the time whether he was awake or asleep.

I knew Papa was very sick, and I was desperately worried. I noticed a large mass in his pants in his groin area. I had been told that when the genitals swell, death is close. I took a deep breath to steady myself. Papa tried to keep a positive attitude, "Look! *Kaun*, my feet are not as swollen, they are getting better. Just keep making the potion for me and my feet will be well again." Papa poked his swollen feet.

I looked at his feet. I didn't see any difference. I said nothing. It was good to hear him be positive so I encouraged him, "Be active. Papa, keep walking fast enough to perspire. Do not sit around depressed; you have to keep moving to help the circulation in your feet."

Sometimes I was mad at Papa because I felt he was not helping himself. In fact, I noticed the people who got swollen bodies all walked very slowly, did not want to talk, and just sat all the time. They all died in the morning. For two days in a row, Papa spoke less and less, refused to eat and slept nearly all the time.

Had I Missed Anything else to Keep Papa?

It was the monsoon season and it rained very hard for a couple of hours each day. When it was not raining, I would walk around looking for someone new who might want the Omega watch, even though I knew it was hopeless. The ground became waterlogged and muddy. In the strong wind and rain, bamboo stalks buffeted each other and made a sound like coconut shells hitting together. If there was no KR, no death, no starvation, this might be a happy sound, like hands clapping, but now the hollow echoes were ominous and foreboding.

As night drew near, I walked barefoot to the river to fill the water bucket since Papa couldn't do this anymore. The muddy ground sucked at my feet like it wanted to swallow me. When I came back, Papa was still sleeping on his side with his eyes closed. While I was washing the mud off my feet at the corner of his bed, he whispered, "*Kaun*, come close to me. There is something important that I have to tell you."

181

These words frightened me; I was afraid of what he would say. I sat on the bed near him and he moved closer to me. I cried and then pushed him away.

"Papa, don't you go anywhere, do not say things like this to scare me."

He closed his eyes and didn't speak again until he said, "I'm… hungry for a chicken." This was not what I expected and I knew it was not what he had been planning to tell me. "I still have a pair of underwear that you can use to exchange for a chicken and coconut juice." He turned to his other side, but then turned back again, facing me. He closed his eyes and covered his face with his hand.

"I will look for it tomorrow, Papa. Be strong for me," I begged him.

"How is Papa, *Aun?*" Unexpectedly my husband appeared at the door.

I was startled but so grateful to see him, "Oh, thank God, how did you manage to get away from work?"

"I asked *Angkar's* permission to come check on you," he said, sitting down beside me.

"He is very sick; he says he is hungry for chicken and coconut juice," I told my husband. "I am so happy to see you today. I need someone to stay with me since Papa is acting so unusual."

Leang moved close to Papa, checking on him. That night, Papa did not say a word. He slept through the night. We three slept in the same mosquito net.

The next morning, I went out with Papa's underwear to find someone who would barter for a chicken. I thought this was probably a waste of time as not many old people still had chickens, only *Angkar's* leaders did. How could I approach the leader for a chicken? Asking the *Angkar* leader for coconut juice was as tough as asking for a chicken. I had heard my mother-in-law say *Pouk* Kreun, our current leader, was tougher and meaner than before. The people were scared of him. She said nobody could approach him for anything anymore. However, my opportunity presented itself. The leader was walking by our cabin, his loud voice cursing somebody who did not work hard enough to meet his expectations. Where I found the courage, I don't know to this day, but before I had time to think, I ran out to the road and called, "*Pouk, Pouk.*"

He stopped and turned to me," What do you want, *Kaun?*" He called me *Kaun* like father would call a daughter.

I was very frightened but I had to do this for my Papa. I opened my mouth and the words tumbled out, "*Pouk*, my father is very sick. He wants just a few drops of coconut juice, if you would permit me to get one fruit. Please help him."

He stared at me for what seemed like an eternity and said, in just as gruff a voice as before, "Go; get as many as you want." Then, he walked away. I was stunned. I couldn't believe my ears. I jumped. I clapped my hands. I laughed and cried at the same time.

"You are very lucky, Ra," said a man across the alley. I didn't know he had been watching my interaction with *Pouk*. He seemed happy for me too. "Let me climb the tree and pick them for you."

He went back inside the house and came out wearing his culottes and climbed the coconut tree that grew next to the bamboo patch. Somehow my mother-in-law knew about this instantly and was at my side to tell me, "Vicheara, don't forget to give one to your father-in-law."

Like I wished, the man dropped down three coconuts on the ground. My mother-in-law sent her daughter to run as quickly as possible to grab one.

"*Aur Kun*, Ra, without you I would never be able to get a coconut," the neighbor thanked me as he took a coconut and walked back to his house, where his wife was waiting with a very big smile. He then helped me to cut up my coconut.

I brought my father the coconut juice, "Papa, you will be alright. You will go home with me. Talk to me." I shook his skinny body, "Papa, I will get the chicken for you also. Talk to me."

He looked at me in a way that I knew he wanted to tell me something but he was having trouble talking. He didn't answer; maybe he didn't hear my question. I moved very close to him.

"*Kaun...*" he whispered. His eyes were closed and his breath came in short, labored gasps. He tried to get up, but he couldn't and dropped back to the bamboo bed. Perhaps, he was emotional about talking to me. Perhaps, he was exhausted from fighting with the illness.

"*Chah*" I cried again, "What is in your mind now? Tell me. If you are tired, lay down, Papa." Nah, he will soon be all right. I lied to myself. I turned to Leang, "Stay with him and watch him closely, *Baung*! I will try one last time to find a chicken for him. Maybe this time, someone will take my watch or his underwear."

Sometimes prayers are answered. I met the right person who had a chicken and agreed to trade it for my watch. She was a lady friend of Papa's who used to bring him his rations and tobacco when I was gone to the fields. Out of compassion, she agreed to cook it and bring it to me in the dark to keep both of us safe. When it was dark, the shadow of a lady appeared next to our little garden, giving me a signal. She bent down, and then walked away. I knew it must be Papa's friend; she must have put down the chicken next to the vegetable patch. I waited for a while to make sure it was safe, that that nobody was around and there were no other shadows that would indicate a spy lurked in the bamboo. Everything looked safe and quiet to me. As I got closer, my nose picked up the smell of cooked chicken, the right gift to heal Papa.

I walked back silently so none of the neighbors would be alerted. Softly, I shook Papa's shoulder, and whispered, "The chicken is here. You get to eat it to give you energy. Drink the coconut juice, it is here too." I scooped the juice with a spoon and brought in to his mouth." Papa refused both.

"He will get better tomorrow," I lied to myself.

By midnight, he was moving restlessly like a child. I woke up many times to pull him back to the middle of the bed and put his head on the cushion. I covered him with the cow blanket. His body seemed very cold and I tucked the blanket tighter around him.

Papa! Don't go without me!

In the morning, near dawn, my husband woke and washed his face to go back to the labor camp. I stayed resting near my Papa. I had almost fallen asleep again when I felt something strong pulling my blouse. It was my Papa. I felt panic surge through me, "Papa, what is wrong?"

His eyes suddenly opened wide and his eyeballs rolled upward. He looked so strange; I did not understand what was wrong with him. I called down the alley for my husband to come back. Papa was trying to grab my shirt; maybe he needed help or wanted to tell me something. I was near hysteria with fear. Then he fell back on the bed. I cried, "Papa, Papa, What is wrong? Tell me what you want me to do. How do you feel? No Papa, do not go without me." I held his frail body that was no more than bones with a thin layer of skin. "Papa, you can't go. I need you. Papa, you can't go without me. I need you here." A flood of tears burst from my soul.

My husband had come back when he heard me cry out. He just let me wail not knowing what to do to ease my pain. "Papa, come back, don't go without me," I repeated over and over. He did not hear me. Through my tears, I watched as he slipped further and further away from me. His eyes closed halfway and I knew he was gone. I don't know how long I sat with him - crying and begging him to come back. No matter how hard I begged him, he left me anyway.

"Now I understand my dream of being chased by a monster. I survived as I was saved by a monk but you....you kept running away from the monk as the monster kept chasing you. You refused to come into the temple. The monster is the illness. The temple was the pink capsule that you gave to me," I wailed, as I held his body.

"Don't cry, sweetheart!" My husband's arms enveloped me, "Papa is not suffering from starvation and disease anymore. We have more suffering to do. His suffering is over."

Was he gone for real? Papa died, *Mak* died. Why was I born unlucky? What is the purpose of them having me? To see both of them die? I rested my head on Leang's shoulder and let him comfort me. "*Anicca* (Impermanence), *Dukkha* (Suffering), *Anatta* (Not-self), his suffering is over.

"Papa, I have no monks to give you a blessing, only these three jewels, *Buddha, Dharma, Sangha*. Take these jewels with you." I prayed as my *Lok Yey* Sem had taught me.

Papa's favorite lady friend came in just then bringing a bowl of rice soup for Papa. "I am very late for his breakfast," she said.

"Papa is gone," I sobbed.

"*Buddha, Dharma, Sangha*," she prayed. "Cook more rice and then set it up next to your Papa," she said. "Invite him to have lunch. Call his name. Call your Papa many times near the bowl of rice to make him hungry and he might come back."

I did as she suggested in case it was not time for him to go yet. I checked the pulse on his neck to see if there was a chance he had come back. I checked his breathing by putting my hand next to his nostrils. There was no breath; his eyes had completely closed, without saying a last word to me. I covered his face with a white handkerchief.

"You are doing the right thing. Keep the handkerchief with you when his body is buried. This is our Khmer belief," the lady comforted me. "The handkerchief represents his spirit that will stay around to take care of you."

I did everything she said, just in case. "Papa, the rice that I got for you is still here, you did not finish it. If you had eaten it, you wouldn't have starved; you would be strong enough to stay.

"Papa come back before they come to take your body away to the jungle!" I put my hands on his cold body and rocked him gently back and forth to wake him up, "Papa, don't leave me alone! I will not be able to live with the loneliness."

The Duty of an Only Child

An hour later, my husband came back to our cabin accompanied by a young adult villager. They carried my Papa's body to the forest on a thin piece of *sangkasey* (corrugated zinc). If I could have, I would have given Papa soft bedding to make him feel comfortable. I watched them carrying my Papa farther and farther away until I could see only his silver hair, and then he disappeared forever in the jungle under the rain. It was so quick! It was so unfair! How could I bear it?

"Papa, do you know that you're going away from me? Papa! I am waiting for you to come back. Why didn't you give me a second chance to talk to you before you went away from me? Where did you go, Papa? Tell me; I will do anything to get you back. Papa, I lost *Mak* when I was eight years old; I lost you at twenty-six. I thought you would stay longer with me to teach me things about life I need to know."

"Papa, when *Mak* died, you gave her a beautiful coffin. Now, it is your turn and I have nothing to give you, nothing; only my words begging you to not leave me. I need you, I love you very much. I miss you! Come back Papa. I can't do this without you. Why have my tears dried out at this time? Why can't I cry anymore, Papa?"

"Papa! I know where we keep *Mak*'s body, but I will not know where to find yours! How can I take your bones home when we are liberated if I don't know where to find them?"

The relentless rain beat upon the roof. I was crying; the heavens were crying and the croaking of the frogs rang in my ears. "Frogs, frogs, are you enjoying the rain or are you crying with me? Maybe you are happy because of the rain. I hate you for being happy; did you lose your papa? No, I lost my loving Papa. Please frogs, beg my Papa to come back. I need more time with him."

You covered your face, laughing in your *krama* when you saw me cutting someone's hair.

You waited for me to come back from work and you smiled at me when you saw me come back home safe.

I remember how happy you were when I brought you a coconut shell full of palm sugar. You grabbed the coconut shell and hid it in your blanket.

I remember you smelled your shirt and said "disgusting" and we both laughed.

You giggled when you saw *'prahok'*. You cracked up when I said you stole *Neak*'s pepper. You gave me the strength to live with the hope that we will return home together, just you and me.

I did not know what day it was. I did remember that this month was the traditional *Phachum Ben* Festival. "Papa! Do you remember this is *Phachum Ben* festival time? It is time to go to the temple to feed the ancestors. Remember we made special food to bring to the temple where we put *Mak*'s ashes so the monks could pray for *Mak*'s spirit? We were happy because we knew *Mak* and other ancestors would be released from suffering and hunger. Now, I have no monks, no temple, no prayer, nothing. You must be very hungry and I don't have anything to feed you as there are no monks. Papa, your smell is still here. I know you are still here but I cannot see you. Papa, you taught me how to care for the bones of the parents. I want to do this for you but how will I, when you rest in the forest and I cannot find you?"

The Hundred Stones Come Back to me

I lay down on the bed, in the same place where my Papa had lain. Suddenly, I felt something hard under his cushion and brought out a little bag. It was jewelry. As I went through this bag, I found two gold chains - one simple and the other mounted with different types of stones, one diamond pendant, one diamond pin in the shape of a tulip, three emerald rings and two diamond rings and many small emeralds – 100 stones.

These stones were the ones that had been stolen by Kilen, our servant. I found them for Stepmother, only to be accused of planting them in the servant's room. Now, these stones came back to me. What good were they now? I tried the rings on my fingers, none of them fit because I was so thin. I knew this jewelry had belonged to Stepmother and my father had somehow managed to hide it all this time. I also found one of his teeth, his silk *sarong*, and his cotton *krama*. These were the mementos that were mine to keep. He could have traded this silk sarong for food for himself but he had saved it for me. What a goodhearted father he was.

I held them to my heart as though they were the richest treasure in the world. Perhaps, his last words were going to tell me about these things, especially and most importantly, the jewelry bag, but he had no strength to tell me. If I had not interrupted him, what else would he have had to tell me? Now I remembered seeing something that looked like a swelling in his pants; it was this bag of jewelry that he hid from *Angkar* after my stepmother died.

God is always Sending me a Message

After his death, the world was empty and had no meaning to me. Everything was an empty space and I was confused. I counted the minutes and the hours until night, where I could escape and dream about Papa. I knew my dreams were the only time I could be with him. Through my tears, I glared at the soy sauce containers, hanging from the bamboo roof beam. I screamed at them. "Why are you here and he is gone? Papa made you for me. You should be gone and he should be here. You hang idly and you didn't save him?" I screamed into the night. "Why couldn't I save him, Buddha? What did I do that was so wrong?" I screamed at Buddha. I screamed at the night. I was so frustrated and angry. I looked at the cushion on which he used to sleep. "You, cushion, you remain in the same place, and you didn't disappear. I hate you; you are still here - my Papa is not. Why couldn't you have disappeared instead of him?" I picked up the cushion and wanted to throw it out into the rain. Instead, I held it close to my heart and buried my face in it. "But, you keep the smell of my Papa. Thank you for that, cushion." I hugged the cushion closer and fell back on to the bed. I cried into the cushion that still smelled of Papa and fell into a dream-filled sleep.

When I woke, it was just before sunrise. The damp cushion was still in my arms. I sat up and looked around me, and loneliness filled me once again. I looked out into rainy pre-dawn darkness. I was scared of hearing the nocturnal bird one more time. I knew he was real and watching us, ready to pick up the next soul. Who is going to be next? I didn't want to believe in superstitious things, but my father was gone. Who would protect me from the bird? Who will make the fire for me when I need to cook? Who will I talk to when I am sad? Who will laugh with me when I am happy? Who will wait for me when I go to the restroom at night?

"I now understand why I couldn't leave you to go to France. You needed me and I needed you. No matter how horrible this has been, it has offered me more time to spend with you before you left this life. I can't imagine you going through this alone, but Papa, now I am alone."

After the rain, the weather turned chilly with the cold winds of October. Now I felt the emptiness of my heart because I was truly an orphan. From now on, I would have to learn to do things by myself, to be strong and brave, to live.

Leang was allowed to come back to visit me the next night. That night I could not sleep. I dreamed again there was a multicolored, bright light that came out from the Buddha's head and shone on my face. I awoke my husband to tell him about my dream. He sleepily said I dreamed too much and I shook him to get his attention. "This is not like the dream I had before we left home. I have a feeling that God is watching over me. Our hope of returning home will be blessed."

My husband mumbled something I couldn't understand and fell asleep again. I continued to listen to the cries of the foxes coming from the forest, praying that God will keep the foxes away from my Papa's body. I still had a fear that the fox had discovered his resting place. By the light of first dawn, I fell into a short and restless sleep.

That morning, Sok's wife came to me with her own sad news. She said that on the day my Papa died, Sok had asked her, "How is *Baung* (my Papa)?" She told him Papa was gone, that he had died that morning. Sok had turned his face to the wall and never moved again. They both died the same day in the rainy season of October, 1977.

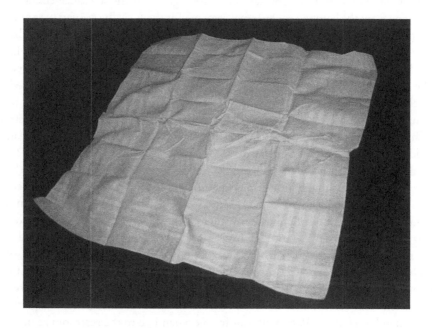

Picture of Papa's handkerchief that represents his spirit

~TWENTY ~

THE NEW LEADER

After my father's death, the KR leader in our village, *Pouk* Kreun, was replaced by a new leader who came from a different district. I knew *Pouk* Kreun very well. He was a short, friendly guy who spoke with a very strong accent of Siem Reap province. His wife was a nice lady who had compassion for people. This new leader was quiet, short and full-bodied; he had not been hungry. Unlike *Pouk* Kreun, who usually chatted with us with a friendly smile, this new leader never bothered to say a word to anyone, nor did he ever smile. I couldn't read him at all and couldn't tell if his silence and implacable face were caused by nervousness, bashfulness or frustration with his new location. Or maybe, he was just angry and mean.

Like the former leader, he wore the black long-sleeved shirt with many pockets and long, loose black pants. Unlike the other KR however, he did not wear black sandals made out of old car tires. He walked barefoot. This incomplete uniform told me that he was not used to shoes which meant he came from a very poor family background, maybe poorer even than the other peasants in the villages. Soon, one of my neighbors told me that, as I suspected, he had been a very poor man, "He was assigned to be a leader because of his ignorance and poverty."

The KR leaders had only hate and disdain for the educated; they believed us to be fatally corrupted. Hence, the advancement of a poor and ignorant man was no surprise. The KR believed an uneducated mind was just a blank of piece of paper. When someone put a stain on it, the stain was noticeable and significant; unlike the educated mind that had been stained by many others things already.

"If the KR only value work done by our two hands, as our ancestors did, without using any modern machines, why do they wear uniforms sewn on modern machines?" asked my brother-in-law, Meng, the husband of Maum.

"You are right. They are hypocrites," I responded. We were laughing at the stupid system.

"Be careful, this new leader is not like *Pouk* Kreun. His red eyes are telling us he has been eating human liver. This crow is a murderer," said Meng. "I miss *Pouk* Kreun. Under his supervision, people felt safe."

"I talked to *Pouk* Kreun's wife; she said he tried to escape on horseback from the new leader."

"I hope he will be safe. He is a good man," Meng said.

"He is," I nodded my head in agreement. "His wife was demoted and put to work like others in the village."

"Doing what?"

"Farm labor," I told him.

"I heard this new leader was sent from the big leader to come here. His mission is to clean out the lazy and mentally ill people. You," he pointed at me, "don't be sick."

This warning made me feel frozen to the bone with fear.

Wife of a New KR Leader

"Meeting! Meeting!" Praub announced at the door. Our conversation was ended.

"What's going on?" Meng asked Praub.

"Go to the leader's house, *Pouk* Kreun's old house. Everyone must go; only the dead are excused. If you don't show up, your rations will be cut off."

"Maybe we are going home," Meng said hopefully. Meetings were very unusual.

"Maybe, but I don't believe that will happen soon," I said.

Only about forty heads were at the meeting, including the sick and the children, both new and old people. Some, like my husband, were away at labor camps far from the village but the population was greatly diminished from illness and starvation.

"There used to be a lot of people, now fewer than one hundred are still alive from the entire village," I whispered to Meng. "Look at those murdering crows! Look at the leader's wife. She is the queen of evil crows. She is ready to eat us alive."

"Sh… listen to what she is going to say," Meng stopped me. The queen of crows announced the opening of the meeting.

The queen of crows announced the opening of the meeting, "*Mit Yeung, Lok Tah, Lok Yey,* and *Mehr* (Mother)! Make sure you all listen carefully to the new *Angkar's* rule. We come here to clean up mental illness and laziness. We are not interested in your excuses." She laughed. "And by the way, good news is a communal eating area will open in a few days." My hope of returning home ceased to exist. "We will all eat in the same area, eat the same amount of food." She laughed again.

Her laugh made me scared to death as I felt my life was in her hands now. I looked at Meng and he looked at me with despair and fear. We had hoped for good news but what we got was a new reign of terror. "Will I be executed by these barbarians? No, it won't happen. I still have hope. I will survive and return home, and then finish my pharmacy degree as I promised Papa," I thought to myself.

"Her smile is cruel. She is really a barbarian," Meng whispered.

The meeting lasted only five minutes, but we had sat for hours in front of the house before it started. The sick and the children were comforted as best we could as the hours dragged on. We learned from the meeting that a communal eating area was ready and we were no longer allowed to cook any food in our own houses. I tied up my *krama* around my hip and walked back home, disappointed.

"We are not going to return home," Meng despaired, coming after me, "We are not to go back home. We will live and die here."

"Maybe we will get more food. How sad that Papa left me before the KR changed the rule. He should have lived until now so he didn't have to worry about finding the wood to make a fire. He wouldn't have starved," I mused, as we walked by the communal eating area. "Why couldn't he wait long enough to walk to this area with me?"

"His suffering is over. We must worry about ourselves now. I am not sure what *Angkar* is going to feed us. I still believe they are not going to give us enough food to survive, maybe this is a new way to kill us quickly if we are not allowed to cook at home," Meng worried. He carried his little son and helped his wife along.

"Wait and see," I said. "I was surprised at how few people are left in the village; have you noticed any other changes?"

"What have you noticed?"

"Before, we heard nocturnal animals screaming every night - the owl, the fox….. I felt evil around us even when the sky was blue and sun was out. Since they have taken away so many souls, I rarely hear the owl's hooting, and the other devil animals screaming. Have you noticed it?"

"Yes, you are right. They're no more elderly and I rarely see sick people. All the weak have died."

"The elders were the first to go; they starved, got sick, and died. Now, it is our turn; we were young and healthy and were able to fight starvation and sickness for a long time but now, we are becoming exhausted." I pointed my finger downward, "Our health is going downhill now, but don't let the evil ones take our souls. We must tell ourselves we are healthy, never be sick."

"I agree," he said.

The Communal Eating Area

Since private cooking was forbidden, a few "Old People" were sent out to every single house in the village and confiscate all our cookware, leaving only plates and spoons. I hid my Le Creuset pot and they never found it.

Our daily routine never varied. At 11:00 AM sharp, mealtime was announced by beating a gong. The sound was ominous and scary - like the drum that beat the cadence during *Mak*'s funeral procession. Slowly, villagers, "New People" who worked nearby and were allowed to come home for lunch, and small children whose parents were working the fields, came out with a spoon and plate and made their way to the communal area. Even the elderly who could barely walk had to make their painful way to the center of the village. The sick who could not walk were the only ones excused. 'If you could walk, you could work' was *Angkar*'s policy, so you had to be at death's door to stay home from work or from the communal meal. If someone missed work for more than a week, the cook, usually the mother in the *Angkar*'s family had the right to torture them to force them back to work. The food was the same morning and evening - one big spoon of rice soup and one small spoon of salt. Sometimes, when the cook was in a good mood, she added fish and vegetables. However, I was rarely lucky enough to see fish or vegetables in my soup, just broth. My friend who usually sat next to me made a joke of it, "The vegetable was eaten by the fish and the fish has jumped out of the pot, that's why we never see it."

We were not allowed to cook anything at home, except to boil water for potions to treat sickness like diarrhea, and malaria; otherwise, we would be reported to the *Angkar* leader. If we violated the rules, we could be killed.

One day I saw a woman tied to a pole next to the communal kitchen. The new leader's wife got our attention and announced, "This is to demonstrate to everyone what happens to a bad person. This woman," she pointed at her, "this woman is being punished for stealing potatoes. Every hair has its own head."

"Every hair has its own head" was a common *Angkar* phrase, meaning that we were responsible for our own actions. *Angkar* had zero tolerance. No forgiving, no forgetting, no compromising.

That woman was very skinny like a skeleton and very weak. She had been beaten by *Angkar* before being tied to the pole. She was left under the hot noon sun without food or water, a common punishment. She was very dehydrated. Next to her, her small child, also very thin, was sitting on the ground innocently eating rice soup. I could imagine the spoon becoming bigger than his hand, too heavy for his little skinny hand to hold. Flies were all around, settling on his eyes and mouth. It was so painful to see this tragedy. I swore to God I would rather die from starvation than have these barbarians punish me like that. I remembered Papa advising me, "Do not forget where you come from." He meant I should live with honesty and integrity. I never found out what happened to this poor woman because we were not allowed to ask questions.

Was he the Soldier who Cut Off the Woman's Breasts?

Late one afternoon, when I got up to make a fire, I was surprised to see a soldier only ten feet from the bamboo bed watching me. I had not heard him approach and had no idea how long he had been there. He was in his twenties and looked like a Chinese Cambodian to me with light skin and small eyes. I stopped what I was doing because I did not want to get caught cooking rice, which was against the KR rules. My heart immediately leaped into my throat with fright. I did not know what he wanted or if I was to be accused of some misdeed. He did not look menacing or angry, but I could not trust him because he was a KR soldier. He might take me away from my husband tonight for any reason.

It started to get darker, but he still stayed in the same place talking to my neighbor but watching me. As it became darker, I dropped the mosquito net, pretending I was going to sleep so he would leave. Maybe a half-hour later, he came close to my mosquito net and extended his hand to show me something. I was surprised and got up immediately. In the dim light, I could see his smile; in his hand he held a small sack of rice and dried fish. It was hard to believe but I was ecstatic to see that food because I was starving to death. My hands trembled with joy and my heart was beating hard like a drum both from surprise and fear. At the same time, I was flooded with sorrow because Papa should have stayed long enough to eat this fish.

"I am the person who took all the jewelry you had hidden under your cushion."

"What did you do with all the emeralds?" I asked him gently.

"I decorated a petroleum lamp," he said with a smile.

"Why do you do that? Don't you know they are precious stones?"

He nodded his head, "I know. I know a lot about the quality of these stones. I was a teacher before Cambodia collapsed."

The word teacher reminded me of the story of Praub's brother-in-law. Could this be the soldier who killed his brother-in-law?! "A teacher! Were you …uh…" I was going to ask him about Praub's brother-in-law, but I thought better of it. "Why did you decide to get involved with the communists?"

"I did not know at that time that I had made a wrong decision…" he stopped because he heard something in the bushes behind my cabin. The expression on his face changed; he no longer looked friendly. I think he suspected that someone was spying him.

"Did you see a green pendant watch?" I did not care about the noise. He nodded. "What did you do with it?"

"I still have it."

"Can I have it back then?" I begged him with a soft voice.

"Wait….! I have to go now, but wait for me, I will come back to bring you a dessert for your *Pouk*. How is he doing?"

"He died," I said.

I was not sure he heard me because he was again staring at the bushes where he suspected a spy was hidden. Then, instead of asking me more, as I expected, he held my shoulder, then touched my chin. He looked at me with soft eyes and said, "You are young and beautiful," and then slipped into the bushes and disappeared. I was confused by the encounter and by his compliment. Although flattering, these words were meaningless. I had a good idea how I looked. I was not trying to be pretty or flirty with any of these people. I was skinny and starving to death, besides I was married. Regardless, at least I had something to eat for now. I was hungry and so was my husband.

A voice in my head told me not to trust the soldier, to not give any information or reveal my real identity to him; he probably was a spy. I might lose my life through his indirect investigation. I feared he would come back so I stayed quiet inside the mosquito net listened for his footsteps. However, he never reappeared. Then, hunger took over my fear. My hunger was telling me to wish he would be back with a big dessert, which would be lucky for me at this time.

The next day, my neighbor, the wife of the man who helped me with the coconut, came running from the fields, "Go, Ra! Run NOW!" She shouted at me. "The soldier who came to see you last night is on his way here. He met me in the rice field asking me if I knew where you were. As soon as he left me and I knew it was safe, I rushed home to catch you before you are sent to 'Thmar Puok District', the severe malaria zone and hard labor camp."

"Where is that?" I grabbed my sandals, getting ready to run.

"You will have to walk about a half day or a day to be there." Thoughts swirled in my head. Maybe God had blessed me and brought this soldier back to me, maybe with more food because he had a good heart. However, my neighbor was pushing me to run to save my life. I was confused. Is it true I have to escape from this blessing? Seeing me hesitate, the woman shouted at me and slapped me on the shoulder, "You will die if you don't escape now. You will not survive in a hard labor camp. It will be fatal for you. Run now!" She pushed me.

I ran into the forest as if wings were on my feet. When I came back to the cabin after dark, I found that all of the remaining teenagers and young adults my age had been forced to go with that soldier to the hard labor camp. Parents were happy to see their children go because they believed they would survive with better food but, in reality, it was a much more brutal and dangerous and few survived it. In my condition, I wouldn't have lasted very long. God saved my life that day! Papa was still watching over me! Thank you, God. Thank you, Papa.

If it weren't for that woman, I would have died in the hard labor zone, as most did. When I told this woman's husband to pick an extra coconut for them, she became my ally. I was very thankful karma had played yet another role in my life.

Seed of *Khlok* from Papa

My Papa had left me a few seeds of *Khlok* (squash) after his death. I did not know how long he had them but I found a small packet underneath his pillow. He should have it planted while he was alive; maybe the k*hlok* could have saved him from starving. Maybe after getting the seeds, he became too ill, and then forgot about it. I planted a tiny garden next to my cabin. The plants grew very well and gave lots of k*hlok* - enough to feed the whole village. The KR lady who did the cooking came to pick my vegetables for the soup that fed us all. Every time I went to the communal eating area, this lady acknowledged me, "This vegetable is from Ra's garden." Everyone looked at me with a smile. "Ra must have put a magic spell in it as I never ever saw any vegetable produce so much."

That should have made me happy but it scared me instead as I worried that this would bring too much attention to me and maybe the idiot KR would accuse me of some crime. The peppers I tried to grow for two years ago just happened to give me one small fruit at that time, also. Why did this damn pepper produce now and never when Papa was hungry for it?

~TWENTY ONE~

CODE OF KILLING

After Papa died, I permanently moved to live with my in-laws and considered them as my own parents. My work assignment at that time was planting sweet potatoes in the fields near the village and I came home every night. All my sisters-in-law resented me. They believed that I was protected by my mother-in-law who did not ask me to do the cooking at home, or bring water from the river. But mostly, they hated me because I ate with them, taking food from their mouths even though I always got the smallest shares. I had to learn to ignore their feelings, their dirty looks, and their hate for me.

Neak continued to secretly make soup out of the vegetables grown in her own garden to add to the food rations. Her kitchen was well hidden in the banana trees. She made the soup in the same kettle she used to boil water and always had one of the family watching for spies.

All the member of the family went to the eating area each mealtime to claim their own portion of rice soup, then came back home to eat lunch together as a family. During lunchtime, *Neak* distributed the soup portions unequally. My portion of soup was much diluted and there were only a few little pieces of vegetable, whereas their portions had fish and more vegetables.

Once a week we received tapioca for additional food from the village leader. However, *Neak* convinced us to save all of it for my father-in-law because he was the man in the family, who needed to spend more energy than the rest of us to work and protect the family. When they went fishing, they saved the good and big fish for their family, only one small fish for me if I was lucky. As time went on, I no longer joined them for meals since I did not want them to be bothered with sharing anything with me. I didn't want to hear their constant criticism either. I was hungry but I remembered who I was and maintained my dignity.

Betrayed

Every day I had to listen to *Neak's* lies. If her lips were moving, she was lying. I ignored most of what she said because they were the only family I had. I had no place else to go and my husband was gone for weeks at a time. One day when I walked into the house, *Neak* and her daughter failed to hear me and I overheard *Neak* say, "We almost lost my jewelry when that soldier came to search our house. Fortunately, I tricked him into going to Vicheara's first and it was her father's jewelry that was taken, not ours."

195

Even though my father had always suspected this was what actually happened, her words deeply injured me. Papa had been right about her. This woman was bleeding me dry. She was still "holding" my wedding jewelry for me and I wondered if it was my jewelry had she used to trade for the fish net? Was it hers or mine?

One day not long after this, I met a lady friend who lived a block away from my in-law's house. We took a bath together in the river where she showed me a diamond ring that I immediately recognized as my own. "I got it from your mother-in-law," the lady said. "She said you were very generous to give her this ring to trade for the fishing net."

These words rang in my head. My mother-in-law was tricking me, she betrayed me, and she took advantage of me. I was so stupid. I was so mad at the whole family, including my husband. I would have gladly given the jewelry to help feed myself and the family; why did she lie to me and then allow the girls to abuse me when the food they ate was bought with my jewelry?

It was fortunate that she did not know about the other bag of jewelry that Papa had saved from the KR soldier. I hid it very well by dangling it on my waist as Papa had done. Over a period of time, the jewelry bag became heavier to me as my body became skinnier. I tried to keep it in my bra but I was so thin that it was obvious and people touched it out of curiosity and asked, "What are you hiding in there?" To avoid the questions, I moved it to my pocket and attached it with safety pins.

A New Way to Please the Mother-In-Law

Neak suggested that I volunteer to work in the communal eating area helping to cook the rice soup and prepare fish and vegetables. The cook who appreciated my squash had spoken to my mother- in-law with this idea since my field work planting potatoes had ended. I was still devastated with grief and paid little attention the first time she suggested this but her persistence and sweet talk changed my resistance, "Vicheara, *Kaun*, you are lucky to be asked. You can hide fish and rice in your skirt and bring it home to feed the family. You are the one who can help us."

I smiled at her but I reminded myself that she would say anything to get her way.

"You want me to steal? What happens if I get caught? I will be the one who get eliminated or beaten," I replied.

"*Neak*, do not be greedy, *Baung* Vicheara knows what she is doing." At first I thought one of my sisters-in-law was trying to protect me, but then I heard her add, "If someone doesn't know how to survive, it is because she is stupid."

I was wrong; she was not standing up for me. Politely, I replied to both of them, "I will try my best to bring home the things you need."

That night, I was called to the eating area to prepare the fish. My mother-in-law was excited about it. She told me to hide some fish in my *sampot hol* around the waist.

Sampot hol? Hide fish around my waist? Was she crazy? I had one *sampot hol* she gave me that I had worn for two years. Usually, silk was given special care and only worn on special occasions. However, I wore it to work in the rain, the heat and the mud of the fields of the KR. Extremes of heat and humidity, rain and cold caused my silk *sampot* to wear out. Over and over, my mother-in-law repaired it for me. Over time, this *sampot hol* became mostly the fabric used for repairs, and it became very heavy when soaked with rain. I had to wash it and dry it at night and wear it again in the morning regardless of whether it got dry or not. I could not care if my *sampot* got a hole in the butt or anywhere else but if it got smelly I couldn't live with it.

"I do not want to smell fish on my body all night long," I complained.

"Do not be stupid! Can you eat the smell or the fish?" *Neak* chided me.

"Oh! God, help me. I do not know how to clean fish. They will be disappointed with my work," I was mumbling at my mother-in-law.

"Chop the head off, cut the tail and throw in your skirt. At night, nobody will notice."

I did it exactly what she told me. When finished, I held my *sampot* and walked back home in the dark. My mother-in-law was very excited to seeing me. She expected fish for a good meal for tomorrow. I dropped the fish that for which she had patiently waited.

"You got only fish heads? Why didn't you take the body?" She was mad at me.

"I couldn't. There was a lady who watched me all the time as I worked."

"So, you picked the heads because they threw them away in the garbage, right?"

"No, they save these for fermentation." I smiled at her, "We can make fish sauce at least."

"Vicheara, you are not smart." She threw the fish heads in a container filled with water. "Go take a bath and go to sleep. I will make the sauce tomorrow," she angrily told me. "Make sure you steal salt for me tomorrow for the fish sauce," she said, as she calmed down.

"Yes, I will" I replied to make her happy. This was a toughest job I ever had; stealing this, hiding that, asking for more of this of that just to please my mother-in-law. I was terrified all the time that I would be caught. This was a new life experience with my in-laws.

Whisper of my Husband

With the new leader, everything changed in the village. Rules were stricter than before. People were moved around; duties were changed as were the food rations. It was all for the worse. My husband was forced to leave us and go to work in a different area very far from home. His duty was to pull a plow as farm animals had done before. He had been gone for over two months and I never heard anything from him. I prayed he was still alive.

One evening, just before dinnertime, I was astonished to see him walk by in front of our house. He walked fast, as if he needed to go to a meeting. He didn't look to the right or left and signaled me to ignore him. In a whisper, he told me that he would be back later. His best friend followed behind him. I didn't know what to think or what to do as I watched them disappear down the dusty road. Suddenly, my sister-in-law came out of the house and asked me in a panicked voice, "Did you see *Baung* Leang?"

"Yes, I did. He signaled to me that he had to go to a meeting down there across the street."

"Are you sure that's what he meant?" She had no confidence in me.

"Just go have dinner; he will be back soon. Be sure we save some soup for him," I said.

As I waited, the sun went down and it became dark but he did not return. Where did he go? I walked out of the house toward to the place where I believed he might be. I waited for him behind a tree across the street. He never came.

The next morning, people started whispering around. I suspected they were talking about my husband's disappearance. We were all worried but I still had hope. That evening after dinnertime, I went to wait for him at the same place, at the bridge where he crossed to a small house on the next street. That little house always had the door closed; no guardian or soldier attended it. I called it a ghost house —that place where my husband disappeared. Where did he go? Who took him? A million questions ran around in my head. Maybe he was held captive inside of that damn house. I decided that if I ever saw someone outside of this ghost house, I would beg him or her to allow me in to search for my husband. I was sure he did not do anything against the revolutionary rules. He was a hard worker. He never came to visit me without the *Angkar*'s permission. He must have gone back to work another way or maybe he was sent to a different camp. Thinking this way released some of my anxiety so I could function.

I kept waiting for him every evening in the same place where he disappeared. I thought of how he looked as he strode by, pretending not to know me to keep me safe, chest bare naked and brown plaid shorts. One evening, I saw a figure in front of the ghost house. I lifted my *krama* to cover my face and walked across the bridge in defiance of the rules and went to confront that man. "*Samak Mit Baung* (Comrade Big Brother)! Did you see my husband? He came in here a few nights ago; he said he had a meeting over here," I begged, with my head lowered.

In the Siem Reap provincial accent, he coldly said, "He was sent to the city for re-education." He then walked away without another word. I crept closer to the house and called, "Leang, Leang, Leang." I stayed quiet for a few minutes to listen for a response from inside of the house. Nothing.......

I went home and told my in-laws what the soldier said and was devastated to hear Maum say, "No! It is not true. He must have been killed that night. Don't you know that "sending someone for re-education" is a code for killing?" My sister-in-law started to cry. "Do not go there and wait for him again, and never talk to anyone about his disappearance if you want to save your life."

I felt his fear and pain running through my veins up to my head. I almost passed out when I heard her words. Leang was gone. He never came back.

My Soul, My Spirit, My World

It was unbelievable to hear I lost him. It was too much to think about it. Was it true I lost the second important person in my life? I remembered the dream of losing all my teeth and that such a dream meant that I was to lose all my family members, including my husband. I was torn between believing this superstition and my rational mind that told me there was still hope that he would be back home someday.

No matter what I believed I was now truly alone. My world was upside down; the people around me were inconsiderate and thoughtless. My spirit, my soul had vanished. I was nowhere in the world. I missed the modest time we had spent together on the bamboo bed when he came home to visit me. He always whispered, "*Aun*, work hard to keep yourself safe." He was a hard worker and I was the opposite. I was the one who should have been killed.

The thrilling romance of our young married life on a soft and warm mattress in a comfortable bed three years ago had been replaced with fear, hunger, misery and despair. I remember looking at his hands and his feet when he was lying down on the hard bamboo bed. I held his hand and brought it close to my cheek. He had looked at me with his eyes half closed and smiled. His words to me were, "My hand is rough now. Do you still love me?"

I kissed his hand and teased him, "Oh, I love a rough hand because it is a manly hand from hard work." I then touched his feet and tried to peel his cracked heel. He pulled it away from me. I was shocked at the condition of his feet and tears sprang from my eyes.

He said, "Let it be. It is better that I look like a peasant; it will save my life so I can come home to see you." I wiped my tears with my *krama*, imagining it was a clean and perfumed handkerchief. My handsome husband, always so clean and well groomed, was two years without soap, or shampoo, or deodorant. His lips that had been so soft had turned dry and cracked from smoking and his harsh life. His clean white teeth were yellow and covered with plaque.

I teased him, "If you don't allow me to clean your teeth, I won't allow you to kiss me."

I pulled out my *krama* to wipe his teeth, but he pushed me away and teased, "OK, then, I will only kiss your hand." I pulled my hand away and we laughed. Now I would give anything to have him kiss my hand again. I was sitting outside in the moonlight talking to myself .....what has this world been teaching me? What is the meaning of my life? I have lost everybody in my family. Why has this happened to me? Why don't the people I love stay with me longer? Why do I have to suffer?

After his disappearance, friends in the village warned me to work harder to make sure the leader kept his eyes away from me, because Leang's wife and family would all be targets if he had somehow offended *Angkar*. Could I believe them? Deep in my heart, I refused to believe Leang was gone from this earth. My mother-in-law believed he was. She prayed for my husband and cried every night. I could feel how sad she was, so was I. All she could say to me was "Work hard and keep your mouth shut; do not talk about your husband's disappearance to anyone." She also warned me that *Angkar* would take the wife next after the husband, but I still believed that God and Papa would always protect me and that gave me hope to survive another day.

Do you Know What an Appendix is?

Early one morning, the barbarian wife of the leader and some of the old people walked around the village waking everyone to water the vegetables.
"*Angkar* needs you."
Neak insisted that I do it. Since we felt that the disappearance of my husband made us all targets, I knew *Neak* was trying to keep her own children from being noticed; so, naturally I was the person the family would sacrifice. I walked toward the river to give the appearance that I was willing, but I was really thinking about how to get out of this very hard work.

My mother-in-law ran after me with two big buckets and a long bamboo pole. She put the big bamboo stick over my shoulders and attached the buckets. "Damn," I said to myself, "it is already heavy already with just the empty buckets." While *Neak* helped fill the buckets, I was asking myself, "Be a hard worker, or be a smart person?" I understood very well there was no way I could possibly carry these heavy buckets back and forth for hours, as the village women did. I simply did not have the strength. If I 'work hard' I would collapse or get severely injured. If I 'work smart', I might get out of this intact.

Angkar's barbarian wife threatened us to hurry, "Work harder and quicker to respect *Angkar*'s rules. Go! Go!"

Neak urged, "Go, work like them, run like them." I tried to do as she said, but the water in the buckets spilled as I hurried along the uneven ground. By the time I arrived at the vegetable garden, the buckets were almost empty and my legs and shoulders were killing me. I had no energy to do one more trip. I knew if I kept running back and forth with the buckets, I would collapse. I remembered my father saying to me as a small girl that I was smart and courageous. I could either be worked to death like a farm animal or I could be smart and trick *Angkar* to save my life. I knew they were all uneducated and ignorant and they might believe me if I could convince them I was injured in some way they would not understand. I sat down in the middle of the road with my hands holding the right side of my tummy. I started to cry with pain.

"What is wrong?" the barbarian lady asked me from a distance. I did not answer, pretending that the pain bothered me too much to talk. As she came closer to me, I groaned, "Oh! My tummy....my tummyyyy! I had appendix surgery a few years ago and I had a terrible infection and it never healed right. Now it is hurting me so badly. I am afraid my incision got torn out from carrying the heavy buckets." Then I pretended I could not walk nor get up.

"What is wrong?" *Neak* asked me, in panic. I did not answer; instead I pointed at my tummy and cried.

"Go home and rest. Do not do any more watering. I do not want to see all your guts come out of your stomach," the leader's wife shouted. A couple of people helped me to go home.

God bless me! I rescued myself. Hell! The buckets are so heavy, I cannot do this or my back will be broken, as I thought to myself.

"I know you faked it, Vicheara," *Neak* said.

"The surgery did bother me a little bit," I said.

This trick saved my life and I was allowed to stay home for a while to take care of myself. I remembered the trick I used when I was a child to save myself from a beating over the multiplication tables. It worked that time with a fake tummy ache and worked this time with the appendix surgery. I was so happy to stay home pretending I was recovering from surgery complications. I stayed home for two months until they threatened to cut off my food rations if I did not go to work. Thus, I went back to the fields.

New Idea of Getting Away from the In-Laws

Neak shaved her head and took out her false teeth to make herself look older and disabled. My father-in-law still worked hard in the forest cutting bamboo to make wicker baskets to catch fish. All the family's children were forced to go to the fields; the youngest children cut baby bamboo under the supervision of the old people. Maum had remained in the village while her child was breastfeeding, doing a light sewing job. Now if she wanted to live, she had to go to work in the fields; the baby had to come second. Her husband was sent away to do extremely hard manual labor breaking rock on the mountain. Since her son was now three years old, *Angkar* said he could stay home by himself. Maum came back at lunchtime to bring food for him then went back to work again. Later, he became very sick with diarrhea. I felt pity for him, but there was nothing anyone could do. Everyone had to go through the same suffering. I was glad that I did not have kids with my husband; it was so hard to watch the children suffering.

I was lonely and miserable. I no longer wanted to live with my in-laws since my life was worth nothing to them; whether I lived or died did not matter. I wanted to go live with my Papa. I decided to look for a place to die, far away from my in-laws. The best way I could think of to die was to go to work in a more distant forced labor camp. I soon got my wish as I was ordered to go to work to build a dam. "A dam? Where would there be a dam? Probably the same place as the stupid canal."

I was not the only person who was curious. I heard the same questions as I followed a group of men and women of my age and older. Lots of people, both old and new from different villages, walked in the same direction. They hoped they would be better fed; they didn't give a damn about the dam.

~TWENTY TWO~

BUILD A DAMN DAM

Arriving at the labor camp, I was surprised with the big bamboo structures, which were completely different from the ones at the canal near my village which had no walls. These were very large and had three walls, leaving the front open. These were divided into compartments with each compartment big enough to accommodate ten people. The roof and walls were covered with palm leaves. Of course, as at the canal, there was no provision made for sanitary toilets anywhere. The kitchen was the same bamboo poles and walls of palm leaves. About twenty long tables and benches were lined up in rows, each seating about thirty people. The distance from the resting place to the kitchen was about a hundred feet. There was no doubt of what the floor would be made. It was always the ground.

Where was the dam, I wondered as I looked around. What does it look like? I saw nothing different, only a large open area with no trees, no grass - only *pakees*, bamboo sticks, shovels, and the damn black crows in their black outfits, swarming about like black ants on sugar palm. They had colorful cotton *kramas* wrapped around their heads or necks. They were throwing *pakees* to the new group of slave laborers who were just skinny shadows as they slowly carried the *pakees* and passed them from one person to the next, and then to the next.

"Where do they dump the *pakees*? Where is the water? How can they build a dam this way?" I was flabbergasted.

"Ha, Ha, Ha, Our *Angkar* fights for this victory...La..La..La..." The KR soldiers laughed and sang revolutionary songs that sounded like gunfire to me. Why are they so happy? Were they insane?

"This is a big dam," a female leader announced. What "big" meant to her, I had no idea. I thought to myself, "The place is big, but I don't see a dam, big or little." I reasoned it hadn't been built yet and it was going to be big because about a thousand people came from different surrounding villages, as well as from Battambang province, to build it.

"Go find your place first and then get out on the field right away, *Mit Yeung*," the same female leader shouted.

I chose the first compartment, which was closest to the camp and the kitchen. My small bag was thrown on the ground against the walls. I sat down next to it to rest my feet from the long walk before I went out to the field. After I took the cow blanket from my bag and laid it on the ground, I gathered all my strength and walked toward the fields. Looking up at the sky and feeling the cool air on my face, I knew we were in for a thunderstorm. I could smell it. Cool air usually warned of an impending downpour. The loud songs of the black crows became more aggressive as they competed with the lightning and thunder. They laughed and yelled at the sky to encourage the rain to come harder and faster.

"God sends us rain to cool down the heat. We need rain." The sound of thunder responded to their demands.

"Shit, you eliminated religion, what God are you asking for rain? What God will do anything for you? You have a lot of nerve praying to a God you don't believe in," I muttered to myself, as I walked slowly to pick up the *pakee* from the ground.

Someone walking next to me heard what I had said and added, "Those who destroyed religion, the temples, and the statues of Buddha will pay the price. Bad karma!" I turned and smiled at a woman in agreement.

"Where are the *pakees*?" she asked me.

"Take your time. It is going to rain soon," I pretended to walk around looking for something.

The crows' wish was granted. They wished for rain so it would cool down the heat. My wish for rain was to make me get sick so I could rest in the cabin without working hard. Rain began to fall in heavy, drenching drops. In minutes, the dry packed earth was turned to a sea of mud. My new friend and I stood still, taking as much time as we could to begin. She found the *pakee*, and put it on her shoulders, and said, "I am not afraid of the rain."

I held the *pakee* up in both hands, "And I am not afraid of the mud."

"What are you waiting for? Get to work." A man's harsh voice from behind scared both of us. "Here is the shovel," he threw it in front of me. "You will dig the ground and fill **the** *pakee*s." He turned to face my new friend, who was even skinnier than I was. "You," he said, "will carry the *pakee*s to that soldier." He pointed at a soldier about twenty yards away, standing in the rain, both hands directing the slaves where to dump the mud.

"It's muddy. We can't walk in the mud carrying these heavy *pakee*s," my new friend spoke up.

"The rain won't melt you and you will figure out how to walk in the mud. If you can't figure it out, your rations will be cut off." He grabbed the shovel from my hand and started to dig the muddy ground. "Go grab the other two *pakee*s. What are you waiting for? I will fill up the *pakee*s and you do the same thing I just told that woman to do. Run... work harder under the *Angkar*'s rule," he was screaming at me.

The *pakee*s were heavy to begin with and became heavier and heavier with the mud and the soaking rain. We were not about to get any sympathy from these screaming crows. For more than two years, I had adapted to the peasants' life and was familiar with the hard work of the labor camps. Carrying these *pakee*s, I now worried about how long I could keep doing this. Would I die here in this muddy field senselessly carrying mud from one place to another to please these stupid crows? I was no longer so sure I wanted to die. My rain-soaked clothes added more weight to my tiny undernourished body; when they became very heavy with mud, I repeatedly fell down. I had no strength to get up; my body shook from the cold and the weight on my shoulders. My hands and feet were cold and numb. The soldier who patrolled us kept pushing me to work harder by threatening me with a stick. Without empathy or compassion, he put more and more mud in the *pakees*. He said, "Your shoulders are large enough to handle more weight." As he said this, he stepped on the contents of the *pakee* packing it down so he could put in more mud.

"Go ahead; fill it up as much as you want, but I am not going to take it. I will find a way to save myself again," I said to myself. I knew if I kept this up I was going to die or injure myself and wind up a cripple for life. I needed to save myself; all thoughts of dying vanished as my survival instincts kicked in. For some reason, the soldier walked away after he finished filling my basket. When he was far enough away, I asked a different soldier for permission to go to the bush to empty my bladder. When I came back, I pretended to be lost. Someone told me to stay with a different group of workers. I thought I was lucky to be digging instead of carrying. I soon found out that digging was not easy either. My shoulders and fingers began to hurt.

I Got What I Wished For

"Work faster and put more dirt in the *pakees!* Why do you work like a child? Your food ration will be cut off." I knew this voice; it was the female leader. If I looked directly at her, she would consider me insolent. Of course, I wanted to smash her in the mouth, knock her face first into the dirt and let her eat the mud she insisted I carry, but I held my tongue and reluctantly swallowed my anger. I did not want my rations cut off. I needed more food, and less work, not the other way around.

As I tried hard to dig the ground, I worked slower and slower. I was exhausted. Hopeless thoughts about how desolate our lives had become occupied my mind. I was out of ideas of how to make this work easier on myself. I started to silently cry. I don't know if it was the rain or my tears that blurred my vision. I mindlessly pushed the shovel into the now soft ground not paying attention or even caring where the shovel landed. My strength was gone. My hope was gone. Then I became angry; angry at Papa and my husband for leaving me; angry at God for letting this happen to me; angry at the KR for taking everyone I loved away from me. Angry at that stupid woman leader who insisted I work like a mule to make a damned dam, for what? For what, God? Why are you putting me through this Hell? None of this makes any sense. With this burst of anger, I slammed the shovel angrily into the mud and felt excruciating pain in my left foot. I screamed and dropped the shovel immediately. The pain was sharp and blood filled the muddy area around my foot. I had chopped my toe instead of the ground. It was bleeding very badly; my toenail almost cut in half.

"My toe! My toe! "I was crying. I didn't look at it.

"Get tobacco to stop the bleeding!!" one of the ladies next to me shouted, "Who has tobacco?"

"I have some, you are lucky!" One of the villagers responded.

"Can you walk back to the cabin?" She asked me, wiping the rain from her face.

"I think so, I will try. Can you look at my toe for me? Is my toe gone?"

"No, it is still here, but the top third of your toe has been badly cut."

"Yah, yah, yah. I lost my toe," I was crying harder.

"Go to your resting place now," ordered the woman leader. I pretended I did not want to leave the working area and dragged myself away. That night the pain was unbearable. I had to wake up in the middle of the night to boil water to wash off the bacteria and cover the injury with tobacco. I had nothing else with which to treat the injury and it soon became badly infected. For that reason, I stayed in the sleeping place for weeks, then a month. I had not meant to injure myself but I had saved myself again.

In my weakened condition, it took a long time for my body to fight off the infection, but gradually I recovered as I did not have to expend any precious energy working. I never let anyone know that I was feeling better so I would continue to have an excuse not to return to the backbreaking labor. I kept the old fabric covering my toe to hide my secret. I walked slowly in front of people and exaggerated my condition. I must have been a good actress because I continued to get away with it. Of course, the labor camp was very large, noisy and confused so maybe I got overlooked.

"KR Gained their Victory with the Aid of China"

One evening a meeting of all the workers was announced over the loudspeakers and communist songs were played to glorify the revolution. I did not attend this meeting because I was still playing the part of an injured person. A lady who shared my living space did not attend either; I didn't know why.

After the meeting, I listened to her son as he reported to his mother, "The KR gained their victory with the aid of China." His mother said nothing as her son continued to parrot the announcements from the meeting: "Our Revolutionary people are independent and self-sufficient. They believe in agricultural production to build our country. They believe in manual labor and hard work under their own sweat and blood to push the wheel of our new revolution without any help from foreigners. The KR fighters are heroes and will be good role models for everyone in the world by going back to the primitive ways, or the year Zero. Many KR were martyrs and all *Pracheachun daup pram pil maesa* – the people of April 17 or the "New People" who did not join their wheel of revolution or were against it - were removed (*vay chol*)."

He went on, "China has been helping the KR fighters to reach their victory; now, we must repay them. Since our land is so rich in rice production and all the

Pracheachun daup pram pil maesa are working together harder and harder with all the revolutionary KR people, we will produce tons and tons of rice to repay China. This is that where all the rice is going."

It was as Papa and Sok had suspected months ago – the KR was sending our rice to China. I listened to him without missing a word, maybe I even forgot to breathe. Then, with a little smile in the corners of his mouth, he said, "After the meeting, all the workers were rewarded with a delicious food ration - green noodle soup made with fermented fish and lemongrass."

His mother still didn't get excited; she didn't react to any of the information. She just said, "*Kaun*, will you bring the soup to me then?"

"*Bat! Neak Maday* (my respected mother)," he got up and left her. This young man was very respectful to his mother – something that had become unusual under KR rule. For a moment, I wondered what their story was but my mind quickly went to the noodle soup and how I would get some. If I show my face at the communal eating area, I will be noticed by the leader and put back to work. To avoid this trouble, I will have to wait until all the soldiers have left but, by then, the soup may be gone.

I asked another neighbor to go get it for me as she often did, but she came back empty-handed. "You have to go get it by yourself to avoid anyone cheating," she said as she checked on my injury. "Can you walk?"

"I will try because I haven't had food like this for years." I waited until it became dark before I limped to the eating area to ask for my food.

"Where have you been?" the cook asked me.

"I am late to join the other workers because my tummy is hurting me."

"Ah, you are sick. *Samlar Nom Banch Chok* – Noodle soup is set up to reward the hard workers, not the sick people, but I will give it to you anyway. Eat fast before the leader sees you."

"I will eat a small amount only!"

Then the cook gave me a bowl of the delicious smelling soup. I would take anything at this time. After I finished one bowl, I asked her if I could have another one. This time, she gave me more noodles and soup than before. I ate every noodle and drank every drop of the broth. When I tried to leave, I could not get up because I overate.

"It is unbelievable to see you eat so much," the cook said. "Usually a sick person can't eat much, but you can."

"I forced myself to eat it because I don't know when I will have such delicious soup again."

She just smiled and turned away like I hadn't said anything at all. I walked back to the cabin as fast as I could, with my hands holding my tummy from overeating. I lay down, pretending I was falling asleep. But in my heart I was so happy for the good food today. Thanks, God! Thanks, Papa, for helping me.

My good luck ran out right the day after that.

"You are to go back to work when your injury gets better. If you can walk, you can work. We never give food to lazy people." This was the message from the group leader who stopped by my cabin to check on me.

"Oh! My God! I hate this work! I hate these people!" As I turned around mumbling, I saw a man in his late thirties who smiled at me and said, "Ra! Come on; work faster to impress our revolution!"

"How do you know my name?" I asked him, as I checked my toenails.

"I heard somebody call your name before you got the toenail injury!" He kept walking toward me and pushed me to walk ahead of him toward the fields.

"Ouch! Do not push me so hard, I cannot walk as fast as I did before my injury!" I gave him a bad look.

"Then I won't put too much dirt in the basket," he smiled. Was he flirting with me?

"It is stupid to make me work injured," I complained. "It is too heavy! I cannot carry all this dirt! The mud is in my wound again!"

"Show me."

"Look, see, it is going to be infected again."

"This small injury isn't going to kill you; keep working or you won't get your food ration today."

"Aren't you even going to look to see if I am telling the truth?" He did not listen. Instead of coming to see my toenails, he walked away from me and shouted at a different group to work harder to get the job done on schedule. Soon, I fell down exhausted from trying to pull my feet through the mud.

"Ouch! Ya! Ya!" I cried loudly with a hand on my tummy.

"What is it, Comrade Vicheara?" asked a woman leader.

"My tummy hurts again from the surgery!" I lifted up my blouse and showed them my old appendix scar.

"Why do you have a scar?"

"I had appendix surgery just a couple years ago; now it hurts me when I carry something heavy!"

"What is appendix?" she asked, poking me with a bamboo stick. I had to lie even though I knew it was wrong, but if being a liar would save my life then I would be a liar.

"In-tes-tine," I said loudly and slowly. "Do you want to see my in-tes-tines come pouring out on the ground?"

"Oh! No! Go back to the cabin and rest. I do not want to see you die in the fields"

"Ha! Ha! This is my magic trick and so far it has worked perfectly for me," I chuckled to myself. If I don't save my life, who will? I walked slowly, hunched over, with my hands holding my stomach.

Bad News and Good News

Next morning, they announced we were returning home. There was no explanation. There was certainly no dam built. It was just over and we were leaving. The idea of going "home" had no meaning to me. Who was at home waiting for me? Were my sisters-in-law dying to see me back? Desolate and lonely, I was still happy to leave the miserable work field.

I walked slowly, following the group of people who were rushing home to see their families in the villages. I did not rush. I walked slower and slower until I was alone on the empty quiet road. As I walked, I watched for any little fish or crabs to appear in the rice paddy along the roadside. Once in a while, I stopped and squatted near the water to look more closely, but there was nothing for me except grasshoppers and tiny frogs hopping freely from one place to another.

Should I eat frogs and grasshoppers? I stopped and looked at them. No, I cannot kill them. I will throw up if I eat them. They want to live like me too. If I eat frogs today, I will still starve again tomorrow. Maybe they are carrying disease and will make me sick. In case I survive, I want to be healthy. It was almost dark when I arrived at my in-laws' house. Strange! It was quiet! Where all the people? Then Meng came out to greet me.

"You are back?" was all he said. This was about the reception I had expected.

My sister-in-law was hugging her son against her chest, "All the rest of family was relocated to Phnum Srok, a different village about two kilometers away from Preah Netr Preah."

This was exciting news to me as I had prayed I did not have to see them again.

"You didn't follow them?" I took off my palm leaf hat and put it on the bamboo bed. Then, I walked to the back door to wash my feet.

"No, *Neak* wanted us to stay and take care of the vegetable patch in the back yard," she grabbed an old cloth to fan herself in the intense heat.

"I was only gone a couple of months and I see a lot of things have changed." I walked back inside and dried my feet with my *krama*.

"Yes, it is quiet now. They sent out more people to work in the camps, only the people with small children, like me, can stay."

I walked outside of the house and sat on the bench near the front door. I looked at the spot where Papa had lived. The cabin had been demolished. Only the squash garden I planted before I left the village remained. There was no indication Papa had ever been there, or anyone else for that matter. All sign of him was gone. It was as if he had never existed. Maum came to sit by me and said, "Most of the other people who lived in the cabin have died, only few stay alive. They have been relocated. Sok's wife died."

"She did?" I was shocked.

She nodded and continued, "The Vietnamese-Cambodian lady and her young daughters died."

"All of them? My Lord!" I was dazed to hear that all the people I had known were gone in the few months I was out in the labor camp.

"The entire village is filled with fear and worry. The old people are humble now as it is clear that this is no communist paradise and those things are going from bad to worse. They appear worried and frustrated. I think they know that we were all in the same boat, live in misery now and die soon."

I took a deep breath, "We all worry and wonder when it will be our turn to die."

She got up and walked inside as her son was crying. They slept inside the house; I lay on the bench outside because I wanted to feel the fresh air after a rain, see the starlight and feed my blood to the mosquitoes as they wanted.

Bamboo Patch! Enough for you

The nocturnal animals came near the lake, screaming with frightening voices just like they did before Papa died. I hadn't heard these screams for a while, as I believed all the souls had been taken. Now that I had come back, their screams returned to try to terrify me in the middle of the night. Only now I was no longer afraid. Whose soul are you going to take next? Haven't you taken them all? You are greedy for souls. Maybe you just want to rub it in that you have all the souls of my family. Go away! There are no more souls for you. You are not getting mine. Go away!

I was not scared of dying if my time was to come tonight or even tomorrow, but those screaming night creatures were not taking my soul. I focused instead on the frogs singing in the bushes, happy with the rain that made a big swimming pool for them. I could hear them sing to each other sending messages of happiness, flirting with each other before making love, whereas I was so lonely. I had no warmth, caring, comfort or love. My husband was not here anymore to hold me close and tell me he loved me. Suddenly, the warm breeze brought a familiar smell to my nostrils. I stood up and looked around me. I recognized this smell. It was my husband's smell. It was not the musky cologne I inhaled on my wedding night but his smell when he lay next to me exhausted and abused from his days at hard labor. It was the smell of sweat and dust. Is he really dead? Is he around me now?

I looked up and took a deep breath. I could hear and feel a breeze blowing from the direction of the place where all of us, Papa, me and my husband, slept together in the lean-to beside the bamboo patch. The bamboo leaves started to move like someone beckoning to me. I stared at the place, where Papa used to sit on the bamboo bed, face down and scratch his toes. I begged Papa to appear now and listen to me. I had so much to tell him. I had so much to tell my husband. I wanted both of them here, next to me. I began pouring out everything I was feeling.

In a whisper I begged Papa, "Please Papa, come visit me, even as a ghost, and bring *Baung*. Come now. I want to tell you how much I miss you. The world is empty, I am alone, and there is nothing left for me. Papa! I force myself to live because I want to honor your request that I finish my pharmacy degree when we are liberated, but it is so lonely, I have no one. The night frightens me. Everything frightens me. Please come back to me."

My tears had been dry since the day Papa passed away; now, they flowed like a fountain. Did you see me cry, *Baung*? My dear husband, you should have stayed with me after Papa died! Why did you have to leave me too? What will happen tomorrow? Will I live or die? If I live, the only sure thing is that I will be hungry again. My life is worth only one spoon of salt and one scoop of rice soup even though I work like a farm animal. Who is calling me? It is neither *Baung*, nor Papa? Is it the bamboo patch? Bamboo patch, don't call me! I knew when I first saw you that this was a place of death. You took away the souls of all people who have lived here. Don't call me; I won't give up my life for you. I will fight to survive and accomplish my promise for my Papa. I will live for all the innocents who died so unjustly.

Now who was calling me? A man's voice was threatening, "If you don't go, you will get no rations because you are fully healthy and capable of working."

I didn't know when I fell asleep, all I knew was I was awakened by Praub, who walked from house to house, ordering the workers from their beds. I had just come back from the labor camp, now I had to go again to the fields for the rice planting.

I did not even wash my face; I just put my Papa's *krama* on my head and followed a group of people. I wondered if there were any leeches in the water.

~TWENTY THREE~

OUR SCHOOL IS PROPAGANDA

What month is the rice planting season? I really don't know....Where is the rice paddy? I really don't know... I just follow the group and do as I am told.

Baby rice plants look like grass; if I did not pay close attention, I might pick grass instead. We not only had to do this back-breaking slave labor but we also had to listen to the group leader ramble on and on about the stupid ideas of the KR revolution: "Technology went too fast and made people lazy. Capitalism taught us to be materialistic like bourgeoisies so they could make money from all of us. As a result, society became corrupt and people took advantage of each other. The smartest became wealthy and continued to mistreat the poor people from generation to generation. We have now opened our eyes and we support our peoples' revolution. We must learn to appreciate all the material and culture that we inherited from our ancestors. In their time, our ancestors used the farming fields as paper and both hands as pens. Our revolution will succeed by the labor of our hands not from desks, comfortable chairs, pens and papers. Our school is the farm, the canal, the forest - doing the same work our ancestors did."

"*Ah Thmil Aut Sasna!*" Angrily, one of my neighbors muttered.

As I heard this propaganda, I became angry that I had to waste my life trapped by such a backward and ridiculous philosophy. I was mumbling to myself, "How stupid and ignorant you are. Life is about moving forward not backward like your evil and idiotic revolution. I will wait and see; soon you will stop talking like this, Parrot!!" I was angry at the situation but not really at the speaker because I knew that if they did not repeat this propaganda, they would be eliminated just as we would be. Maybe they didn't know they had been lied to from the top to the bottom; the rice crop was to pay back China. Or maybe they were too uneducated or just too dumb to figure it out.

I am Comfortable With your School Now

I had rolled my pants up to the knees to avoid being soaked but soon sat down to pull the young baby rice plants.

"Ra! Work faster!" one of the revolutionary girls shouted at me. "Ra! If you are lazy you will have no food!" I looked up and found her staring at me. Whenever I looked up, she was still there staring.

I thought to myself, "I am never lucky enough to be left alone. Everywhere I go, I always get in trouble! If I cover my face with my *krama*; I get in trouble! If I talk, I get trouble; if I do not talk; I get trouble! My name never gets called for a good reason."

When I filled the *pakee* with the small rice seedlings, I carried it to a flooded paddy for transplanting. I did this over and over until my legs became tired and I slowed down. The leader kept adding more space for me to finish planting before lunch. I fell further and further behind as I grew more exhausted. Finally, I was told to stay there working alone while everybody else went to get their mid-day soup.

"Ra! You cannot go for lunch until you have finished!" my nemesis said and left for her own lunch.

How could I change my name? Ra! Ra! This name was not lucky, maybe that was my problem, I wondered as I waded in the foot-deep paddy to plant the rice. As I worked alone through the lunch hour, one of the soldiers passing by asked, "Why didn't you go for lunch?"

Should I ask him for pity? No, it will give me more trouble. I just said, "I will eat later." I decided to keep my dignity and strengthened myself not to give in to the hunger. As I worked, I had another thought – why was I being so careful of each young rice plant? No one was watching me. If I care too much for each rice plant, I won't get lunch. So, I started to plant very quickly even if the plant did not stand up straight or went too deep into the ground. I didn't fix it. I just kept going until I filled up the land.

"Poor rice, I do not mean to kill you but I have to think of my tummy first!"

I got up and put both hands on my hips, angrily looking at the sky. I finished my work at the same time the others came back to the field. I went straight to the eating area and asked for my food ration.

"Ra! Shame on you! You do not know how to plant the rice!" the cook laughed at me.

"I am much better at it now, it won't take me long from now on," I said and smiled at her. When I finished eating, I looked around me and noticed that a couple of people were sick with pink eye. I wished I could be sick with pink eye so I could stay home, but I felt healthy. I walked back to the field and did the same work as in the morning, but this time I became more comfortable with the planting, "Who cares?"

Pink Eyes

Next morning I woke up feeling like someone had punched me in my eye. "Do not look in the mirror!" my neighbor said.

"Too late! I want to see if I got pink eye from you!" I said.

"If you look in the mirror, both eyes will be infected."

"Really!" I went to see the lady leader about my eyes hurting. She looked at my eyes and screamed with panic, "Ra! Go home; I do not want you to give pink eye to me!"

"Give me my rations and then I will go home as quickly as I can, just as you say!" I acted miserable in front of her to make sure she wouldn't change her mind.

"Good! Go home!!"

On the way home, I took turns closing one eye, then the other, to avoid the sunlight. Frequently, I wiped off my eyes with Papa's *krama* to clear my vision. Arriving home, my sister–in–law said that next I would probably give pink eye to her and her family. That night, the pain in both eyes increased until I screamed in agony. I asked my sister-in-law if she could give me the milk from her breast to calm down the pain. This is an old Cambodian remedy. Unfortunately, it did not help. Finally, I decided to walk in the middle of the night to the house of the shaman (traditional healer) of the village. People called him Mr. Herbalist because he knew how to use herbs to treat minor illnesses like diarrhea, malaria, high fever, and cough. He also knew how to put spells on people. I used to say, "Why doesn't he put a spell on the communist troops?"

"Wake up, *Pouk*! I need medicine for my pink eye!" I called to him three times.

"Who is this in the middle of night? Why don't you wait until the morning?" his voice said from inside the house.

"*Pouk!* My eyes are miserably hurting me!" I got on the stairs of his house and called him again. This time, he did not refuse to get up and the moonlight showed me his skinny, bent form in his doorway.

"Oh! Is it you, *Kaun* Ra!" Everybody in the village called me Ra rather than Vicheara.

"*Pouk,* why is the pain miserable at night and okay in the morning?

"It is pink eye!"

"I know."

"You have to get milk from a breast-feeding mother!"

"I did that already."

"I do not know how to treat it," he said and started to walk away.

"Do you have sugar palm? I am hungry; maybe I will feel better after I have sugar palm." I knew he had the sugar as it was an ingredient in many traditional medicines, especially the Rabbit Shit pills.

"*Kaun*! Unfortunately I do not have it now," he replied, coughing.

"I also knew your answer, you are selfish, *Pouk*!"

I went back home with nothing. If I had brought gold to him that night, his answer would have been different.

The Same Person did a Good Thing for me

The next day I was desperate. I had to do something. My eyes felt like someone was stabbing needles into them. At noon, I decided to sneak across the street without a permission slip and walk to the house of the former leader, *Pouk* Kreun, hoping that his wife would have something to treat my eyes. I was fortunate to find her home at naptime. She asked me to come into her house and showed me some medicines. I feigned ignorance and asked her to choose. She was always nice and caring to everyone, even after the disappearance of her husband. She couldn't give me any more palm sugar, but she said she had something better. She put some liquid in my eyes, "Let's try this!" she said.

"I can barely see, *Mehr!*" I did not care what kind of eye drops she used on me; I just wanted to feel better so I could fall asleep.

"Come back again if it works and you feel better tonight."

"*Aur koun, Mehr!*" She then encouraged me to keep working hard as the new leader was stricter than *Pouk* Kreun. She warned me that the new leader was determined to "clean up" the lazy and mentally ill people.

"What is his name? He had just come before I was sent away."

"His name is Kim. He is from the province of Kampot. He was ordered by the *Angkar Leu* (Superior *Angkar*) to replace *Pouk* Kreun and reorganize our village. He is very strict, with a cold heart. You better go back home now before you are noticed."

I said goodbye to her and hurried back home before the new leader saw me. That night my pain gradually diminished like she had put a magic spell on me. I went back to her house again the next day for the second drop, but she was not home. I went back again a third time, she was still not there. Someone next door told me she had been sent to the fields. However, whatever she put in my eyes seemed to do the trick. My eyes rapidly healed. I was very fortunate to find her before she disappeared forever. I believe that she knew the new leader had killed her husband and that she was next.

My *Pou* Va

I had stayed home to recover from pink eye for weeks, hiding in the house, pretending I was deathly ill. I slept under the cow blanket and dreamed about all the good food I craved. Now I was hungry for something for real. I was thinking about sneaking out during the siesta to look for someone who would trade food for my diamond pin or maybe, if I was lucky, I could get something good for free. Why not? If I stayed in bed, food wouldn't hop into my mouth. I got off the bamboo bed, covered up my face with Papa's *krama* and walked quietly out of the house, just following my instinct, to the alley leading in the opposite direction of the main road. On both sides of the alley, every single house was empty; I kept walking along the alley, hoping to see someone, until it ended at the forest. At the very end was a small cabin built away from the others. Seen from a distance, it looked scary and I was about to turn away when I heard my name called. My wish to find someone to give me food had guided me to find my *Pou* Va's wife. She looked older and skinner, but her heart was still the same – a good woman who cared about me as family. Since the house looked very quiet, I started to worry about her family.

"Where is *Pou*?" I stood on my tip-toes to see if *Pou* was nearby.

"He left us."

"Left you? Is he crazy? Is he…"

"He may be dead already because he had no fear of death. In his mind, staying with the family or leaving the family would have had the same outcome – starvation. So, he chose to leave."

She smiled when she finished telling me. She probably had no fear of death either. She was strangely unemotional and seemed disconnected from reality. All her children were sick; she fought alone to make an herbal potion to treat their problems.

"How did you know I was here?" She asked as she poured the boiling potion into a kettle and brought it inside for her kids. "Drink this," she said to her oldest daughter.

"I didn't know you were here." I followed her inside to check on her children. "I came looking for anyone who could give me any food."

She started another potion. "This potion is to help clean the wound. My oldest daughter has an infection on her leg." I was about to ask what the difference was between the two potions when she took a deep breath, letting out her frustration and pain. "If your uncle was here, at least he could carry water from the lake while I took care of the children. Oh well, he was not that nice when he was here; he was very mean to all of us; he was the father but fought over food with his own children. I am happy he left." But, then, her tears began to fall again to belie her words.

"I am so sorry to hear this, dear Aunt." I was about to cry with her, too.

"It is good to see you. I am worried about my daughter who is seriously sick. She was my big helper." She invited me to come inside and have lunch with her. How could I do that to her when she had nothing to feed her children but wild vegetables cooked in salted water? Seeing her family in this condition was heartbreaking.

Still smiling, she said, "I wasn't going to stop him. It was his choice. He lost his mind. He said that he will die if he stays, he will die if he goes. He said he chose to go because he might get lucky and meet someone who will take him in and give him food." She told me she had lost her youngest son a few months earlier to diarrhea and was now worried that she would lose the next ones too. I couldn't stay and listen to any more tragedy. I said goodbye to her and wished her and her daughters God's blessing. She wished the same to me. This was the last time I saw her and her family.

~TWENTY FOUR~

WE ARE GOING TO DIE

'It was time for the rice harvest; it must be February'

My sister-in-law encouraged me to go back to work for the rice harvest and together we made a bra that had big pockets where I could hide grains of rice. I liked the idea of going not to just to be a slave but to pick rice for our own purpose. Ever the optimist, my imagination went wild as I calculated that if I could steal one can a day, it would be a lot in a month, then I would be rich, and I would not have to eat rice soup anymore. My sister-in-law would be grateful for the rice and be nicer to me and later, with the rice I saved, I could do black market trading for gold or something else I wanted.

My Plan Fell Through When I Saw the Rice Field

With all these happy plans, I volunteered to go the next morning. The field was dry and golden. The leader, a young woman around twenty, gave me a *Kadiev* – a long knife in the shape of the crescent moon, and showed me how to hold the plants as I cut them. The people around me were experienced and worked comfortably; they cut the stalks and lay them on the ground for the worker behind them to collect and tie in a bundle. I cut very slowly the first hour leaving a big space in front of me between me and the cutter. "Everyone! Leave a big space for comrade Ra since she is a laggard." The leader mocked me for my slow work.

Hearing this made me very angry. I wanted to kick her in the butt to keep her mouth shut. A half hour later, she came back to check on my work and reassigned me to tying the rice plants into bundles.

"It is not fair to have only me to do the work for twenty people. Look at all the bundles you left for me to tie up," I put my hands on my hips and shouted at her.

She shouted back at me, "Ra! You cannot eat if you cannot do the work!" What could I do at this point except grind my teeth to hold back my anger?

"Just do the best you can, do not talk back," a nice lady next to me said and she helped me when the devil leader walked away. In couple of hours, I became more comfortable with tying and was keeping up with the others. I decided to help an old lady who was as slow at cutting as I had been. I ran back and forth cutting rice, helping her to reach the front line and then going back to tying bundles. But it wasn't long before I cut something other than the rice stalks - my little pinky finger on my left hand. I was not brave enough to look at the finger, "Please help me with the bleeding. How far did I cut off my finger?" I asked my neighbor.

217

"Your fingernail is cut. I will put tobacco on it to stop the bleeding before I can tell how bad it is." Fortunately my whole finger was not cut off.

The different leader came up and asked, "Why did you stop working?"

"I cut my finger with the knife."

"Oh! No! Stop cutting right now. Do the rice tying instead," she ordered. I sat down and looked at the injury, "My poor little finger! I will have a scar for the rest of my life. Maybe I will lose my finger." I asked the leader to go home so I could treat my injured finger before it became infected. Fortunately, she let me go.

When I returned home, my sister-in-law looked at me with a soft smile; she expected me to steal some rice and bring it home. When I came home empty handed and with an injured finger, her face changed. She was not happy.

Rumor by the End of 1978

I did not know what day or month it was, as we had no calendars, watches, personal radios, or clocks. We got no official news and relied on gossip and rumor to find out what was happening outside the village.

Unexpectedly, my in-laws arrived back in the village. What had happened to make them to come back? I heard *Neak* saying she didn't like the leader and she had lied to him that her daughter was seriously ill. However, my father-in-law provided a different explanation to Meng. He said he wanted to be reunited, as a family, in case of civil war.

My father-in-law said, "I noticed KR troops in trucks when I went to work. I overheard they talk about battles between Vietnam and the KR. It looks like the war will be near us very soon, but I don't know anything for sure. I pray something will happen very soon to eliminate these black crows, destroy their regime. Nobody wants it. They use humans to replace machinery and buffalo and then starve us, so can we push the wheel of their stupid revolution?"

"I fear whoever is fighting with these devil crows may kill all of us as well," Meng sighed. "There must be a battle between the Vietnamese and KR over there -look at the smoke." Everyone looked in the direction Meng pointed. We had seen smoke before but had never thought it might be from a battle.

"We are so weak. We wouldn't be able to resist invaders if they wanted to kill us. It would be easy for Vietnam to invade Cambodia and kill the rest of the survivors."

"That doesn't sound right to me. Why would they do that?" said Meng.

"If Vietnam invades our country, we, the survivors, could escape to Thailand," My father-in-law sounded optimistic.

"The Thais would kill us too. You know Vietnam and Thailand are both waiting to absorb Cambodia's land," said Meng.

"Shush… don't talk anymore. Do you want to be killed by the KR before liberation?" mother-in-law warned from inside the house. Meng and my father-in-law lowered their voices.

Hope of returning home started to fill my heart. Seeing smoke and hearing gunfire that grew louder day by day encouraged me to stay alive. Something would happen very soon that would lead to our rescue, I was sure. I still believed I would survive until the liberation.

No one in the fields talked about the possible Vietnamese attack, or a civil war. We all heard the gunfire and saw the smoke. At night, the fury of the battle appeared on the horizon like a forest fire, but we were told by our KR masters that *Angkar* had won the war with Vietnam. Some KR soldiers and their old people allies sang the revolutionary songs, danced, and giggled. These songs praised progressive work on the farms, the happiness of the farmers with revolution, and victory in the war with Vietnam:

We are the *Komar Chhean mouk* (role model for children),

We serve the *Angkar,* and we will die for the *Angkar!*

Ding, Ding, Dong, Dong.

You make my life! We have to eliminate all the people

Who are trying to shove the wheel of revolution backward.

Victory! Victory! Victory!

Mother, Father, brother, sister, children,

Help move forward the wheel of revolutionary rule.

Ding, Ding, Dong, Dong.

Cooperate with our *Angkar* to eliminate our enemies.

Victory! Victory! Victory!

I was physically weak but my mind was not dead

We lived in constant despair as the food rations continually diminished. My health gradually worsened due to starvation, hard work and untreated illnesses. Diarrhea bothered me every night. I lost the last little bit of fat on my body and became merely skin and bones. I looked like a little girl of about nine. My skin was dehydrated, very dry; my legs sometimes felt heavy and freezing. My energy was gone, my spirit exhausted. I was physically weak but my mind was still searching for something to keep me alive. I kept my ears open for any rumors; I was always looking for any way to escape this misery. I heard a rumor the leader of the village was looking for a person who had sewing skills. I went to the leader and acted as if I had this skill. The leader's deputy could not assess my skills because she was a peasant. The few skills I had learned from my stepmother, such as using a sewing machine, fooled this ignorant woman and I got the job.

We had three women in our group of sewers; one lady was about thirty years old, another one about twenty. I got along with the older woman but the young one seemed very suspicious of me. To my face she acted very friendly and nice but she asked me nosy questions, "What did you do for a living when you were in the city?"

"My family sold food for a living. We had a little food store in the city," I lied to her.

"It seems you are a poor liar. You must be from a high-class family."

"Everything I said about my life is the truth," I said innocently.

The next day, she started in on me again, "Ra, you do not know sewing. If the leader finds out the truth about you, she will remove you and will send you back to do farm labor."

My older friend said not to be afraid of her and to work harder to avoid problems. One day they got into a fight. They argued back and forth and I felt I was a helpless little chicken in-between them. About two months later, I was called by the leader, "You are fired from this easy job. Women your age have to work on the farm."

I had to kiss an easy job goodbye. Luckily, I got a couple of white cotton *sampots* as a gift when I was hired and I had sewed a more traditional bra for myself with the fabric left over from sewing shirts for soldiers. Best of all, I had gained a little weight during two months sewing in the shade and eating enough with my older lady friend.

Do not say, "Fountain, I never Want to Drink your Water Again"

A couple of days later after getting fired from my sewing job, the leader of the village ordered me to go to the fields to cut the rice. I was sent to new area; I had not been here before. The shelter was just a roof, no walls and hard packed earth for beds. So far, nobody knew where the working area was or how far away it was. My feet were already killing me from the long walk; sweat ran down my back and chest like rain water off the roof during a storm. I un-wrapped my *krama* from my head as soon as I got in the shade, then looked around to see if I knew anyone.

There were many new faces; so few people survived in my village that workers had to be brought to the fields from many different villages. Soon the structure was filled with the noise of shuffling footsteps and the clang of aluminum plates and containers. Men and women with children, as well as single men and women rushed to claim a sleeping place. Their belongings had been reduced to only aluminum containers, spoons and plates. I didn't see how it would make any difference where I slept; there is no good spot in Hell, why waste my energy to looking for the perfect place. They didn't see me or anyone else as a human being. We were animals to be put to work and whipped with less compassion than they would show an ox or buffalo.

I dropped my meager belongings - a few meaningful things of Papa's, at a small space between two quiet women. I couldn't decide if the women were widows like me or if they were young adults, or teenagers, without asking their age. One of them looked dirty, skinny, weak and defeated; the other one was not as dirty, skinny or weak but looked as discouraged. She was dressed all in black and had the trademark KR car tire sandals. I was immediately suspicious of her. Could she be KR? How could that be? I wasn't going to ask her.

My stomach had been empty for what seemed like an eternity. I would sometimes dream of having a full tummy and being able to laugh and run just for the joy of running. I craved food every second of every day. I swallowed my saliva in an attempt to satiate the hunger. Sitting between these two women, I looked at them and knew they felt the same as I did. The walk in the hot sun had used up all the energy our scoop of rice soup had provided. I was sure my bellybutton was touching my spine as I curled into a little ball hugging my knees. I wanted to cry, to scream to anyone who might rescue us from this Hell we had been tossed into and forgotten like unwanted toys in the bottom of a closet; the faces of the two women had the same hopeless, defeated sadness in their eyes.

I looked around for the black uniforms that would indicate where the kitchen area was located. I listened for someone to call us to go for food. It was not time yet. The two quiet women seemed to know better and lay down, covered their faces with their hands and slept. They were as physically and emotionally exhausted as I was but they found solace in sleep while I sat, sure we would be called for food any minute. I didn't want to miss the call by sleeping. I looked at them and wondered, were they alone like me? Had all their family succumbed to starvation as mine had? I wanted to make friends with them, listen to their stories, but what good would that do? They would just die and then I would be alone again.

I untied my bag, took out my other *sampot* to make a bed, carefully hiding my sandals underneath. These sandals had come to mean a lot to me and I guarded them carefully. Most had long since worn out whatever sandals they had and would steal from anyone who was fortunate enough to have a pair, no matter what shape they were in. Mine were very worn and mismatched. The soles of my sandals were the original that I had brought from home. Over time, the heel of the left sandal developed a large hole and my husband had attached the sole of a sandal I found to the original and fastened it in place with wire, even though it was a different size. I never did find one to replace the right side which also had a hole. After he was gone, this was all I had left of him. The sandals had become my best friend and I had to keep them safe from covetous eyes. I massaged my right foot, the unlucky foot that had to deal with the hole. As I massaged my aching feet I realized that both were swollen and cold. Was this a sign of death waiting for me nearby? No, I won't die.

"Everybody, come claim your food," a familiar voice yelled from the kitchen area. As he passed by me, I couldn't believe it. It was Praub, Papa's friend. I looked at him. He wordlessly looked at me but acted as if he didn't know me. Did he not recognize me in my present condition? Did he not want to acknowledge me as someone he knew? My thoughts whirled. Shall I approach him? Could I trust him?

The sound of anxious voices and aluminum plates clanging against each other like clapping hands, joyful to receive any morsel of food offered, interrupted my thoughts. As I attempted to get up, my swollen feet refused to allow me to rise. At that moment I was overcome with exhaustion. I felt as if the ground had drained all the energy from my body. Now all I wanted to do was sleep. As I was about to lay back down, Praub screamed at me, "Stay awake and go get food now, you will get nothing later. You will be called to work soon. *Angkar* will eliminate the lazy." His warning tone scared me and I forced myself to hobble to the kitchen on my sore feet.

At the kitchen area, I met a Malaysian lady who came from the same village. If I saw myself as skinny, my body was still in a good shape compared to hers. Her hair had become thinner; she was almost bald. I didn't know how small her body and legs were as they were all covered by her loose pants and shirt. She looked like a zombie to me. When she spoke, I was surprised. Her voice was strong and clear and didn't match her physical appearance. She smiled at me as soon as I met her. I didn't have any energy to smile back. I asked her where her baby was.

"If I stay home with my baby, we all die together. I left the baby behind in hope of her getting my food ration in the village. I didn't tell anybody that I left the village for this camp. Don't tell Praub that I am here; he will report to the leader at the village to cut off my food ration. Please help save my ration for my baby."

"Who is caring for your little one?"

"I left her with someone who can breastfeed her. I have no milk to feed my baby. I cannot feed myself, how can I feed my baby?"

"Hum! Poor baby! I am glad I did not have a baby."

"What have you found out about Leang?"

"My husband? The rumor is that he has been killed but I don't believe it."

"Poor Ra, we are living in the same basket."

"If I were you, I would bring my baby with me. I would live and die with my baby."

"Well! I sometimes send rice soup home to my babysitter to repay her for her kindness in breastfeeding my daughter."

"Rice soup? Do you have enough for yourself?"

She smiled ignoring my question. "Life is unpredictable for everybody. I do not worry too much about it."

After she received the food, she quickly walked away from me before I asked again where her place was. However, I found she was about ten feet across from me. I came back quietly to my own place and finished my food slowly, watching her. I saw her take out little things here and there from a container. Then she made a fire to cook something with wild greens. I watched so intently I didn't know how many spoons I had scooped from the aluminum plate, only that when the spoon touched the bottom of the plate, the noise startled me. I looked down, so sad to see my food was nearly gone in just a couple of bites. Even with that small amount of soup, my tummy swelled out like someone squeezing a full bag of water.

I began to have diarrhea after eating and more often during the day when I had nothing in my tummy. There was no bush nearby to hide myself during these moments, only the abandoned rice field; the shitty water would have to be good enough for me now. I hurried there as fast as my swollen feet would take me. It was an open area where everybody could see what I was doing, but I was beyond caring. The KR didn't care about modesty. It was obvious that the field had been used by many people before me based on the dried feces scattered all around.

Disgusting, smelly and dirty and we were expected to live with it. We had to live with it. We couldn't escape; the only escape was death. I made it going down to the field, but, coming back, my feet couldn't move very fast. My inner voice kept pushing me to move, stay strong; don't let death get me easily. "Remember Papa's advice," I told myself, "don't forget where you come from." I had to fight until my last breath. My swollen feet and the coldness of my extremities were not severe enough yet to kill me. I took it as a warning to push myself and move before it was too late. It was all about the mind. If the mind won't allow something to happen, it wouldn't happen. I believed this and I lived every day planting trees of hope. I would not give in to despair; I would not let the KR win. I would fight with every bit of hope I could glean from everything and everyone around me.

My Work Schedule

After I became familiar with the camp routine and the level of supervision, I manipulated it to my advantage whenever I could. If I thought I could get away with it, I would claim sickness and stay sleeping. If they cut off my food ration, I would get up to work pretending like I was recovered. I lied, yes; but it was necessary to save my life. "Look at my foot," I would say, "it is swollen. I can't work. Look, I am sick. I had diarrhea all night and all day. I can't work. Look at me, I am very skinny and too weak to work."

I obeyed *Angkar*'s rule that said sick people would have to stay still until they are well. I proved it by staying asleep all day. This tactic worked for me and probably saved my life.

My regular schedule to work was to work hard for three days, stay sick two days or vice versa. One day, I found the Malaysian woman very sick also. I went to where she rested to see how she was and she spoke to me in a low voice, "Ra, sooner or later we are all going to die. Why let yourself starve?"

"What do you mean?"

"Come and steal rice with me. Aren't you hungry?"

"Yes! I am hungry! Every day I am hungrier than the day before."

"Do you want to take a risk with me?"

"Doing what?"

"Follow me at noontime when the leader takes a nap. We are going to go a half mile away from here to steal rice."

"Did you ever do this before?"

"I cannot do it by myself. It requires two people."

"How?"

"I cannot tell you how, just follow me at noon."

I checked in my big bag to find a small one to fill with the rice. When we were sure no one was watching, we left the working area and walked to the village where the rice warehouse was located.

"I am already so tired from walking; how will we ever get back on time before we are caught?" I asked her.

"Do not worry; we will make it on time."

The village was quiet at noon. Everyone was sleeping, including the dogs. The warehouse was built of wood and was not very secure; we could climb the wall easily and crawl inside through the hole between the roof and the wall. The wall was not high enough to scare us.

"It is not very hard to climb the wall from the outside, see?" She asked, "Do you want to go first, or shall I?"

"You go first," I whispered.

I waited for her outside; I was afraid. I leaned my ear against the wall listening to her footsteps inside the warehouse. Then I heard a noise; something had been thrown through the space between the roof and the wall. It was a sack of rice she had thrown from inside the warehouse. I looked around me to make sure we were safe. Then my friend appeared in the space and jumped off the wall. She smiled at me and encouraged me to go next, "It is your turn to go get rice."

I don't know how I did it but I climbed up the wall and was inside of the warehouse. I saw lots of big rice sacks and in the middle of the warehouse was a little bed for the guardian. "Where is he today?" I wondered.

Suddenly, I heard a little voice from outside, "Hurry! Get the rice before the soldier comes to take a nap." I filled up my little sack as quickly as I could and threw it like my friend did earlier.

"But how do I climb this wall?" I asked her from the inside.

"Do you see the chair next to the bed? Use it."

When I stood on the chair, I was able to reach the top of the wall. I could crawl through the space and jump to the ground. We smiled at each other with satisfaction. We left and walked back to the working area happily. When we arrived, my friend left to go to work; I decided to stay to recover my energy. That night I had one lady come to talk to me secretly to ask if she could trade her gold ring for the rice I stole. We could not come to an agreement. I decided to keep the rice; she decided to keep her 24 K gold ring.

My Greediness became Big

The next day the Malaysian woman approached me with the same request. This time I strongly refused her idea. She only laughed and said, "Don't tell the fountain that you never want to drink its water again."

"I know you have stolen rice before you came to me. You told me you paid your babysitter with the rice."

"Of course I have. I like you and I want you to live until we are liberated."

My hunger urged me take a chance again. "Yes! I want to go again. This time I will be rich. I will have enough rice to trade for the gold ring and also enough for myself to survive for a couple of days."

This time I took a bigger sack and I volunteered to go in first. My hands were shaking with fear and happiness. I filled my big sack with rice and then tied it up before I was to throw it out to the outside. The sack was heavier than I could handle.

"What can I do? I cannot even lift it up?" I ran to the wall, whispering at her.

"Tie up your rice sack with the scarf you have on your head and then throw the tail to me so I can pull it up from outside." She helped me but I was soon exhausted. I tried to use the last of my energy to climb up the wall.

"I cannot find the chair to climb on. What can I do? I have nothing to step on."

Before she answered my question, I heard the door at the opposite end of the warehouse being unlocked. Terrified, I hid between the tall rice sacks behind the door. My heart was beating out of my chest, and my legs felt paralyzed. I had a horrible feeling that this was the last day of my life. "Papa! Please help me; please hide me from this soldier," I prayed. From my hiding place, I saw the door open and the soldier walk in, followed by his dog. "Will I have to stay behind the sacks while he is napping? The dog will pick up the smell of a stranger very soon," I worried. I began to perspire all over thinking about the dog. "Oh! The dog will discover me very soon and bite me, the soldier will beat me with a baton, maybe kill me."

I watched through a hole between the rice sacks as the soldier took off his shirt and picked up his keys, then walked out the door followed by the dog. He closed the door. "Oh! God! He isn't going to stay for a nap as usual. Lucky me!!" I ran back to where I thought my friend could hear me and asked her to help me get out. She threw another cotton scarf to me. "Tie this to your scarf to make a loop that you can put your foot in." I did as she told me.

"I cannot move my legs, I have no energy."

"Step in the loop; I will pull you from outside." I tried to regain my strength and concentrated on rescuing myself. My friend worked very hard to pull me up to the top of the wall. As soon as I got on the top of the wall, I jumped off. With no time to waste, my friend rushed to complete her turn. Again, we both made it successfully. On the way back to the work area, we were delighted with our success and happiness and how smart we were. However, I told her, "I swear to God I never want to go back to steal again. I got enough rice today."

I lay down like a dead person when we returned to recover my energy and to think about how brave I was to take a risk like this. That night I was not hungry a bit, instead I was dreaming about eating crabs. Some of the people in my sleeping area had walked to a nearby stream and found small freshwater crabs. They made a small fire and boiled them. The next morning before work, I approached my Malaysian friend to exchange rice for her crabs.

"You know how to crab, I do not. Can I exchange my rice for some of your crabs? I am hungry for crab. I cannot stand seeing you guys eating crabs every day."

"No! Heh! Heh! I do not need rice, Ra!" She must be laughing at me. Before she left, she hid her container of crabs under her blanket.

I went back to my place and lay down again disappointed. When the leader called us to get up for work I remained unresponsive, pretending I was sick under the cow blanket. I wasn't lying; I was not feeling well from severe diarrhea that I had for a long time and was getting worse. Later, when everybody else had left for the fields, I stole some of my friend's crabs to punish her for her selfishness. I cooked rice and the crab for a meal, cleaned my dish, washed my hands, and then quietly lay down.

At noon, the workers came back for lunch. I pretended like I was innocently and calmly sleeping. Suddenly I heard my Malaysian friend shout with anger, "Who stole my crabs? Ra, did you see anybody come to my place?"

I sat up and said, "I was sleeping all morning, I do not know anything." I lay down again, ignoring her anger. Later I heard her say, "I will tell the *Angkar* about the stolen crabs and I know who stole them."

A few minutes later, Praub came in and checked my belongings. He discovered the rice I used as a pillow and took it away. I was told to follow him to see the chief who was sitting in a hammock; his eyes were red and he was dressed in the KR black shirt and pants with a red cotton *krama* around his head.

Interrogation

"Where did you get the rice?" asked Kim, the evil crow leader.

"I exchanged my gold ring for it."

"Tell me the truth, where did you get the rice."

"From a peasant who stopped on the road."

"I recognize this rice type. It must have been transported from south of the village." I was quiet; getting ready to answer his next question. Then he asked me the same questions over and over again.

"Why don't you believe me? "I asked.

"If you do not tell me the truth, I won't let you go back to your place."

"Tell him the truth, we won't do anything to you, Ra!"Said Praub. I looked at the chief before answering his question, looking for pity, for compassion. I could see in his eyes his roughness, hate, inhumanity and selfishness. His voice was intimidating with the accent of villagers from the south of Phnom Penh. This was the voice that frightened me for the last three years, the voice that punished me for working too slowly, the voice that lied to me about my husband's disappearance, the voice that forced me to work like a slave, the voice that commanded the murder of millions of innocent people, the voice that starved me, my Papa and my family to death. I hated this voice; I had to sit in front of him being asked if I committed a crime. The black uniforms reminded me there was a deep hole of darkness in their minds and hearts.

He cruelly smiled at me, showing his power, "Tell me the truth Ra! Where did you get the rice? I know where you got it from." He threatened me, "I do not want to beat you to discover the truth. Be honest with me." I was about to tell him the truth as I felt I had no escape. It seemed to me he knew what he was doing. Suddenly, someone walked in and caused an interruption. After whispering in his ear, this leader turned to me and said, "Go back! I will ask you again tonight."

Last Chance of Living

I was quiet when I got back to my place, mad at my friend who had told the chief on me. My mind was working furiously – looking for a way out. I doubted the punishment for stealing rice could be execution. I told myself that if I told the leader the truth probably I would be forgiven. All I was worried about now was to choose the answer: truth or lie. However when the dinner time arrived, my belief in forgiveness from the leader was long gone. As terror got the best of me, I felt coldness starting to rise up from my legs; my head became light and my heart started racing. I felt like I was watching a film that was playing way too fast. Faster and faster my thoughts whirled in my head until I was startled by the threatening voice of a woman ordering me to hold up my plate. "What?" I looked around and found myself in line in front of the kitchen. I looked at the cook and the plate. Without wasting any more time with me, the cook grabbed my plate and filled up with a scoop of rice soup, then thrust it at me.

"Here," she said and pushed me to move forward with the plate. "What is wrong with you? Are you deaf?" I heard her, but I was more worried about the leader than I was about her.

At near dark, Praub came back, "Let's go. It's seven o'clock." He looked at his watch. When I saw him, I felt my time was up. I had no way to refuse, nowhere to hide, so I got up and followed him without looking back. No one around me cared about my predicament. Only Praub and I knew what would happen in next few minutes. When we arrived, I was told to sit on the ground and wait until he got permission for us to come in. Praub, my father's friend, sat next to me and said, "Tonight the chief will beat you badly to get the truth."

"Are you sure I will be beaten?"

I knew Praub couldn't give me a direct answer, but looking in his eyes I saw what he could not say.

"I feel sorry for your back; it will hurt your soft smooth back and leave scars. I do not know how hard he is going to beat you." He scratched the ground with a little stick, and drew a little picture on it. This man had known my Papa very well, he had spent time talking with my Papa about the cruelty of KR. He had expressed his feeling of hate of this regime to my Papa. He was a small man of medium build. He was a quiet person and usually talked only when asked a question. We both squatted on the ground about fifty feet away from the place the leader stayed. As we waited, I scratched the ground, drawing with a little stick to hide my fear.

Praub asked, "Who are you, Ra?" Obviously, he had not recognized me.

"I am just a daughter of a small business man," I replied, looking at my drawing.

"What did your father do for a living?"

"He had a little food store, we were not rich at all, just kept our heads above water," I lied to him.

"How much education did you have?" This time, I stopped drawing and looked up to see his eyes. I wanted to see in his eyes the real purpose of asking me this question. I wondered if he felt pity for me or was just curious.

"I just finished my 11th grade," I said and I looked in his eyes again. His eyes had plenty of pity and compassion mixed with sorrow that he could not help me out.

He mumbled with a trembling voice, "Ra! You will be beaten today!" Then we were silent.

In my silence, I kept praying to God and Papa to rescue me. Did Praub pray for me to be released too? I knew he had more to worry about than me; his duty put him in the middle. We waited for an hour for the chief to call us. Praub grew anxious and said, "Wait for me here; let me go see what is happening." Moments later he came out and told me "Go back to your place!"

"Will I come back tomorrow?"

"No, he is not here," he said and brushed off his pants as he walked away in a different direction without giving me any more explanation. I rose and walked back to my place very confused - happy that I had stayed out of trouble tonight, but not sure about tomorrow.

My neighbor who wore the KR black uniform and car tire sandals looked up and asked, "You are safe?"

I was surprised and frightened that she knew what had happened and responded, "What do you mean?"

"Ra, I was a *yotear* (KR soldier). My eyes, my ears, my nose are like a cat's. I was sent here because I had violated *sellator* (Angkar's rule)." At the time, I believed she was having sex outside of the marriage. She lowered her voice as she was going to cry, but then raised her chin to preserve her dignity, and said. "I was demoted. I have to pay for my mistake."

I slowly untied my *krama* from my head to buy time as I thought about this frightening revelation. I had been suspicious but now my fears were realized and I had something new to worry about. This *yotear* woman had slept by me, yet she never looked at me or spoke to me. Now she was confiding in me? How could I trust her?

"I have been watching you and I know you are a good person." A brief smile crossed her face. Hearing this last sentence, I was on guard. Because of my naivety, I had been underestimating the duplicity and falseness of people around me for years. *Neak* cheated me while she smiled and called me *Kaun*. If this woman was a snake, she would bite me. I suspected that she might have been sent to spy on me after Leang's death. Who knows?

My suspicion must have been obvious because she quickly moved to reassure me by telling me to check her plate as she had left something there for me, "You must be hungry now."

She gave me her plate where I found rice and a piece of dried fish. I was way too hungry to let suspicion stop me from eating; I grabbed a handful hand of rice as I asked her, "Why are you giving me your food?"

"Don't ask, just eat it." As I gobbled down the food, she started to talk more until I felt comfortable to share my feelings, not all, but enough to appear sincere. Then she told she would stay around for only a short time and then would return to her duties with the KR.

"Where?"

"I cannot tell. This is *Angkar*'s rule."

In the early morning, we were informed that the chief was permanently gone and that a new chief had replaced him. Where did he go? Why did he disappear without any advance notice? Why was he replaced? Nobody knew the answers. Yet, my new friend, who had introduced herself as Pheap, knew. She didn't say much, only one word – *reansot* (re-education). That chilling word was code for execution as I had learned when I lost Leang. She told me not to worry about the old chief and my previous problem; it would be forgotten along with the chief.

Well, at least my stolen rice problem was resolved and I was still alive. I would just have to wait for malnutrition and forced labor to kill me. Die now or later.

I saw the new leader who replaced Kim. He was about twenty five years old, tall and skinny. He had a pleasant face and I hoped he would be kinder than the previous leader and that things would get better for the workers. But, I knew better than to judge a book by its cover.

Miracle

As I felt safe, I decided to take a bath and wash my clothes, which I had not done for many days. I went to the canal where the crabs were found; the water from the canal was funneled into a large pipe which carried it under a small bridge. The water was so clear that I could see through to the small rocks and little fish swimming along the bottom. As I got into the water a little upstream of the pipe, I was swept into the middle of the stream by a strong current. My *sampot* was stripped off my body. I was naked but I still held my *sampot* between my toes. I caught the edge of the pipe and held on. I had worried about dying many times but had never imagined I would drown in a pipe!

I was thinking about whether I should keep holding on or allow my body to go through the pipe to the other side when a soldier appeared. He was almost past the pipe; then turned as he heard my screams. He walked toward me and pulled me out of the water with one hand. I was very small and skinny and very light to him, I guess. I was rescued.

I lay limply on the side of the canal, too exhausted to move. When I looked around to thank the soldier, he was gone. Who had rescued me just a few minutes ago? If he walked or rode a bicycle, I would still be able to see him. He couldn't have gotten very far. Where did he go? There were no hills or bushes around me;

it was a rice paddy. Looking around again and again, I still couldn't figure out how he was disappeared so quickly. Was he a ghost? Did he come to haunt me? No; I had seen him, a real human, dressed in a soldier's uniform a few minute ago.

As I lay there naked and exhausted, I looked at my body; my skin was dark and dehydrated with stains and dirt on it. I scratched at the stains until my skin bled. It was not dirt and stains; it was the skin on a body that had lost all fat, muscle and elasticity due to the extreme weight loss. My waist was tiny; my chest was skeletal like a zombie's. My breasts were gone, like a little girl. I could see capillaries and veins over my tummy and arms.

When I recovered enough to stagger back to the camp, I couldn't stop thinking about the soldier who just disappeared without letting me thank him. My eyes searched for him everywhere to no avail. Was he an angel sent from Heaven to save me? I believe he was.

~TWENTY FIVE~

VOODOO DOCTOR

When the harvest was finished, the chief announced that we would move on to another job in the *Phnom* (Hill) *Srok* District. I didn't know how far away it was but to me it was a long, long way as I had difficulty walking. To make it worse, there I surprisingly met my in-laws. I had no choice to escape from them. They welcomed me back. I decided to temporarily live with them, as they suggested, until I felt better. I never bothered asking them when and how they got to this new place. My health was getting worse every day; I started getting weird feelings in my body. The diarrhea continued throughout the nights. My feet remained cold, numb, heavy and swollen. My in-laws still treated me very poorly. I saw what they did to me, but I tried to be patient. I believed my patience would cool down their hearts.

Beef Stew

Unbelievably, one afternoon, *Neak* somehow managed to get some beef. Everyone in the family was busy helping cut the beef into small pieces, cooking it secretly to avoid the eyes of *Angkar*. Lony and Vanny were sitting outside of the house in the palm leaves watching for *Angkar* or his spies. They were to give a signal to hide the soup pot if a spy or an *Angkar* leader passed by. I was not given a job and was told to stay away from the kitchen. Since I had nothing to do, and was exhausted from sickness, I lay down on my mat listening to their chitchat.

Was I excited about the meal to come? No, I knew I wouldn't get much of that delicious soup; this party was not for me. Once in a while, Srey growled at her mother for nagging too much. In return, she growled at her daughter to put the lid back on quickly to avoid the smell that might be noticed by the neighbors. I did not know how *Neak* could have gotten beef at this time when no one in the village could find it and nearly everyone was starving. She would be punished or even executed if caught.

At night, I slept on the floor in the kitchen as the house was very small and there was no other space for me. Because I was treated so poorly by them and never given a fair share of food, I promised myself that I would steal some beef that night when everyone fell asleep. As they started to snore, I got up quietly and crept to the pot. Silently, I opened the lid with one hand and, with the other, grabbed a handful of meat. I happily ate very well that night. I got even with them. Unfortunately, after eating this unfamiliar food, my tummy started to grumble. I got up and quickly crept toward to the door which was always left open, even at night. I became very sick. It didn't taste the same coming back up.

In the early morning, before I got up, I heard *Neak* come to the kitchen to check the soup. I heard her whisper to Srey, "Maybe a rat crawled into the pot at night to eat the meat." She blamed her daughter, "You forgot to put a heavy object on the lid."

I stayed feigning sleep because I was exhausted from being sick all night. At lunch time, mother-in-law served beef soup to everyone, including me, but I was given only a small portion of the broth, no meat. I was right. If I did not steal it last night, I wouldn't get anything in the morning.

After the beef soup, it was tapioca for dessert. Again, I knew I would be lucky to get any. I did not expect to see *Neak* throw a piece of the tapioca root from behind her back to me. I understood that she was hiding my portion from the others because none would approve of me getting any. She turned to me and said, "Hurry up, finish it before your sisters come in."

I tried to eat it as she encouraged me, but, it was the toughest part of the root and impossible to chew. I threw it back to her, "It is just wood, there is no meat."

"You got a bigger piece and you still complain?"

It was almost funny to hear her say that I was luckier than her children because I got a big piece of tapioca, while they only got a small piece. She wouldn't give a big piece to her own children; big pieces were old pieces and very woody and tough. Only the small pieces of the root are young and have lots of meat.

I felt hurt and did not understand why I could not do something to make myself valuable to this family. "Keep the bigger piece for yourself, *Neak*." I replied to her.

"You do not bring anything home like your sisters-in-law." That hurt me more than ever.

"I suppose I shouldn't eat anything more than my rations," I agreed with her.

Impressed Mother-In-Law

I saw the *anchoat* – fishing basket that was sitting next to the house and I got the idea of going to the lake to get fish. Bringing fish to *Neak* would certainly raise my standing in the family. Perhaps my two little sisters-in-law would stop insulting me. Without saying a word to anyone, I took the basket, which is shaped like a large shell and made of thin strips of bamboo, and went down to the lake. I promised myself I would not stop until I could bring home fish.

To protect myself from leaches, I tied a very tight knot in my shirt and tucked it into my pants. I tied the legs of the pants up with string. I started out in the shallow water first. I did not see any fish; all I found were little escargot and water plants. I threw them away. Then I went deeper and deeper, hoping I could catch a big fish. Thinking about getting a big fish motivated me to keep going deeper into the water.

The water was about chest level; but still the fish did not come to my basket. As I checked to make sure everything was safe from leeches, I found something big and black laying flat across my chest next to the knot of my shirt. I slapped it thinking it was just a water plant stuck on me. It was not. It was slick and attached to my skin. It was a giant leech. I got goose bumps but I tried to be brave and not scream. Slowly, with my eyes closed and grinding my teeth, I pulled harder until it released its grip on my skin and then I raced out of the water in a panic.

"I must eliminate my pride. I do not care what abuse my parents-in-law give me, it will be better than being sucked by leeches," I said to myself as I went home ashamed, without telling *Neak* where I had been.

My living with my in-laws was of no benefit to them. My young sisters-in-law complained everyday about keeping me as I was one more mouth to feed. They were right; I was not able to help the family. I did nothing but eat and sleep. Frustrated with this unresolved situation I was glad to go back out in the fields again, to escape from the hostility.

Escape from the In-Laws

It had been raining for a couple of days and we had to walk about a mile in the mud to get to the farm. By the time I arrived at the field, I could not move my feet. I fell and needed help to get up as the bottom of my *sampot* was so heavy with mud. My sandals grew thicker and thicker with mud and made it harder to walk. My little bag of jewelry became very annoying because it also felt heavy after a while.

We worked under the sun for a while and then it rained again by the late afternoon just before we got off work. I hated rain, I hated mud, I hated walking back home with the mud stuck on my *sampot*. We had to walk one more time to get our rations, which I also hated. The next morning, I had nothing to replace my muddy *sampot* so I wore the same one all morning and all afternoon from wet to dry and back again. I went to work regularly for one week, and then my body became exhausted.

One afternoon, when we returned to the sleeping area, I asked my friend who was going to the village if she could help me by exchanging one of my gold necklaces for rice. While she was gone, I fell deeply asleep since I was exhausted from the hard work. Sometime later, I heard my friend come back from the village and say to her husband, "I got twelve cans of rice for Ra! Where is she?"

"She is taking a nap," her husband replied.

"I will cook the rice for her; go wake her up now."

Her husband came close to me, "Ra, rice is here, do you want rice soup or cooked rice?" I was too tired to answer or even open my eyes.

"She must be really tired," the husband said.

"We can let her sleep until the rice is ready, honey."

Half hour later maybe, she came to wake me up again, "Ra, wake up, the rice is ready."

I did not want to wake up and did not respond to her, nor open my eyes.

"Ra, wake up!" She touched my body and slapped my cheek to wake me up. I still did not want to answer because I felt very depressed and discouraged with my life. I did not even want to open my eyes for rice.

"What is wrong with Ra? Ra! Ra! Help me! Ra has something wrong in her body. She won't wake up." She did not leave me alone as I had hoped and expected.

I thought my silence would make her leave for work without me but that was not to be. She continued to try to wake me up by slapping very hard on my cheeks, and pinching my arms and legs. Other voices joined hers. I heard all their conversations, but I was floating somewhere and did not want to come back. I recognized her husband's voice – he sounded like a grandfather even though he was a young man. A few minutes later, I heard another man's voice. I recognized this voice and the smell of tobacco on his clothes. But I did not want to come back for him either. "She probably has a bad spirit in her body," Loun, the leader said.

"How can we help her?"

"Poor Ra, she is truly sick. Someone told me she was probably faking. That is wrong," Loun said. I heard him command my friend to take me to the village and have me treated by the traditional healer. This was not a doctor but more of a shaman or a witch doctor.

A Special Spell

They used a small oxcart to bring me to the village. On the way I heard people asking my friend about me, but I did not want to open my eyes at all. I was happy floating in the ether. My friends brought me to their house. Although it was evening, they asked the healer to treat me right away. He pinched very hard on my arms and legs to wake me. I did not scream a bit. However, when he pinched my neck, the pain brought me back to reality and I reached up to grab his hand and stop him.

"Oh! Ra is awakening!"

"Must be a bad spirit got into her body, I have to use another spell to catch the bad spirit." Then he pinched me again on the neck and again I pushed his hand away. Then he squeezed my tummy very hard. "Oh! The spirit stays in the head and tummy! I have to get this creature out!" Then he spit something on my face and squeezed my tummy even harder.

"Ouch! Ouch! It hurts," I screamed.

The healer said, "Hum… if the spirit was still in her body, she wouldn't feel the pain. I don't know what is causing this." As I heard his words, I was scared he would report that I had been faking. "But …" he paused, "Ok! I am done. The spirit has been caught and thrown away in the bushes. She will be all right later." Then the man left for home.

I lay on the bamboo floor at my friend's house for the entire night without moving or talking. I was so depressed that I didn't care if I lived or died. In the morning, I heard the husband say to his wife that the rice that I exchanged my necklace for was almost gone. They both worried what they should tell me when I awoke. They had eaten nearly all my twelve cans of rice. I heard the husband tell the wife that they wouldn't need to save any for me as I would probably die. Fortunately, I heard the wife said she should save a little in case I woke up. At this point, I knew I had to get up if I was to get any of the rice; besides that, I had to go to the bathroom.

I opened my eyes and looked around me, "Where am I?"

"Ra, do you want to eat now?" My friend asked as she came to my side.

"Yes! I am hungry," I answered as I massaged my back that ached from staying so long in the same position.

"Do not eat too much, you just recovered. Do you know I exchanged your necklace for twelve cans of rice? We finished five cans already while you were sleeping."

"I knew that, but, at least she is being honest," I said to myself.

Shockingly, my father-in-law showed up that night. As soon as I heard his voice, I closed my eyes pretending to sleep. My mind was wondering how in the world he and I were back together again.

"Is she awake?" he asked.

"She is all right," the wife responded with a big smile.

"I want her back under my supervision soon."

Damn! I didn't run away far enough. After he left, my friend asked me, "Do you want to go back to live with your in-laws?"

"No, I do not want to. Nobody misses me. They do not love me."

A couple days later, my father-in-law showed up again to check on me. When he found me, I was awake, eating rice soup. Without any greeting, he barked at me, "Your *Neak* wants you to come back home now!" Then he looked down at the ground before he continued, "Everybody is worried about you!"

"Hum!" I didn't believe it.

"It is my responsibility to take care of you now since your father is gone." It sounded very nice, but I still didn't trust him.

"Hum!..I..." I was undecided.

"Let's go home now; this is not your family." Silently, I turned around to look at my friend and her husband who were curious about what I would decide.

"We all love you as a younger sister if you want to stay with us," her husband said.

I looked at both of them, and then put my face down to think before making a decision. After a few seconds, I looked up and told my friends that I would have to stay with my in-laws. I believed it was my best decision as I could see my in-laws had a better life than my friends. I also believed that if something bad happened in the future, my in-laws wouldn't abandon me, my friends would. I asked my friend if she would give me the rest of the rice I had traded for my necklace.

"Can you leave some for us?" she said.

"How much do you want to keep?'

"One can."

"OK!"

I followed my father-in-law to his house located about a block away. As usual, *Neak* was busy sewing. She was sitting in the doorway to get more sunlight. As soon as she heard our steps, she looked out and asked, "Is Vicheara here?" I smiled at her. "We were worried about you," she smiled, peering over her reading glasses. Srey, Vanny and Lony did not say a word; they walked away after scowling at me.

"What is in your hand?" she asked, as she took off her reading glasses and raised an eyebrow.

"Huh! ...Rice...." I hesitated to tell her the truth.

"Rice! Rice! I will cook rice for you. Your father-in-law is lucky today. You will save his life." She grabbed the rice bag from my hand before I could even offer it to her.

The next few days that I stayed with my in-law's family were like living in Hell again. Nothing had changed; they still treated me like dirt. I could understand if they cheated me due to starvation, what I really minded was not being treated like a human being.

~TWENTY SIX~

"WHO DO YOU THINK I AM?"

Since the rice harvest was still going on, I went back to work to get away from my in-laws. During the mile-long walk to the fields, I decided to change my attitude. I made a commitment to work hard, stay on the job and do better than before. I often touched my jewelry bag in my pocket to be sure it was safe. Once at the camp, I met lots of women friends, including the Malaysian woman who had reported me to the leader for stealing her crabs. She smiled at me first and said, "How are you doing?"

I ignored her.

"Oh, you are mad at me? Don't you think I should be the one who is mad? You stole my crabs!?"

"Yes, right! Those two crimes are the same?! I could have been killed by the leader! Are you happy with what you have done to me? And even after you reported me, I didn't tell Praub that you were cheating on your food rations," I looked in her eyes without smiling.

"You didn't? Thanks, that's because you have a good heart for my baby. But, anyway, stop thinking about it. We can be friends."

"You taught me a good lesson. If I were you, I would have shared food with a friend."

I looked for a different place to sleep, away from her. I tried to avoid her whenever possible. She never could be my friend again. Finally, I chose a place next to a woman whose oldest sister had lived next to my house in Phnom Penh, three years ago. I made friends quickly with her as she seemed friendly and nice. I lay down to rest for a while after the long walk from the village. My new friend, her name was Ry, asked me if I wanted to go to the eating area to get our rations. I was very dusty and I wanted to take a bath in the canal first.

"You go first; I will go later, after a bath," I said to her. I saw her grab her bowl and leave. I wanted to wash my blouse since I had not done so for a long time, because the jewelry bag was hidden in the pocket. I thought that it would be safe to leave the jewelry hidden in my clothes bag for a few minutes while I was bathing.

I enjoyed the clear water of the canal; it made my body feel fresh and clean. It was the hot season and we were very sweaty. I re-dressed in my wet clothes and walked back to the sleeping area. As I picked up my clothes bag, I could tell immediately from the weight that the jewelry was missing. I opened up the bag wide and shook it. It was gone.

More Heartbreak

I was suspicious of Ry. I asked around and looked for her. I was told she asked for permission to go back to the village quickly.

"Why? She just got here," I asked the leader.

"She said her son was very sick."

I threw caution to the wind and said, "She lied. She stole my jewelry."

"What does it look like?"

"The bag contained 100 loose stones - emeralds, rubies and sapphires, five diamond rings, one diamond pendant and one gold bracelet."

He scratched his head before answering. This showed me that he did not know what to do. "I do not know where to find her. But I will arrest her when she comes back."

I was surprised that he believed me and said he would help instead of threatening me when he found out that I was hiding jewelry. I was either brave or foolhardy to tell him the truth; what if he had decided I was the bigger criminal and eliminated me in the forest? I waited and waited for Ry to come back that night. She did not come back then or the next morning.

I asked the women who slept next to me if anyone of them knew where she lived. Finally I got the answer, "She lives in the same village you do, but her cabin is located at the end of the valley. Ask around, everybody knows her; she does jewelry trading as a business."

"Ah! I am worried she is going to sell my jewelry before she can be arrested."

I went back to the leader asking for permission to go back to the village to recover my jewelry. He looked at me for several long moments and then said, "Work for three days and I will let you go."

Three days might as well have been three years; it was too late. Now I had nothing else to be stolen except for the fancy French bras. They were now way too big for me and nobody in the camps or the village wanted a French bra; many had never even worn a bra. Losing the jewelry was like losing my life. I got a permission slip to go back to the village on the third day and rushed to find Ry's house. Her neighbors told me she was off somewhere with her son selling jewelry but I didn't believe them and finally just went inside and discovered her hiding there.

"Where is my jewelry, Ry?" I asked her.

"What do you mean, Ra?" she said innocently.

"You stole it from my bag."

"I never knew about it. I swear to God I never did that. We are all in the same boat, how could I do that to you?"

"Please, give me back what you have not sold. I want to keep it as a remembrance of my Papa."

"I never had it."

"Yes, you do."

"I swear to you, God will punish me miserably, I will suffer by the KR regime, and I will live miserably for the rest of my life if I stole it."

"God will do all these things to you. I've never done anything to hurt or betray anybody. Whoever steals from me will receive God's punishment."

I went back to the camp empty-handed. One more heartbreak.

As long as I was there Ry never returned to the camp. I don't know how she got away with that. But, by far the oddest thing was that the leader never followed up with me. He didn't ask about Ry or the jewelry. There was no consequence for me hiding the jewelry or for her stealing it. Maybe he didn't know what to do and was happy to let the whole thing be forgotten. I don't know. People had been killed for much, much less so I felt blessed, no matter what the reason was.

He Buried her Alive

Life in the labor camp was the same every day; I knew everybody in my group as they were all friendly. One day, I noticed the disappearance of one of the village women who used to sing and flirt with the leader. One of my co-workers said she and that man were gone.

"What happened?"

"That man was married; he betrayed his wife"

"You're kidding."

"Yes, it's true. He fell in love with this woman and then got caught by the *Angkar* leader."

"Uh! Was she killed then?"

"He wanted to show his love to this woman but she said she wouldn't make love with him if he was still married to his wife."

"What happened?"

"Don't you know? He beat his wife until she lost consciousness. Then he buried her alive."

I froze in fear. "That is very horrible! I would hate a man who could do this to his wife. I would not marry such a man if I were the other woman."

"Then, at night, his wife awakened and tried to crawl back home. When he saw her, he killed her and buried her again. She is dead for sure now."

"That's unbelievable!"

"He came to claim that woman as his wife. But he got caught. Both of them have been killed, leaving two small children behind."

"Oh! I am sorry for the children. They will never be able to be proud of their mom."

"I heard from the person who executed them that they both asked him to untie them so they could kiss each other before giving themselves to the executioner."

"Hum, very sad. And what happens to her two children?"

"They will be adopted by the *Angkar* leader."

"Then they will grow up to be them. Poor kids."

"No! They will have a better life than us," she said and bent down to cut the rice as she saw the soldier walk toward our group.

"Keep moving when talking," he said.

"Did you see the woman who used to dress up sexy and sing in the field next to me?" she asked the soldier.

"Why? Do you want to betray *Angkar's* rules like she did?"

We did not talk to him anymore.

I stayed working in the fields until the harvest season ended. Then we were all sent back home to await the next order. The idea of returning home was depressing to me. I was not surprised to see them looking at me with hate when I arrived home. My mother-in-law informed me my father-in-law had been sick for a week with serious diarrhea. She was right, he was very weak, could not get up, nor talk. He had lost a lot of weight.

Equal problems

One day soon after that, after leaving the communal area, I walked back home using a short cut through the bamboo bushes instead of walking by the house of the *Angkar* leader. I couldn't stand to see them laying out all kinds of food while I was starved. I couldn't stand the smell of delicious food tickling my nose when passing by. About halfway through the bushes, I heard a male villager, Sareun, a man that I had known for years, softly call me to stop, "Ra, Ra, come here."

I was surprised; usually he only smiled when seeing me pass by. I looked at his hands hoping he had some food, but he was empty-handed. What did he want? I had no problem with him because he was always friendly with me, but his wife was a creep. I was astonished when he said, "I care about you so much; I want you to be my mistress."

My heart started to pound faster because I felt danger; accepting or not accepting was an equal problem. He then stepped closer and grabbed me, touching me inappropriately. "I feel compassion for you since the disappearance of your husband. Living as a widow is not an easy life! You need a man. I can support you by stealing food from my *Angkar* leader for you. But, you cannot tell my wife!"

"I will be executed if I do this, please leave me alone. If you truly have compassion for me, just give me food," I begged him in a soft voice. Without listening to me, he pushed me to the ground and forced himself on me.

"Nobody can see us in this bush, hurry!!"He ordered me to pull down my *sampot*. I fell on the dried bamboo leaves, without the strength to push him away. Was rape now going to be part of my life? My body became limp and paralyzed. Death was inevitable. If I accepted his offer, I would be executed by *Angkar*, when his wife reported me. If I didn't accept him, he might wrongly accuse me just to punish me. Suddenly, the idea of pinching his penis came to me and I did so as hard as I could. He screamed only once with embarrassment and got off me immediately. He then kicked me toward the bush and threatened me, "I will get you next time."

A good pinch had worked on the pedicab driver when I was only four years old, and it worked again – at least for now. Walking back home, I decided to keep the incident secret. Who cares about me? Not anyone in the village, but I was still afraid this man would come back to follow through with his promise. I was not sure what he might say to manipulate *Angkar* against me. Should I go to tell his wife on him? I didn't know the right answer. I just had to wait and see and hope for the best.

~TWENTY SEVEN~

KICKED ME OUT

As I climbed the stairs to walk into the house, *Neak* came toward me, acting very sweet and sincere. This was not right. Her behavior was telling me she wanted something from me. She started with a question, "I know you still have a silk *sarong*, right?" she asked me.

"You mean my Papa's?"

"Yes. Maum saw it in the bag that you left at their place in *Preah Netr Preah*. The reason I ask is that someone has asked for this type of material."

"I cannot give it away; I need to keep it to remember my Papa."

"Listen! Your father-in-law is sick and hungry for palm sugar. The person who has sugar will exchange it for the silk *sarong*. Don't you realize he is the man of the family? He supports us. We cannot live without him. And he is very sick; he may die soon without sugar.

I knew she was trying to make me feel guilty. "Let me think about it because it is the last thing I have of my Papa's."

The next day, I saw my father-in-law eating sugar; I saw also my mother-in-law distributing a little spoon to her children to taste. She hid it from me.

"*Neak*, did you get the sugar already?"

"Yes, Maum brought your Papa's *sarong* over here."

"But I never said I agreed!" My heart was boiling with anger. When I looked at her face, I didn't see her, but my Papa's *sarong* that I would rather die than give up. Now, this woman had not only stolen everything I had, she had also robbed my heart and took the only material thing I had left to remember my papa. I ground my teeth, controlling my anger; otherwise, I would do something very violent to get back my Papa's *sarong*.

"Do you want to see your father-in-law die miserably in front of you?" she asked in a threatening voice as she took off her reading glasses.

I knew I had no power, no control, so I walked away.

After eating the palm sugar, my father-in-law got his energy back. Soon, he could talk, walk around the front yard, do light work around the house as well. His health improved gradually.

Several days later, I was shocked by his sudden shout, "Vicheara, damn you. Get out of this house. You never bring any luck to my house!!"

"Don't go anywhere, Vicheara," *Neak* protested.

My father-in-law stared at me with fury and hate. "You ruined our luck in this family, get out, fuck you, Vicheara," he shouted again.

I was not too surprised that my father-in-law exploded with anger. Lony and her sister had been whispering to their Papa during the three days of his illness. They would have told him every reason they hated me. I did not pay too much attention to them because it was not new that they hated me. However, this time I wondered what new lies they had told to make him explode with anger. I never could understand why Vanny hated me so much. Did she know that her mother lied when she said that the soldier took her jewelry as well as mine? Did she know that her mother took advantage of me by stealing my jewelry to get the fish net that benefitted her whole family while I had only few little scraps of fish and a big bowl of watery banana leaves?

Her mother didn't just steal once; she had deceived me several times. I could let it go and forgive Neak because I could understand that, as a mother, she should fight to get as much food as she could to feed her own children to keep them alive. I felt that my mother-in-law patted my shoulder with one hand while her other hand drove a knife into my back. She was a hypocrite; she did bleed me dry like Papa had warned. Maybe if I had challenged her after she lied to me, I would have been treated better, maybe given credit for my contributions? It was my fault that I had chosen to keep quiet and avoid confrontation; it encouraged her to continue to take advantage of me. Now that they had taken every single thing of value that I had, I was to be kicked out of the house as a person who didn't bring luck to the family? Perhaps my father-in-law did not know that he got the sugar from my Papa's silk *sarong* or maybe they had told him that I was angry about it. I don't know.

No regrets

With all the dignity I could find, I grabbed my clothes bag and my pot and left the house without regret. My clothes bag had nothing but the three French bras and Papa's *krama*.

"Do not listen to your father, Vicheara. Do not go. Keep your mouth shut," I heard *Neak's* voice behind me. It seemed very caring, but these words were not sincere. I had to leave because I had no more to offer. If I stayed, next time could be worse. Maybe Lony will run to *Angkar* telling them to execute me. I told to myself to close my ears, my eyes and keep walking forward without looking back. I have had enough with this family. They fight to live by stepping on my shoulders. If I die, I'd rather die by myself in a different place. If I stayed alive, it would be in a place where I never have to see them again. I continued to walk without knowing where to go. I passed by houses without looking back.

I was asked about my quick decision to leave the house by a man I met.

"He kicked me out!" I began to cry. "He got better with the sugar we got by trading my Papa's silk *sarong*. He paid me back for my generosity." As I finished talking, I felt shocked with pain like an arrow in my heart. I wasn't sorry to leave them but the injustice was hard to bear.

"Poor orphan Vicheara, God bless you forever," the man prayed for me. I asked how to get to the revolutionary hospital and he gave directions. But he warned me, "If you go there, you will be walking into the gates of the cemetery. You will die soon."

Die? Am I scared to die? Am I scared to see you, ghost? I have no soul. I am a dead person now. I want to see what else I will suffer with. This is what happens when you are not around to protect me, Papa. I remember when my *Mak* was very ill and you were not around the house to protect me. I was left alone in my bedroom and was molested by my cousins at night. Now, I get kicked out by my in-laws. If you were still alive, father-in-law would think hard before he did this. I can see clearly now. I have to stand up for myself, won't let this family treat me like I am worthless anymore. I have to stop crying and move forward.

I kept walking forward with no regret. I ground my teeth and told myself that if I had to walk through fire just to get away from my in-laws, I would not hesitate. My Papa is always here to protect me. The man called after me, "You will walk by the forest; it is haunted."

Haunted? I wanted to see it if it would scare me. I had been scared to see my Papa die; now, he was gone, and my husband was gone, too. "What do I need to be scared of? I have nothing left," I answered him.

The revolutionary hospital was the only place that could keep me from being called to work every morning. If I happened to die there, I could die on my own terms without hearing anything hateful or having to endure any more cheating and criticism from my in-laws. Usually I would need a permission slip to get out of the village and to present to the hospital caretaker; however, I did not think about getting one. They must have allowed me to leave because I was obviously very skinny and sick. Or maybe nobody noticed or cared. I don't know.

I walked by a mountain that was very quiet and scary even in daylight. I had heard the story that many 'New People' had been killed near this mountain and that was why it was haunted but I heard nothing but the sound of my feet dragging my worn out sandals. Now, alone in the middle of nowhere, with no one to see or hear, I could let out my pain and I burst into tears. I thought I had no tears left but I did. I wailed and sobbed. I just kept going, praying that I would not see anything that would terrify me. I thought about the bitter lesson I had learned from my in-laws. People can be cruel and hypocritical. No one will love you and care about you as much as your parents. Once, just once, I looked back to see if there was a chance that *Neak* was coming after me, that she really did care about me – that I wasn't truly alone. But, I was alone – completely alone.

I remembered the dream I had the evening before we were all forced to leave our home in Phnom Penh. I woke Leang to tell him that all my teeth had fallen out. I had feared that the dream symbolized the loss of my family. It had. Once again, my worst fears had become my reality.

~TWENTY EIGHT~

THE HOSPITAL OF DEATH

I do not know how long it took me to walk from the village to the hospital of death. When I finally staggered in, teenage attendants dressed in black *sampots* and black blouses with long sleeves, their heads covered with *kramas*, helped me to find a bed next to the entrance door. The hospital, as we called it, was just a simple wooden house containing about twenty beds sitting on a dirt floor. The patients who were sent from the village to have treatment here were suffering with malaria, diarrhea, and swollen bodies. They all looked like zombies to me; I'm sure I looked like one to them. The place was very dirty, dark and unhealthy. I called this place a cemetery because people who went there all died sooner or later since the hospital had no doctors or medicine except a guava potion for treating diarrhea and the Rabbit Shit pills. The KR had murdered all the medical professionals that they could identify.

The teenage girls who worked in this "hospital" were cruel to the patients. They treated us like animals. At mealtime, they distributed rice soup; sometimes the soup spilled to the ground if we could not give the server the bowl quickly enough. Once spilled, it was rarely replaced, it depended on their mood. We were at their mercy. They dumped out leftover soup rather than giving us more. When patients suffered from malarial shivering, they just watched them and laughed. When patients died, they laughed again and treated the bodies without respect like we were garbage. They said "Here it comes - another one, bury it ..."

In front of the hospital, a sheet of *sangkasey* lay on the ground next to long bamboo sticks. It was used to carry the bodies away and then left there for the next body. I heard this metal sheet was haunted. I wanted to see the spirits so I could talk to them, but, I never did.

I made friends very quickly with the patients, then with the "Old People" in the nearby village. *Pouk*, a local healer or shaman, was an elder who distributed the Rabbit Shit pills at night, walking from bed to bed, giving pills to every patient without asking what kind of illness they had. Those pills were a peasant placebo used to treat every malady from malaria to exhaustion because there was nothing else. I knew it was nonsense but what did I care? It had been a long time since I had tasted anything sweet and even this tiny treat was appreciated – particularly since I did not have to plant rice for twelve hours to get it. When he arrived at my bed, he faced away from me, his hands crossed in the back. He hid extra pills for me in his hands. I laughed and opened up his hand, grabbing them. Why didn't he give them to me like the others patients? I didn't know. I didn't care. I was his favorite and happy to be.

Next to my bed, was a young child, around eight years old, who cried all day, either from the pain of his swollen legs maybe just from hunger? For days I watched him cry as his swollen legs kept getting bigger. His mother, a Malaysian woman, fed him only the rice soup provided by the hospital girls even though she managed to find additional food for herself. He would see her eating and beg to share the food but she refused. "No, you cannot eat it because it is going to make the swelling worse," his mother told him.

The more he was starved, the more he cried. Every day he cried, and screamed at the mother. Once I heard her scream back, "Do not shout at me, or I will leave you alone to die here." This scared him into silence.

She even hid the Rabbit Shit pills which she trade for food that she did not share with the starving child. He knew it, but what he could do? He was too weak and sick to even get up. So he wept and begged.

I had seen many terrible things in the last four years as the people around me were starved and terrorized. Living in Hell changed people. My *Pou* Va left his wife and children; I remember my aunt complaining that he had fought over food with her. My neighbor, a Vietnamese mother of three children wanted to report to *Angkar* because one of her daughters didn't share food with her! Small children were trained to belong to *Angkar*, love *Angkar*. Their parents became worthless in their minds. They spied on their parents as well as others. Who knew what they could report to *Angkar* on their parents. Normal life had ceased to exist. This was the "upside down" life that *Pou* Ban, a fortune teller, had warned me about.

They were still people whose loving natures remained despite the nightmare we were living. Sok's family remained intact. I never heard them fight and scream over food. But the regime had turned many normal people into uncivilized brutes. My husband's family had not turned on each other but they had turned on me. Even in the hospital of death, I felt I was in a better place - away from my two little sisters-in-laws who resented me sharing their food. If I had stayed there longer, they probably would have reported some lie to *Angkar* and caused my death.

Despite all that I had witnessed I was still astonished that a mother would not share food with her starving child. Since she was not a patient, she had to go to work in the fields each day and care for the child when she returned. She was not allotted any food by the hospital and had only the soup distributed in the labor camp. She was starving too, but not at death's door like the child.

The next compartment was even darker with only a few beds holding the very sickest patients, very skinny and dehydrated. Next to their beds was an aluminum container for their rice bowls; it was covered with flies. These patients could no longer get up to eat and just waited for death. When I looked at them, their eyes acknowledged me and they sent back a little smile filled with sadness and pain. Their skin was very dried, very pale. Their faces and feet were very swollen, and their mouths hung open. Flies settled around their mouths and noses but they no longer had the energy to shoo them away.

New Neighbor

One day, a new lady about my age arrived. Unlike most of us, who staggered in without possessions, she carried many bags and was followed by a pathetic child, so starved he was but a little skeleton. Yet, she seemed quite healthy - it seemed to me that she would smash him to dust if she accidentally stepped on him. Before we could see her arrive, we could hear her verbally abusing this tiny victim. "Lazy boy, why don't you walk faster?" As she came into view, I saw her slap him on his tiny arm. The force of the slap was enough to almost knock him over. In response to it, the child began to wail and I could see every bone in his naked chest as he inhaled. As she raised her hand to him again, he ran from my view.

I looked at her with wonder. Hell! She has a lot of meat on her compared to her little child. What the hell was she doing here? Her bags filled up the entire space between the beds. As soon as she took ownership of the bed next to mine, she started working on mounting a curtain to separate our beds. It didn't bother me since I also liked more privacy. She didn't seem to be a very nice person, but this didn't stop me from trying to get to know her quickly in case she had any food in those bags. She introduced herself as 'Amy'.

"Is the child your son?"

"He is the son of my sister, but she died."

"How about the father?"

"He died too."

"He is an orphan."

We were interrupted when the boy came up to us. She asked him, "Did you find anything for me to make a fire?"

"Yes, Auntie." Surprisingly, he came back with a full hand of tiny dead branches. He seemed to know his duty very well. His face showed he had wiped away his tears with his dirty little hand.

"It is not enough, go find some more," she criticized.

"Later, Auntie! I am hungry now." Amazingly, this little boy challenged her authority. He answered in a clear and strong voice, much stronger than his skinny body would have indicated.

"No! Go find it now; otherwise, I won't give you anything to eat." He resisted and without hesitation, she slapped his face. Quickly, he took off again, crying.

"Why do you treat him like this? He is very skinny, very young, and an orphan. Don't you have pity for him? He is your nephew?"

"I do not care; he is a smart-mouth child." I saw her put something in her mouth. She was eating something without sharing with her nephew.

At meal time she said, "Ra! I like you. I have a brother living in the US right now. I will introduce you to him as my new sister-in-law when we are liberated." We laughed together. "Are you married?" she asked.

"Yes, but my husband has disappeared and I fear he has been killed."

"My husband, too," she said. "We are all widows."

"How come you are not skinny? It looks like you have not been starving while we have." I asked.

"The parents of my nephew left me a lot of jewelry after they died. I exchanged it for food."

"Why aren't you nicer to your nephew; he looks very hungry?"

"Fuck him. I wish he would die too. Maybe he won't come back; maybe he will die in the forest." Then the little boy showed up with a bunch of wood. "Good boy, you can eat now. Make sure to go out again and find some for our next meal. If not, don't come back."

I watched him eating happily, paying no attention to what his aunt was saying. Innocently, after finishing his meal, his childish voice assured her, "I will go out again to find more wood." It broke my heart that he assumed she appreciated his good work.

Survival in the Hospital of Death

A rice grinder was located next to "the cemetery hospital". Collecting any rice accidently spilled on the ground could make the difference between life and death for "patients". Of course, it was strictly forbidden and we were told that if we were well enough to go out and pick up grains of rice, we would be judged well enough to return to the fields. Regardless, those who were able would slip out during the daily siesta for the workers and glean every grain we could find. We would hide the grains in secret pockets sewn into our sarongs or in small sacks that we could hide in our clothes.

I was taught to dig a hole in the ground next to my bed and line it with cloth before I ground the grains of rice by hand with a piece of rock. Sometimes, too many patients ground rice at the same time, producing an unusual noise which caught the attention of the teenage attendants who came right away to identify the noise. When this happened, we quickly covered the holes with wood, hid the rice under our pillows and pretended to be asleep. As soon as the girls left for their house, we gave a signal to each other with a fake cough. We ground the rice so it would cook quickly in a little water and supplement our meager rations. We were allowed to boil water so if we had a pot or a little container, we could add the rice flour when no one was looking. This was one more horrible life experience in the "cemetery hospital".

She could be Dangerous

Sometimes, I slipped out of the hospital during the siesta and went to the nearby village. Occasionally, a compassionate person would give me leftover food -not much, just enough to fill my tummy, one day at a time. Even with the extra food I earned, I still couldn't feed my body enough to stay healthy and I gradually deteriorated. I began to have more difficulty walking; soon, even rising to my feet seemed like an enormous effort. At this time, I noticed my feet were swollen when I woke up in the morning and I suffered with serious diarrhea like other patients. My swollen legs and feet always felt cold; the skin was tight and shiny and I could feel the fluid underneath the skin. I knew well that this was an ominous development and sometimes I just wanted to poke my legs with a needle to drain out the unhealthy fluid, but I knew it would be the end of my life if I did such a foolish, unsanitary thing. I felt like I was carrying heavy weights on my legs and I was very slow and had trouble maintaining my balance. Just walking drained all my energy and I had to stop to rest after even a short distance.

Amy still had food so she expended no energy trying to find an extra mouthful. She mostly lay on her bed and watched me and the others who could still walk. One day, after she had ordered the little boy out to find firewood, she got up and called me, "Ra, I have a mirror for you." She handed me a small piece of broken mirror; I didn't know where she got it or what made her think I would need it. She laughed when she gave it to me. I was suspicious because I couldn't imagine what was funny but I was also curious because I hadn't actually seen my reflection for a long time. I could only see a portion of my face at a time but I had to look again and again to make sure I saw myself, not somebody else. My teeth were yellow, my lips were dark and dehydrated, and my hair was thinner and my eyes hollow. I tried to smile at the mirror. It was not the same smile I had before. It was a zombie's smile. I now looked like the dying who could not move from their beds. I looked at my body and realized I looked like a bamboo stick compared to Amy. My dimple had disappeared while both her dimples remained on the corners of her lips. She had plenty of food in her bag and she did not share. I walked like a zombie, while she walked fast and her footsteps were heavy.

As I was still absorbing the shock from the mirror, I was distracted by a child's shriek. Amy's nephew was running off and covering his ears as his aunt chased him. "Fuck you! You steal my food," she yelled at him.

I thought to myself, how could she treat him that way? He is her flesh and blood! This cruel woman chased the boy as if he was her prey. Along the way, she chucked whatever she could get her hands on: rocks, dirt, baskets, and knives. The poor boy ran with all his energy, dodging the projectiles. He pleaded her to stop, "Don't hurt me Auntie!"

But this only angered her further. "Go! Die in the forest!" She panted. The poor boy disappeared for a whole day, but came back next day after lunchtime when Amy had left. He went through the food in her bag and raced away when he had finished eating without even talking to me.

I was crouched next to my bed blowing through a hollow bamboo to encourage my small fire so I could boil water. Suddenly, I heard the fast heavy steps of someone walking toward to my bed. Without warning, I was pushed hard from behind toward the fire. I felt both hands pushing my head down close to the fire. Then a familiar voice threatened to kill me; I knew right away it was Amy. I did not have enough energy to scream and push back at the same time. I tried hard to keep my head away from the fire but I smelled my hair burning. Then she released me; someone else had stopped her and pulled her away from me. I tried to get up but fell back exhausted. I looked at her without saying a word; she was screaming that I had stolen her food. Now I understood the problem. Someone next to her bed explained to her, "I saw your nephew looking in your bag and leaving."

"I will wait for my nephew to make sure he did it. If not, I will kill you." Impatiently, she walked back and forth, in and out, around her bed, but the child did not appear until the next day, around noon. She did not ask him anything, but beat him with a stick until it broke. She then got a string and tried to strangle him. The lady next to her bed screamed at her and pulled her nephew away, "You are stupid to kill a little kid."

"He is my nephew. Leave him to me, I will kill him."

The little nephew cried very hard and called for his dead parents, "Papa, mama, help me."

After she calmed down, she came to apologize to me but it was too late. I had enough of her; I never could trust her again. My friendship with her was never the same. I did not talk to her unless she spoke to me first. I told her, "You do not know me. I would rather die with dignity rather than steal your food."

She laughed and patted my shoulder, "Okay, Okay, my future sister-in-law."

"No! I would never want to be your sister-in-law."

Suspicious Man

Later, there was a new family who moved in next to my bed. So I was in between this new family and heartless, nasty Amy. These newcomers were not sick and had plenty of food every day but they did not share. I wondered where they got it and why they were allowed to stay in the hospital. They all got along very well with the hospital girls. They had adopted one young man who seemed retarded. Every night, the girls played with this guy and teased him. I observed him often and had a feeling there was something peculiar about him. It appeared to me that he faked his disability.

Every night, he came back from somewhere with a bunch of vegetables, perhaps stolen in the dark from someone's garden. At a distance, I noticed that he walked like a normal person. When he approached my bed, he whispered to me to hide his vegetables from the hospital girls. Then he again acted retarded. To confirm my suspicions, I hid some of the vegetables he had begged me to hide for him. When he came back to claim them, he noticed the difference. "Did you take some of my vegetables?" he asked me.

"I thought you were retarded," I answered as I gave him the hostage greens. He just stared at me without answering. Next day, he sat next to my bed. When no one else was paying attention, I whispered, "What is your name?"

"Why do you want to know my name?"

"I am right, you are faking it."

"Shit…. I have to pretend like I am retarded to entertain the KR so I can have an easier life."

"You are smarter than me. I should follow your ploy."

I was serious about doing it, but then, he told me, "It's too late for you. If you don't do it right, you will be killed."

He didn't know he was talking to someone who had tricked the KR a time or two herself.

"Heh....next time when you have vegetables, please share with me. I am hungry too and will hide them for you again. Also I won't disclose your secret to *Angkar*." He did not answer but the next day he shared vegetables that he had hidden behind his back.

I had now been in the revolutionary hospital for three months. During that time, I heard more rumors about the war between Vietnam and KR. I heard people in the hospital worrying about our lives after an attack by Vietnam. We might be killed during the attack or executed by *Bo Doy* (the Vietnamese soldiers). Another rumor was that the KR had prepared a huge hole to bury us alive. This rumor spread quickly among the patients saying. "We are all going to be buried alive by KR. No one will be left behind."

"They want to get rid of all the Cambodian people, especially the men and bring Vietnamese or Chinese men to the Cambodian women survivors, so that the kids in next generation will have no full Cambodian blood. This is the way Vietnam and China want to eliminate our land and our culture from the map just like the people of Champa and Khmer Mon, who now live only in history." Amy gave me this explanation, hoping she could kiss my ass, as she had heard me express this view before.

I did not care about the rumors. I told people in the hospital that if we go to the water there will be a crocodile that will try to kill us; coming back, we will have to look out for the tiger. We will die either way, why should we worry?

PART V

DEFEAT OF THE KHMER ROUGE

In 1979, the KR government fell when the North Vietnamese invaded and occupied the country. Pol Pot and his allies fled to southwestern Cambodia and engaged in guerilla warfare against the new Vietnamese-backed government, while *Samdech* Sihanouk fled once again into exile in China.

~TWENTY NINE~

NOTHING LEFT

One morning, like every morning, everyone woke up, washed their faces and waited for the rice soup distribution at 10 AM. I still lay on the bamboo bed since I was thinking about a new plan to fill my stomach for today. I looked at the ceiling and thought about what I could do to have vegetables with my rice soup. My body felt like I was carrying a big heavy rock this morning, even heavier than yesterday and the days before. It was a struggle to move. I looked down at my legs; they were swollen. Swollen legs were the sign of final stage of starvation. If the swelling continued up the whole body and face, death was next. I tried very hard to get my energy together and rise from the bed. I had fought with starvation for four years; I wasn't going to give up now. I told to myself, "I have to survive!" I set out my aluminum bowl and spoon ready for the hospital girls to come out to give us one scoop of rice soup. Time passed and everybody was still waiting and waiting.......

"What happened to the hospital girls?" It was the voice of a Malaysian lady across from my bed. This lady was still relatively healthy. She was here to take care of her husband who had problems with swollen legs like me and others. The wife was healthy because she knew how to fish and then traded the fish for other food which she cooked next to her husband's bed. She walked outside towards the hospital girls' house. "There is no one here!" she shouted from a distance.

"What has happened? Why is it so quiet?" another lady asked, worriedly.

"I usually see the girls up early to water the vegetables but now the kitchen is quiet and I do not see anybody there," said the Malaysian lady as she walked toward us.

Suddenly, the guy who was faking being retarded appeared with two live ducks in his hand. He loudly announced, "All the communist girls disappeared last night and KR are running away before the Vietnamese troops arrive."

The lady next to my bed shouted, "Are we liberated?"

Could it be? Was it possible? About the same time people that I recognized from my village began to appear on the road in front of the hospital with bags on their shoulders. They carried infants and small children. They were rushing to reach the national road about one hundred yards away from the hospital. They shouted at us to leave as soon as possible because, "If you delay you might be killed by the KR, they have a big hole ready to receive your bodies."

Zombies Walk Out of the Nightmare

It was a miracle! Oh, *Mon Dieu!* Were we dreaming? We all hugged each other and wept tears of joy. "Everyone, let's go home!" my neighbors exclaimed.

"Ra! We can go home!" Amy jumped with excitement.

"I'm going home!" I used what little energy I had to try to jump with joy but I could not.

For a few moments, I hesitated to leave because I was felt like I was leaving Papa. But, another part of my heart wanted to rush out so I could look for my husband everywhere on the way back home to Phnom Penh. I was surprised when a little finger touched me from behind and a little voice said, *"Baung,* I want to go with you too. I have nobody. I am orphan."

It was a tiny girl about 10 years old. She smiled at me showing her yellow teeth and dried lips. She was giggling to show her shyness. "Is it you? I have observed you for a long time. You are cute and smart," I said to her.

"If you let me follow you, I will be helpful with finding fish and cooking rice for you. Also I can help you with carrying your stuff."

"All right, now I have a friend and will not be lonely. What is your name?"

She was giggling again and swaying from side to side, "Leung!"

I knew very little about her only that she had stopped by my bed a couple of times when she was hungry and I shared food with her. She used to help me by watching out for the hospital girls while I was grinding the rice. The reason I did not know her better was that she was like a butterfly, flitting in and out. I only saw her when she was hungry; when she had special food from somewhere she ignored me. Sometimes, she disappeared from the bed for a couple days; there was no one who seemed to care about losing her. Sometimes she returned to the hospital in a bad mood.

I tied up the clothes bag and put it in a basket with couple of light aluminum dishes and my Le Crucet pot. Little Leung carried a small sack of rice that we stole from the rice grinder. She combined it with her few possessions and carried it on her head. Amy, the mean aunty, had many more things to carry, but it was okay as she was bigger and stronger than any of us. She, too, put all in a big sack which she carried on her head.

We moved out into the stream of people flowing away from the village onto the national road. This road had been forbidden to us and silent for four years; now, this morning it became noisy, filled with the survivors - children, parents, the widowed, and teenagers. They were leaving the Prison Without Walls. Still afraid and uncertain, our frustration and sadness mixed with happiness, all the new people rushed as quickly as we could to get out. No elderly walked back home with us because they all, like Papa, rested in the forest. No "Old people" were on the road, because they did not have a life, a home, or someone waiting for them in the city. They belonged to the village.

Am I really, really free today? Did I just wake up from a nightmare? I touched my body and looked at myself in the little broken piece of mirror again. It gradually became real that I was still alive. How did I survive until today? That was another miracle. God must have known that I was not ready to go yet. I knew I had more to accomplish in my life. I had lived in the darkness for four years, now I had a future. My heart that had been dried out with disappointment, hopelessness, fear, depression and sorrow now filled with a new emotion. I did not know how to describe it. It was not excitement, but more like awakening from a nightmare. When I looked back, I saw only hurt and loneliness so my feet needed to move, to walk away from the bloody well of death. This tiny bit of courage helped me to move forward, to keep moving and moving as far as I could, because this place reminded me of the tragic lives of the "New People", the death of my family, pain, sorrow, tears, hunger, hate, fighting, and anger.

I held my Papa's *krama* to send him a message that I missed him and how I agonized that I had not been able to help him fight with death. I put the handkerchief that I used to cover his face after his last breath in my pocket. These few mementos gave me courage and hope; they made me feel protected as I went to find a new life. I wished I knew what my Papa had been trying to say as he lay dying and I told him to save his strength instead of talking. That wisdom had disappeared and gone with him; what last advice would he have had for me?

Now my tears came down in a waterfall, tears that had been hidden for years in a mind occupied only with hunger and sickness and survival. My thoughts raced and tumbled in my head. The nocturnal birds and foxes that came to scare me every night won't exist anymore because I am going to live in the city. I am not going to sleep on a bed of bamboo covered with a cow's mosquito net anymore. I am not going to hear the frogs happily singing with the raindrops as I grieve for my Papa. I won't have to see all the things that remind me of Papa's death - the muddy ground, and the scattered leaves, and the forest where my Papa was buried and eaten by the foxes. I would no longer have to fear the darkness knowing it hid the KR spies listening to our conversation, looking for information to cause our deaths. Darkness was the time when KR came for the new people, escorted them to the forest and executed them. It was the time when shovels, axes, and bamboo rods, which should be tools to help us, instead were used to kill us. Today, from now on, I am not going to hear anymore the stupid Khmer communist songs singing about the victory of the April 1975, and the power of *Angkar*. "This is real sunshine......I AM FREE...

I did not know how long I walked lost in my thoughts, but the voice of Amy shouting at her tiny nephew brought me back to reality, "Hurry, lazy, you walk too slowly. I will leave you here."

Because both the children and I were so weak, we had to take frequent rests and sat at the edge of the road. "How do we know which way to go?" I asked Amy.

"Just follow the crowd," she said.

"To your left is Siem Reap province, to your right is Kampong Thom," came a voice from behind us. "I choose to go left, because it can lead me to Battambang province, then straight to the Thai border. I have no more interest in living in Cambodia. It is too painful to be the only who walks back home surviving the cruel regime of Pol Pot. The other eight of my family members died in the jungle like animals."

"Me too, I want to go to Siem Reap and cross the Thai border if possible." Amy said. "What month were we liberated, Ra?"

"Do I have a calendar with me?" She laughed. She then came close to me trying to grasp both my ears with excitement. I stopped her because I was still afraid she might try to kill me again. "I think it is November or December because it is kind of cold and windy in the early morning." I said.

"It is hot now. I am exhausted and thirsty," she said. "Nothing to drink here except the dirty water which fills the cow tracks after the rain. Are you going to use that water?"

"No, I am liberated now. I do not want to die from drinking this dirty water," I muttered.

"We can stop right here to cook rice, I am hungry now," I said. My little girl went down to the muddy ditch to catch fish. I asked her how she knew fish were there.

"Sister, fish live in that muddy water. I will splash the water out to the other side to make it easy to catch the fish."

"OK, I trust you. Go find a little branch for me to make a fire."

Amy ordered her nephew to go with Leung to catch fish, but he hesitated. She got angry and smacked him on the shoulder. "Aunty, you are hurting me, you are mean," he cried.

She insulted him again, "You eat my rice for nothing. You are lazy!"

A half-hour later, my little girl came back with a big smile. Four years of starvation and neglect were evident in her wasted body and yellow teeth but she glowed with pride as she gave me the little fish she caught. This made Amy jealous and angry again. She got up and hit the little boy again, "You are worth nothing!"

After eating, we continued our trek; the weather became extremely hot and humid. The crowd moved faster than we did, as my little orphan and I were very weak and slow, leaving only four of us on the road as the day passed. Once in a while, a military truck drove by and waved a flag at us. We waved back to them to show our gratitude to them for saving our lives. We weren't sure who they were but there were not KR. "It looks to me like they are *Bo Doy* in those trucks, did you see them?" I asked Amy.

"It may be. Maybe they chased the Communists away?"

I was too tired to think or answer. I looked at the children and said, "Amy, "Your nephew is tired."

She yelled at him instead of showing him any compassion, "Stupid boy, walk faster, or I will abandon you." She stopped and waited for me to catch up to her. "He has nothing to carry, but he is slow and lazy," she said. I didn't even try to reason with her; she was a miserable person.

We walked until dark, and then stopped where a group of men, women and children camped on the roadside. I heard a man tell his life story to his neighbor and felt sorry for his loneliness. Miserably, he died that night after eating; it could have been from overeating. The next morning, we saw a long line of military trucks with soldiers wearing the same uniforms that we saw the day before, driving from the direction of Kampong Thom toward Siem Reap province, the same direction we were going. Our fellow travelers told us these soldiers were Vietnamese; they all wore khaki uniforms with a white handkerchief underneath their hats. The soldiers appeared happy and excited and waved to us

We rejoined the stream of refugees and moved on. Unexpectedly, I saw a woman I recognized walking rapidly against the tide of survivors. It was Pheap, the *yotear* KR that I had slept next to in the labor camp. She had been punished because she violated the *Angkar*'s rule. I saw her walking as if being chased, and called to her, "*Samak Mit* Pheap, why do you look so nervous? Do you want to come with us? Don't you want to live in the city with us?"

Hearing me, she stopped and smiled, "I know where I want to go. I have to hurry. You!" she pointed at me, "leave quickly as there is a battle ahead of you between the KR and the Vietnamese." She then hurried away.

"What did she say?" I asked Amy. "Did you hear what she just said?"

"I don't believe it," Amy replied, but we moved faster.

"It could be true, that's probably where the soldiers are going."

"What should we do?" Keep moving forward or walk back to the village?" Amy asked hesitantly.

"We need to keep moving forward. If we are caught by the KR, we will stay with them and die. But, if we are not caught, then we will arrive home. I am not going to take one step backward," I made my own decision and started to lead Amy. The crowd that was walking behind us kept us moving forward and then passed us.

"Hurry, Ra!" Amy pushed me. "Move your legs faster, dummy," she said to her little nephew.

"Come on, hurry up," my little girl smiled at me.

"I've run out of energy now. My legs cannot move anymore," I said desperately. We decided to rest for few hours, sleeping on the ground, and then got up to follow the crowd before we lost them again. My little orphan girl was stronger than me, with a smile on her swollen face; she encouraged me to move forward. I teased her, "Where do you want to go, little Leung?"

She smiled and said, "I will follow you."

"Do you want to live in the city?"

"*Chah.*" She was giggling and swaying.

My Little Friend Followed me

Especially frightening along the road were the many dead bodies; I did not want to look at them or remember them, for fear they would haunt my dreams. My little orphan looked at, and then described, the ugly shape of one dead body. I stopped her with a little smack on the cheek, "It is not nice to say such things." Some still looked bloated so I knew they had died recently. At first I thought it was a dead animal, round and brown, but as soon as I got closer it clearly was a human body. I covered my nose with my scarf.

"It is a corpse, sister," said Leung.

I said, "Do not tell me more, or I won't be able to eat lunch today."

I was startled by a shout from Amy, "Ra! I lost my little nephew." She called for him and asked people around us to send him to her when they found him. Now, she was crying, feeling sorry for losing him, "Maybe he could not follow me, because we walked too fast without checking on him," she was mumbling.

"You never treated him nicely, maybe he followed somebody else after the last time you smacked him so hard."

"He did not know that I still love him. I did not do this on purpose."

"We don't know when we lost him," I said.

"We cannot wait for him; we have to keep moving, hoping we will catch him, maybe at the front of the line. Hurry!" she replied.

"He may still be in the back of the line. I remember at the last stop you threatened to make him carry a big bag. How would he dare follow you?"

"No! He may have disappeared on purpose. Oh! God! He warned me lately that he wouldn't follow me. He hates me. I did not believe that a little boy like him could become brave enough to leave me."

"You never had children of your own, that's why you did not have a good heart to raise him."

"You are not better than me, Ra! I saw you slap your little orphan too."

"Yes, but she is still following me, see. This means I am bad?"

Then she turned to talk to my little orphan, "Leung, come live with me."

"No, you are mean to your nephew," Leung answered with a smile.

"See, I am right."

"Ra is mean to you, too"

"Yes, right, I remember you tried to kill me in the hospital, you are a cruel woman!" I had enough of her.

"I like you, sister-in-law. I will tell my brother to sponsor you to the US as soon as we get back home."

"I do not want to be part of your family. I never liked you anyway and I do not want you to follow me." She did not care what I said; she still kept calling me sister-in-law along the road.

On the second night, we were encouraged to slow down by the people who were walking in the opposite direction. They told us the KR resistance was in front of us. They said the KR lost the battle with Vietnamese and then escaped to the jungle. The KR resistance fighters were capturing and coercing both new and old people to follow them.

"Oh! It is scary; I do not want to go back to living with them anymore. We lived miserably for four years," I worried. "If they come out of the forest, they will catch us and force us to follow them."

"Do not be scared, dear." Amy encouraged me.

"I am scared too," my little orphan said. We decided to spend the night in the middle of the road with the others. The next morning we decided to keep walking forward, but a little faster with only short stops. Finally we arrived at a river, where we found many people arriving from different directions.

"We made our trip safe, finally!!" said Amy.

Instead of agreeing with Amy, I chose to talk to my little Leung who always waited for my decision. "Find a shady place to rest, I am tired and hungry," I said to Leung.

We found a shady place next to a brick house where we all sat on the ground. I sat on my sandals to protect my behind which was just skin and bones. Amy had a large piece of fabric to lie on the ground and she untied her bag to sort out her dried food. She was not just mean, but also selfish. When she ate, she acted like she was a stranger. She talked to me only when she had finished her meal. The loss of her nephew did not seem to worry her at all. I wondered what she had in her two big bags of black fabric, one that she never opened. It appeared to me that she had lots of dried food but she never told me how she obtained it. I remembered she told me she had inherited all her sister's jewelry; I wished I had the same skill to keep mine. As I thought about the lost jewelry, I realized that I should learn a big lesson from the loss. I never believed Papa's advice telling me to not trust my mother-in-law. Now, I blamed myself for being too naive, passive, and quiet with my in-laws. Why had this family changed my personality? I used to be smart, assertive, and talkative, but not with this family.

Suddenly, Amy interrupted my thinking, asking me how we could get to Phnom Penh.

"If I go, you are not going with me." I said.

Ignoring my last statement, she said, "Do you know Ra? We have walked safely for three days and three nights?"

"Yes, we are so lucky to be here safe," I agreed, looking for Leung, who had gone down to the river to try to catch a fish.

"You are so lucky to have a country girl with you who can fish," Amy said enviously.

"I do not know how long she will want to stay with me," I responded, with no interest in talking to her about Leung.

Is my Husband Alive?

I was thinking about my Papa and my husband - if they were here, they would join me for a meal. Why didn't Papa wait for another year so he would have been safe and walk home with me? I hid my tears in his *krama*; I felt he was with me everywhere I went. I could feel him when I touched his scarf. As I thought deeply about my Papa, something caught my eye on the other side of the river. There was a man wearing shorts that I recognized. Who was wearing my husband's shorts, brown plaid shorts? He was walking fast and disappeared into the crowd of people. Could my husband be alive? I went to edge of the river and called his name twice but no one answered. I ran along the river to catch the man as I believed it might be my dear husband, but there was no sign of him and I couldn't cross the river. I stopped and took a deep breath, "Huh...if I cannot find him here, I will find him in Phnom Penh." I told myself to be patient.

Now my imagination started running wild. What if my husband had a new family, what should I do? Will he come back to me? Will I accept him and his family? The answer was not quite clear, what I would do? Yes, I still want him back and will love his children as my own. Or no, I will leave him alone with his new family, but......Oh! I do not know what I would do.

Then I began to worry about the money Papa hid at our house. My husband knew where Papa buried the suitcase; maybe he would take Papa's money and cross the border to Thailand. I don't remember the hiding place; what should I do? The only other person who knew the hiding place was *Pou* Sunthary, but little unfortunately, my little uncle was gone, too.

Meeting a Princess

As we rested in the shade, I saw a lady in her mid-forties walking toward me. She had one leg shorter than the other and walked with a cane. A second woman walked behind her, carrying her luggage and acting like her servant. A small girl trailed along behind them, whining and complaining. The older lady approached me and sat down by me and we introduced ourselves to each other, including Amy. Judging from her cultured language, she came from a high-class family, she told me she was a cousin of *Samdech* Sihanook. So, she was a princess. I felt confident to share my family background with her. After listening to me, she said that she had guessed right that I must have been belonged to a high class family. She said, "Ra, stay with me, I am single and lonely; I will adopt you as my stepdaughter."

At that point, I had no idea how I would survive the trip on foot to Phnom Penh and my rice supply was almost exhausted, so she seemed like a gift from God. I readily agreed and called her "Auntie Princess." She told me that she wanted me to take care of her luggage as she had something very important in it. I thought that it was very curious that she could have kept nice luggage for four years without any trouble from the communists. But, by courtesy, I could not be nosy and ask the questions in my mind.

It was very comforting for us to sleep in a familiar group with her, the small girl and her mother, Pheun. I learned that Pheun served the princess by scavenging rice and greens from the fields and cooking. Thankfully, Amy met her youngest sister's family and went to stay with them. I was glad to see what I hoped was the last of her. Her nephew never resurfaced and I prayed he had found some compassionate people to travel with. There were many unaccompanied little children like Leung who were alone in the world and struggled each day to live.

~THIRTY~

HOMELESS WOMAN

With no other way to find food, people fought and killed over what remained in the food storage abandoned by the KR. The strongest fighter won and carried off the sacks of rice. He could eat all he wanted and trade the rest for gold. Auntie Princess traded her jewelry to buy rice to feed us. People were desperate and began to prey upon each other. Robberies, killings, and shootings began.

The *Bo Doy* provided what little security there was but they were mainly interested in finding any KR that might be hiding among us or in the surrounding area. At first, the real KR were arrested, but later, innocent people were accused by neighbors of being KR due to the fights over food and other jealousies. It became harder to prove who was or wasn't KR, and soon the makeshift prisons brimmed with both the good and bad people. The place we were staying became crowded with people from different ethnic groups and many parts of the country.

Somehow Auntie Princess was able to move us to an abandoned brick office. There was no door; it had been used for firewood, but it provided more shelter than most people had. Every day, Princess walked around the encampment, visited people she knew friends, and made friends with newcomers. Meals were cooked by Pheun and her little daughter. I accepted my duty by watching her luggage carefully; I never left unless the princess was there herself. After a while, Auntie Princess began to complain, "I don't have enough jewelry to buy rice for everybody." She waved her hand at me. "You! Get up and find food or I will not support you anymore."

I understood her dilemma and obeyed even if I didn't want to. Pheun, her daughter and I went to the rice fields and collected all the grains we could find, but the princess wasn't pleased with our paltry results. After being berated for our inadequacies, I spoke to Pheun, "Hell, I cannot believe how she has changed to a different person."

"I don't know how to make her happy. I cook, I provide water for her bath, and I collect food and firewood. I do everything for her; she acts like a queen."

"Are you really her servant?" I asked.

"No, after liberation she asked me to follow her. She told me that when she arrived in the city, she would provide everything for us." Pheun turned around to pat her daughter's head. "My daughter is treated like a servant, too."

"Do you like Auntie?"

"She was very nice in the beginning."

"Would you stay with her forever, even though you feel mistreated?"

"For my daughter's sake, I want to live in the city. I want her to get a better education and marry a city man. Life is nothing on the farm."

From that day, my duty to watch her luggage was lifted. She made me another one of her servants and ordered me sleep outside. In my spare time, I walked from one family to another trying to find someone I knew, or a member of my family, so I could leave the princess. But I found only unknown faces.

I Sweated Over an Open Fire to Serve People

I soon heard from other survivors that we were camped quite close to Angkor Wat. I was surprised as I had never seen on a map where the labor camps and the village where I lived were.

About a month later, a market was set up, but we still used rice as currency. The merchants sold meat, vegetables, dessert and fabrics, like a real market. Once the market opened, Auntie Princess became more cautious about her rice cache. She worried that we might steal her rice to trade for a dessert or something else from the market. She was especially suspicious of me as I was skinnier and hungrier than the others. My little orphan, who had followed me from the village, sometimes stayed with me, depending on her mood. She wandered around stealing food from people, especially from Amy, who settled next to our house much to my disgust. Everyone called my little orphan my stepdaughter. One day, she stole beef jerky that Auntie Princess had left to dehydrate on the roof. Knowing I would be blamed and punished, I became so angry that I beat Leung. She then left me and I never saw the little orphan girl again.

Auntie Princess taught me to make a special dessert. She bought gluten rice and showed me how to cook it just right. She then rolled it like meatballs but bigger. She explained how to sprinkle yeast powder on the rice balls, and then keep them fermenting for three days in a covered pot, my Le Creucet pot. I checked it at least twice a day because I wanted to know how the fermentation process worked from beginning to end. The smell tickled my nose on the third day. She ordered me to check if it was ready, so I ate one piece. Her eyebrows pulled together, "I said to taste, not eat it."

"It's sweet and delicious," I said, as I enjoyed the wonderful treat. I expected she would give me more, since I was the one who made it, but more guests and friends of the princess kept coming in as lunchtime approached. "Damn, they are going to eat all the rice and then all the dessert I made," I worried and I was right. The rice was gone. She told us to cook more. "They're going to eat the beef jerky, too." She kept giving them more because she was crazy about their compliments on the food. But I was the one who worked very hard in the house. Why did I get less than guests? I tried to drag out eating my rice, hoping Auntie Princess would distribute one more piece of jerky.

"You eat too much rice," she said

"I'm just slow."

"Eating slow is eating more."

Finally, she told me to take out the dessert and serve a piece of fermented rice ball to each guest.

Nothing was left for me. I wanted to kick her. Now my duty was to clean the dishes with only the smell of the dessert left to tease me. I couldn't stop the tears from coming. Pheun wrapped an arm around my shoulders, "Don't cry, Ra! I didn't get any either. She is mean."

A couple of days later, newcomers joined the princess's family - a woman and her son. The woman was talkative and very smart, tiny at five feet tall, skinny, with dark skin and surprisingly big hands and feet. She had naturally curly hair, big lips and a mole on her cheek. Her son, Chroch, was about six years old, skinny and small, due to malnutrition. She told me she originated from Kampot province, and was what we called "Black Chinese". In the city, Black Chinese had a reputation as smart, mouthy people who were good with business matters. This lady did not like me from the beginning and only spoke to me when she had a criticism. Soon, she became a favorite of the princess. She didn't talk a lot but was a big screamer. Nobody knew this new woman's name. We called her "Chroch's Mom", which was respectful in our culture.

~THIRTY ONE~

DEMOTED ME TO SERVANT

As soon as Chroch's Mom joined us, Pheun lost hope that the princess would take care of her and her daughter because Chroch's Mom took her place. Pheun and her daughter decided to leave; she found a man she felt she could depend on despite the fact that she had only known him one week! A week made her feel comfortable enough to be his wife without the benefit of a wedding ceremony. I said it was a good idea to find someone who loves you now, rather than staying with the princess who was obviously just using all of us. Unfortunately, with Pheun's departure, I now became the target whenever the princess was displeased.

Auntie Princess decided to start a small business making and selling a popular Cambodian dessert, "Banh Chnoek", in the market. Refugees who had survived on rice soup were hungry for any sweets and would trade rice for them. Then she announced that I would sell the dessert in the market.

"I don't know how to sell in a market," was my horrified reaction but this response didn't save me from what I perceived to be a great humiliation.

"If you want to eat, you will do it. Now!"

Shit. This woman was ruthless. Sending me to the market to sit on the gravel, selling desserts? What if my friends, my relatives see me? To what face can I change? This is so humiliating. Why doesn't she send Chroch's Mom? Her face, her skin, her voice, her accent are perfect for this job. Why did she choose me? I was about ready to walk away from this Auntie Princess that day, but my next thought stopped me, "Maybe this will be a good opportunity to search for my husband in case he is still alive, or at least, I may meet relatives who will take me away from this princess. OK, Auntie Princess devil, I accept your job offer, but not for the reason you think but because I am taking advantage of the opportunity to find a way to get away from you.

Banh Chnoek is made with gluten rice powder, coconut milk, sesame seeds, and cooked beans that have been mashed like mashed potatoes. She shredded the coconut and extracted the milk four times over the course of several hours, adding a little water to the squeezed coconut each time. She set aside the first extraction. In the meantime, she cooked the beans, mashed them and rolled the mash into small balls. She made a paste with gluten rice powder and rolled the bean balls in the paste. The balls were then cooked in boiling water. In a different pot, she brought the coconut milk to a boil and transferred the balls to the boiling milk. She added a piece of smashed ginger and some palm sugar as well as a pinch of salt. When done, she ground sesame seeds and sprinkled them over the top.

"The dessert is made," she said. "All you have to do is sit in the market selling it. You will be helped by her boy," she pointed her finger at Chroch.

I agreed, thinking I would have some dessert when I was away from her. At 7 AM, I was given a big container filled with the rice balls and another smaller container of the first extraction of the coconut milk, which was the richest. She counted the balls and instructed me, "Sell four balls for one can of rice. I have forty gluten balls, so that should earn ten cans of rice."

I peeked inside the container. "How about the one that is broken. Did you count it? I bet the customers won't want it." She said if the customer didn't want it, then I could have it.

Genocide Survivors

The market was just an open field where merchants laid out their wares on the ground. It filled up between 7 AM and 10 AM, when all the vendors flocked in looking for the best spot to sell their wares on both sides of the road. They would spread a little thin *krama* or worn cloth on the gravel to display their goods. As there were no aisles to separate the merchandise, vegetables, meat, desserts, and items like laundry soap and *sarong batik* were spread willy-nilly with no particular plan. They were spaced well enough for shoppers to walk between looking for what they needed.

The heat was relentless and the lack of security made it necessary for everyone to be constantly vigilant for thieves and robbers. Shoppers, refugees as well as uniformed *Bo Doy*, wandered around looking for a good deal. Khmer shoppers insistently bargained for the best prices while sellers stayed firm. Despite their experiences of the last few years, it did not appear that either buyers or sellers had learned humility. Fights would break out when they could not agree. The frustrated buyer would yell, "Burglar. Go to Hell! I rather give money to a beggar than to give it to YOU!!"

"Who cares?" the seller would scream back. "I would rather feed it to the dogs than sell it to you."

However, when an agreement between the seller and buyer was met, the amount of rice was calculated in 16 ounce cans, like those used for condensed milk. Money had been replaced with rice. Each buyer carried a bag containing rice and a can when going shopping. The richer buyers carried gold to buy *sarongs batik* and other sundry items. The most popular place in the market was the place that sold stereos. People of all ages would stand around listening to the loud music. No one had heard anything but the revolutionary music forced upon them for four years. To compete with other stereo sellers, each turned up the volume trying to drown out their competition. It was a cacophony but it was wonderful to hear music again. Next to each vendor was a place for his wife or whoever was the cashier; they had small scales in little boxes to weigh gold when it was offered in payment. Buyers with gold had an air of superiority, as they were richer than the rest of us. Not many people shopping in the market had gold to pay for what they wanted. Everyone had to be extra cautious about thieves.

Watches! They sold watches! There were many watch vendors and each had many watches securely strung together and worn around their neck like a giant necklace. It did seem to weigh them down but they didn't have to worry about thieves and the vendors could walk around approaching people as they shopped. Rice was sold in big sacks.

And then there were the small, poor sellers like me, no different from other dessert sellers, paid only with rice. No one paid gold for my little desserts so I didn't have to worry about thieves either. If one appeared, I just hoped they wouldn't knock over my pot. I wanted some of those rice balls for myself. I had only one bowl and it was dipped in a small container of water after each customer ate from it, and then used for the next customer. Nobody complained and nobody seemed concerned about sanitation. It was much better than during the Genocide and people were grateful they were fortunate enough to have survived to be able to enjoy any dessert at all.

A lady sitting next to me begged the customers to buy her dessert; in my heart, I begged them to not buy mine so I could have them all for myself. Unfortunately, I came home with nothing left. This motivated the princess to send me to the market every day. She became greedy and increased the number of *Banh Chnoek*. The greedier she got, the harder we had to work. The harder she had to work, the bitchier and stricter she became.

I had to come up with an idea to have some of the dessert for myself. One day when I arrived at the market, my regular place was taken by a woman selling durian, mangoosteen and rambootan. Fortunately, when she saw me looking lost and hesitant, she offered me a small place next to her. She then asked to buy a dessert from me, "I will be your first customer and bring you good feng shui. How much does it cost?"

I smiled and put down my pot, "For your good feng shui, it is three pieces for only one can of rice. I'm sorry that I cannot also bring you good feng shui, but I have nothing in my pockets to buy fruit. The best I can do is to enjoy the fragrance of your tropical fruit, especially durian."

"Will the smell make you too hungry for my fruit?"

"Nah! I am OK with just the smell. I have controlled my appetite for four years; I can survive without durian." She laughed and put her arm on her forehead to cover her face from the blazing sun.

As she brought her arm back down to arrange the fruit, the reflection of her watch shone on my face, momentarily blinding me. She had a watch. I had none. I had exchanged my Omega watch for a chicken and malaria pills to try to keep my Papa alive. I looked at my empty wrist with sorrow for not being able to save Papa. I then looked down to the pot of desserts and realized that I needed to transfer three balls to the small bowl for my new neighbor. Of course, Princess had told me to exchange four balls for a can of rice but this lady had not even tried to bargain when I said three balls. The excitement of saving one ball for myself made me forget my troubles momentarily.

I Sell and I Eat because I am Hungry

I'd been dreaming about eating delicious dessert for four years, but how could I eat it with Chroch watching me all the time? Maybe I could trick him. I pretended to be surprised that I had left another small container home and told him to run back to get it. He ran fast but he was not as fast as I was. I opened the pot and enjoyed one of the rice balls. The boy came back quickly to tell me the small container was nowhere to be found and I then "discovered" it under my *krama*. I then continued to sell three balls for one can of rice. I sold enough to earn ten cans of rice and then prepared to eat the rest! But then I felt sorry for Chroch; I called him and offered him a piece.

"Do not tell the princess, okay?"

He ate it without saying anything. When I got back home, the princess stormed over to me. "The boy reported you have stolen the desserts."

"Only the broken ones I could not sell; you promised I could eat them. I have brought back all the payment you expected," I answered as I handed her the rice.

"You are very smart, Ra!" She said staring at me, narrowing her suspicious eyes to small slits.

When she turned away from me, I went outside to find Chroch, who was hiding behind a tree. I caught him by the shirt before he could run away and exclaimed, "You are a moron! Did she give you anything for reporting on me? I was doing you a favor. I won't give you anything next time. You are stupid and you deserve nothing."

I went to talk to his mom later, "I do not understand why you guys keep spying on me. Does she pay you extra? We are all in the same boat, she orders us around like we are slaves. Why don't we help each other?"

"I understand, Ra! I don't think it's a good idea to spy on you, but since she provides us food, I have to do as she asks."

"Before you got here, she treated me the way she treats you now. She told you to spy on me, right? Before you came, there was a family of two, Pheun and her daughter, who had served the princess for a month. Both of them were treated well before I came, and then treated poorly after I arrived. Now, you have taken my place; I have become Pheun. The pattern will continue after I leave the princess. Get the picture?"

At this point she cried rather than answering. I revealed the truth about my family and my background. She said, "I agreed with the princess that you were a bad person before, but now I know you have a good heart."

"You know that the princess uses us as her servants. I will not be living with her for the rest of my life. As soon as I find a job in the hospital or maybe meet my relatives, I will leave her because I have lost all confidence and trust in her."

Days and days passed. Auntie Princess continued to make dessert for me to sell in the market, and I used the time to look for anyone familiar. Chroch helped me bring water from the well for cooking and washing dishes. Chroch's Mom helped with cooking as the princess started to invite more guests for lunch and dinner. I wondered what her game was. I still didn't know what was in the luggage or how she managed to retain all her belongings through four years of the KR.

I continued to look for a better situation for myself. Pheun still came back and forth when necessary, to help with the cooking. Amy was still next to our house with her younger sisters' families. They stayed in the open air next to us, doing nothing every day except eating and sleeping. This gave them plenty of time to watch me serving the princess which humiliated me. Over time, Princess got too lazy to get up early and make the rice balls. God blessed me! Papa saved me! I won't need to sit on the ground selling dessert any more.

Le Grand Hotel Fourteen Years Ago

But I rejoiced too soon. Auntie Princess came up with a new idea of sending me to Angkor Wat to purchase food from the peasants who brought it in from nearby districts and then re-sell at our camp to make a profit. Now I had to leave not at 7 AM but at 5 AM to arrive before the merchants who came from around Angkor Wat or other districts near Siem Reap. This business was "first come, first served." If we were late, all the merchandise was sold to somebody else.

Chroch's Mom and her son were sent along with me. They carried a big sack of rice that we were to use as currency. I carried nothing because I was so weak and skinny. Once in a while, I would glance at Chroch's Mom who walked quickly without saying a word. Chroch kept running behind his mother, sometimes, he ran faster to pass her and then ran around her laughing.

"*Ah* Chroch!" she yelled, "I am not playing with you."

Chroch teased her, "*Mehr*, you too slow because you have short legs."

His mother stopped and bent down to pick up a little gravel which she threw at him. "I don't have time to play with you. I am worried that we may not catch the merchants. Keep away from me." She kept her eyes on the road to make sure we were going in the right direction. I just followed her like a little baby duck following a mother duck, until we hit the main road.

As soon as we were on the main road, a familiar building, Le Grand Hotel, appeared in front of me. My mouth fell open and I stopped dead in my tracks. My heart began beating so hard, it shook my entire body. This was the luxurious and famous hotel where Papa, Stepmother and I had stayed about fourteen years earlier. I began to tremble and I could hear my heart beating in my ears. Tears burst from my eyes like an ocean wave hitting the shore in a tsunami. Memories rushed back with the flood of tears. They filled my heart with a mixture of memories, ending with pain, hurt, and loneliness.

I was stunned with the change in the magnificent Le Grand Hotel. The once immaculately landscaped gardens in front of the hotel were overgrown with knee-high, pale yellow grass. The faded hotel stood alone, quiet and empty.

I looked down at myself. I saw a dirty, worn out *sampot hol* with many patches. My long-sleeved blouse also had many patches. This was the outfit I had worn constantly for what now seemed like a lifetime. Like the hotel, I was a pale and faded ghost of my former self. Like the hotel, my fortunes had completely reversed.

"Why do you stop? And why are you crying?" asked my companion.

I stared at her through my tears, "What? This is the ….." I couldn't finish the sentence because I couldn't believe my eyes; I had thought I would come back to this place again to relive my memories of Papa, but not now, not like this. "Let's wait for the merchants under these big trees," I said.

Against my will, I could not keep myself from staring at the hotel. When I was a teenager, I had walked under these *romdoul* trees and enjoyed their shade as a visitor to Angkor Wat. The trees were now in bloom. I closed my eyes and deeply breathed in their unique fragrance. I felt lightheaded, and in that moment, I was back with my family again, with Papa and Stepmother, feeling like a princess, as Papa had wanted when he brought us here. He had wanted us to feel like royalty and be treated like royalty. I had, and Papa had been a king in this famous Le Grand Hotel.

"What are you doing? Are you asleep?" Chroch asked, jolting me from my memories.

I looked again at the hotel. Everything had changed. I had changed – now a ragged orphan walking along the road instead of a princess riding in a fancy car. I had once slept here in a clean bed with white sheets, and now I slept on the ground covered with a little piece of cloth and Papa's *krama*. Papa had brought me to a dining room where we were served delicious food on an immaculate table, where waiters and maître d's attended to our every whim. Back then, many bellmen greeted us by opening our car doors and bringing our luggage to our room. Now I sweated over an open fire to serve strangers in order to keep on living.

Think Smart - Act Smart

The day's heat and humidity began to build and broke my reverie. I wiped away the sweat and tears with Papa's *krama* and I turned to look at Chroch's Mom, who was sitting on the ground, her face also drenched in sweat. I felt compassion for her and her son, and a little sorry for myself. She and I were in the same situation, no hope, no future, it seemed. Chroch's Mom, I still did not know her name, was not really my friend; fate had brought us together. I felt it might be a good time to improve my relationship with her but I didn't know how or where to start. How could I earn her trust? She looked away from me; maybe she was tired or worried about what princess would have to say if we returned home with empty hands. How could she know what Le Grand Hotel meant to me? I wiped the sweat from my face many times before I gained enough a courage to ask her, "Why do you stay controlled by the Auntie Princess? It seems you are stronger than me because you were born to do this job that I have never done."

Surprisingly it was not as tough to approach her as I thought. In a sad and calm voice, she answered my questions. She told me the same thing that Pheun had said - that the princess promised that when she went back to the city she would allow both of them to stay in a nice house and she would provide for them. However, now she was looking for ways to move out of the princess' control, because she felt they had no life with her; Auntie Princess was selfish and unkind.

Her answer encouraged me to ask more question, "Why do you spy on me?"

Remaining calm, her response was, "I am very sorry that I did mean things to you, I thought I would be treated nicer if I gave you trouble. I was jealous of you at that time. But, I have come to like you."

I was pondering her words when a sound from the bushes surprised me. It was *Bo Doy*; I turned around and saw a couple of other soldiers sitting together eating. The boldest of them flirted with me. I had not spoken Vietnamese in years but I understood "*Anh thoeung em* - I love you, come here, I will give you food." I smiled and answered back very tartly in Vietnamese. They laughed but he still did not leave me alone.

To tease them back, I said in Vietnamese, "I would love to talk to him if he gave me the key to his truck."

One of them handed the key over; this young soldier obviously did not believe I would be able to drive a big military truck. To prove it to him, I got in his big truck and started the engine. They were laughing and joking in Vietnamese but stopped laughing when they saw the truck was moving. Laughter turned to panic and they ran after the truck but I kept driving, very slowly, making them run after it. Then, I backed the truck up to the bushes and stopped there. They were sweating, "*Choy Euy, Chet Roy*", that means "Oh gosh! You kill me."

Many of the *Bo Doy* were college students. Well, I let them get into the truck and drove back to where they were before.

"All Cambodians speak French, right?" one young soldier, handsome and friendly, asked me.

"*Oui, je le parle* — Yes, I do," I said with a smile and asked, "*Qui es-tu* — Who are you?"

They told us they were drafted because the KR attacked Vietnam's border.

"*Eh, quoi* — And what?" I asked. "Did you really come here to rescue us? It was really to defeat the KR who had invaded your country, right?" I looked straight into his eyes to dig out the truth.

"This is what *Ong Leun* — Superior leader told us."

"Do I believe you? Don't you come to occupy our country since so many of us have been killed by the KR?"

He said, in French, "I was forced to leave my family to help my country. My mother cried and prayed for me to come back home safely."

Chroch's Mom never stopped laughing about how I made those *Bo Doy* run after the truck. She also heard me speaking both Vietnamese and French and saw me making friends with others easily. She used to see me quiet in front of the princess, but not this time. From that day, I noticed she showed me more respect. Both of them, mother and son, started to regard me as an educated person, stopped spying on me and treated me with compassion.

Memory of the Pyramid

I had been stalled in Siem Reap province for almost two months now. The population increased because the liberated used this province as a central meeting place to reunite families before they started a new adventure, either going back to Phnom Penh or crossing the border to Thailand. Some came to get a ride to other provinces or to the city, with *Bo Doy*. Once in a while, we waved to the soldiers who drove by in tanks.

Later, Princess added one more person to the family. He was related to a royal family too, and was single. I never asked him his name and he never told me; I just didn't care. It wasn't long before he made it clear that he was interested in me but I ignored him. After I rejected him, the man hooked up another woman in his royal family line. The new woman got pregnant, and he was forced to marry her.

The wedding ceremony was set up at Angkor Wat. They obviously had hidden their gold well because they still had plenty to buy food and prepare a little wedding ceremony. Friends had been invited to join this ceremony by walking to Angkor Wat to witness their marriage in this magical place. I was not invited; I was nobody to them but I followed the procession, not knowing what I wanted. Arriving at the temple, they chatted and teased each other. They brought bunches of lotus flowers in place of roses. The exotic smell of curry soup wafted to my nose, mixing with the strong fragrance of the tropical fruits they could afford with their gold. There was the sound of dishes clinking and clanking as they arranged offerings on the ground, in front of the statue of Buddha.

I didn't care what they were doing. I looked for a place where I could enjoy my time alone. I walked to the pyramid with the scary stairs that I had regretted climbing fourteen years before. My heart was searching for memories that I had buried – memories of my Papa, of the voice of the guide I was so impatient with, of Stepmother's unhappy face, of Papa's worried face looking up at me while I waved from the top of the pyramid. My father's reassurance that 'we can come back to visit at any time, our country won't run away' was true, but I did not come back as a visitor and the country had not left, but Papa had.

I put my foot on the step to begin the climb up the pyramid but the stairs seemed to stretch out higher and higher. Why expend the energy? There was no Papa waiting for me. There was no one to impress. I turned and looked at the spot where he had stood all of those years before. I wanted him to see my daily life - how I survived with the princess. I wanted him to know how his absence had changed me physically and mentally. I wanted him to help me find a way to go back home, so I could search for my husband. I wanted to let him know that his words telling me to not forget where I came from had encouraged me to be strong when I was my most desperate. I had to go back where I came from. I had to finish my pharmacy degree as I promised my father. No matter what, I still searched for his approval. As I stood there in Angkor Wat, I knew I was dirty, ragged and penniless, but I knew who I was. I knew what I must do.

It was Meant to be

Some days later, my fortunes changed. As usual, Chroch's Mom, Chroch and I had left for the market at 5 AM but the "first come, first served" trading business had not been prosperous for us that day and we were returning with the same sack of rice we started with. Today, like the days before, we were tired from many hours in the hot sun and dehydrated. I had no more energy left and straggled along behind Chroch's Mom, thinking about what Auntie Princess would have to say about our failure.

As usual, I walked straight to the well first before meeting Auntie Princess, just to drink and rinse off the dirt and sweat from my feet and face. As I did so, the voice of Princess surprised me, "Someone was looking for the daughter of a congressman; I believe it must be you."

Slowly I turned to her as I didn't believe my ears. As my eyes met hers, she smiled with greedy excitement, "And maybe this person has money from her father and is ready to give this money to her so she can go to France! You have to go see her." She then gave me directions to find the surprise visitor.

Wow! A big surprise alright! But I knew someone was confused. I had no father to send me anywhere but I was very curious to find out who this was. I responded with a doubtful, "*Chah*, it's probably me."

Before I left, I told her that there were no merchants at Angkor Wat and that we would have to get up earlier next time. She told me to not worry about it, an unusual reaction – did she think my fortunes might be going to change and she should not abuse me?

Without being Able to Help

The directions were easy to follow and within minutes, I was overjoyed to find an aunt I loved so much, my *Keo* Phon. Five years earlier, she used to come to see my stepmother during our lunchtime as they were traded jewelry. I remembered she was hesitant to come into our house when my Papa was around because he disapproved of stepmother's business, but I always encouraged her to come in and have lunch. As soon as our eyes met, she jumped with joy, "You are alive! You are blessed."

I ran to hug her and wept, "I am by myself." I wiped my tears with my sleeve.

I was amazed to hear her say, "I lived in Kompong Cham province for a while with your father-in-law's family but saw it was a good time to get into business if I were to regain my wealth. I chose Siem Reap province. Your father-in-law told me everything about you."

The words "father-in-law" and "Kompong Cham Province" worried me so much that I couldn't hear what *Keo* Phon was saying next. If my in-laws were already in Kompong Cham, my father-in-law might get to Phnom Penh before I did. If that happened, I knew that he would first go to his own house to dig up his treasure hidden beneath my husband's bed, and then do the same at my father's house. Once again, I would be penniless.

I looked up to the ceiling and prayed, "Oh! God, please help me. I pray that my husband didn't tell his father about Papa's hidden treasure."

"Vicheara, I am talking to you." My *Keo* brought me back to reality with her question, "What are you thinking about?" She smiled the same loving smile as when she came to my house five years ago. I knew she still cared about me, and wanted to take care of me to pay respect to my papa.

"About my father-in-law," I said. "He was mean. He kicked me out of the house because--"

"Stop worrying about him. He told me to look for you and to let you know he misses you and wants you back. He even asked me to take you to Kompong Cham province to join him."

"Oh, No! Never!" I raised my right hand to stop her.

"You can stay with me if you don't want to stay with him."

"What kind of business are you doing?"

"I bribe *Bo Doy* for a ride to the Thai border to buy goods that we can bring back and sell at a profit. We also bribe the soldiers to truck goods to Phnom Penh to sell. My oldest son-in-law, Vann, and his brother, Sunny, have made the run many times while I stay home, handle the finances and set up the plans. They trade such things as *sarong batik*, food, precious stones, laundry soap....etc. They are paid in gold when they trade the goods in Phnom Penh."

"Uh....uh."

"Well, you don't have to decide now. Come and eat with us anytime."

"*Aur koun*, dear *Keo*. I will think about it and come back with a decision soon." *Keo* looked at me, disappointed, but I not about to get tied up with my in-laws again and I knew that what I needed to do was to get back to Phnom Penh. However, just knowing that some of my extended family had survived was a blessing and brought such joy to my heart.

My luck had surely changed because just days after I found *Keo*, I met an old neighbor at the market. She used to live behind my house in Phnom Penh five years ago, before the KR invasion. We had been neighbors for many years. "*Baung* Sien!" I jumped to my feet like a tiger when I saw her pass me in the crowd.

"*Aun* Vicheara!" She threw her arms around me. "I can't believe it. Is it really you? Where is your father? Your husband? How is your family?"

"All my family died. How about yours?"

"My tragedy is the same; I lost most of my family and my husband. He was executed by the KR when he became sick. I remember watching him disappear from my sight. His last words to me were to take care of our daughters." Now, both of us were weeping, tears streaming unchecked down our cheeks.

"Your daughters -where are they now?" I asked, dreading the answer.

"They're at home."

"Home?"

"Yes, they are fine! We survived! We have a house here - let's go see them! Ta and Thom will be so happy to see you." She looked at my ragged clothes and my miserable little business. "Why don't you stay with us for a while, Okay?" I looked into her eyes and felt she was a person whom I could trust to begin a new life with.

I said goodbye to Auntie Princess that same day, and moved in with *Baung* Sien and her daughters who welcomed me like I was truly part of their family. I was filled with warmth and acceptance. Had I finally found my place? Both girls called me "Auntie" as if I was their true aunt. They had grown so tall. I used to see them running around on the balcony of her house, giggling and happy.

The house we were staying in at Siem Reap was big with stairs leading up to the front door and coconut trees on either side. The owner was single; her parents died during the KR regime. She stayed in one of the bedrooms and let *Baung* Sien and her daughters stay in the big living room; they pulled a curtain to provide a little privacy at night.

Baung Sien, at about 5'6" was tall for a Cambodian a woman. She had light European skin, with lots of freckles on her arms and back. Her hair had a reddish tinge, which was also very unusual for Cambodians. She had intelligent, honest, and patient eyes. Her lips were pink and wrinkled, with triangular points on her upper lip. In the Cambodian tradition, we believed that these points meant the person would be a very articulate speaker and, when she spoke, everyone would listen intently and with respect.

Everyone who met *Baung* Sien admired her for her intelligence. She spoke Vietnamese, French and Chinese fluently and never seemed to stop talking in one language or another. She wasn't traditionally beautiful, but she seemed prettier the more you got to know her. She blossomed with every word.

Baung Sien taught me to prepare fresh fish, cook, and do the grocery shopping. Neither my stepmother nor my mother-in-law had ever let me do these things. Every day, I counted the cans of rice that *Baung* Sien earned by exchanging gold and other goods with *Bo Doy*. She gave me five cans a day to barter for groceries at the open air market, which was near her house. She made her living trading with high ranking *Bo Doy*. I learned more Vietnamese from her and from the soldiers that she invited to her house every day for lunch and dinner. I admired her soft-spoken but effective communication skills as well as her proficiency in business, both skills that I needed to learn. I became familiar with many *Bo Doy*; one of the soldiers was very kind to me, but very shy and quiet. His name was Chi. *Baung* Sien teased me that Chi was interested in me. However, I was not interested in him or anyone else. I just wanted to make friends and improve my language skills.

Anyone who knew Vietnamese would have more respect from others and maybe gain a good position in the new regime. *Baung* Sien earned respect from the owner of the house by helping her with translations that were necessary for her to conduct her own business.

I went to see my *Keo* later to tell her my decision. She looked happy to see me find a real home and real family.

I never could Forget What you Did to me

A month later, my father-in-law showed up at *Baung* Sien's house unexpectedly. I was very, very surprised to see him. Only months ago, he said I was bad luck and kicked me out of the house. What did he want from me now? Why was he looking for me? I knew I couldn't trust him; I also knew he could smooth talk and change his personality to accommodate the situation. Did he feel guilty for being mean to me? I think he had expected I would die and there would be no memory of what he did to me. *Keo* Phon must have told him where I lived.

Despite his past behavior, I still treated him respectfully.

"Vicheara," he said, "forget about the past. Come to live with us." My heart started beating with fear. "All your sisters-in-law are waiting for you in Kompong Cham province."

I had heard this sweet talk before. Instead of giving him his answer, I decided to ask about his wife. "How is *Neak?*"

"Besides losing Leang, we also lost Phanara. He didn't return home, so we have to assume he has been executed. Your *Neak* died of a heart attack after liberation."

What? *Neak*...gone? Despite the way she treated and cheated me, I still felt compassion for her. My mother-in-law was an unhappy person before the KR took over. Her husband was not faithful to her. She had a minor heart attack a couple of times during KR but nobody in the family had changed anything to make her any happier. In fact, my father-in-law said she was faking illness to get her attention. She was devastated about the disappearance of her oldest, my husband, who was her favorite. She sang sad songs in remembrance of him, my Leang. The loss of another son must have been too much for her heart to bear.

"Thanks for finding me," I said, "but, I am happy to stay here."

I wanted to tell him that the Vicheara he knew had died in the hospital after he kicked her out of the house. The Vicheara he saw now was a new Vicheara, but one who still remembered what he did to her. However, I decided it wasn't worth it and I kept it inside. He may have been disappointed, but he would not show it because he was a strong man. I knew I wouldn't miss any of them. I would not go back. My future was here and in Phnom Penh.

"Have you ever heard anything about what may have happened to your husband?" he asked.

"I saw someone I thought might be Leang walking on the other side of the lake a few months ago, but he disappeared in the crowd before I could get to him. If he is alive, he will find us in the city."

During this short conversation, he expressed his strong belief that my husband and his brother, Phanara, had been executed as neither of them had appeared after liberation. He left the following morning and I felt free and happy.

I had few important duties while living with *Baung* Sien other than eating, sleeping and gaining weight. *Baung* Sien warned me not to eat too much too quickly since we had been starving for so long and our bodies were unable to adjust quickly to the new bounty, just as it was unable to adjust four years ago to plain rice soup broth. I giggled, "No, I won't eat much."

"Oh sure, 'Miss Don't Eat Much'! You eat more than anybody else," *Baung* Sien teased me and laughed.

I Need to Go to my Paternal Home!!

I was happy and became healthier over the next three months in Siem Reap province with *Baung* Sien and her family. As I became physically stronger, my mental health also improved and my depression lifted. One morning, I woke up with clarity of purpose for the next stage of my life. "What am I doing here? I need to go back home and finish my Pharmacy degree as I promised." This thought came in as clearly as if Papa was in my head. Also, I needed to look for my husband. Then, the money and jewelry that Papa had buried also hounded me. There was a chance that it had not been discovered and stolen. Oh, *Mon Dieu!* I don't know exactly where it is but I had better find it before somebody else discovers it.

I went to *Baung* Sien after breakfast and told her, "I need to go home as soon as possible, maybe today or tomorrow."

"I think you are right. It's time; I need to go too, but just for a visit so see what has happened to my house and to the city."

We decided to ask Chi for a ride to Phnom Penh. Luckily, he was driving to Phnom Penh that week, so we were very lucky to ride in the front seat with him instead as cargo in the rear. *Baung* Sien told me to sit in between her and Chi; we had so much fun on the trip, teasing and flirting with him. Our stop for the night was in Kompong Chhnang province, home of the flooded village where my family was dropped off by boat at night when we thought we were returning home. This time I stopped at the same place, but I was headed in the opposite direction, not to Preah Netr Preah District, the Prison Without Walls, but back to my beloved home.

Wrong Assumption

Baung Sien and I could not go inside the military compound where Chi had to take the truck and stay with it for the night so he left us at the gate. Later, *Baung* Sien suggested I walk inside and look for Chi to see if he could give us some rice. I finally found Chi resting in his truck. Respectfully, he cleaned up his truck to make room for me to sit and talk to him. He had no rice to give us, only cooked rice for his own meal.

I don't know how long I spent talking to him, but when I tried to leave to get back to Sien, I found the gate had been closed for the night and I couldn't leave. Chi warned me he would be in big trouble if the *Ong Leun* found out I was with him in the truck. I stayed with him, sharing his food and slept in the back of his truck while he slept in the front seat. There were a couple of soldiers who walked by the truck and teased him as if I was his girlfriend or maybe a "one-night stand." Chi told me to remain quiet so he could hide me from those wild soldiers who wanted to have their way with me. Neither of us slept very well because the mosquitoes buzzed at our ears, biting us every chance they had. I prayed for the sun to rise so I could escape from this new nightmare.

In the morning, when the fence opened, I went back to find *Baung* Sien. Rather than showing any concern about my absence last night, she accused me of escaping from her to sleep with Chi. Had she lost her mind? She told me to go get rice, and then she forgot what she said? She wouldn't believe anything I said. She was unhappy to have been left on her own outside the compound; I didn't blame her.

As we got on the truck with Chi that morning, we were quiet. It was apparent *Baung* Sien believed I had been sleeping with Chi, and Chi believed I was interested in him. Chi smiled at me and held my hand; sometimes he put my hand on his heart. *Baung* Sien laughed and looked away saying in Cambodian, "He is madly in love with you". What a mess! Both couldn't have been more wrong.

Coincidence

When we stopped at Prek Kdam, I got out of the truck and walked around. To my horror, I spotted Sareun, the village man who tried to rape me in the KR time. My heart raced. Did he see me? His wife stood next to him; but looked in a different direction. She seemed to have no idea how evil her husband was. Suddenly, there was a panic around us. A Cambodian woman was in labor and seemed to be in trouble. *Baung* Sien went to help and then asked Chi to help find immediate transport to the hospital in Phnom Penh. Very quickly, Chi found transportation for the woman and we got approval from the *Ong Leun* to go to the hospital with the pregnant woman in a small car. We left so quickly we had no chance to say goodbye to Chi.

About half an hour later, we were dropped off at the Calmette hospital where *Baung* Sien provided translation services for the woman and we soon left the hospital. This incident was a stroke of luck for us because across the street from the hospital was a house that belonged to *Baung* Sien's in-laws before the KR. It appeared the house was now occupied by someone else but we didn't know who, so we went to find out.

It was Dr. Mey and his wife! My heart was overjoyed to see both of them alive, I hoped my Cousin Thor was also alive. Dr. Mey was about six feet tall and scrawny with dark skin. His wife was also tall and very beautiful. Unfortunately, she was also a betel chewer. This couple looked like Beauty and the Beast.

"*Mon Dieu*, I bet she married him only because he was a doctor," *Baung* Sien whispered.

"I love both of them. They were good friends to me and my family."

They seemed genuinely happy to see us and we all shed tears as we shared our stories of what had happened to our families. We were invited to stay for dinner. At the dining table Dr. Mey gently told me that my cousin Thor, had been murdered. He said he had been with my cousin in the operating room, performing surgery on Thor's father, when the KR burst into the clinic. "They came right into the operating room and forced everyone to leave immediately, regardless of their condition. We all tried to protect the patients, but KR told us to leave or they would kill us all right there, right then. Dr. Thor's father died from the unfinished surgery." He relaxed. "My wife was with me at the clinic, but Dr. Thor could not get to his family so we left the city together and took refuge at the Pralom temple and provided medical aid to the monks, expecting that the KR would respect the temple and the monks. However, we quickly found out that religion was forbidden and the monks were told to remove their robes and assume the same status as everyone else. Soon, the stored food in the temple began to run out and the soldiers began threatening the monks."

He paused to take a sip of water and clear his throat, then continued, "My wife and I left the temple first; and continued our bitter adventure to Kompong Thom. We had to stop when the car ran out of gas. We stayed in this province from the beginning until the end of KR regime."

He couldn't tell me any of the details of my cousin's death but he assumed that most of the monks and my cousin were probably killed soon after he left.

"How about his wife? Have you heard anything about her and the children?"

He shook his head in sorrow, "Recently I met Dr. Thor's chauffeur who survived. He told me Dr. Thor's wife and three small children had left the city with three servants. They walked to Kampong Cham, about 30 kilometers from Phnom Penh, where they all later died from sickness."

We all sat in silence as we absorbed these stories. I thought I was too numb too feel any more grief but I had prayed that these beloved cousins had survived and my heart were broken again.

A young man then walked into the room and joined us at the table. He was about twenty five and I was surprised as *Neak* introduced him as Savy's future husband.

"Savy has not married in France?" I asked, surprised, since I remembered that Savy had a boyfriend in pharmacy school.

"Well, Savy has known this gentleman," she turned to smile at him, "for so long waited for him to show his devotion." I knew that was nonsense but wisely kept my opinions to myself and instead asked, "But, how will he get out of Cambodia to join Savy?"

"We will send him through Khao I Dang, the Thai camp, very soon. We are now negotiating the payment with the guide," *Neak* said, smiling.

"How much does it cost to take a person across the Khmer border to the Thai camp?" I asked, wanting this information because I might not stay in Cambodia either.

"About one *damleng* (37.5g) of pure gold." I took a deep breath. Neither of us could afford that. *Baung* Sien had two daughters, so it would cost her three *damlengs* of gold. There was no way.

After the dinner was over, we were fortunate to be invited to stay with them temporarily.

PART VI

THE GHOST CITY

~THIRTY TWO~

A STRANGER IN MY HOME -MY RICHES STOLEN

The next morning after breakfast, *Baung* Sien rushed me to get moving. "We need to see our houses!"

"Do we have to walk? We're going to die in the heat!"

Baung Sien gave me a disgusted look, "We didn't die in Pol Pot, why should we die now?"

We walked the three miles down Monivong Blvd. to find our homes. The streets were empty. It was very different from four years ago when we had been herded out in huge masses, like cattle. All the restaurants, houses, buildings, and theaters along the boulevard were deserted. Windows hung open like hollow eyes, the streets were littered with trash, and shadows played in abandoned buildings like *Khmouch* (ghosts). It would be very scary to walk there alone and *Baung* Sien and I clung together. Once in a while, a small car drove down the road, not a brand new one but a rebuilt car, perhaps restored by a mechanic.

No electricity. No markets. I now had a clearer picture of the extent of Pol Pot's destruction of the urban people. He had scattered the people to the four winds; he had destroyed the schools, burned the books and the temples, and executed the Cambodian people who knew and cared about such things. During the two hour walk, we began to worry that our houses would be occupied by strangers. We turned left on Samdech Ponn Street where there used to be a Chinese restaurant at the corner where Kilen would buy me noodle soup in the morning. The restaurant was now neglected, silent and dark. The karate club across the street from the restaurant, next to my house, was now used for furniture storage.

All the houses around my home were empty, dead, and wretched. There was no sign of the former inhabitants. Maybe only their spirits were floating around to guard their homes. *Baung* Sien and I stood alone on the familiar street looking at my beloved house, the home I had longed for, the home that Papa and I had waited so long to see again. Papa's initials were still stenciled on the gate, and the number 182 was still carved into the brick. What had the KR thought of the initials 'KH', for Kim Houn? They probably had no clue; most were illiterate.

My house! It, too, was a dead house! Pain stabbed my heart as the faces of my family rolled through my mind. Everybody who had lived in this house was gone, everyone. I was alone. As I looked at my house, I felt like I was leaving my body.

I looked at myself and at my house and looked at the past to see if I could have changed it to prevent the horrible fate awaiting my family. Even though my house looked as uninhibited as the others in the neighborhood, it was too painful to accept that it was empty. Surely, when I went in, my family would still be there and I would awaken from this horrible dream. Papa, my grandparents, *Pou* Sunthary - they were not just memories; I knew they must be here. The rocks that Papa put in the front yard still existed, as did the coconut trees in front of the house. Then, as I looked around, reality returned and I noticed the changes. Gone were the jack fruit, guava and jasmine that bloomed and scented the air. Now there were banana trees everywhere, taking over even the spot where my grandfather napped in the hammock. Why would the KR do such a thing? Were they morons? There was only silence and emptiness where the yard used to be filled with the sounds of my Pekinese dogs running around, chasing each other and playing with me. My stomach dropped.

The KR had turned my house into a farmhouse; traces of chicken nests were outside and inside. I peered through the windows; it seemed empty; only a few pieces of furniture were left, probably because they were too heavy to carry away. The china cabinet remained by the window but the drawers were filled with chicken nests. My favorite daybed when I was a child—made from hand-selected wood and crafted by my grandparents' hands—had been moved out of the house and sat in the front yard; it had been used by the stupid *Angkar* to grind rice. I longed to have it again but there was no way we could carry such a heavy bed. The door was open and we went in.

We checked my grandparents' rooms. A lady in her 40's, who appeared quite panicked at the sight of us, occupied the space. I tried to calm her, "I'm the owner of this house. Don't worry, I'll be leaving soon."

Her expression changed to a friendly smile, "Go ahead, please visit."

Rich Ghost!

In Grandpa's room, there was a hole in the wall where the air conditioner had been. The lady said, "You can live upstairs. Nobody stays there because it's haunted."

"Haunted? That's not possible."

I went to the dining room where the communist leaders had dinner with Papa. All the antique silver plates had disappeared from the china closet. The dining room had been turned into a bedroom complete with air conditioning. The air conditioning unit was indeed the one removed from my grandpa's room. I left *Baung* Sien talking to the lady and went upstairs. The portrait of my *Mak* and all the furniture in my room had disappeared. There was nothing left in Papa's room, not even the big safe remained.

Remembering of Papa's Last Words

I did find the safe, unopened. The KR had thrown it out the window to try to break it open. I wanted to take it, but I couldn't —it was too heavy to move and I didn't know the secret code. Papa's last words popped into my mind, "Come here," he had said, "I have to tell you a very important thing."

I knelt in front of the safe, realizing that the code to open it may have been the "very important thing" that Papa had to tell me. Now I knew why his room was haunted; Papa's ghost must have been trying to protect the big safe. I should have let Papa talk more; now his soul haunted the safe, scaring people away and waiting for me, but I was still unable to open it. Gently, I put my hand over the lock to let Papa know everything is over; I will start my life over with my education and my two hands. I wanted to release his soul to heaven. If an angel appeared, asking me to choose one thing for my future, my answer would not be whatever riches were in the safe but the lives of my family back.

I climbed up to the ceiling hole where Papa had hidden his gun. Nothing was there; I knew it wouldn't be. I checked everywhere in my room one more time. I wanted to find any small memento—but nothing remained, not even a little piece of hair. I took a little peek at the balcony and saw the sun glint off some small object in the far corner. When I went outside my heart soared! One small memory of my family! I knew this was a gift for me. I couldn't believe my eyes; a little container of pure silver was still here on the balcony, waiting for me for more than four years, while everything else in house disappeared. Papa had haunted everyone who stayed upstairs just to protect his last gift to me.

I ran back downstairs to show it to *Baung* Sien, "This container was my *Mak's*. After she died, my stepmother used it to hold jasmine scented water; she never let anyone else use it. I don't really want any reminders of her—but I could sell it."

Baung Sien couldn't say anything more than, "Oh, *Mon Dieu!*"

I turned to the lady. "Has anyone come to this house before me?"

She smiled, "yes, someone was here; he claimed to be sent by the owner of the house. It was a man in his mid-fifties who came looking for treasure in the garage."

"Are you sure that the man was in the mid-fifties? Might he have been around my age, instead?"

"No, he was old."

I had hoped it might be my husband, "Did he have a mole on his upper lip?"

"No mole on the lip."

"Hmmm…then it couldn't be *Pou* Phan, either."

"Who is *Pou* Phan?" *Baung* Sien asked, worry in her voice.

"He was here helping Papa hide his wealth the night before we left the house."

"How about your father-in-law? He came to claim you back in Siem Reap province," *Baung* Sien offered.

"I can't accuse him, but who else could it be, if not him?" I tapped my right hand on my head, and bit my lip with anxiety as I agreed with *Baung* Sien.

"Ah, now I remember. When *Keo* Phon was looking for me she told Auntie Princess that my father had money and wanted to send me to Paris. It must have been my father-in-law; after he got the hidden treasure, he was guilty and thought about giving some to me. Since I refused to go with him, then he kept it for himself." I turned to the lady, panicked, "Treasure, you said. Did he find anything? Do you know who he was?"

"He said he was sent by the owner's child, a son, who couldn't come personally due to the illness."

"A son?" *Baung* Sien asked, raising an eyebrow, "The child was a son?"

"No, not a son. A daughter. Me," I said to the lady. "He lied to you." I narrowed my eyes. Something felt off.

"He didn't find anything except a metal container, "the lady said, and now I was feeling really suspicious. Could what she said be true? I knew my Papa had hidden a suitcase filled with American dollars and jewelry. Could he have transferred the treasure in the suitcase to a metal container? Had I forgotten? I rushed to the garage where she said the man had been digging. The hole was bigger than the size of the metal container she mentioned. My *Pou* Sunthary used to talk about the hiding place where he and my husband had helped my father hide treasure. I hadn't thought about this in four years and I couldn't remember what he said. Now, someone had taken my treasure, and I suspected it must have been my father-in-law, since he'd been here first.

"Either way, if he is a good person, he would have to tell you the truth. But, humans are corrupt and greedy. When you didn't come with him, he probably used your papa's dollars to find a guide to help the entire family escape the country. They are eight people and it would cost a big fortune. Don't you think? That's why he didn't tell you," reasoned *Baung* Sien.

I wordlessly nodded my head to agree; her idea made sense. I was frustrated but maybe none of this wealth was meant to be mine. Everything had conspired against it. My father's last words that I was too frightened to hear, the safe that couldn't be opened, the theft of two bags of jewelry that we had hidden for so long. Or, maybe, I was just unlucky? But then, I was alive, and so many others were not, so maybe I was the only lucky one. I didn't know. This is what life's about, I decided, uncertainty.

After I searched my house from upstairs to downstairs, I left a message on the wall of the dining room for the next person—maybe my husband—saying, "I'm alive. Find me at Dumex, the pharmaceutical plant."

Memories sometimes were not Painful

Baung Sien and I walked to the backyard, hoping to find something else. I looked at a single longan tree that remained in the yard. After this tree bore fruit the first time, my grandpa told me not to touch them and then counted the longan every day to be sure I had not disobeyed him. He got so mad at me when one longan disappeared; I tasted it before he did!

"What do you smile about?" *Baung* Sien asked me.

After I told her about my on-going battle for fruit with my Grandpa, *Baung* Sien laughed. "You are a mean girl."

Next to the longan tree was a guava tree. I hated guava so it was in no danger from me but he guarded it anyway. "*Lok Tah*." I shook my head. "He fought with me over the guava fruit, too."

"What did you do?"

"One day the fruit disappeared and Grandpa was furious with me; he did not believe that I wouldn't eat guava."

"I know you," *Baung* Sien teased. "You picked it."

"No, I didn't. I didn't even like it."

"Did you find out who did it?"

"No."

"Then everyone assumed it was you."

As I thought about this, I realized how silly and small-minded the whole thing was. We had plenty of money to buy fruit; why in the world had he been so mean to me over fruit?

"*Lok Tah* counted every single fruit and all the coconuts. Of course, none of this stopped me. As soon as he heard a coconut fall on the ground, he ran out to protect his fruit from me. Now, I am so lonely I even miss his screaming and his angry face, a face that I can never see again."

Baung Sien laughed gently and soothed me, "It's over now."

"I need to check if I can find any trace of my dogs."

I walked around the walls, sniffing like a cat to catch the smells. I called their names everywhere in case they were still alive, hiding, but there was no response.

"They couldn't have lived this long. Come on, I want to see my house," *Baung* Sien said and walked toward the wall in the back of the yard.

Jewelry in the Well

We walked through a hole in the cement wall in the backyard to *Baung* Sien's house. She hoped to find the silver and the jewelry she threw in the well that was in front of her house, before she left in 1975. This had been her dream for the four years — that she would reclaim her wealth to begin a new life. She had often told me, "That treasure will help me build my business and ensure my family's survival."

Finding the well intact gave her hope, "I'll need help to get down there," she said, as we made our way to the well.

"If you ask someone to go down the well, you need to pay him."

"I don't mind. But what if he wants to split my treasure in half?"

"Will you?"

"No way. My treasure was inherited from my parents." We leaned over the side and looked down the well; I didn't know what it should look like, but she did and she screamed with rage and disappointment, "It is dry and empty! Everything is gone!" She rubbed her chest, and then collapsed to the ground, crying, "Who could do this to me?"

"It's so dark down there. Deep, too. How could someone have emptied all the water?"

"What difference does that make? The well is dry, if my big bag of treasure was there, we could see it. Someone else got here first."

"I didn't get my treasure, either," I tried to make her feel better. "Let's get out of here. I need to go to my father-in-law's house."

We walked back through the same hole in the fence to my back yard. The lady occupying Grandpa's room was in the yard and asked *Baung* Sien politely, "Did you find anything from your home?"

"Everything is gone. I hid my jewelry and a big bag of pure silver in the well. Unfortunately, the well is still there but it is dry. Dry and empty - neither jewelry nor silver remains."

"It may have been found by the Vietnamese troops who went through the houses using metal detectors."

"Vietnamese? Really?" Hearing this, *Baung* Sien cried again in frustration and rage.

"Did you see them doing that? Or is it just a rumor?" I asked.

"It's no rumor; think about it, the city is empty, nothing is left. Did you notice the entire house was empty? All the furniture was gone? Where did it go? The KR couldn't take it when they fled. Who came to the city first and chased out the KR?"

We both just stared at her as we began to understand the second stage of the looting of the city. "Well, come visit me sometimes, if you want to come back to your house, you are welcome to stay upstairs, like I said before."

"I am welcome? This is my house. I would say you are welcome to use my house. I may not come back soon but this is my house. Good luck and take care of my house. I hope one day, I can come back and live here again."

As we walked away, I looked back at 'KH', with mixed feelings of anger and sorrow, "What would Papa have to say, if he had walked back home and his house was occupied by someone else?"

"What do you think? If he was alive, that woman wouldn't be here. Your Papa would kick her ass out."

The mental picture of this made us laugh and the laughter released my anger and made me feel better, "Just imagine, Papa screaming and chasing her all the way to the main street." We laughed again.

Baung Sien pointed at the karate club, "Well, now we know why the karate club is a furniture warehouse."

Underneath his Bed

We walked about one mile to my father-in-law's house. When my husband was still with me, he told me his father had hidden gold in a hole underneath his bed, so if I found an empty hole in the main bedroom, it would confirm my suspicions that my father-in-law had been in the city and took the treasure from both his house and mine.

We walked through my father-in-law's house looking for any sign of my husband. When I went into the main bedroom, I found a big hole in the middle of the room, just as I had suspected. I left the house with bitter disappointment. Why did my father-in-law treat me like this? Now I was sure it was his guilty conscience about looting my house that caused him to look for me after liberation. I was increasingly discouraged about finding my husband since there had been no sign of him at either house. *Baung* Sien squeezed my shoulder, "We still have one more place to look. Be strong."

Dr. Mey had told us that Dumex plant, was trying to restart and that if any pharmacists had survived and returned to the city, I might find him there. We decided to walk the two miles to the company to see who we could find, and, hopefully, be offered lunch.

This Man could Smile

When we reached Dumex, the first person I met was professor Nim, my husband's cousin. "*Lok Krou* (Male teacher or professor)! I come here to find Leang." I greeted him formally as my former professor.

I remembered him as a very quiet man who seldom spoke other than to say yes and no. Today, when seeing me for the first time after liberation, he was very friendly and caring. Miraculously, he could even smile, "Vicheara, we are alive. Where is Leang?" He looked at *Baung* Sien with disappointment, as he verified that Leang was not with me.

"I was praying you could tell me." My eyes filled with tears as my last hope was dashed.

"Be patient. If he is alive, he'll be here soon." Again, he smiled. He was still very thin and seemed shorter, but other than that, didn't seem to have changed much. He certainly looked better than I did. Who knew? Maybe, after he arrived in the city, found sufficient food, slept well without worries, and worked in a building rather than under the brutal sun, he had returned to his former self.

"I still cannot believe the KR didn't raze this company to the ground like other buildings in the city. I hope my Papa's company won't have a lot of damage. Are all the machines still intact and ready to function?"

"Well, I came in first, and then, later, more pharmacists arrived." Suddenly, several of my friends from pharmacy school appeared behind him. I was elated to see them alive, and looked around for Savy's former boyfriend, Ban, Hor.

"We have not seen Ban, Hor," my friend, Cheam said, as if he could read my mind. "We still don't know who is lost and who may yet come back."

"You," Cheam pointed at me, "need to come help us here. Where is Leang?" I shook my head and everyone knew what I meant.

"We all worked very hard to clean up this place, make it look ready as you see it now. It was a big mess and as dirty as a dumpster before," *Lok Krou* added. "You need to join our team." This invitation excited me. However, it still couldn't replace the emptiness in my heart since my Leang was not here.

"Go to the dining area. Fill up your tummy first, we will talk more later," *Lok Krou* sent us on our way.

In the canteen, I met Siv Nay, the girl who bullied me by pulling my short, permed hair at the Sutharot elementary school. It was amazing to see her at Dumex also. She looked at me and laughed with delight, *"Mon Dieu*, are you alive?"

"What kind of wind blew you to come to see me today?" I pretended to pull her hair, but she got mine first. We all laughed - in joy that we were alive and in sorrow for all that we had lost.

Baung Sien laughed with us and said, "Laugh louder...after the tears is laughter."

"I no longer have short hair; don't you have anything else to torture me with?"

"Now? Yes, I do. Pol Pot time is over, take off the black uniform, silly." She then playfully chased me to pull off my ugly black shirt.

"You never change. Fortunately, I am now taller than you and you cannot torture me anymore, or I will kick your ass."

Baung Sien and I ate like pigs, as we were starved. We really enjoyed the food we were served, even though it was only rice and water spinach – food we would have distained before the Pol Pot time. When it was time to get up to find a drink, I couldn't stand up straight from overeating. Nim appeared at the door but quickly left without saying anything. His quick presence made *Baung* Sien wonder if he was checking on her. She pulled my shirt to stop me from getting up, and asked, "Where is his wife? Does he have children? Is he alone now? Do you think he is staring at me?"

"His wife is my age and she is a snob. I remember I had to call her *Baung* to buy her respect, even though she was my age. If she was here, she would come to see me now." Hearing this conversation, Siv Nay volunteered that *Lok Krou's* wife was on the way to Phnom Penh and that he had lost his two children.

"Oh, No. They were so cute."

"I am right. If the wife was around he wouldn't stare at me like a dog looking at raw meat. You know men!" *Baung* Sien was sure Nim was interested in her.

I left Siv Nay without asking her more details about her life. I thought we'd talk more when I started my job at Dumex, but it was the last time I saw her. I never found out why. When we walked back to the factory floor, I found *Lok Krou* and other pharmacy friends back at work creating office spaces and assembling supplies. Cheam was singing softly to himself as he repaired a broken chair. When he saw us, *Lok Krou* came to meet us in the hallway and offered us the use of his room upstairs if we needed to rest but I refused, "*Baung* (his wife) would kill me if she found us in your room. I know her."

He smiled, "Yes, she will be here soon. However, when you return to work, there is a room available next to mine. You can stay there." I smiled back but hesitated to accept because I knew it would mean trouble with his wife.

"When you are ready, let me know," he said and walked away. We said 'goodbye for now' to this group of friends and left.

The House of Grandaunty Houn, the School Principal

The next day, *Baung* Sien and I went to see my Grandaunty Houn's house, on Samdech Pan, one street away from my house, to see if there was anything left to bring to her surviving children. The house was very big as they had eight children and they all lived with the parents. The oldest son and daughter had left for France before Cambodia collapsed. The first floor of the house had been a dental clinic as her husband was a dental surgeon. The second floor had the parents' bedroom and the living rooms; upstairs were bedrooms for all the children. Behind the big house were rooms for the servants and the kitchen. Like everywhere else we had been, the house had been thoroughly looted. I found only one photo and a purse.

When I went into Grandaunt's living room, I found a man I guessed to be in his early forties dressed completely in black. He sat alone in the middle of the big living room as though he was waiting for someone. Even though he was indoors, he wore dark sunglasses. When I greeted him and asked his name, he told me I would find out his name later because he was a "special man who came to reorganize the country." He frightened me; he did not look friendly. I never found out who he was. It was probably a lie to scare away the rightful owners…it certainly worked on me.

Little Tour of the City

The next day, a new friend of *Baung* Sien's gave us a ride in an old car around the city. We were stunned to see that all the important buildings like the National Bank, state offices, and the libraries had been ransacked and the contents destroyed. Documents, books and photos were piled everywhere in the street, rotting in the rain. The KR had grown bananas on the lawns inside my secondary school, Preah Norodom College. The streets that used to be clean and drivable had become like farm roads, flooded and muddy. Furniture, mangled household goods, and trashcans were all over the roads in heaps that made the city look like a huge dump. In some areas, the houses had been burned down; in others, homes been demolished into piles of rubble.

The KR obviously had an obsession with banana trees. They were growing everywhere, even in front of the Royal Palace, along the *Tonlé* Mekong, and the *Veal Mean* where *Samdech* Sihanook used to hold public meetings. How did planting banana trees further a revolution? What kind of imbeciles were they? I heard people marveling that that the KR drank water out of the toilet; they had no idea what the toilet was for. My experiences in the fields had taught me that long ago.

As we drove to check out my Papa's pharmaceutical business, we passed by *Psar* O'Russey which had been the heart of the city's daily commerce. It was now a dump. Much of the city reminded me of a cemetery. Another shock hit me in the heart when arriving at my Papa's business. I would not have recognized Papa's company, if the name had not still been on the building. All the doors and windows had been destroyed. The sophisticated machinery was pulled outside and rusted into junk.

Once again, fanaticism had triumphed over common sense. I had nothing left to start my new life but one last hope - to find the man Papa had been in business with in Thailand, "Mr. Chhorn. I will find him when I find Charanay, niece of S.E. Phlek, Pheun." I told myself.

Meeting my Nephews

The next day, at Dr. Mey's house, I was called downstairs to meet visitors. I was ecstatic to see my cousin Phach's two older sons, Naith and Ridh, alive and in good condition. They both gave me a hug; I was delighted but surprised because in our culture we rarely hug each other. They brought me new sandals, which I badly needed, and told me that they were so lucky during the KR régime, because they were adopted by a KR leader. Then, after the liberation, they were taken in by a peasant lady who loved them like her own children and treated them like princes.

"Will you leave her when you find your mom?" I asked.

"Don't know."

"How did you find out I was here?"

"From Dr. Mey," explained Naith, the oldest brother. "He is now the president of the medical and pharmacy schools, and they are searching for students who may have survived the Genocide. Granduncle Chhun..."

They did not get to continue, as I screamed, "He...is...ali...ve..?"

"*Bat*," they responded, in unison.

"I need to see him.....I need to see him....he is my favorite step-uncle. And then?"

"He works with Dr. Mey at the medical school, too. Naith exhaled and continued, "He lives at Kbal Thnal, working as director of the hospital there."

"I'll go see him soon. Where is your mother?"

"I still don't know anything about her or my siblings," Naith replied.

"What will you do now?"

"I'm not sure."

"Where do you live now and who else has survived?"

"We found a place near the post office, on the 2nd floor."

"How about cousin Deun's family and Or?" I asked.

"All butchered in Chhlong District, Kratié province, six months before the defeat of KR."

I gasped with horror and rubbed my chest to show my sorrow. "Only six months ago?" I couldn't believe it – to have survived so long and be killed just before liberation. I took several deep breaths to regain my composure but it was so painful to talk about. They told me that the KR was particularly savage in Kratié. The victims' hands were tied behind their backs; they were blindfolded with black cloth, lined up and beheaded with an axe - one after another. The music played loudly to mask the sounds and prevent panic. Sometimes, their poor bodies were disemboweled and filled up with grass. Babies and small children were smashed against the trees or thrown into the air and shot.

"But *Pou* Many had survived and is living with his parents."

"*Mon Dieu*, I want to see him. I used to see him when he was a kid, now I probably wouldn't recognize him."

"His face hasn't changed. You will know him right away," Ridth assured me.

"This is too painful to hear," I said, wincing. "How could the KR kill small and innocent children?" I took another deep breath to control my emotions. I couldn't imagine how terrified and agonized my cousins were to know their family was being murdered. They couldn't escape; there was no one to rescue them. This news erased the bitter memory of the night my cousin Deun molested me when *Mak* was very sick and Papa was not around. I forgave him. My anger was replaced with sorrow that he and his family suffered through Hell. I remembered cousin Deun teasing me every time he came to my house. He once took a picture of me crying in front of the house, pooping my pants. The last time I saw him he was with his wife and two small kids.

Naith and Ridth were very shy and quiet. They spoke little and smiled a lot. I told them about the death of all my family. They did not cry, just were sad. Finally, Ridth asked me, "How about you, my Auntie? I never thought you could make it."

"I don't know. I was lucky and I tricked them whenever I could." My nephews said goodbye and encouraged me to go see *Pou* Chhun.

~THIRTY THREE~

MY FAVORITE UNCLES

Kbal Thnal was about ten miles from Dr. Mey's house. Nonetheless, *Baung* Sien and I decided to walk to there to see my *Pou* Chhun. At midday, it was very hot and humid and we were soon tired and thirsty. We wished we had enough money to buy a bicycle or at least pay for a ride on a bike but we were way too poor. At that time, bicycles were so valuable that people would trade jewelry for them. We were almost at Kbal Thnal when someone called from behind, "*Neak Neang*", which means "My Highest Miss" in Cambodian. This phrase was used by servants of high class families to address young women in the family. I turned around and saw our former chauffeur, Un, smiling at me. He now made his living transporting people on a bicycle. I spoke with him for a short while and he offered me a ride the rest of the way, but I couldn't leave *Baung* Sien behind and we both couldn't fit on the bicycle. Instead of accepting his offer, I gave him the new pair of sandals I brought for my uncle. This was the last time I ever saw Un.

Started a New Life with Pain

Soon, the temperature was 90-100 degrees F and we were sweating from head to toe by the time we arrived at Kbal Thnal. A market had been established - selling fish, dried fruit, desserts, and clothes. We carried rice with us to barter for these goods. One can of rice would buy one big dessert, like a donut. This donut was made of white flour mixed with palm sugar and baked. When it was ready to eat, we put shredded coconut on top. I used to hate it but now I was dying to have one and *Baung* Sien bought one for me. We asked around to find our way to the hospital and to see if anyone knew my uncle by name. I reasoned he must be well known because he was the first doctor to return to the hospital at Kbal Thnal. I was right; everyone knew his name. I was very impatient to see my *Pou*. We found the hospital about two blocks from the market and began asking everyone we met where to find him. We finally were sent to the right room, and when I saw him, I ran to him, "*POU!*"

He was skinny, but that was normal; his hair had all turned grey. He turned around and jumped with surprise. He was so emotional he didn't seem to hear what I was saying, and so I had to tell him again and again that his parents and my Papa's entire family had died. He was devastated to hear this tragic news. He took off his reading glasses to wipe his eyes and look at me. "How did you survive?"

"By luck and trickery."

"How did my parents die?" He kept asking me, without allowing me to answer. "Where did you bury them?"

"Prek Chi Heung."

"Where?"

"I do not know for sure where it is." Then the dam broke and we all began to weep for the lost. I wept as if they had all died yesterday; all the pain that I had pushed away to protect my sanity flooded into my heart in the safety of my *Pou's* presence. I was afraid to ask him about his family since I was overwhelmed with death of my own family and terrified to get any more bad news. After we regained our composure, he volunteered to share his story.

"I lost my second wife and the youngest children because we were forced to leave the city separately when the KR invaded Phnom Penh. I left with Phan's and *Baung* Srun's (his oldest brother) families. We walked to Kampong Thom province."

"Wait…I remember *Pou* Phan came to our house, stayed overnight, but left us in the morning on April 18," I interrupted. "He told us he would go to Kampong Thom province. He must have gone to get you and then went to that province later." He first agreed with me, but he then shook his head, "Unum…I don't know; he didn't say anything about that."

He walked to a little table next to his desk, filled three cups with hot tea, and then came back to sit at the desk, giving us a cup of tea. He gestured for both of us to sit and continued, "After liberation, when I returned home, I met our servant who told me that my wife had become very sick and died. Four of my older children were killed by KR. She didn't know what had happened to my two youngest boys who were living with their mother until she died. Our servant was not sure if they are dead or alive since she was in a forced labor camp until liberation. We still haven't found the boys; if they are alive, they may grow up and be strangers to us." He got up again to turn on the electric fan and, I am sure, to collect himself. "Our servant is a good person. I felt a great obligation to her since she remained loyal to my wife and children as long as she was able. I rewarded her the only way I could; I married her."

I was surprised that *Pou* Chhun talked so much. All my young life, I rarely heard him say more than two words. I told him the story of *Pou* Va, who left his family because he couldn't deal with starvation. *Pou* Chhun told me he had met the youngest daughter of *Pou* Va who came to see him in the hospital, with an uncle on her mother's side. She was the only one to survive.

"I can't believe they all passed away as I remembered seeing them, especially his wife, not so long ago and she wished me good luck."

Pou Chhun wanted me to meet his new wife who worked with him in the hospital as a midwife. "Midwife?" I raised my eyebrows in surprise. "How could she become a midwife so quickly?"

"She is very intelligent and I taught her everything I could about methods, treatments, and medicines. She is very brave. She also trained with a midwife supervisor. She learned quickly; we need a lot of emergency help here since midwives are in great demand and few of them survived."

My *Pou* was called then to see a patient, so we left, promising to meet his new wife soon. It was sooner than we had imagined as she was on her lunch break and, after a short conversation with her, she left work and walked back to their house with us. She used to be the servant, but now she was the wife of my *Pou*. Since I loved my *Pou*, I would have to respect and love her and accept her in the family. Even after four years in the KR, this was quite a shocking turn of events. I called her 'Auntie'. Her name was Nidd.

Pou's house was a big row house with three stories. It was in pretty good shape but still needed a lot of cleaning. Old dumpsters were right in front of the doorway; they were so obnoxious that we had to hold our breath as we walked past them. I couldn't believe that my *Pou* hadn't picked a nicer house since he had been an early returnee to the city, but Auntie Nidd explained that since he lost his family, he had no interest in anything material and really didn't even seem to notice his surroundings. He was very depressed.

When we got to the house, I found out that another uncle, older brother of *Pou* Sunthary, had also survived and had returned to Phnom Penh. He, his wife and two beautiful daughters lived in the same house with my *Pou* Chhun, but in the first floor. *Pou* Chhun had been so emotional; he had forgotten to tell me. We also visited *Pou* Srun, the oldest brother who lived behind the hospital. He looked the same but his circumstances were very changed after four years with the KR. He stayed home doing the cleaning and his wife supported them by baking desserts to sell at the market. She was a hard worker and a very sweet and friendly person. This was my last memory of them.

~THIRTY FOUR~

CHANGE FOR A REASON

A month had gone by quickly for us as we had searched for family and friends but, for Dr. Mey's wife, it seemed to have gone very, very slowly. She had been nice on the first day, but by the end of the month, we noticed that her servant followed us everywhere. Annoyed by her constant presence, I confronted her and asked, "What makes you think you need to spy on us?"

"My mistress has told me to keep my eyes on you both to ensure you don't steal her rice since food is still scarce." Her tone was very disrespectful, her chin raised and a superior smile played on her lips. I was surprised with this behavior and with her direct, confrontational answer.

However, *Baung* Sien took over the difficult situation. She wasn't shocked by anything and wouldn't give this rude woman any power, "Are you sure you didn't invite yourself to do this job because we are homeless and poorly dressed?"

"I don't know anything about that; I just do what my mistress tells me. Don't get mad at me. She told me to ask you where you got your rice from," the woman retreated from *Baung* Sien's attack.

"Wow, what kind of person is she? How dare you talk to us like this? Did you see us steal any rice?" *Baung* Sien drew close to the servant and glared at her.

I don't know why I was still shocked by suspicion and mistreatment. Everything was upside down. The social order had changed. Kilen threw a pot at my Papa. This servant doesn't see me as the same person she respected before because of what? Because I am now a homeless person? Because I wear a shabby black outfit, just as she does? More importantly, because I have no place in society, as does her mistress, the wife of a MD? Because I am of no benefit to this family? Why should they, she and her mistress, respect me? Should I be mad at this servant? No, she just repeated what she had been told to say. She had no clear picture of what she should or shouldn't say to me. It was just like the little KR crow soldier, repeating nonsense like a parrot. Her mistress doesn't have to treat me as she did before because I am a homeless beggar, no longer the entitled, pampered daughter of a wealthy, famous father. She could treat me like shit. How should I deal with this? Should I fight back and teach them a lesson? What lesson? Why humiliate myself for a few grains of rice? I know who I am, what I want in my life, and where to go. Fighting with her is just like beating my head against a wall; it will not change anything.

297

"I don't plan to stay here for the rest of my life. I have a lot of things that need to be accomplished. You are doing what you were told. Please tell your mistress not to worry about the rice. I cannot take advantage of her kindness and her hospitality any longer," I said with as much dignity as I could muster.

"Have you heard enough?" *Baung* Sien asked me, clearly irritated. The woman left before we could say more.

"It is our mistake for staying too long," I said.

"I cannot believe that all she has been through in the past four years has not softened her heart and humbled her a little more. It has just made her greedy. *Aun* Vicheara, I need to go back to Siem Reap province to be with my daughters." *Baung* Sien sighed dejectedly, "I have had enough of this paranoid family. They don't trust us. Why should we stay?"

I moved out the same day *Baung* Sien left for Siem Reap. Professor Nim offered me a small apartment in the Tan Pa's building, where I lived with other pharmacist friends. Because of Papa's reputation, I was offered a job as a temporary lead pharmacist at Dumex, responsible for the syrup production line. I was paid in rice. The apartment was close to where I worked which was important because we had no transportation. Every weekend, I took a four-hour walk to visit *Pou* Chhun. He was always happy to see me and encouraged me to live with him. He had never put me down or intimidated me like the other *Pous* on my Papa's side had when I was a child.

They didn't Recognize their Father

About a month later, when I stopped by at the hospital to see *Pou* Chhun, he had astonishing news. He had found one of his missing sons, in nothing short of a miracle.

"One of our employees went to the market in Kbal Thnal for noodle soup. He saw two little boys sleeping in the dirt near his table. One of them, the youngest, had a wound on his right leg. Out of compassion, this employee brought the child to the hospital to have the wound treated and, as I was the only doctor here, I was called in. Once I saw this little boy, I recognized a scar on his left leg and began to question him. After asking him his age, I began to believe that, by some miracle, my son was here in front of me."

"Oh, *Mon Dieu*! What did you say?"

"I asked his name first. Thy, he told me. He also remembered his siblings' names, as he had grown up with them. I knew this was my son because he recited the names of my own children."

"How come Auntie Nidd didn't recognize him?"

"She was forced to leave my wife for the labor camp when the boys were two and three years old. Remember I told you earlier?" I nodded my head. "They would have changed a lot since then. But, all is not well because I have problems keeping him in the house because he doesn't remember me and won't accept me as his father."

"It will be very hard as there had not been a bond between you and him."

"Yes. I have to be patient with him. He runs away all the time and we have to go out, search for him and bring him home; the boy is traumatized."

We ended our conversation as he was called away for an emergency. Before he left me, he told me to stop at his house to see the boy. I went right over and found things in an uproar with the boy screaming, "*Kdouy mehr vear.* Leave me alone. I do not have any father. I want to go back where I came from."

The boy ran past me, hitting my hip, and then my auntie ran after him, calling him to stop. I joined the chase and soon caught him. The boy was furious and kicked me very hard and spit on my auntie. Softly and gently, she consoled him, "*Kaun*, don't run from your real home, your real family. We prove to you that you are our son because we won't let you go back to where you came from."

"I am hungry," he screamed. "I want to eat leftover noodle soup at the market." He howled and kicked and refused to follow us back home. Auntie gave me a signal to lift up his legs; she grabbed his arms and we carried the hysterical child, who alternately sobbed and cursed, back to the house. Auntie gave him a bath, dressed him in clean clothes and then fed him. He gradually calmed down and ate like a normal child. I was impressed with her command of the situation and with her devotion to the child. She was an intelligent, kind, and loyal person. What right had I to look down on her because she had been a servant? I had been a slave in the KR after all. I was so proud of my *Pou*'s decision to marry her. She was really good for him and the boy – unlike Kilen, my servant, who had been a careless mother.

I introduced myself to the child as his cousin and then asked him, "It is amazing that you found your way to this market. How did it happen that you came here? Did you know where you were going?"

Thy was not a timid child nor irrational, despite his traumatic experiences. Obviously intelligent, he answered succinctly, "My older brother and I just kept following people until we got kicked off the Vietnamese truck at the last stop which was the Kbal Thnal market." His voice was clear and his eyes darted around the room as we talked. He told me more of his story and how he needed to find his brother. Auntie Nidd told us that my *Pou* had gone back to the market many times looking for the older son and had been told that the older boy had been taken by a couple who decided to adopt him.

I gave Thy big hug and told him to be a good boy. I turned to Auntie and asked, "How about his brother? Do you still hope to find him?"

"We will always have hope but we have no idea who his new family is or where they have gone. We have left many messages for them at the market but we do not know how to find them."

"Good luck, Auntie. It is God's purpose to guide him to his father."

Another Lesson

I went to see *Pou* Phan's family; they did not live far from Dumex. That visit once again slapped me in the face about how my world and my place in it had changed. Five years earlier, *Pou* Phan had worked as a payroll clerk for my Papa's company. He was always very pleasant to me. But, as a privileged and elitist young woman, I was not particularly respectful to him because I considered him and his family lower class. As a result, I called him *Pou* Phan (as opposed to just *Pou*); however, in our culture, young people were never allowed to call older people by their given name unless those people were of a lower class. To me, my *Pou's* family was in a lower class so I could call him anything I wanted. Now things had changed. Now, when I greeted him as *Pou* Phan, instead of being surprised and happy to see me, he chose to lecture me and insult me for my disrespect.

One statement he made stayed in my mind, "You do not know who you are now?" He not only said the words but his cold and angry eyes threatened me. I backed up one step while trying to collect myself. I couldn't believe that someone I loved and missed so dearly had just terribly humiliated me.

I clearly understood *Pou* Phan had never liked Papa and resented him. He couldn't wait for the time to come to put us in our place. He got what he wished for. He had the power now. My Papa was gone and I was now poor and homeless. But, I still had trouble thinking of myself as lower class. *Pou* Phan no longer had to show me respect as he had when my Papa was rich and powerful, and his boss.

I had to continue to learn to adapt to this new world and figure out my place in it. I changed the way I addressed him but he still would not talk to me. In fact, he avoided me. He hasn't talked to me since that day.

In a conversation with his wife, Aunt Sichoeur, I learned that her sister Si Theur (the prettiest girl, and the one who caused the family conflict) had committed suicide during the KR regime due to severe sickness. "Wow!' I said, "She was so brave. She must have felt her husband had to care for the children and he didn't need to care for her too. She committed suicide so he could move on. Where is he? Did he remarry?"

"Yes, you know men, they can't say alone for very long. She knew he would remarry and the kids would have a mother to look after them. He looked up his ex-girlfriend and married her. Now the kids have a new mother."

"I am hungry. Where's my food?" a booming, angry voice abruptly interrupted us. "Don't you have anything better to do than sit there and gossip about worthless things that mean nothing?" *Pou* Phan demanded. Aunt Sichoeur finished her stitch, put down her sewing and went to do his bidding, winking at me as she left.

I knew *Pou* Phan didn't like me and didn't want me around, but what else I could do? I felt powerless. I had very few choices. I had no place to cook in my room and I received only rice as pay. I had no money. The tables had turned and I was now the poor, needy relative. I had to depend on his generosity just to eat. This was indeed a new and humbling experience for me. It was like begging for every morsel of food, pretending to see nothing, hear nothing.

~THIRTY FIVE~

REAL SAVIORS?

Mid-year, 1979.....

The victorious North Vietnamese had taken over Cambodia and imposed a communist government, not communist like Pol Pot's 'return to Year Zero' but communist, nonetheless. All KR survivors were required to attend three months of training, called "Political Morality" before working for the government.

"Political Morality? What does that mean?" I couldn't wrap my mind around this statement. I had to take a leave from my job at Dumex for this political re-education. The school and the students were housed where the National Pedagogical Institute had been four years earlier - on the way to the Pochentong airport, a mile from University of Pharmacy. The classrooms on the upper floors were turned into a dormitory, with four beds in each room - males on one side of the building and females on the other. The classrooms were on the first floor. Students were divided into cadres of fifteen and each had a leader. Ours was a man who had been a teacher before the KR regime. We referred to him as "*Lok Krou.*" He spoke slowly and calmly like a stream of water running over rocks.

Purpose of Learning Political Morality

On the first morning, all student survivors met in their designated classrooms. Our classroom was eerily quiet as we waited to hear what *Lok Krou* had to say. He began by explaining the communist principles and the role the Vietnamese played in releasing Cambodians from their "Prison Without Walls." We were taught about the Treaty of Peace, Friendship, and Cooperation and told this was the Vietnamese strategy to save Cambodian lives.

"No, it is not true. I met one *Bo Doy* in Siem Reap right after liberation and he told me that the Vietnamese came because the KR had invaded Vietnam," my voice seemed to fill the entire room and everyone stared at me in surprise.

Lok Krou seemed unaffected by my outburst. He just smiled, and in a voice that seemed even quieter than usual, gently said, "Whatever you have learned, please keep it to yourself, for your own safety." Everybody was silent. "You will learn to understand the meaning of the old proverb: "Going down to the water, you could be bitten by a crocodile; coming back from the water, you could be eaten by a tiger," *Lok Krou* said in a slow and steady voice and then asked the group what it meant.

After a short silence, Sokou, an opinionated woman and the oldest among us, volunteered, "It means there is danger and deception all around us. You can't trust anyone. Pol Pot wanted us dead; the Vietnamese want to control us."

"We'd rather be controlled by America. But, they didn't offer to help us rebuild our country. Why?" Sothy directed her question at me.

"I don't know. Americans have a reputation for helping other countries. Why do they turn their backs on us, ignoring us, acting as if nothing is wrong with our country?" I searched the faces of other students for an answer.

"Let's wrap it up and think of what we have learned. It's time for our lunch break," *Lok Krou* clapped his hands, his signature signal for the end of class.

Chicken Soup or Water Spinach

The lunchroom was filled with large round tables, closely spaced. On each bare, wooden table was a stack of ten small bowls with ten pairs of chopsticks. "What will we have for lunch? My guess is we will have something good, like chicken soup," I joked, when we were all seated.

A woman came from the kitchen using both hands to carry a big tray with containers of rice; she left one at each table. Like everybody else around the table, I was grateful to be freed from the Prison Without Walls. I had a porcelain bowl instead of the aluminum plate that I used for four years. I had a clean spoon and chopsticks that had been washed with soap and rinsed with clean water, not wiped with my grimy *krama*. I sat on a chair, not on the dirty ground. An electric fan cooled me; I was not in the blazing sun, drenched from head to toe in sweat. A cheerful cook, who I knew I could trust, served food with a friendly smile, and she didn't wear a black outfit. I had friends to sit with and talk about "peace" and "freedom". We laughed, we teased each other, and played like children; so different from hopelessness of the past four years, where our time was spent quiet, scared, and miserable. But the food was awful.

Next, the friendly cook returned with a container of veggies, brown and greasy, "Ç'est de liseron d'eau – it's water spinach, *ou quoi* – or what?" I asked her. "Anything else?"

"We don't have anything else besides water spinach. It was brought by *Ong Leun*, the Vietnamese boss," she replied with a smile.

"Just eat it. We are hungry; don't complain so much," my girlfriend, Sokun, said to shut me up. "We don't produce anything yet. C'mon, the Vietnamese like this veggie. We have to be like them now."

"Yuk, we are going to have *Reak Ach* (diarrhea)," I groaned.

"Disgusting," another girl, sitting next to Sokun, agreed.

Devastated

At 2 PM, after lunch and the traditional midday nap, we returned to the classroom to learn about Prince Sihanook and Pol Pot. What did Pol Pot do to

Cambodia? We learned that Pol Pot's real name was Saloth, Sar. He was born in Kampong Thom province in 1928 and joined the communist party, the "*Cercle Marxiste*", when he studied in France, where he became a leader. He married Ponnary in 1956, in Paris, and then eventually returned to Cambodia to begin a revolution to bring communism to Cambodia. We were taught that that Pol Pot and his KR troops were reinforced by China with millions of dollars a year in weapons as they took over Cambodia and began the Return to Year Zero. Eventually, there was a conflict between the KR and Vietnam over the Khmer border. This dispute caused the relationship of KR communists and the Vietnamese communists to fall apart and Vietnam attacked Cambodia and overthrew the KR. However, Vietnam's official view of this was that they acted in self-defense.

After his defeat in January, 1979, Pol Pot fled to Thailand and hid in the Khao I Dang camp under the protection of the Thais. We were taught that Pol Pot's plan was to eliminate all Cambodians and bring the Chinese to our land. Without Vietnam, we would all have been executed. They were our saviors.

"Bring the Chinese to our land?" several young men that were sitting in the back of the room shouted their question in disbelief. I had heard this before but it was news to them.

"Our saviors? Hmm, it sounds a lot more complicated than that to me. Pol Pot and the North Vietnamese were allies; they knew what he was doing. Now, Vietnam is our savior? This gives me a headache," Sokun said.

Lok Krou cleared out his throat, "I was told to tell you that Vietnam came to rescue us. We need to appreciate Vietnamese kindness. They voluntarily rescued us from Genocide." We were all quiet for a while. Then, still smiling, *Lok Krou* asked, "What did *Samdech* do to Cambodia?" He waited but there was no answer. He continued his lecture, "One of the most difficult things for most common Cambodians to wrap their minds around is the role our "God-King", *Samdech* Sihanook, played in the destruction of our country and our families. He was not just our leader; he was deified in Cambodia, as his forbearers had been before him. Of course, in reality, he was a selfish hypocrite who betrayed his country and his trusting people for his own political ends. He exiled himself to Beijing, living in luxury with his wife, while allowing his people to be executed, and to die from sickness, forced labor, and starvation.

"Why did he call himself the Father of Cambodia?" He, who most of the ordinary, unsophisticated population believed in and trusted, had turned into a devil prince using history and ignorance to ensure that Cambodians would love him forever. This spell has still not been eliminated in Cambodian minds, especially the farmers and peasants. It is like a carving on the wall of Angkor Wat, never to be erased.

"Look at this picture," *Lok Krou* showed us a photo in which *Samdech* stood smiling next to Pol Pot, (aka Ieng Sary, the mass murderer) clapping his hands. "What was he celebrating other than the deaths of millions of innocents? Notice that he and his wife, Monik Sihanook, who also was shameless, are dressed in the

KR black uniform and *krama*. Nonetheless, he remains a popular figure to the Cambodian man on the street."

"At the end of the three month session, we will go to all the provinces, districts and villages to explain this to all Khmer farmers and peasants so they will understand the real face of *Samdech*. He is not a 'God-King', as these people believe."

For the most part, the student survivors were silent. We knew that we were being fed Vietnamese propaganda mixed with truth and rumor. We also knew that there was nothing we could do about it. There was danger and deception all around us.

Eating Water Spinach

Dinner time had arrived. We got the same water spinach and rice again. "*Mon Dieu*! My teeth are going to be stained black like the North Vietnamese from eating too much water spinach," Sithon, a goofy girl, said. She was the youngest girl in our group, very talkative and had a loud belly laugh that made her popular.

"There is a lot of Vitamin B12 in water spinach but I had diarrhea already. Maybe tomorrow we'll have something different," I tried to be hopeful.

"You complain a lot, but you also ate more than anybody else," Sokun laughed.

"No, I didn't eat much," I said, as I started on the second bowl of spinach that the cook had just brought out for me.

"That's your second bowl! Show me your teeth," Sithon demanded, as we both giggled.

"No," I said, covering my mouth with my hand. "Don't make me talk when I am eating, it is very impolite and ugly." I continued to chew the veggies; they were so tough it was like chewing a piece of beef steak.

"Ah, your teeth are stained, too, aren't they?" I teased, pointing at Sithon.

"So are yours," she said pointing back at me. We all laughed through our hands.

Many people were still severely malnourished and food was still very scarce. Rice and water spinach at both the lunch and dinner was better than the KR rations but was not enough to return people to health. Yet, that was what was available under Vietnamese occupation because water spinach was a common food in Vietnam and readily available. Everyone had brown stains on their teeth from the water spinach. Nonetheless, it was better than the KR time.

Autobiography

At about eight that night we were asked to return once again to the classroom. "Is *Lok Krou* crazy? I don't want to go. I'm tired," I whined.

"You have to go. *Lok Krou* will come looking for you if you don't. This is mandatory."

"This will be a very emotional session and there will be a lot of tears," *Lok Krou* began. "Each one of you will tell your experience during Pol Pot regime. Telling your story will make it easier for each of you to deal with how it has affected you."

Sokun began by telling how her husband was buried alive in Pursat province in the western part of Cambodia. She cried uncontrollably. Everyone cried with her and for each story as it was told. *Lok Krou* mourned the death of his child who died from sickness. The rest of his family, his wife and other two children, had survived. Sothy lost his brother; Wilson lost his parents. Sithon had no personal loss to share with the group because her family all survived but she was just as moved as everyone else with the horror of what had happened. When I told my story, I had everyone's sympathy because I was the only survivor in my family of nine people. I cried, maybe longer than everyone else had, for the loss of my husband and my Papa.

Sympathy

The next morning when class reconvened, I heard a soft whisper from behind me, "I want to share my sympathy with you." I turned to see Dararan, a male student who nodded his head and smiled at me. His smile was gentle and I felt an uncanny attraction for this stranger. His smile made my heart light and his voice was low and melodious. Every time I attempted to steal a glance at him, I met his eyes. I couldn't believe my luck. Here was someone, handsome, brilliant, and nice. He was alive, healthy and interested in me.

"He likes you," Sokun whispered. I smiled my agreement.

I continued to steal glances at him and his eyes were always on me. I wondered if he was looking at me or another woman. I looked around. Sokun? – No. She's too old. Sithon? – Impossible. Mony, a young girl sitting next to Sithon? – Definitely not, she's married. I was happy to conclude it had to be me. After the class was over, I left quickly with the other girls instead of staying to talk to Dararan.

"Am I escaping from love?" I asked myself. No, I am just nervous. I felt giddy and alive as I had with my husband. Dararan's smile, his face, his voice were with me all night. What do I want? Kisses, hugs, or just to get to know him? I was confused. I wished the night were over so I could see him again. But days went by and I did not get a chance to talk with Dararan.

"Hurry, Dara wants to talk to you," Sokun said excitedly one night about a week later as she came into the room.

I bounced off the bed and ran to the door. A friendly smile greeted me as I opened the door. "Can I talk to you?" Dara said eagerly. He was another man in my class who was friendly and seemed very pleasant.

"*Chah*. About what?" I kept walking toward to the balcony, so we could talk.

"I have a picture of you."

"What picture? When did you take a picture?"

"A week ago, when I brought my camera to class."

"Oh, now I remember. Where's the picture? Why did you do with it?"

"You know I live with my sister. She has been like my mother since I lost my parents. So, before I make any important decisions, I discuss them with her first." He paused; I looked at him curiously, having no idea why we were having this conversation.

"I gave your picture to her. I told her about you based on what you told us in the classroom. She likes you and she agrees I should ask you to get engaged."

I was shocked. What? Engaged? I barely knew this man and had never spent a moment alone with him.

"Dara. I am flattered but I need time to think about it. I didn't know you were thinking of me in that way. Just give me time."

Dara smiled at me. He seemed very happy after telling me what was in his heart, but just moments after he said goodbye to me, Dararan appeared at my door. "What did he tell you?" He asked me very familiarly, as if we were longtime friends.

"He wants us to become engaged."

"Engaged?" I nodded.

"Honey, please tell him you have me. Let him go."

"Honey....?" I looked at him in shock. "You have me?" I repeated his words. "When did it become you and me?" Was I losing my mind?

"Honey, I love you from the bottom of my heart. I know we are meant to be together," he said and kissed me on the forehead. He squeezed my hands and hugged me. He held my face in both hands and looked into my eyes, "I love you and I promise I will heal your pain of the loss of your family."

"I do not have the courage to tell Dara I cannot marry him. He will be hurt because he told me he loved me first."

"I will tell him for you. It doesn't matter that he said he loves you before I did. I love you more and I am the man you are meant to be with," he assured me.

An Angry Lion

From that time, Dararan and I spent all our time together, eating at the same table, talking more often on the balcony. On the other hand, Dara still appeared very happy, very confident. He hung around me more often. His behavior confused me. I hoped that maybe Dararan had told him the truth and Dara decided to keep our friendship going regardless but I soon found out what was really going on. One night, about a week later, someone pounded loudly on the bedroom door. Sokun shouted, "The door is open, stop banging."

The door flew opened and there stood Dara, red faced and acting like an angry lion. He threw a picture on the floor and left. Sokun went and picked up the picture. "Vicheara, it is your picture. Wait! There is something written on the back." She read aloud, "Don't ever come back. What does it mean, Vicheara?" she asked.

"I don't know," I walked to Dara's room with my picture in my hand. Someone answered the door for me and I saw Dara sitting on the bed, facing the door. As soon as he saw me, his face grew dark and he shouted, "Get out and don't return." I backed out. After that night, Dara avoided me like the plague.

~THIRTY SIX~

REGIMENTAL COMMANDER

The most surprising part of the political re-education was a mass meeting with Hun, Sen, a Cambodian man installed as temporary head of the government by the Vietnamese. I can't remember exactly how he introduced himself because his dialect sounded like the KR that I had heard for four years, and it startled and dismayed me. I actually felt sick at hearing it again.

Amazingly, in front of the hundreds of Khmer survivors who attended this meeting, he declared that he was a former KR regiment commander. We forgot to breathe. How could this be? KR? Here? How the hell could this happen?

Then, after this shocking admission in front of an audience of survivors, he began a bizarre diatribe on the evils of adultery. Adultery? He spent more than a half hour just talking about and criticizing adultery with inappropriate words. People looked at each other in a combination of shock and bewilderment. I looked at him - trying to figure out the meaning of his speech about adultery. Was it a code for something else or was he serious? Was he crazy?

"This speech doesn't make sense to me at all. Listen to him; he is not an educated person. I smell danger to our country in the future, believe me or not," I whispered to Sothy, who sat next to me with his eyes closed. "Hey!" I gently pulled his shirt to wake him up.

"Yes, I heard what he said. I just want to rest my eyes." He sighed.

"Are you listening to him?"

He chuckled. "What do you care what he says? I expected to hear something interesting other than his opinion on adultery. His speech made me fall asleep." He closed his eyes again.

"Hey," I kicked his chair and whispered, "Did you hear how he identified himself as a former KR regiment commander? If that is true, he is a murderer of over two million Khmers. He must have participated in many murders to become a commander. Why should we be here so he can identify us as educated people so he can kill us later?" I stared at Hun, Sen who continued to speak in front of us with no shame.

"Listen," Sothy kicked my chair back. "He wants us to believe that he was a hero who fought with the KR to save his country. This man was part of the KR who murdered our families, tortured us and put us in the Prison Without Walls. This man ruined millions of lives and he is droning on and on about adultery. This is surreal. I can't believe it."

When I heard the words "KR commander," it was like slap in the face. I was shocked and horrified. I asked myself if my life would once again be jeopardized by the KR? I was so shocked and frightened that I stopped listening. What I remember hearing clearly was he said he lost his eye in combat.

"His eye is gone; he looks like a pirate but he must be smart," said Sothy.

"Hun, Sen is flexible. He knew how to survive," Wilson was listening to us and shook his head and laughed bitterly.

"Are you laughing at Hun, Sen?" I turned to him.

"*Bat*, I cannot believe our country now has a leader who participated in mass murder. I cannot believe he revealed his true identity to us. He must have a reason; I think he is laughing at us. It must be, don't you think?"

Sothy shook his head again and said, "What does this say about the *Ong Leun* who has put him in power? He must have deserted from the KR and run for help from the Vietnamese; if he didn't, he wouldn't be here today, in front of us. Why in the world would they choose him instead of an educated person?"

"The Vietnamese don't look for educated people; they want followers, not leaders. Didn't you learn anything from Pol Pot's regime? Did they keep or kill the educated people? And then, what happened next, after the uneducated people took control of our lives?" I asked, in irritation.

"Hey kids! Let's talk about it when his speech is over," Wilson hissed to us over his shoulder.

"I am not a kid, Grandpa, and look at people when you are talking to them. Looking away is disrespectful," I retorted.

"Ho, Ho…I'm now looking at you in the eyes, face to face," Wilson stuck his face in mine. I backed away to avoid the smell of his smoking. "You call me grandpa. Can I call you girlfriend, then? Now I can see your eyes are beautiful."

"In your dreams, maybe."

It had been a long evening listening to first Hun, Sen's ridiculous speech, later to more propaganda from the Vietnamese boss. On the way back to our rooms, I mentally reviewed what I had heard from our new leaders that day. Disappointment and depression descended on me as I thought about the implications for me, for my friends and family and for my country.

"Why are you so upset? Didn't you get any sleep during the speeches?" Sothy teased me.

"Be serious." I said. "Regardless of whom Hun, Sen is in this new phase, he is still KR. He is the same person, just wearing different clothes. How could this happen without the help of the Vietnamese? Why did they help him? What does this mean for us survivors? What is the unspoken message when Vietnam, his boss, our unwanted boss, is behind Hun, Sen making him even stronger and more powerful, and making us more insecure about our country and our safety? Is this all part of the historical Vietnamese strategy of "Nam Tien" or colonialism towards their neighbors?"

Wilson was walking behind us, "Yes, I heard about Nam Tien or the Southward March strategy. The Vietnamese plan is to take over their weaker neighbors like Cambodia, Laos, maybe Thailand."

"Oh, now you want to be serious? What do you know about Nam Tien?" I asked.

Wilson laughed and shared his ideas, "Vietnam's invasion is not to save our lives but to take advantage of our weakness. They think the survivors are so debilitated and traumatized that they can brainwash us. They think they can put thoughts in our minds and water spinach in our mouths and that we will accept re-education because we are so weak and so exhausted from the barbarian regime of Pol Pot. And to a certain extent, they are right. We are hungry; we need to feed our bodies before we can begin the intellectual task of finding out how this happened to us. We are not going to obsess about political intrigue when our stomachs and our babies are crying for food."

Wilson surprised me with his analysis; I had not thought of him a serious person until then. I answered in the same vein, "However, throughout history, I can see that the Vietnamese alone could not have easily succeeded unless they had help from corrupt, selfish and misguided Cambodian leaders like King *Chey Chetha* II, and now Pol Pot, and *Samdech* Sihanook."

"You are right Vicheara. I know about King *Chey Chettha* II and what he did to Cambodia," Wilson agreed. "I remember he ran for help from the Vietnamese."

"*Chah*, this Khmer King had been married to a Vietnamese princess," I said.

"Right." Wilson's face was getting red as he warmed to the subject, "To please his wife, *Chey, Chettha* allowed the Vietnamese government to occupy the city of *Prey Nokor*, which was Khmer land. The Vietnamese never left *Prey Nokor*; first they changed the name to Saigon, and now to Ho Chi Minh City. You know that Ho Chi Minh is the leader of the North Vietnamese? *Prey Nokor* has disappeared from the Khmer map permanently. History does seem to repeat itself in Cambodia. Since the fall of Angkor, Cambodian leaders always have asked for foreign intervention - Vietnamese, Thai, and French, when they fought each other. *Samdech* Sihanook supported Pol Pot, and now Hun, Sen, to save his monarchy which obviously is more important to him than saving Cambodia and her people."

We said goodnight and went to our rooms but I could not sleep. My mind was whirling as I thought about what had happened to me and my country. Cambodians are Buddhists; we all believe in forgiving and forgetting. Many forgave Sihanouk for his devil heart, betrayal and hypocrisy. I did not. His popularity was more important to him than his crimes against millions of Cambodians. He joined the evil empire of Pol Pot for revenge against the Lon Nol government and the Cambodian citizens who overthrew him on March 18, 1970. The lust for power turned him and the KR into devils. Because of their inhumanity, their devil hearts, I lost my dearest father, most of my extended family, and I was almost lost myself in the hole already dug for my tiny body by the KR. My innocent husband was executed just because KR was given the authority to kill anyone whenever they wanted with no government to protect them. Should I forget this horrible life and forgive Prince Sihanook, his wife, and his KR associates?

How long it had taken me to understand the western adage that those who do not know history are doomed to repeat it. Now I realized that learning history was very important so we would learn the lessons of the past and not make the same mistakes over and over. How many times had Vietnam and Thailand used their tricks to try to swallow our country? I remembered that my aunt, the first wife of my *Pou* Chhun, used to remind me that the Vietnamese mistreated the Cambodians because of our lack of sophistication. They called us morons. I remembered Dr. Mey saying that when our city was empty, it allowed neighboring countries, mainly Vietnam, to take advantage of our disaster. He said that if we do not know how to take care of our country, somebody else will do for us and they will expect to be rewarded. He meant Vietnam felt entitled to confiscate anything they could from us because we killed our own people.

Kouk Toul Sleng

In March 1980, a week before finishing our training, all the students went to visit the *Kouk* –Prison of *Toul Sleng*, S-21 (Hill of the Poisonous Trees) to see firsthand the evidence of how Cambodians were massacred by Pol Pot. *Toul Sleng* was formerly College of Toul Svay Prey. All the classrooms had been transformed into prison cells. Razor wire was used as fences surrounding the school.

Guides took us through the prison and told us the grim story of the brutal torture these poor people suffered before they were murdered. Every effort was made to humiliate and de-humanize them. They were stripped of all their possessions and most of their clothing; they were photographed, interrogated and then shackled in utter misery twenty four hours a day. We walked into one of the cells where we still found traces of dried blood where the victims' legs had been shackled to the bars and their wrists restrained by brackets. The blood still looked fresh. I couldn't stay any longer because of the pain in my heart for these people massacred so horribly. I could not imagine how the KR tortured their fellow human beings with no mercy. I saw the pictures of the victims on the wall and, even though I knew intellectually how widespread the murder had been, it shocked and frightened me when I saw the pictures of the children and the babies. I searched the photos and lists for the names of my husband and my missing relatives in case they had been sent there. But, I did not find any. So the uncertainty continued; they could be alive, or perhaps killed somewhere else. I just had to wait and see.

Outside of the building there was a big, big brick jar set up next to a pole. Victims' arms were tied to the pole and they were fully immersed in the jar which was full of caustic fish sauce. This continued until they "confessed" or died. We learned that each province had organized the elimination of enemies in different ways. Towards the end of the KR time, the KR were killing each other as well as killing us. This reminded me about *Pouk* Kreun and leader Kim who "disappeared" from the village right before a new leader arrived. I also learned that the KR was not as organized and disciplined as we had thought and had become more disorganized as they began to fight internally.

I saw the ten KR rules for the prisoners. Of course, they were in Cambodian; the words below are a somewhat mangled English translation that was added some years later.

1. If I ask a question, you must answer right away

2. Don't test me; you must answer the truth when I ask you a question

3. You are a prisoner of the revolution, because you are not smart

4. Answer me right away, no thinking about your answer

5. I don't care about your opinion of our revolution

6. No crying, no matter what your punishment, even electric shock

7. Do nothing, sit still and wait for my orders. If there is no order, keep quiet When I ask you to do something, you must do it right away without protesting

8. Don't make pretext about *Kampuchea Krom* in order to hide your secrets or the fact that you are a traitor

9. If you don't follow all the above rules, you will be whipped many times with electric wire

10. If you disobey any of my regulations you shall receive either ten lashes or five electric shocks

Across the street from this building was another small office where the school security guard had stayed when the buildings were a peaceful school. That little office was used by the KR to torture people by pulling out their nails with pliers and then killing them by electric shock. I could not stay in that building either as I could not stand the pain as I felt the cries of the victims begging me for help.

It began to dawn on me that the Cambodian leaders, including Papa, may have thought they understood the KR tactics, principles and system but that they did not understand their enemy at all. They behaved as though they were negotiating with a centralized government when, in fact, the KR leaders could not speak for the whole movement, but only for themselves and their small band of communists. Who knew how many "leaders" that the KR had set up in their organization?

There was no central plan other than punishing and killing the "privileged" and the idealization of a simple, agrarian life. Generally speaking, it seemed that the peasants killed the urbanites, the non-educated killed the educated, the poor people killed rich, and then KR killed their own members. Everyone had an enemy but who would be Cambodians when they all got through killing each other?

Now I understood where all the rice went and why we starved in one of the most fertile countries in the world. The rice all went to China to repay their support of the KR; I recalled Praub, the "Old People" who was Papa's friend, telling us exactly that. This evil doctrine of Pol Pot was a study in hatred and betrayal. The poor were promised a better life but wound up betrayed, starving with the new people. The KR betrayed each other from the top to the bottom, from the leaders to the soldiers because it was a system without a moral compass, they made up their own rules; they betrayed all the Buddhist principles that value life. Papa died, my husband died, so many of my extended family died, more than two million Cambodians died because of a lust for power and the cowardice of many in the face of madness.

I stomped my feet on the floor in frustration as I thought of this injustice and betrayal. This was why I lost my family.

.....If they were alive, I would never have been so lonely....

~THIRTY SEVEN~

RE-EDUCATE THE PEOPLE

The three months of political training by our "Vietnamese saviors" ended. Now our obligation was to go off into the countryside to present this propaganda to the villagers. We had no choice; if we wanted to eat and work, we would do it. Again, we were divided into groups of about fifteen people, each assigned to a province where we would educate Cambodian villagers about who was the murderer of millions of people, and who was our savior.

I was initially assigned to Takeo province, about eighty-seven kilometers from Phnom Penh, in the southern part of Cambodia but I asked if I could go with Dararan to Kompong Chhnang and was happy when it was approved.

At 7:00 AM, all the students assembled, attendance was verified and we were assigned to Vietnamese military trucks. Fifteen people would be a tight fit in the back of the truck and this morning I saw more than fifteen.

"Where are we going to sit?" I asked anxiously, remembering other very long rides, standing for hours, as we were moved by the KR.

"No chair for Your Highness?" responded Wilson, back to his usual sardonic self. "We will be packed in the truck like cows."

"This should be a lot of fun," I said to Dararan.

"Stay by me, Honey," I moved next to him. There was room for everyone and my fears subsided.

Sithon never stopped laughing and giggling about anything and everything. When the engine started, everyone screamed with excitement. Me too, as it was a new experience for me. The Vietnamese driver was obviously in a hurry and didn't bother to slow down when turning corners or going over bumps. When the truck made a turn, everyone fell on each other, and then came the scramble, along with the screaming and yelling, "Don't fall on me. You're sitting on me, get off! Can't you see?"

I watched everyone and couldn't help but laugh because everyone was so unreasonable; especially the men, when one fell on another. But, if a woman fell on them, they made no attempt to remove us. Remarkably, my Dararan, who never allowed himself to sway or fall, held me close and prevented me from falling or losing my balance.

After about three hours, we were dropped off near an abandoned hotel in Kampong Chhnang province, town of Kampong Chhnang, and set about finding where we would sleep and find food.

The Legend of Rithisen Neang Kang Rey

Kampong Chhnang is west of Phnom Penh, about ninety kilometers from the city. Before the devil communists took over, handmade pottery was a mainstay of the local economy. The potters worked from their homes and many people traveled to Kampong Chhnang to buy these unique pots. Every house would have jars sitting outside drying; it was also quite a spectacle as the potters transported their pots from home to the market by oxcarts. The pots hung from hooks on the carts, spaced perfectly to avoid breaking any of the valuable handwork. People came to the market from all over and it had hummed with vendors selling the beautiful earthenware, fish, and vegetables of all kinds, tropical fruit, desserts and many other wares. Walking through the market, one could smell delicious noodle soups with deep fried garlic, coffee, tea and fermented fish. These scents, mixed with ox manure, were the unique aroma of Kampong Chhnang market.

My personal memories of Kampong Chhnang were much more recent and painfully acute. This was where my family and I had been dumped after we were tricked into thinking we were being returned to Phnom Penh by boat. I remembered how panicked Papa had been when, blind but for the moonlight, we had struggled off the big boat, carrying all our belongings. He had believed all of us would return home when *Angkar* ordered all the "New People" to the boats, instead we were transported to this province. The image of Grandaunt Hieng, exhausted, dehydrated and starved, lying on the ground waiting for *Pou* Sunthary to carry her on his back, was still very vivid in my memory. That night, both sides of road had been flooded due to monsoons and we had waded through the water to find a dry place to sleep. I felt the spirits of my family all around me and I sent my prayers to them, "Papa, Leang, and *Pou* Sunthary, all of you made me come here so I wouldn't forget you. I know all of you may be walking with me right now, but I can't see you. I wish I could see you. I wish I could hug you. I miss you."

The town was quiet like that night four years ago, but today, I didn't feel the panic and worry. I wondered where all the inhabitants had gone? Those talented potters had been "relocated" just as we had. It was evident that they had suffered the same fate as everyone else. Damn the KR!

The distant beauty of the mountain of *Neang Kang Rey* was unchanged by the four years that had changed so much of the rest of Cambodia. When I was young, Papa brought us here many weekends; I would ask him to take me to the mountain but for some reason he always managed to put it off, promising he would take me 'next time'. Now, I was here again and it still did not seem that a visit to *Neang Kang Rey* would happen. "Maybe I will never visit you," I said to the mountain.

This famous mountain was located along the *Tonlé Sap*, about fourteen kilometers from the town. A centuries-old local legend explained its shape of a woman sleeping on her back, her face looking up to the sky with her long hair flowing beside her. "Do you know the legend of *Rithisen* and *Neang Kang Rey?*" I asked Sithon, pointing in the direction of the mountain.

"No, I don't think so, what is the legend?" she stopped giggling and looked at me quizzically.

"Look, what do you see?" I pointed in the direction of the mountains. "What do those mountains look like to you?"

She stared at them for a few moments and said, "They look like mountains. What am I supposed to see?"

"This is the mountain of *Neang Kang Rey*. It is supposed to look like a sleeping woman. See there is her head, and then her breasts, and over there are her legs, bent at the knee." My fingers traced the silhouette of the sleeping giant woman while Sithon watched intently. "And that," I pointed to the trees at the base of the mountain, "is her hair flowing beside her as she sleeps." Sithon squinted and then her eyes opened wide, "Yes, I see her; it really does look like a sleeping giant woman." She was excited; she looked like a little girl hearing the story for the first time.

"It is a Khmer legend called *Rithisen* and *Neang Kang Rey*. As a child, my servant told me this story almost every night before I went to sleep."

"I didn't have a servant to tell me stories, how can I know this legend?" she giggled.

"She doesn't even know how old she is, how she can know Khmer legends. How old are you now?" Sokun was also listening and looked disgustedly at Sithon.

"Uh…I guess, 22, or maybe 19…I don't know. My mother forgot too." She looked up to the sky, "But, it is not my fault. Oh….I remember, I was told I was born in the time when the tamarind gives flowers."

"What? It is strange that someone wouldn't know their birth date."

"Wait," she changed the subject, "I remember my mother did tell me this story. She said *Neang Kang Rey* was a deer and died or something."

"You should know this famous legend when you are born a Khmer. Once upon a time, there was a very poor couple who gave birth to 12 baby girls."

"Twelve babies would have to be small like rats to fit in the mother's tummy. Yes, I remember this too. My mother told me this story," Sithon interrupted, taking my hand.

"As the girls grew up, this poor couple could no longer afford to feed them. They decided to take the girls deep into the jungle and leave them there. Once they were far from home, the parents made an excuse to leave the girls and never returned. The king at that time loved to go hunting in the jungle. While hunting one day, he came across the twelve beautiful girls sitting by a small stream crying. He was so smitten by their beauty he took them back to the palace and announced his marriage to all twelve. Sometime later, the king was bored and wanted to hunt again. Guess what?" I asked Sithon, to ensure she was following me.

"I think…..he found another twelve women to marry," she giggled.

"This time while hunting, he saw a deer that seemed to be peeking at him from behind a large palm tree. The deer lowered her head and looked at him though her lashes. Her large brown eyes drew him in as if she had cast a fishing line and snagged a catch. Her body moved like water rippling in a gentle stream, beautiful, serene and graceful. He suddenly had no control over himself or his actions. She entranced him and he had no choice but to follow her cute little twitching white tail through the jungle and soon became separated from his guards. When the doe was sure the guards were far enough away, she turned herself into a beautiful woman. The king was mesmerized as he watched the transformation. He had never seen such a stunning woman before. The king decided to marry her on the spot. The woman, who was in reality a giant monster, had what she wanted. She had fallen in love with the king when she saw him hunting in the jungle and watched him many times. It took her a while to think of this scheme to have him marry her. The king and the woman found the guards and returned to the palace. Now there was a problem. Can you guess what that was?"

Sithon shook her head and took a deep breath, "No…Oh, maybe she got into a fight with the other twelve wives."

"No. Remember this woman was really a giant monster. Turning herself into a human did not alter who she really was inside. After eating all the women servants in the palace, she wanted to eat the twelve wives. But, it would not be as easy as eating the servants. Can you guess why?"

"Me? Again?" Sithon pointed at herself. "How am I supposed to know what is in a monster's head?" Sokun laughed with Sithon this time.

"She will come to find you and eat your head tonight." Wilson came at Sithon with his hands clawed to scare her. We had attracted quite a few listeners.

"Bastard." She slapped him on the chest.

"Fairy tales! Why are you listening to this crap?" Wilson laughed and walked away.

"Pay attention, Sithon," I reclaimed her attention. "She told the king many lies about the twelve wives to make him hate them. She and the king now had a daughter of their own and the king believed all her lies and decided to get rid of the twelve sisters. He told his guards to take them to a cave in the jungle and leave them there. He told the guards to remove their eyes so they couldn't find their way back to the castle. Before the guards left, the monster woman told them to bring the eyes back to her. The youngest of the twelve wives was the most beautiful and the guard who was supposed to remove her eyes couldn't take both her eyes. So, without the knowledge of the rest of the guards, he only took her right eye and, therefore, she was able to go foraging in the jungle for food to feed her sisters. This was difficult as her sisters were very hungry. As it turned out, all twelve of them were pregnant and began giving birth. Because they were so hungry, they decided to eat the babies. It was up to the youngest to divide the babies into equal parts since she was the only one who could see. When she did this, she decided to save her portions. As she was the last to give birth, she gave her sisters the eleven portions she had been saving and did not kill her son.

"Unbelievable. How can they eat their own babies?" Sithon was horrified.

"It is a legend, remember?"

"But still, who would think up such a story!" She just couldn't fathom such a thing, real or not.

"Years later, the baby grew up, found his way out of the cave and was responsible for bringing food for his mother and his aunts."

"Wait!" Sithon stopped walking, and looked at me," How could she hide her baby for so long until he grew up? Let say, about six or seven years until he knew how to find his way out of the cave? Didn't the baby cry?"

"Sithon, this is a legend. You can't make sense of legends, so just shut up and listen," Sokun straightened herself and sat quietly, waiting for the rest of my story.

"Hurry up; we can finish the story later," *Lok Krou* motioned us to walk faster as we neared a group of tall buildings.

"OK, I will continue the rest tonight but you must remind me if you are interested." Sithon agreed and we all picked up our pace.

Our Resting Place was Protected

I looked up at the five-story brick houses. Luckily, the doors and windows were still in good condition, but the walls were pock-marked with bullet holes. Maybe the Vietnamese shot at the devil black crows to chase them out of this place.

Lok Krou, who always took the lead, turned to the three of us who were trying to keep up with his long steps. "There are *Bo Doy* staying in the next building to protect us, but we were warned to take our security seriously. There is still the threat of KR who are hiding in the jungle and come out to steal food from the people who remain in the town. They could come into our buildings, so we must be vigilant."

"Don't worry," Dararan whispered to me, "stay close to me, I will protect you." I was comforted to have a man who wanted to protect me. I didn't think I would ever have that sort of comfort again after the deaths of Papa and my husband.

Surprisingly, the building was clean. "Why is this building clean?" I asked *Lok Krou* as we climbed to the second floor.

"I was told they prepared well for us and they chose this place as the safest place because the black devils wouldn't come this far down. But, we need to be careful. Who knows?"

"Who are 'they'?" I climbed the stairs behind him, carrying my little cloth bag on my shoulder.

"*Bo Doy*. They lived in this building and others in this town." We reached the second floor where the evening breeze was coming through the windows. Some of the men unbuttoned their shirts to feel the fresh air. I felt fresh air coming through every window; I took off my sandals and walked barefoot on the red and white floor tiles. Everyone dropped their clothing bags on the floor to breath in the fresh, cool air.

"I will stay on the second floor," *Lok Krou* said and turned to Sokun, "you and all the women will stay here also." She was busy hunting through her bag without paying attention to *Lok Krou*.

"Did you bring the whole house with you?" *Lok Krou* teased her as he took his shirt off.

"Women always carry a lot of necessary stuff, like this little pillow, a *krama*, a comb, and other totally necessary things. If we didn't, we would be men," Sokun replied, without looking at him.

"I had hoped for a nice bed in each room," Sithon said.

"Nonsense. How can we have such things when everything has been destroyed by the black devils?" Sokun spat out irritably.

"I can't believe the devils destroyed all the furniture. They probably took it to their farms. Don't you think they would enjoy furniture since they never had any? Remember, in the city every single house was totally empty. They either took it to their farms or totally destroyed it. Maybe they used it all for firewood or something, but what happened to the appliances? Why would they take them to their farms when they don't have electricity?"

"Maybe they sold them to make money for their cause?" Sokun speculated.

"Sold it? To who?" Irritated with their conversation, I decided to tell them the truth. They would have to think harder before believing the KR destroyed all the furniture and appliances. "The KR know nothing about anything. They drink water from the toilet, what does that tell you? Have you ever seen any farm houses with furniture in them? How would the farmers transport all those things? With the oxcarts?"

"Vietnamese then?" Sithon asked.

"Now you are thinking!" I replied.

"It's time to cook. Who's going to cook?" *Lok Krou* cut off our conversation.

"Sithon," Dararan suggested. "She has had good opinions today, so she should be rewarded by cooking for us."

"OK, I will do it, but *Baung* Sokun will be my assistant."

Sokun didn't answer, just glared at her and got up looking for the cooking area.

"The kitchen is on the first floor. The earthen jar is full of water for cooking. We will have dried fish with our rice tonight," *Lok Krou* took dried fish from his other bag and gave it to Sithon.

"Honey, I will sleep outside on the balcony tonight," my boyfriend whispered, his hot breath close to my ear." Come sleep with me if you want." I smiled with anticipation.

"Dara!" *Lok Krou* said, "You can go to the third floor with the other guys if you want because it is crowded here with all the women. They will be fine here as the door is metal and well locked." Dara grabbed his bag and went upstairs followed by a couple of the other men.

"I will go to the fourth floor. No one is allowed to choose this floor," Wilson stated.

"There is no restroom on the fourth floor. I will lock the door and you won't be able to come downstairs," one of the men threatened. Wilson looked around to find out who said it, but everyone covered for each other.

"Good, I will go to the fifth floor balcony and piss down on your head."

"I am just kidding," came the same voice.

"Ya.....Don't know me much…hah?" Wilson huffed.

After dinner, we got together for a short meeting. "Each night, the men will take turns providing armed security since there are still KR resistance forces in the area and KR hidden among the citizens," *Lok Krou* said, as we all sat together on the floor. He wiped his nose and said, "The KR come out at night to steal food and anything else they need. Security is a serious position so be careful with the gun and if you are tired, please let me know." He smiled at Sithon and Sokun, "Thanks so much for cooking for us." Everyone clapped their hands to close the meeting.

The Legend Continued

Suddenly, Sithon whispered in my ear. "Can you finish the story of *Neang Kang Rey?*"

"I am proud of you, Sithon." I tied my hair up with a barrette to allow the breeze to cool me.

"I am proud of you too. I cannot believe you still remember this."

"Well, this was my favorite bedtime story; my favorite servant would tell it to me almost every night when I was young. She told me I should tell this legend to anyone who was interested. That is how legends get passed down through the generations. You will tell this story to your children who are interested in learning Khmer legends."

Sithon smiled her cute, childlike smile. She was a friendly, easy-going, nice girl. Her skin was darker than most Khmer people, her full lips were pretty, and her brown, almond-shaped eyes sparkled. Her nose told me she was not a pure Khmer girl. I was curious, so I asked her, "One of your parents must be not a pure Khmer."

"My parents are Khmer, but my great-grandmother was a black girl. Don't ask me how she met my great-grandfather. Nobody talked about it, because as you know, our culture doesn't appreciate mixing blood that way."

"Ok, I won't ask. Now, remember, my story is not perfectly correct. I tell you based on what I remember." Sithon nodded her head and smiled. "Do you remember where we left off?" I noticed Sokun and *Lok Krou* were also interested in my story.

"The boy was in and out of the cave to bring food for his mother…uh!...what was the boy's name?"

"*Rithisen*. So, one day, the boy met a hermit who accepted him as a student. After many years of learning and training, he became a warrior. Before he left the hermit, he was told it was his duty to retrieve the eyeballs of his mother and aunts from the daughter of the giant woman monster. The daughter, *Neang Kang Rey*, lived far away in a royal palace. Rithisen was given a very powerful, magical white horse as his transportation and protection. This horse had wings and could fly!" Sithon, wide-eyed, nodded her head, without interrupting with questions like before.

"The horse flew him to meet the King-father and kill the woman monster. His aunts and his mother were then brought back to live in the palace with the King-father. His next mission was to go get their eyeballs and return them. He followed all the hermit's instructions to find *Neang Kang Rey*. Oh, I forgot to tell you one thing -before *Rithisen* left, the hermit also gave him an important letter and told him to bring it to *Neang Kang Rey*."

"What did the letter say?" Sithon asked.

"It says as soon as Rithisen arrives; marry him regardless if it's day or night."

"Wow, marrying someone without knowing each other?"

"In any case, she did marry him. However, she didn't know *Rithisen*'s reason for seeking her. She was so much in love that she trusted him and told him where her mother had hidden the eyeballs. *Rithisen* threw a big party and made everyone in her palace, including her, get drunk. When everyone had passed out, he took the eyeballs and left her and the castle. Soon, she woke up and look for *Rithisen*. She ran outside just as he mounted his winged horse and prepared to leave her. As she called his name and ran to catch him, the horse left the ground and flew into the sky. Devastated, she refused to return to her palace alone to avoid being labeled a "deserted woman". *Rithisen* loved her very much and it broke his heart to see her like this, but he needed to accomplish his goal - the eyeballs for his mother and aunts were his first priority. From the sky, he begged her to return to her palace, and told he would return when his mission was accomplished but *Neang Kang Rey* believed he was leaving her forever. Seeing her running after him, he threw his magical baton to the ground. When the baton hit the ground, it turned into a big lake that we now call *Tonlé* Mekong. *Neang Kang Rey* stayed by the lake waiting for his return until she died. When she died, she turned into a mountain. That is why the mountain range has the shape of a woman resting on her back, looking up the sky."

"Too bad *Rithisen* couldn't have flown in and rescued two millions Khmer; he should have arrived on his white horse and destroyed the KR," *Lok Krou* said sardonically as he arranged his sleeping mat and mosquito net.

My Heart is on Fire

I slipped out to the balcony to meet Dararan who was there waiting for me; he pulled me close to him, intending to kiss me. Gently, I put my hands against his chest, "Honey, it is neither a good time nor a good place; there are too many eyes and ears about." He groaned in mock disappointment but agreed.

When he listened to me and controlled his passion toward me, I knew I was right to love him. I will give him everything he wants, but in a bedroom with just him and me, on nice white sheets. He pulled me close for another kiss and his hands began to rove over my back and neck. I felt soft, full lips kissing my neck, then my shoulder, then my chin, then moving down; I didn't want to resist this passion that I craved. I reminded myself we'd better stop before we got to the point of no return. One more kiss and I feared I would be to that point. I gently pushed him away. "Honey, I love you. But, I need to go back inside."

He held me closer and then reluctantly released me. I kissed him on his lips before I got out of the mosquito net. Coming back into my own mosquito net, I untied my hair and laid down thinking about his hands, his lips, his kisses. I wanted him now, but....I cannot. I caressed my neck with my hand imagining it was his fingers caressing me. I let my fingers retrace the place where he kissed me seconds ago just to feel him, his body, his smell, his heart beating, his warm breath and his soft yearning eyes pleading passionately with me. I love him...I love him...I love him.

A Cranky Baby

"Vicheara, are you dreaming?" Sokun's voice woke me up. I looked around me; everyone else was up as their bedding and mosquito nets were put away.

"Oh, I am ....I think you interrupted my dream. Oh...ummm ...the sun is up." I pretended to look out through the window at the sky but really looking for Dararan.

"What did you dream about?" asked Sokun, smiling as she patted her face dry.

"Uh...uh...my Papa. I saw him come in smiling at me," I lied. "Where is *Lok Krou?*"

"He went out to wash up," Dararan said, as he came inside.

"How was your sleep?" I looked at him and smiled, "I woke up late."

"Because the men are responsible for security, *Lok Krou* has directed that the women take turns doing the grocery shopping, as well as cooking. There's a little market set up down the street. So, do you want to cook today?" asked Sokun.

I looked hesitantly at Dararan; I had already confessed to him that I was a terrible cook. He shook his head negatively. "No, I'd rather do something else," I replied to Sokun.

"Grocery shopping?" she asked; he nodded positively.

"Yes" I answered. "But I will need a man to go with me because I cannot carry the rice sack. Maybe Dararan?" Sokun and I just looked at each other and smiled; I wasn't fooling her.

"I'll go, too; it'll be fun." She stuffed her belongings in her bag and we all went downstairs to find some breakfast.

The marketplace was not as big as I remembered but it had some things I had not seen since the fall of Phnom Penh - Khmer desserts! My favorite pumpkin pudding steamed in banana leaves, palm cakes, and palm fruit in coconut milk drove me crazy. I wanted all of them for myself now....now....but, there was no way I could use the group's rice to barter for dessert, so all I could do was look. I turned to Dararan for sympathy, saying "Look." And pointing at the desserts displayed on the ground in bamboo baskets, but he just smiled and plodded along like a little donkey carrying the heavy sack of rice. Sokun did not seem to have a sweet tooth either as she walked from one vendor to another to bargain for a better deal.

As I gave up my hopes for sweets and looked around the market, my eyes were drawn to a face that seemed familiar to me. She was also staring at me. She was about my height, a little chubby, dressed in a black *sampot* and blouse. As our eyes met, I could see she was talking to herself. Even at a distance, I could understand that she said, "Who is she? She looks like Vicheara."

My heart exploded. I jumped into the air with happiness and ran to her, "Cousin, you are alive! Where are all my nieces and nephews?" We laughed and cried; neither of us had expected that we would ever see each other alive. This lady was my beloved Cousin Phach, the only cousin who loved me as her own daughter. I had found my favorite cousin! She was alive! We clung to each other in the middle of the crowd and cried with joy. Sokun and Dararan had joined us when they heard our screaming; everybody in the market stopped their activities to view our happy reunion and shed tears of joy and tears of sorrow with us.

"How in the world you were able to survive. Incredible!" We hugged until neither of us could breathe. "I never expected you to survive the genocide," she laughed and cried and we swayed back and forth together, unwilling to ever let go. "Cranky baby, slept all day cried all night. Are you really alive?" She examined me like a mother checking her newborn baby: my hair, my fingers, my face, and then she rechecked my middle finger, "You still have your middle finger. Good, you are not a ghost!" She cried and looked at me and couldn't believe we were standing there together alive. "It is unbelievable," she hugged me again. "It means we are supposed to be together, Cousin. Where is *Tiev*? And the rest of the family?"

"All died. My husband was executed." The laughing was over, now was time for sorrow. "Honey, I have to go with my cousin to her house." I said to my boyfriend and turned to explain to Sokun, but she needed no explanation.

"Vicheara, don't worry, go!"

"I don't want to lose her after just finding her. Please explain to *Lok Krou*," I asked them.

I followed Phach to her house where I was so happy to see two of her daughters. They had changed so much in four years. They were all grown up. "Where are all the rest of my nieces and nephews?" (In Cambodia, we call younger second and third cousins 'nieces and nephews')

"I lost three children from sickness and wound infections. Sivanna, (the third oldest daughter) was married just a couple of months before liberation. They are on their way to join me. I still don't know what has happened to my two older sons; they were in Phnom Penh when the city fell."

She wept, missing her children, when talking about them. I was overjoyed to be able to tell her that I had met her two oldest sons in Phnom Penh. She screamed with joy, "Really? They are alive. Oh, my dear sons. I never expected them to survive, like I never expected you to survive."

"Be happy. They are doing well and living in a comfortable place with an old lady who really takes good care of them."

"Who is she?"

"She lived in the same village during the KR time. She loves them like they were her own and treats them like kings."

Phach laughing and crying at the same time, and said, "God took care of them for me since I prayed every night for their health, safety and security."

"How about you? How did you survive?" I was anxious to hear her story.

"When Phnom Penh fell, the province of Battambang was not affected very much at first. Do you remember before the KR time, my husband had cheated on me, and I decided to leave him and his new girlfriend to live in Battambang with all the younger children? To put the food on the table, I sold fermented fish at the market. Later, when the KR came to Battambang, my family was forced to leave the city for a village only three km away. God always took care of my family and me, because I never did any harm to anybody. For this reason, I was never forced to do hard labor; I was fortunate to be liked by the *Angkar* leader's wife who allowed me to do a light duty job. My oldest daughter also got an easy job working with *Angkar's* lady where she used her sewing skills to make shirts and did alterations for *Angkar* leaders and soldiers. A month before Vietnam's invasion, she was forced to get married to a man in her group."

"Poor Sivanna, she was forced to get married to a KR?" I asked, in horror.

"No, no, he is not. Her husband is a nice guy. He used to live in the city, too. My second and third daughters worked in the children's camp chopping down trees in the forest. They both worked away from me, and only came to see me once in a while. Later, Srey Peuv, (her third daughter) was sent home because she had an infection in her leg. She died in a month."

"Oh, *Mon Dieu*, poor niece."

"Guin (the fourth child, a son) died from diarrhea."

"Oh, No! My little nephew, Guin. And how about Peuv? Where he is? Don't tell me he…" I looked at her, too afraid to complete my sentence.

"He died, too; I don't know what exactly; he had a swollen stomach." Tears flowed down our faces in rivers as she told me of the deaths of her children. She told me she felt especially sorry for her fifth son who never made her worry about anything during the KR time. He worked hard. He usually saved good food for her for an additional lunch. He was respectful. Before he passed away, he told her, "I am sorry that I could not stay longer to take care of you. I have so much pain in my tummy like a stick poking me." He kept talking to her until he passed away.

Touch and Ngeb came to hug me tightly. "Do you love me, Ngeb?" I caressed her hair. She didn't speak but squeezed me hard to replace her words. "Do you remember me, Ngeb? You have grown taller, both of you. I cannot believe it. How old are you now?" She squeezed me again, without response.

"She is eight and Touch twelve," Phach responded for her.

"It is a miracle to find you here. Why did you decide to come here, my dear Cousin?"

"I came here intentionally looking for my husband, but, people who had known him told me he was taken by *Angkar* a week after the invasion."

"He must have been killed."

"Yes, I think that must be so."

"*Chum Reap Sour, Neak Baung* – Hello, dearest older sister!" Dararan's voice interrupted our reunion and he respectfully greeted my cousin in the traditional Cambodian manner.

"*Chah*, God bless you," Cousin responded, as she greeted him, she gestured for him to sit on the bamboo bed.

"*Neak Baung*, you and your kids look great," Dararan complimented her.

"Well, I did gain a little weight since we have no more worries; we now eat enough."

"Yes! Look at me." I got off the bamboo bed and posed for her, "I have gained weight, too," I said as I wiggled my still very skinny bottom which sent my nieces into a fit of giggling.

"How did you survive with *mes petite mignonnes* – my little cuties?"

"I traded my jewelry for fish, fermented it and sold it to the merchants at the market."

"You are a heroine, my lovely cousin. I remember my step-mother used to make fermented anchovies at home, but I didn't like it and never wanted to learn how to do it."

"I know you. I am surprised you stayed alive, my little cranky baby," she gently knocked on my head with a laugh and then the girls giggled too.

"What are you laughing about? You were not even born yet so you don't know what a brat I was," I affectionately squeezed each one. "Now," I put my hands on my hips, looking at my boyfriend, "how did you find me?"

"Easy. I can smell you everywhere," Dararan smiled at us. Then he gently suggested I return to the group for lunch because *Lok Krou* didn't want me to stay away from our group very long as it was not safe. We said goodbye to Phach and promised to visit her again the next day. Ngeb followed me back to the group like a baby duck following its mommy.

Excited to find my cousin, I shared this news to *Lok Krou* and the whole group. "Well, you can take them back home to the city with us if you want to," he said with a smile.

Resentment

That night, around 10 PM, when Dara was serving his turn as the armed guard, he shot the gun into the air and screamed that he wanted to kill Dararan and me! I knew he was still angry but that level of emotion was completely unexpected.

Lok Krou called a meeting of the entire group right away to change Dara's thinking. *Lok Krou* was obviously upset and everyone in the group was alarmed; he spoke firmly to us while we all sat as still as statues.

"This is the worst kind of inappropriate behavior. The purpose for coming here is to be good role models to the Khmer survivors, and to educate them to understand our purposes. We did not come here to resolve our personal problems and talk about killing each other. Dara, I order you to stay away from Vicheara and Dararan. Since I can no longer trust you, you will not be allowed the honor of sentry duty and are forbidden to handle any weapons." Dara was obviously embarrassed and ashamed but I could tell that he was still angry.

Despite this embarrassing and bizarre incident, Dararan and I grew to love each other more with each passing day. We took care of each other. When it was his turn for sentry duty, I stayed beside him. He told me he was crazy about me; I felt warm, safe, loved, and happy when I was around him. I felt needed all the time. He filled my heart so that the painful memories of my Papa and my husband began to fade little by little. He said that he would love me more than my Papa or my husband. People in our group were happy to see us in love. They called us Oliver and Jennifer as in the "Love Story" movie. It was silly but I loved it.

Dara avoided us for the most part but when he found himself in our company, he acted very rudely. He insulted us indirectly by loudly comparing a girl to a snake with two heads. This meant a woman was a cheater, pretending to love her husband, but having an affair behind his back. When I accidentally met his eyes in a group meeting, the anger and jealousy in his eyes frightened me. In the next group meeting, the leader talked indirectly to Dara to let him know that if his behavior did not change, he would be sent back to Phnom Penh and would be reported to the *Ong Leun*. This warning scared Dara. Everyone in the group advised Dara to give up his revenge and forget about me, as I was not meant to be his.

Meeting with the Khmer Survivors in the Village

That night, *Lok Krou* called us together with final instructions for the next day. He divided us into groups of three and told us which of the surrounding villages we were to visit. "Remember what I told you to say. When you are not sure, don't answer; write down the question and ask me later. Keep track of all the most asked questions."

I didn't remember who went with whom at that time. Since I found Phach and her children, I felt I was living in a dream. *Ong Leun's* re-education meant nothing to me - I had my beloved cousins, I had my boyfriend and nothing else seemed to matter. They wouldn't let me return home now anyhow, I would have to stay working for them like a little puppet walking from village to village under the hot sun, singing the praises of *Ong Leun*.

"Remember to let our fellow Cambodians hear this:" said *Lok Krou*, "The Vietnamese are our saviors, Vietnam is like GOD. Vietnam is our important friend. Vietnam should be rewarded. Vietnam will help Cambodia to rebuild after Pol Pot's Year Zero. We should all learn Vietnamese. We should be nice to the Vietnamese. We should support *Bo Doy* in any way we can as they keep our country safe. We need Vietnam to help us to reorganize our economy, administrative offices, banks, schools,"…blah, blah, blah. We all looked at each other and rolled our eyes. We had heard it all before, ……..propaganda.

Lok Krou calmly persisted, "Remember in class?" We looked at each other as he paused, "Each one of us told our story about our time under the KR? You will do the same thing when you visit the villagers. Let them talk so they bring all the bad memories to the surface." He looked at us to see if we understood and we nodded. "Then you explain to them about how *Samdech* Sihanook betrayed us and how Vietnam saved us. Make sure you don't forget to tell them the real face of Pol Pot and his purpose when he devastated our country."

"Do we have to explain everything you said to every house we go in?" Sokun asked.

"Yes. This is our mission. But, if they live close to each other, it best to invite them to come together in one place and then speak to all at once." He paused again to collect his thoughts, "And make sure you write down their names."

"Dam Tè pheuk – Shall we make a tea?" (Khmer slang used to criticize someone's opinion with disrespect). Wilson asked sarcastically. We were all bold enough to crack up at the absurdity of what we were being sent to do but, surprisingly, *Lok Krou* didn't seem offended by this teasing, he just patiently waited to regain our attention and softly repeated a Cambodian proverb that is hard to translate exactly but means "the fish dies because its mouth gets it into trouble." The atmosphere in the room changed very quickly.

Each small group of three was assigned to different villages and again reminded to go to every single house. We were to make contact with as many people as possible. My partners were two young men, Ratana and Houng neither had much personality. Houng carried a notebook and stuck his pen behind his ear. Ratana carried an old worn-out briefcase that contained nothing but a pen and a notebook. I carried nothing and was only thinking about getting some fresh coconut juice.

We found devastation and despair everywhere. All of the houses were the same, burned half way down with only the pole structures remaining. The thatched roofs had been burned and the doors demolished. People were living in whatever shelter they could create; many had no home to return to. In the smaller houses, people had made makeshift roofs with old broken aluminum sheets, and walls with whatever they could find to afford them some privacy. One of the families I met had returned to their own house and found only the cement floor intact so they made a shelter on the cement with different colors of plastic they picked up somewhere. What sense had it made to the KR to destroy these villages? I could not fathom their thinking.

In three hours, we had only contacted five families in five separate houses. Most of the time, Houng did the talking, and Ratana and I listened. We left the fifth house and started down the path into the countryside; it was about 11 AM and getting hot. The surrounding area was very quiet and we saw no signs of life. I remembered walking by the haunted mountains to the cemetery hospital the previous year. It felt the same – eerie and isolated. We saw neither animals nor people; there were no voices in the distance, no smell of cooking fires, no animals to indicate a nearby farm. The ground was loose and sandy, and seemed to grab at my feet so I quickly became tired. It began to feel like the heavy mud of the rice paddy where I had labored to build the canal. There was no shade, only an occasional coconut palm and the hot earth began to burn my feet through my thin sandals. Exhausted and thirsty, I was now also feeling panic welling in my chest and I stopped and turned to my companions, "Can we stop now? Let's go find *Lok Krou* and join his team. I don't feel safe to be isolated from the group for so long. I don't think we are going to find any more families that live this far away from the town. We have walked a long way and *Lok Krou* warned us to not go too deep – that it was not safe."

I think the two men were relieved and they agreed with me immediately, "Yes, you are right. Follow me," Ratana said. "I know where *Lok Krou* and his group will be."

It took us about a half hour to backtrack and make our way to a village where we found *Lok Krou* talking to a group of about twenty in front of a house that was newly repaired with aluminum sheets. A lean-to in front of the house provided a nice shady spot for *Lok Krou*. The villagers were listening attentively, either sitting or squatting on the ground around him. There were men and women as well as children, but no elders. As in my family, very few had survived the genocide. Little children, too young to pay attention to speeches, ran around playing. Seeing us walk in, *Lok Krou* paused to send us a warm smile and continued. As soon as he saw us, Dararan came to me right away, "I have been waiting for you. Is everything alright?"

"Oh, I am just tired and thirsty. Is there anything to drink? Why is your group here?"

"There was coconut juice, but there's none left. You are late; we finished in our sector and came here."

Politely, the homeowner got up and greeted us, then sent someone to climb a coconut tree. I knew many Khmer peasants were uneducated and, therefore, naïve about politics. Historically, they had trusted whoever made them feel protected. They obviously regarded us as good people, probably the same way they had regarded *Samdech*. They were incredibly poor and coconut juice was the only thing they had to offer us to demonstrate respect and hospitality.

They didn't know we were political pawns sent there to further the Vietnamese political agenda. I felt like a fraud and a criminal. If I could have sunk into the ground, I would have, because these good people were once again going to be used for a political agenda and I was part of the problem. However, *Lok Krou's* subtle warning about the fish's mouth causing its destruction had been clear - I lived under a communist dictatorship and I had neither free speech nor any power to change the current circumstances. If I wanted to live in society rather than in a prison in Vietnam, I would repeat the propaganda as I had been taught it, avoid giving any information that was not necessary and, therefore, cause no problem to myself. So, after relaying our personal stories of our life in the genocide, Houng talked about the Vietnamese saviors; Pol Pot and his crimes were spoken of by Ratana; and I told the villagers about Sihanook's betrayal.

Emotions were raw as the villagers shared their personal tragedies. I recognized the cleverness of the communists' agenda as *Lok Krou* repeatedly asked, "Who rescued you?" and they answered, "*Bo Doy.*" The realization that rural Cambodians now saw the communist Vietnamese as their saviors without understanding any of the political complexities was very disappointing but understandable.

One man firmly declared that, "Without *Bo Doy*, we cannot stay here safely. The KR still come out sometimes at night looking for food but are chased away by *Bo Doy*. We don't have any weapons to protect ourselves. Without them, we would all be killed."

I began to wonder about that. If the KR come here, they must not live far from the village or could it be that they hide among the villagers? Could there be KR here right now? Which ones are they? Without their black uniforms, everyone looks and talks the same. Would they try to kill us? Then I thought, "Well, the KR are communist, the Vietnamese (from Hanoi) are also communist. Surely they would realize we were also here to promote the Communist propaganda, just in a different phase? Even the names we called the leaders meant the same thing – *Ong Leun* for the Vietnamese top leader and *Angkar Leu* for the KR leader. Why would they kill us?"

As these thoughts swirled around in my head, I began to feel a rising panic and started to hyperventilate. Mercifully, Dararan took my hand and brought me back to reality with, "Here, Honey, coconut juice."

I looked at the villager standing in front of me with a friendly and honest smile. He handed me a coconut with the top sliced off and said, "I selected the best coconut fruit for you. The juice will be sweet and delicious."

Instantly, my mind went to the time when the KR leader allowed me to have coconuts to help my Papa. Everyone had been so hungry and the one coconut I had shared with my neighbor had meant so much to them. I also remembered how his wife had returned the favor by risking her safety to warn me to hide from the soldier coming to take me to the labor camp - how she had said, 'you are going to die if you go'.

"*Aur Koun, Pou.*" I received it with both hands as I deadly thirsty. But, then I noticed his naked child crying and pointing at the coconut in my hands. I felt so guilty; I was part of a propaganda team and now I was also taking one of their few coconuts? The father lifted the child up in his arms and comforted him with, "I will get one for you later."

"No, he can have mine. I am allergic to coconut."

"Really? I never heard of anyone allergic to coconut." I gave the coconut to the child.

"Honey, you have a good heart and I love you for it," Dararan said.

"He gets coconut juice every day, but is never satisfied." He put the child down so he could drink out of the shell.

"He is just being a child. Is he your youngest?" I asked, trying to forget how thirsty I was.

"No, the baby is still breastfeeding," He turned to a woman sitting at the bottom of the staircase. "She is my second wife. My first wife died in the genocide. I married my second wife according to *Angkar*'s rules: ten couples at the same time, vows taken in front of the Leader with no monks to give a blessing, no traditional music."

I thought of my own wedding and knew that I had been lucky to have a traditional ceremony from the beginning to the end, even if the music was competing with the sound of bombs.

He continued to tell us his story, "My youngest daughter from my first wife," he was pointing at a teenager standing next to his wife, "survived but is traumatized. Today she seems fine, but yesterday she was crazy; she screamed as if someone was coming to kill her. She doesn't talk much, usually stays by herself and only speaks when asked a question."

"What is her problem?"

He began to weep as he told us, "When she was only eight years old, she was forced to watch as the KR killed a man horribly, cut open his stomach while he was still alive and filled it with grass. She was screaming....and screaming...until she passed out. It has taken her a year to become somewhat normal but she has also become a stranger."

I rubbed my chest with pity. I looked at her, standing mutely, listening to *Lok Krou*. I turned to her father and said, "This is what we are here for ...to strengthen your spirit, to empower your will so you will never ever be influenced by them (KR) again. Right now they are hidden; they come out only for food. If the KR ever come back to power, they will displace your family and ruin your homes again, they will murder and starve you."

The villager nodded his head and said, "*Bat, Bat...Bat*," to every single word I said.

"Do you now realize what Sihanook has done to us?" I asked.

"*Bat, Lok Krou* told us about it. I am astonished to hear this. Where does Sihanook live now?"

"Still in Peking with his wife."

"If I see Pol Pot, I will slice his skin like slicing a fish and ferment him alive with salt. As for Sihanook, our God-Father," he steepled his hands as if in prayer, "bad karma will return to him."

"We all have tasted the Communist power. We lived with it. We have become traumatized because of it, you, me, her, your daughter. Your wife died. Your parents died. My parents died. Remember all this tragedy and loss. The KR killed over two million of us."

"Oh, *Mon Dieu!* I learn now, no more communist or socialist. No more KR, no more Sihanook." He was visibly shaken.

"Look at my back." A man in his late thirties joined us. He lifted his shirt, exposing a big scar across his back just below the shoulder.

"What happened?"

"Pol Pot. *Ah Norok* (devil). Please God," he placed both hands together palm-to-palm and raised them up in the traditional Khmer way when praying to God, "Please punish them and make them suffer the same way I did. He tied my hands in back, covered my eyes," he demonstrated by putting his hands over his eyes, "and pushed me to the ground with other victims. They killed hundreds of new people as we sat there in terror and waited for death to claim us. I heard the voices of the murdered screaming in pain and begging for help. Some women had the courage to insult the KR and put a curse on them, but these curses only encouraged the murderers to kick and rape the women, before beating them to death with axes. I didn't know how many murderers there were, as I couldn't see them, but I know there were many. I hate this regime. I despise Pol Pot, Sihanook and all their comrades. They need to be brought to justice."

I was so amazed to hear one of the villagers call for the KR regime to be brought to justice. "They will, and we need all of you to stand up strong, fight together to completely eliminate this evil from Cambodia. *Kouk Toul Sleng* in Phnom Penh is proof they killed innocent people with no mercy." I then told them about the "10 rules" for the prisoners, and described what I had seen: the equipment, robes, metal beds, the tiny prison cells and the earthen pots that filled with fish sauce to torture and drown the victims. Then I turned to the younger man and asked, "How did you manage to survive?"

"When it was my turn, I was pulled up and thrown against a pole. I still couldn't see so I don't know what weapon was used but I think they beat me with bamboo. I remember the pain and that he laughed as he beat me. He laughed at us while he killed people like they were rats. I lost consciousness, I don't know for how long, when I woke up it was night and I found myself in a big hole full of dead bodies. I could move and I crawled over the dead and into the jungle."

"It is a miracle. How could it happen?"

"I believe the killers got exhausted after so many victims. When it came to my turn, his hand was not strong anymore; maybe the bamboo broke. Fortunately, when I got out of the hole, I made my way back to the village and then was told that all the KR had been chased away by the Vietnamese the night they tried to kill me."

"God bless you. They must have smelled the danger coming and run away," I exhaled to release my anxiety and try to calm down.

"If I see that killer, I will cut off his fingers, his hands and his feet, one by one and cut his head off last."

"How will you know it is him since you did not see him?"

"I will recognize his voice."

"Do you know people around here very well?"

"*Bat,* they used to live here before the genocide, before being sent to labor camps."

"Where did you go?"

"Battambang."

"I went there too. What district?"

"Phnom Srok. How about you?"

"Preah Netr Preah. Are you scared to stay here?" I asked.

"*Bat,* we all are scared. We don't know what is in the minds of the KR now; they no longer attack us and came in only for food at night but we know we cannot trust them. We have nothing to protect ourselves. There are not many *Bo Doy* here; we need to have more *Bo Doy.*"

"Please report to the top leader that we are not safe and we need security. I am so scared of being raped again." I looked at the woman now joining our small group. Her fear of being raped instead of being murdered was telling me she had been outrageously raped many times in the genocide. "I am so happy to see all of you come here to meet us, and that you are concerned about us. I lost too many people in my family; I don't want to lose anymore. I have only my mother left and one child, ten years old. My mother was blinded from pink eye. The KR leader believed pink eye was just an excuse to avoid work and forced her to wash her eyes with something that smelled like urine. If she hadn't done it, they would have killed her; instead they blinded her."

"Incredible. I got pink eye, too, but I was so lucky to be treated with the right eye drops by a goodhearted woman, a former KR leader's wife. Her husband became a victim of his own comrades because he wasn't cruel enough."

"My husband, father, sisters and brother were all executed." She now dropped to the ground weeping. "I cannot believe Khmer killed Khmer. Sihanook, the devil *Samdech,* killed his own people. I want to kill Pol Pot now. I want to know what his brain is made of." She then hugged my feet, "Please forward my message to the top leader to protect us. We are not safe here. I have been raped many times, too much for my life. If I get raped again, I will kill myself."

"No! Please don't. That why we are here, to see what you need. I promise I will report to *Ong Leun* to send more *Bo Doy* to this area. While you are waiting for their help, you will need to use your strong will as a weapon to avoid being manipulated by a small group of defeated KR. Remember our proverb: help yourself first, God will help you later?"

"*Aur Koun,* Please God bless you," her mother prayed for me.

I almost burst into tears as it became clear that we were the only hope these people had. I had no idea what the *Ong Leun* would do and I had no power to influence the situation. I was promising to help but was I just a liar trying to get out of a terrible situation? I had felt bad about doing this job from the start – now I felt even worse. In order to prevent them from being influenced by KR, they need security. To provide the security, I must now become a messenger. We are all messengers. What happens if *Ong Leun* won't respond to their needs? We all become liars! Will I lie to my own people?

"Vicheara, is everything all right? We need to return to our living area, rest and eat," said *Lok Krou* as he appeared in between the people in my group.

I pulled myself away from them and whispered to him, "No, I am not OK. How can I promise them security will improve?"

"Don't worry too much. I'll take care of it."

We said goodbye to the villagers and began the long walk back. It had been a very emotionally and physically tough day. As we got out of earshot of the village, *Lok Krou* said, "We won't come back here again. Too many safety concerns."

"Really? Why do you say that?"

"We don't know what is going around here. After listening to these people, I suspect KR are hidden among these good people."

"I feel the same. Now I worry our presence was just stirring up the water. They know who we are and they might come to harm us."

"I doubt that but, to be safe you just have to stay with the group, don't go off on your own without letting me know. I will talk to the group in the meeting tonight."

After a long day and many miles on foot, we returned to our rooms, exhausted and hungry. At 8 PM, *Lok Krou* called us together to share what we had heard. It was clear that safety and security were the top concern of the vast majority of the people in the villages. This was hardly a surprise since we all knew the defeated KR were still hiding in the jungle around the villages. The message was so clear that *Lok Krou* decided that one of us should go immediately to Phnom Penh to report to the Vietnamese leader that reinforcing the safety and security plan must be a top priority.

"Who can go?" *Lok Krou* asked for volunteers. Nobody answered. "Vicheara, can you go since you speak both Vietnamese and French? All the top Vietnamese know you better than anybody else in the group because you have often translated for them."

"*Chah*, I can go."

"Don't forget to ask for more hammocks for our group and more rice," Wilson said.

"I will, I promise."

Under the Moonlight

That night I stayed with Dararan longer than usual. "Honey, can I have your shirt? I cannot go to sleep without thinking about you. Your shirt has your smell and I want to keep a little bit of you with me while you are in the city," he asked.

Happy to hear this, I gave him my favorite shirt. Under the moonlight, Dararan's eyes were filled with passion and warmth. He watched me everywhere I went. Every time my eyes met his, I wanted to wrap myself up with him. I wanted every part of my body touching his for the rest of my life. I wanted to kiss his heart shaped lips; I wanted to feel those lips all over my body again and again. I was not sure if I was in love with him or not, but I certainly was in lust with him. Was he in love with me? I didn't know that either, but I certainly felt a strong sexual attraction to him, stronger than I had ever felt with Leang. Was it love? I didn't know.

He was so perfect - his skin, his voice, his body, his attitude, his hair. I found no faults with this man. Who wanted to lose a man like this? We stayed up whispering, as my roommates and my little Ngeb, who was staying with me, settled in for the night. As Dararan went out to the balcony where he slept, my feet started to move, following him to the private spot where we could not be seen. I tried very hard to resist; I turned my face to the street looking at the light, pretending to ignore him. But, my feet just kept going. I couldn't escape as his arms wrapped around me, pulling me close to his chest so I could hear his heart beating. I could hear the sound of my own blood rushing in my head as his lovely mouth kissed my neck and then my cheeks until finally his tongue parted my trembling lips. I closed my eyes and allowed my body and soul to melt into his embrace. Every breath I took filled me with his scent; I was living in a dream of love and desire. Once in a while, a whispered moan escaped from one of us. The gentle night breeze cooled our skin but not our passion. I threw all caution to the wind as his hands caressed my waist and then moved up to my breast. I would belong to him tonight.

I rose before the sun in hopes no one would discover that I had spent the night in Dararan's mosquito net. Noiseless as a cat, I slipped barefoot back to my own mosquito net and pretended to fall asleep next to Ngeb who was so sound asleep she was drooling. As soon as I heard a sound, I turned around yawning as if I just awakened. "Sokun, are you awake? *Lok Krou*! Are you up yet?" I didn't even feel guilty with this little deceit; I felt wonderful.

Lok Krou's answer got me moving, "Well, I slept so good last night and had many dreams. I think this morning we need to send you to see *Ong Leun* before the rice is gone."

I woke up Ngeb, washed her face and told her, "Honey, I need to send you home while I am in the city. When I come back, I will come find you and you will stay with me. OK?" She smiled like a little flower blooming under the first ray of sunshine in the morning, showing me her dimples. She gave me a hug and took off. Before the Genocide, Ngeb was only four years old and I never would have thought she would remember me but since I had appeared at her mom's house and showed them much affection, she had showered me with love. From that first day, she stuck to me like glue. Quiet and shy, she only spoke when asked a question but her sweet smile brightened every room.

The Snake that could never be Caught

Around 9 AM, a Vietnamese military truck stopped in front of our place to pick me up.

"I'm coming with you, Honey," Dararan said, as I was about to get in the truck. He had gotten permission to accompany me. I was thrilled. *Lok Krou* had instructed me on the message to give the leader, and the entire group saw us off.

We arrived in the city about 11 AM. Dararan was dropped off at his home while I went to the office of *Ong Leun*. I knew this Vietnamese official from the three months in the program as I had often been called to translate. He was a good-looking man in his late middle-age with short, silver hair. He had seemed very nice and trustworthy.

I entered the two story building and went directly to his office but the door was closed and locked. That was odd. Usually busy and bustling with people, the building seemed strangely quiet, almost deserted. Where was everybody? The lights were off and many doors were closed. Fortunately, I came across a Vietnamese man who seemed unsurprised to see me and gave me detailed directions to where I would find *Ong Leun* on the second floor.

It was a small room at the back of the building; this seemed a strange place for the office of such an important official. My knock was answered, "*Entrez* – Come in."

I opened the door, found *Ong Leun* in a hammock in a short sleeved white cotton shirt and white cotton shorts. I was quite taken aback and wondered to myself, "Why has he scheduled to meet me during his siesta? Why has he not gotten up? Why is he dressed like that?" The words I actually got out of my mouth were, "Should I come in or not?"

"*Alors! Ç'a fait rien* - It's fine. *Ç'est toi* - Is it you? *Viens* - Come in! *Qu'est-ce que tu veux* - What do you want?"

"*Salut. Comment Ça-vas* - Good morning. How are you?"

I reported to him about the Khmer villagers' concerns and requested more rice and hammocks for my group. I was preparing to leave when he reached out to grab me. "*Approaches-toi* - Come closer!" He ordered.

I started to back away, feeling extremely uncomfortable. He got up from his hammock and came towards me. Now I could see he was a short man, maybe three inches shorter than me. With his wrinkled face and thin chest he was an unattractive man and, to my horror, as he came toward me it was obvious that he had an erection. Oh, my God!

Before I had a chance to turn and run, his hand shot out and grabbed my breast. I was angry and shocked and roughly pulled away and escaped out the door. I was shaking; I couldn't believe this person, *Ong Leun*, whom I trusted, dishonored me. I was about to scream for help, but stopped myself. What was the point? He had power, I had none. If I screamed, nobody would believe me. I remembered the Khmer proverb that warned if you were going to catch a snake, make sure you know how to do it right. He was a high ranking Vietnamese official. If people didn't believe me, I could get into serious trouble, and I could lose my job, my reputation. And then, this damn *Ong Leun* would laugh at me. It was all about power; if my Papa was alive, he would take this damn man down.

He had followed me out the door and I told him, "I need to go back to the province. NOW! NOW!" My voice rose despite myself and it must have alarmed him. I was so angry and frightened that I was shaking.

"Ok, I will send for the truck," he said and walked away.

"I need more rice and hammocks for my group," I said loudly, to his retreating back. "And this is the report from the group leader: our people need more security!" I threw it on the floor and fled down the hall.

From behind me, I heard him say, "OK, OK."

When the truck driver stopped at Dararan's house, he immediately noticed how upset I was and put his arm around me and asked, "Honey, what happened? Why are we leaving so soon?"

"We need to go back to Kompong Chnnang now. I cannot believe what just happened. I don't trust anybody anymore," I looked away from Dararan's concerned eyes.

"What's wrong, Honey?" he asked, holding my shaking body. "What happened?"

"I'll tell you later when I settle my nerves. I cannot talk about it right now." He said nothing more and just held me.

Everyone was surprised to see us back sooner than expected, "Is everything all right?" *Lok Krou* asked.

"*Chah.*"

"He will do what you ask him to do. He likes you," *Lok Krou* teased.

"*Chah*, but don't send me to see this *Ong Leun* again. He is a bastard. Send a man."

~THIRTY EIGHT~

THE MASK IS REMOVED

The assignment to re-educate the people was over. The three months of Political Morality training was completely done and my group could return to our lives in Phnom Penh. All my companions were was elated and looked forward to reuniting with family members: "I get to go back home to my family!" "I left my wife for three months; I hope she still remembers me." "My children will be happy to see me back home!"

I was not so happy. Staying here or there was all the same to me, I had no family to go home to and my daily interaction with Dararan was ending. "Are you happy, Honey?" I sadly asked my boyfriend.

"*Bat*, Honey, I am happy and I will continue to love you more and more every day. Remember! I am your man and no one can steal you from me. I will take care of you." Hearing this made me smile, filling my heart. If we were alone, I would jump on his chest and kiss him all over. But, we were in public. Our culture wouldn't allow such a public display.

"Hey *Pros*! (Boy or man) I have a letter from home," interrupted Dararan's brother, who was in our cadre.

"Who is *Pros*? Is this your nickname?" I asked, surprised and a little amused.

"It is," he confirmed. I liked everything about him. If his name changed to monster or shit, I would still love him. There is a Khmer saying that when you are in love with someone you see shit as a flower. This couldn't have been truer than it was for me at that moment. He was my perfect man, no matter what his nickname. Did he think the same of me? I was sure he did.

"What did the letter say," I asked him.

He smiled as he replied, "It's just a letter from home."

"Is it from your mother?"

He put his letter in his pocket and smiled passionately at me, "It's nothing important. We are more important than anything else."

Happy Reunion

Phach and her family returned to Phnom Penh with us. We were all housed in the tallest building in the city, a former hotel, Sukhalay, on Monivong Blvd.

"You have to stay here until you are picked up by family or the government," *Lok Krou* explained to us. "Don't wander around or be curious and go downstairs checking out other floors because they have not been cleaned yet. We have been ordered to stay on the fifth floor and all women can stay in the same room if you want."

My cousin's sons came to pick up their mother and her remaining family. Their reunion was joyful and also heartbreaking as they shared their stories. "Are you going to stay with that old lady or your mom?" I asked my cousin's sons.

As usual, they smiled first before talking. "I will live with my mother," Naith responded first.

Then Ridth said, "I have told her (the old lady) that she should forget about adopting us. She was very upset and disappointed when she heard our decision and said she would return to her home village. She said some nasty things about my mother; she seems really jealous of her." This probably seems odd to the western reader but in Cambodia, sons were social security for one's old age. This was exactly the situation that had caused so much conflict in my own family – stepmother saw Koy as her social security if my father adopted him and she became the official mother. If I was my father's heir, she knew her future was not assured so she tried to create a rift between me and my father.

"Well, it's hard to blame her; she wants you for herself. Perhaps she loves you so much and wants to keep you as her own sons. It must be very hard for her to accept that you have found your own mother who needs you to take care of her first. So, do you have any idea where you want to live yet?"

"I picked *Psar* O'Russey – O'Russey market, near the market area. There are many empty houses in the city, but I like *Psar* O'Russey. I picked the fourth floor for my *Mak* (cousin Phach), and the second floor for my sister when she comes, but in a different building, across the street."

"Why not the first floor?"

"Too dirty and smelly," Naith explained, and held his nose to demonstrate.

"It is a good idea to live at *Psar* O'Russey. I think it is the right place because it will be possible for me to do a little business selling desserts for a living," Phach said.

Should I Leave my Boyfriend?

I was happy for my cousin and her family as they began to rebuild their lives together and I was hopeful that Dararan and I would begin to do the same. But fate did not have that in store for me and karma was ready to deal me yet another betrayal.

I found out that Dararan had deceived me.

My beloved was not single. He had a woman at home and a son. I saw his brother bring another letter; when I questioned him he quickly admitted that it was from Dararan's wife! His wife! I was outraged that they had hidden this from me. His brother had been with us for months in the provinces, he had observed our growing romance and, in all that time, he never told me about Dararan's family. I was so devastated and disappointed; I didn't know what to do next.

Surprisingly, Dararan showed up at the door of my bedroom. I rushed to go out to talk to him, "Why did you hide this from me?" I asked, so angry I choked on the words. I put my hand on his chest, but stood straight in front of him, eye to eye, mouth to mouth, so Sokun wouldn't hear our words.

"We are not married. She is not my legal wife." He pulled me out of the room and closed the door after us.

"You have a kid with her, and lived with her, and then you tell me she is not your wife. What kind of man are you?" I was furious.

"Honey, do you feel my heart beating? It is because I love you. You have to trust me." We walked through an empty room to the balcony, next to my room. He then knelt and begged me to listen to him, "We were at a New Year's party in 1975 when the KR occupied the city. She could not get back home at that time so she decided to stay with my family. We had no choice but to go together and then live together in KR. She and I have never gotten along; we fight like cats and dogs, and she said that she would leave me after liberation." I believed him because the latest information I had gotten from questioning his brother was the same. "Honey, listen to me. She will leave me and take our child."

I let my heart make my decision. I decided to continue our relationship hoping she would leave him. No one could separate us. That evening after dinner, my boyfriend told me more of his story during the Pol Pot time and why they had survived. "She and I were forced to go to Kratié province, next to Rathanakiri province, where the *Phnong* (primitive Cambodians) live."

"Did the *Phnong* become communists too?"

"*Bat*, Honey. But *Angkar*'s rules were different there than in the other provinces."

"How could the rules differ from one province to another?" I was suspicious but I had heard this from some other people also. My original view of the KR as a monolithic, well organized entity had altered as I talked to survivors from other areas. I wanted to see if Dararan would slip up, giving me proof that he and his woman were really husband and wife but as I listened, my anger and disappointment subsided. I wanted to believe him; I wanted to have a future with him. I so wanted to believe he loved only me and that he had been thrown together with her by the circumstances and not because it was what either of them wanted. I melted as I watched his heart-shaped lips caressing each word. Each expression on his beautiful face cast a spell on my heart.

"We were worked very hard but we were fed enough for the entire four years. We were far luckier than anybody else in the entire country."

"I believe you," I said, as he finished and reached for my hand. I believed everything he had said and there was nothing to prove to me that he and she had ever been in love.

"If you had lived in my province, you would have been executed because of your light skin and your handsome looks," I said in a soft voice.

"I love you, Honey. I love you to death. I will do anything to please you." My heart was melted by his sweet words. I believed him, this handsome man that I was sure God had made just for me. Sokun appeared beside us unexpectedly; I hoped she had not heard our conversation.

"You are so lucky, Dradran," she said. That statement convinced me that she had not overheard us.

"Who is Dradran?" I asked her.

"Sorry, I can never remember your name," she answered, a little embarrassed. Looking at my boyfriend, she asked, "Can I call you Dradran instead?"

"Go ahead, I don't care," Dararan replied.

"You make a good couple. You, Dradran, are so lucky to have Vicheara. "Don't leave for a minute. I want to show you something," she said and went back to her bedroom. She was back seconds later with a photo. "This is a picture of my husband and me, when we were married."

"How did you hide it from the KR?" I asked as I looked at the picture. "I am so sorry about what happened to your husband. He was so handsome and you made a beautiful couple."

"I found it after I came back to our house. This photo is always with me wherever I go, asleep or awake."

I passed it on to my sweetheart. He looked at it, then shook his head in amazement, "I cannot believe you found it; tell us your story again."

"I told a little bit in the classroom. Remember? At the 'Political Morality' training?" She led us back to the bedroom, sat on the bed and sipped a glass of water.

"I heard them but there were so many and they were so upsetting that I just couldn't listen anymore. Tell us again," I coaxed her.

"*Chah*, I probably will talk about it until the day I die. I will never forget my pain. I will never forgive whoever killed my husband. His face is always in front of me, crying for help. He didn't do anything wrong, but he was treated like a criminal." She paused. "Are you sure you want to hear about my tragic life in Pursat province?"

"Sure, if you want to tell us," we encouraged her and she sat down beside me.

"I lost my husband and other family members in this province." She began to weep, "I will never remarry. I saw *Angkar* hit my husband twice with an axe on the back of his head. I sat holding his bloody body until midnight wishing I could die with him, but then I heard my husband whispering to me. He was still alive; I was so happy. I took him back to my cabin but the next morning, *Angkar* found out that he was still alive, dragged him out again to the same place and finished him in front of me. I cried and screamed at *Angkar* asking them what my husband did wrong but they told me to be quiet and go away or I would be finished with him."

We cried together; I comforted her and tucked her in that night.

Khmer Culture

Within a week, people in our group started to leave for job offers in different government departments. Dararan was called to work with the Indochina Bank as an administrative lead and I was finally called back to work in the Dumex pharmaceutical company, responsible for syrup fabrication. As before, each month

I was paid with rice. This was a burden on me since I didn't cook, had no cookware, and had no kitchen in my small apartment.

"What should I do?" I asked my friend Chang, when I met him in the Dumex hallway.

"Sell it. Easy," he responded.

"Where and how?"

"Give it to me. I will pay you in dong (Vietnamese currency); how does that sound?" Chang looked at me.

"I love this idea. What will you do with the rice?"

"My wife will sell it to a merchant and make a profit."

"Aha! Mr. Businessman! It's good for me because I need the currency to buy other things that I need."

"You have only one mouth to feed; I have a wife and children. I need to make extra income to support them or my wife will kick my ass." He laughed. "You told me you don't cook. But, how and what will you eat?"

"I eat here and there, one day at *Pou* Phan's, another day at my cousin's."

"I like your *Pou* Phan. He is funny." I nodded. "He said he was your Dad's payroll clerk, right?" I nodded. "It's good to have a relative offer you a meal."

"No, I eat at his house once in a while, depending on my auntie's mood. I eat out a lot, you know. That's why I need dong - to buy a meal. *Pou* Phan is never happy to see me. He doesn't even look at me or talk to me either," I said sadly. "I know I must be different now; I need to learn to bend down my head, kiss his ass and ignore his rudeness."

Chang just listened with no comment. At last, he said to me, "People are different after surviving the genocide. Some change from good to bad; some the other way." He patted my shoulder, "Don't be lonely. Look for a husband," he said and laughed again.

"Are you laughing at me because I am a widow?" I glared at him.

"No, I said it with compassion. You know how our Khmer culture is about widows and divorced women, never anything good to say. Women think the widow will want to steal their husbands; they see her as a potential whore. Men see a widow as weak, comparing her to a house without a fence, meaning she has no protection. So, men will seek you out just for sex."

"Or maybe to keep you as a mistress," I finished his thoughts. I felt hurt and secretly humiliated for being in a relationship with a married man, Dararan. My mind began to whirl: "Am I one of those desperate women? What happens if my friends find out I have a relationship with a married man? I will be shamed and embarrassed. But, my boyfriend doesn't love me only for sex, he really loves me, he told me so. He certainly never referred to me as his mistress. He told me he will marry me when his fake wife leaves him."

"Well", said Chang, oblivious to my secret thoughts and fears, "I wasn't suggesting that you be anybody's mistress. You are beautiful. Look for a foreigner. If you look, you will meet someone single. There are plenty of them who came to work with us in the pharmaceutical industry. Vicheara, do you hear me? You are good with foreigners." He pulled my sleeve to get my full attention as my thoughts continued to race.

"Do you think it is easy to make a connection with foreign men? You know we are prohibited from having a relationship with foreigners. They will put me in the prison if I do so."

"Ah, don't worry so much. It's easy; you speak French fluently. You speak Vietnamese better than us. You are single and beautiful. You are educated. Who wouldn't want you?"

"You are right, who wouldn't want me?" I repeated after him, without knowing what I was saying. I stopped talking when I saw my pharmacist supervisor walking toward me. Vuddhy was a very nice and sweet person, and I liked him a lot. He used to work at my Papa's pharmaceutical plant four years ago. "Stop, that's enough. I will find a man when I want one." I gave him a signal to knock it off.

Vuddhy laughed and tapped on my shoulder, "Come talk to me, in my office." He put his hand on my shoulder and steered me in the direction of his office. Chang turned and went back to work. We smiled at the people we passed in the hall until we were in his office. "Who are you staying with? Do you have anyone to take care of you?" I felt like someone was poking an open wound. I knew my wound hadn't yet healed and this time it exploded. I burst into tears, folded my arms on his desk and put my head down on them and sobbed until Vuddhy got up and offered me a napkin to wipe my tears.

I could say only one word, "Alone."

Softly he comforted me, "If you want to have lunch at my house, you are welcome at any time. I loved and respected your father. He had treated me very well, now in return, I will offer help to you. It is not going to be a big burden to feed you, just one mouth." I couldn't respond, but kept crying. "If you need anything, like western medicine, come to see me. I heard my employees saying western medicines were selling big on the black market. You can do this to get by." I nodded my head to agree with him. However, I still couldn't say a word to him, but I was reassured by his caring and compassion.

After that day, my income from my sack of rice was supplemented by selling medicines I made and those offered by Vuddhy. He didn't just give the western medicines to me; he also shared with other pharmacists friends as well. These were things like cough syrup, injectable vitamins, and aspirin tablets. Comparing my life to my boyfriend's, I was better off than he was. My sweetheart had nothing but the rice from his job at the bank, which was barely enough to support his family. Every night, after work, he came to see me and stayed with me all evening. His visits to my apartment didn't go unnoticed and my friends and colleagues were happy I had a boyfriend. If they knew the truth, what would they think of me?

Adultery is Prohibited

Months later, my brain started to take over my heart. I admitted to myself that I was living a fantasy and Dararan was not going to leave his wife, and his wife was not going to leave him. They had a son together.

I had been arguing with myself for months about whether I should stay in the relationship or say goodbye and move on. I decided that I would tell him that night that I couldn't continue to commit adultery whether he was legally married or not. Adultery was against our religion and it promised that when I died, instead of Paradise, I would be thrown into boiling water and would suffer for all eternity. I was not particularly religious and reasoned that I had already done quite a bit of suffering but it scared me anyway.

My boyfriend came to my apartment at 5 PM as usual. I decided to take him to my Cousin Phach's for dinner so we could talk on the way. We had walked for about a quarter of a mile as I got my courage together when Dararan broke the silence, "Are you sad?"

"*Chah!*"

"I know what you're sad about."

I looked at him. "You think you can read my mind, but you can't, not this time."

"I don't understand you, Honey." His eyes were full of concern.

"I feel it is not right to steal you from your wife. She is really your wife, no matter what you say. What happens if she finds out about us? She will be upset and may be pissed enough at me to do something to ruin my life and my job."

"She already knows about us." This really surprised me and I felt a blush rise up my neck. Would there be a battle between two women for one man?

"Did you tell her?"

"No, but she told me she heard a rumor about us." I relaxed.

"What did you tell her?"

"She and I never get along."

"That is it?"

"Yes, this is a code of dissolution."

I yelled at him, "What the hell does that mean? Does she understand your code? How about her code?"

"Honey, don't yell in the public. Everyone will look at us. It is very embarrassing." I laughed at him, without saying more. "No, Honey, our relationship will be dissolved very soon. I don't love her. She doesn't love me. She is looking for an opportunity to leave me."

This promise sounded realistic. It made me think that patience may pay off and we would be together. I wanted so badly to be with him and to start a life with him. All my resolution and strength melted away and, at my cousin's house, we acted like a real boyfriend and girlfriend. She accepted Dararan as family without knowing the whole story. I decided to not tell her and did not want her to get involved because I was not sure what direction I should go.

Despite my patience with him, our relationship continued to be shaky. I needed things to be black and white. As much as I loved him and wanted to be with him, I continued to doubt him. When would this woman be out of his life? Then, as if someone turned on the lights, I remembered he said that his wife was looking for an opportunity to leave him. It didn't make sense to me. Why did she need an opportunity? Why couldn't she just leave? How long will I have to wait? And why wouldn't he leave her? I needed to take the blinders off and read between the lines. The conclusion was obvious; Dararan was not telling me the truth. He was not brave enough to make a decision. However, it was very hard to dissolve the love between us because he came to see me every night and I was alone and lonely. When I was face to face with him and looked into his eyes, I clung to the flicker of hope that his wife would leave him.

My relationship with Dararan continued for six months, then almost a year; he did everything he could think of to please me, but my patience was running out. My hopes of marriage and a life with him were fading. I wanted to wake up and face the reality of the situation but he was like a drug I had to have. I spent hours building the courage to leave but, in his arms, the courage dissolved like sugar in water. Every time he came to see me, I pushed him harder and harder to make a decision. Each time I told him I would leave him, each time I didn't. He didn't believe me, who would? I was like a stuck record.

~THIRTY NINE~

NEW LIFE OF KHMER SURVIVORS

The first real market was opened in the city, next to Dumex. Open all day, it signaled the beginning of a new life for the Khmer survivors coming back from "Year Zero." More and more people arrived in the city, occupying the row houses from the first floor to the top. Slowly, they filled the city and it returned to life.

Those on the first floor had the opportunity to run their own business or rent to someone who had a skill like running a restaurant selling noodle soup and coffee, a popular breakfast for Khmers. Others sold goods like soap, cigarettes, and medicine.

Food stands were set up in front of the row houses, selling lunch and dinner to those of us without kitchens, like me. When I lived at home with my family, I would never have eaten street food. Now I ate everywhere whenever I was hungry. How my delicate sensibilities had changed. Now the varieties of dishes available were attractive to me, and I used the plate and fork and spoon that the vendor provided, despite the fact that I knew one small container of water was used over and over to wash the dish and that no soap was involved.

The food smells made my mouth water despite the dust and the smell of the four year old piles of garbage that were everywhere on the street. The piles became rotten, muddy, and smelly under the rain. People continued to dump their daily garbage on the pile making it bigger and smellier by the day. Public services were practically non-existent. It was certainly not pleasant to sit down on the curb for a meal, but I did it anyway. Even in my reduced circumstances, people saw me as rich because few could afford food along the street.

Once in a while when I got more money from selling on the black market, I would go to a restaurant and actually sit on a chair and be served. The delicious smell of deep fried crispy Chow Mein with Chinese broccoli would entice me in from the street. When served hot and spicy with chilies, who could resist coming in to taste it? Since the restaurant was right next to *Pou* Phan's house, his little son was always hanging out there watching people eat and enjoying the lovely aromas. Occasionally, he would see me sitting there and come in to share my food. This made both my little cousin and his mother happy.

On the street, farmers, who didn't have the money to set up a stand, sold their vegetables and fish from wicker baskets. There were also vendors for dried fish, fermented fish, meat, prawns and clams. All different kinds of dessert were a treat the survivors craved. We used Vietnamese currency and rice to buy their merchandise; later rice was no longer accepted, only dong.

345

Phù Lam -The Vietnamese Camp

Weary of my chilly reception from *Pou* Phan, one day I walked to the market to buy lunch and unexpectedly ran into my cousin Charanay. I had heard nothing of her since the KR came into power. Seeing me, she pointed her finger and laughed aloud with happiness, "You are alive!!?"

"You also are alive!!?" I pointed back at her in delight.

Besides being thrilled to see her alive and well, seeing Charanay gave me hope that I might still make a connection with Mr. Chhorn. If I met him, my dream might come true. I wouldn't care if he couldn't give me a lot of money, just some. Surely he wouldn't refuse to help me, I reasoned.

"What are you doing here?" I could hold the question about Mr. Chhorn for later.

"I just came back from Vietnam by boat. I am living there in a Vietnamese refugee camp."

"Why did you come back?"

"Do you have any medicines?"

"Yes, I do. Why?" She told me she came to Phnom Penh to buy any kind of medicine to take back to the refugee camp to sell for a profit.

"I need money now. I cannot wait until you come back again to bring me money."

"I will come back again next week. I go back and forth all the time."

We went back to my house and I gave her what medicines I had on trust. The next week, she came back with the money. I became convinced this was a way out for me and I should escape with her by boat to the camp in Vietnam. The plan to leave Dararan and start a new life would become reality. Tonight, when he knocked on the door, I wouldn't be there for him anymore. What would he do?

"You can live with us in the camp until you have your name called for relocation to a third country." Charanay seemed to be positive about what she said.

"I want to leave my boyfriend. This is a perfect time to let him go," I sadly told my cousin.

"Does he want to come with us too?"

"No, he has wife and son."

"Screw him then," she laughed. Charanay was a very nice person, tall, skinny and beautiful. What I liked the most about her was her giving heart, her generosity. We had a lot of things in common like being westernized and easy-going, with a sense of humor; but Charanay had a better business mind and was braver. "Do you know how to swim?" she asked me. "In case the boat has an accident, you will have to rescue me. I don't swim." She laughed but I was alarmed.

"I don't want to go, then." I hesitated

"C'mon, make up your mind. If you die, you die, and then you will have really escaped." I decided to be brave and trust her. Taking only my clothes and telling a work colleague that I was sick, I followed her to the boat. "Now, remember, if the Vietnamese ask you for ID, tell them that you have a husband who lives in Vietnam and you are joining him and don't say any more." I nodded my head

After a one-day trip, we were in Saigon. Charanay took me to her depressing little house in the camp. "This camp is called *'Phù Lam'*," she told me. It was not a big like *'Wat Chan Reangsey'* (closed later), and the Khmer refugees of about 1,000 families who lived in the camp were not provided with food rations. They had to provide for themselves. Since the camp was located next to the main bus station, it gave the refugees the ability to leave the camp during the day to make a living such as buying and reselling rice, other foodstuffs or medicines. Richer refugees could run small businesses such as a restaurant outside of the camp. The camp was very poor and primitive; all the houses were built off the ground about three steps, very close together and made of bamboo and palm leaves like in rural Cambodia.

It didn't take long for me to realize there was no future for me there. I had very little hope that my only relative in France, my Auntie Leng, would send me enough money to live on; I didn't know what the Vietnamese agencies would require for me to get an ID; and I had no desire to return to my life as it was with the Princess – selling desserts in the market. I wasn't going to live like that again.

"This is where we have lived for four years since we escaped from Phnom Penh."

"You make enough money to bring enough food to the table?"

"Well….mostly we depend on our relatives in France to send us money."

Just as she finished her story, an enraged male voice shocked me, *"Mee samphung!"*

"Shit, he comes to torture me again," Charanay sighed.

"Where have you been all day? What are you doing? Where is the money?" A man staggered in and railed at her but was so drunk he couldn't even stand up straight.

"I don't have any money," she responded. "C'mon, get away from him. He is drunk." She pulled me into her cabin. "He is my unwanted husband. He abuses me every day, torturing me to look for money for him. This is my life. It looks like I am a happy person, but it's only on the outside. I will leave him and go to a third country very soon."

"How soon?"

"I don't know," Charanay sighed and wiped her eyes.

"I want to leave my boyfriend. You want to leave your husband. But, I don't think the camp is a good plan for me; I have no way to survive economically. I need to talk to Mr. Chhorn about the money that Papa left with him."

Charanay shook her head negatively and calmly told me, "He is miserably poor now. All the business he owned in the past failed and he lives in a very poor studio in France. Poor cousin."

"Oh no…" I bit my lips, "He was my last hope."

"He has no money to give you now."

"You have his address?"

"Yes!"

We were again distracted by her drunken husband. I never got the address from her and no reason to doubt her description of his financial condition. One more miserable disappointment that I would have to overcome.

Forgiven

Three days later, Charanay accompanied me back to the Phnom Penh; after that, she returned often to visit me and buy medicine. The very next morning, when walking around the market, I ran into one of my friends who used to work for Papa. This meeting brought me some very unexpected information about Papa's mistress.

Her name was Chiet; I decided to go see her, mostly out of curiosity. I expected someone who "married" Papa for the power and money would be beautiful, but shallow. When I met her, I changed my mind about her and her motives. She was about 5'2", lighter skin, very friendly, and mature. I could see her real beauty even though she wore no make-up. I did not wonder why Papa was involved with her because she still looked so young and pretty even after living through the horrors of the KR life. Her generosity and good heart made me forgive her for her adultery with my father. I certainly had no right to judge anyone when it came to illicit love affairs.

She cried very hard when I told her about Papa's death and said, "Stay with me, I will take care of you."

This statement, while generous and well meant, held no attraction for me. It reminded me about too many experiences living with somebody who said they wanted to take care of me. My mother-in-law deceived me over and over; my father-in-law kicked me out of the house after eating the sugar he got from stealing Papa's silk *sarong*; and the Auntie Princess I met after liberation who treated me as a servant.

Instead of refusing her offer right away, I politely asked her about her life, "What do you do for a living?" She got up and filled a glass with soda.

"I am a trader." She gave me the drink and filled one for herself.

"Aur Koun." I guessed her business was similar to my *Keo* Phon in Siem Reap province, who went back and forth to the Thai border for import/export.

"What I do is," she took a nip of her drink, "ride the Vietnamese trucks to the Thai border to buy goods to trade in Phnom Penh." She smiled.

I thought, "I was right about her business. If I had wanted to be in such a business, I would have accepted my *Keo* Phon's offer months ago." Deep in my heart, I knew I couldn't accept her offer because she and I lived in different worlds. I continued to ask her about her life and how she survived the KR.

"I lost all of my family - mother, brothers and sisters and father – all were executed in Takeo province." Her story was so familiar; like me, she was alone.

I finished the drink, ready to get up and leave. "I will be back to visit you again," I promised but I never saw her again.

New Idea

I returned to work, acting like nothing happened despite the fact that I had been gone three days. Many people asked where I had been and I lied and told them I had been very sick and stayed at my *Pou* Chhun's house.

"I thought you had left for Khao I Dang camp." said my friend, Sothy.

"Khao I Dang?" I was surprised. "Why would you think that?"

"A lot of people escape to the Thai camp. Don't you know that?"

I pretended such an idea had never crossed my mind," Yes, I know about the camp, but I don't want to leave my country."

"Vicheara, nobody wants to stay here. I want to escape too, but I am still looking for a reliable guide. Just be careful, don't let anybody know any plans for your escape......It's very dangerous......You would go to jail if you got caught." He looked straight into my eyes to be sure I understood how serious he was and then walked away.

This worried me, but excited me, too. I didn't know how to go about escaping but I knew I had to leave. Since I didn't have the strength to stay away from Dararan and I knew he would never leave his wife and child, I needed to make a fresh start. That was particularly clear to me now that my last hope of recovering any of Papa's money was gone.

"Hey, Vicheara," another pharmacist said loudly from the working area, "I thought..."

I was startled and jumped with surprise, "Don't scare me like that, pig."

He cracked up. "I thought you were at Khao I Dang already,"

"Yes, everybody said you were gone," said another employee.

"Hell! No, I have been sick...and all of you stop this conversation, it will provoke a problem for me."

At 6 PM, that night, my boyfriend unlocked the door from outside. Of course I missed him and was happy he was with me. "Honey, I came here every night waiting for you. Where have you been?"

"Vietnam." I kissed him.

"Vietnam? I nearly went crazy. I thought you were mad at me and left me."

After I told him about the camp in Vietnam, my boyfriend crushed me to his heart so hard I couldn't breathe. "I know what you want. If you want to escape the country, go with my mother. She is working on finding a trustworthy guide to escape to Khao I Dang with my son."

"Your wife isn't going?"

"No, she is staying."

Hearing that his wife would stay with him, I became furious. "You are laughing at me because I am a widow, lonely and naïve. You want me to be your mistress. I will never be anything more than your mistress. You didn't tell me you were married until I was already in love with you and I have been stupid enough to believe everything you say. I love you and I don't have the strength to tell you to fuck off."

"My mom is encouraging us to get a divorce."

"So, why don't you?" I asked.

"Let's get married now!" he said, holding my hand, but not answering the question.

I snatched my hand away, "What you are really asking is that I agree to be an illegal second wife to you. No! I won't be second in anybody's life. I have to be number one or nothing. You won't leave her for me. You have a son with her."

"All I ask is that you love my son. He is a nice boy."

"No, I will not marry you. I am too ashamed of our relationship. I'm an adulteress and I don't like it. I am not selfish. If she leaves you, I will marry you, but you have been promising that for far too long. I don't want to live like this."

"Honey, she won't let me win. She wants to find a man first before she lets me go. If she finds out I was unfaithful, she will find a way to stop us from being together."

"That doesn't make sense. You already told me that she did know about us and was looking for an opportunity to leave you. Well, so am I looking for an opportunity to leave you," I said, and I meant it.

"You won't leave me."

"What makes you say that?"

"Because I love you more than life itself. I will steal you back from whoever has you."

"You don't love me enough to leave your wife and risk your job and reputation. Honey,....." I kissed him. "Let me go."

"Nobody loves you like I do." He grabbed my hands and brought them to his heart. He kissed my hands passionately as if he was afraid they would disappear.

"I lived through Hell for four years and survived; I will hate myself if I continue to make myself suffer every day by loving you. What is the difference? I suffer from starvation and illness or I suffer from a broken heart because I can't have the man I love all to myself. I have to share you and I don't want that for myself."

"I know that. Real love is hard work. I promise you we will be together eventually."

"Eventually, I can't wait for eventually. Eventually may never come and I need to move on."

"Please Honey, trust me," he pleaded over and over.

I wanted so much to trust him but his promises had worn thin; I couldn't trust any more promises. When he fell asleep, I listened to his breathing and did a lot of thinking about my life, my career, and my future as well as my love for Dararan and how intertwined they all were. What was my priority? He believed it was him but I knew I needed to make my future my priority.

"Honey? Wake up." I said, pulling my arm from under his neck.

"What is it?"

"I know a man, a friend of *Baung* Sien's. I've known him a long time; he can be trusted. He has trades at the Thai border so he could be my guide to Khao I Dang. I will approach him when he comes to visit me next time. I feel it is my time to go.

Leaving you will break my heart but when you go home every night, my loneliness makes me feel cheap and worthless. When I look around, all I see are families. Cousin Phach, my uncles, my friends - all have families to love and care about. I have no one. When my parents were alive, I couldn't wait to be independent. Now with my parents and grandparents gone, I am independent but now I know that life alone is lonely and difficult."

My boyfriend put my hands to his lips. I continued, "If Papa were alive, he would care how I lived, what I ate and what I did with my life. When I was sad, I would have Papa to show me affection, and to coach me. When I was happy, Papa would share the happiness with me. It is never the same with people who are not your family."

"You are right, Honey," he kissed me deeply, from his heart. This kiss, in fact, motivated me to talk more, "Papa's love had no conditions. When I was in trouble, Papa would stand with me when others would walk away. I want that unconditional love again and it will never happen in the love with no future that you are offering me. I need to be strong and take my future into my own hands."

"Honey, if I could swallow you to keep you safe in my heart, I would. I don't want you to leave but I will support you in any decision you make. I want to support you because I love you. But, I have a feeling that you will come back to me. You can't leave a love as strong as mine. No one can love you as I do but I will trust your decision."

We just looked at each other for a moment and then I asked, "You're not going back home tonight?"

"No, I am staying with you. I don't care what anybody thinks at home."

"Can you stay with me again tomorrow?"

"I won't guarantee it, Honey, I don't want her to find out we are here."

I pushed him off the bed, "Just go home and don't come back."

"No, I will stay tonight and tomorrow too."

"Staying with me tonight will be good to remember our love. Staying with me one more night will prove you are going to miss me. This is what I want before I leave you."

My boyfriend put his head on my breast, his hand caressing mine. Once in a while, he brought my fingertips to his lips. What was he thinking? He stared out the window for a long time then turned to look at me. I looked at him and we both began to cry. "I won't stop you. When you are happy, I will be happy." We fell asleep in each other's arms.

A Piece of Cake

About a week later, the guide that I had been waiting for showed up at my apartment. After telling him about my plan, Ty didn't hesitate to say he would help me.

"Going to Khao I Dang is a piece of cake for me. I know the directions by heart. However, the road is risky because we have to first pass the Vietnamese troops who guard the forested borders in Battambang province and Sisophon District. Then we have to pass through a KR camp, and then the *Chumrum Thmey* territory. These groups fight each other constantly to maintain their territory. I will do my best but I can't guarantee your safety along the road. Also, you will need to have at least two *chees* (one *chee* =3.75g) of 24K gold with you. You never know what may happen and we may need to bribe one or more of the guards along the way."

"I don't care. I want to go. I have to go. I won't be scared. I have a pure silver bowl; how much can I get from selling this?" I gave him my silver bowl.

"Depends on the weight." He balanced it on his hand and took a guess, "I'm not sure exactly, but you will get at least two *chees* of gold."

"Perfect," I said happily. "So, when will you go back to Siem Reap again?"

"Two days. Meet me at the bus station; dress casually, and act like a merchant."

"It sounds good to me. I'll be there." I let him stay at my apartment, so later he and my boyfriend could meet.

~FORTY~

FIRST ATTEMPT

Dararan met Ty that evening and questioned him closely about the potential dangers we might encounter on the escape. Ty described the route and how he avoided the various insurgent groups and assured us that he had done this successfully many times. After Ty left, Dararan and I talked late into the night.

"Honey, I agree with you that leaving for a third country may bring a brighter future for you. I think we can trust Ty. He seems sincere and honest and his knowledge appears genuine. I believe he will help you to safely reach the refugee camp, without being caught. However, my main concern is…"

"He will take me to the camp out of compassion. I won't pay him a penny. He will help me sell the silver pot to get the gold I will need if I get into trouble along the way," I interrupted him.

"Honey, my concern is…"

"Honey, I will have at least two chees of pure gold from selling my silver pot. I can survive on the road until I enter Khao I Dang camp," I interrupted him again.

"My concern is," he put his hand over my mouth as I was going to talk again, "will he be honest with you and really take you there for free?"

"Yes, I trust him. He is a good person."

My boyfriend looked down at the floor thinking. "Is he married?"

"Single," I cuddled my darling. "We will go to Siem Reap and stay with *Baung* Sien before trying to cross the border."

"I am worried for you, but I believe in you. Honey, make sure you don't tell anyone at work about your plans. You know," he reminded me, "whenever anyone misses work or requests vacation, everyone is immediately suspicious that their only goal is to cross the border. You wouldn't get very far before they found you."

"Don't worry, I will just disappear from work; I won't request vacation. By the time they find out I have escaped, I will be in Thailand." I hugged him with excitement, "Please stay with me tonight, so I can inhale your scent all night long and remember it. Talk to me all night so I can keep the sound of your voice in my ears forever. Look at me when you talk so I will always remember the shape of your mouth." I ran my fingers over his lips, and he kissed my hand, "I will see your heart shaped lips in my mind when I am asleep. I will smell the essence of you in every flower. I will hear your voice in every song. I will see your beautiful eyes in every star in the sky. You will always be with me."

"Please continue to love me. This is what I want from you," he begged. We stayed in each other's arms all night.

At 6 AM, before our neighbors awoke, Dararan gave me a ride on his Vespa to the bus station. I didn't know if I was making the right decision or was making a huge mistake, but I had to go. I had to change my life; I was both sad and excited. I loved to travel, but it would be better if I knew what I was traveling to. I knew I had to think of this as a wonderful and exciting adventure, a beginning, not an end.

At the bus station, my heart started to beat faster with excitement and fear. I was sure everyone in the bus station could hear it pounding as we made our way through the crowds. I was excited because I was taking such a huge step and I was afraid of being caught and punished for my attempt. I was worried but I knew that worrying about something that hasn't happened yet was not the thinking I needed and I tried to push the worries out of my mind. "I am a tiger, I jump from one place to another, and each time I jump higher to my new future in this new country," I said in my head, to reassure myself I was doing the right thing.

I looked around at the people; all seemed to be rushing to catch the bus just like me; I didn't see anyone I thought was a spy. I looked like anyone else focused on their destination. I avoided eye contact with the policemen who watched the commotion. "Don't look at them," I told myself. "Pretend to be indifferent." If they suspected anything, I would be pulled over and asked for identification. They would notify my pharmacist supervisor and then what? Would I be sent to prison? Without watching where I was going, I bumped into a woman vendor who had been following me to try to get me to buy her goodies. She bumped me again to get my attention.

"I don't have any money! Stop hitting me with your basket," I said, irritated.

"No, you are rich. Look at your face, your complexion. Please help the poor people like me. I need to survive."

Before I could answer, my boyfriend pulled my shirt," Honey, keep going. Don't talk to her."

Ty was waiting where he told me he would be and we easily found our bus. Before boarding, I held Dararan's hand for the last time. Instead of giving him a kiss on the lips, I just closed my eyes and took a deep breath as if I was kissing him from a distance. My sweetheart said nothing; maybe he was breathing the breath I just released or maybe he forgot to breathe. His eyes glistened and filled with tears, as did mine. "Honey, I want you to love your wife and forget about me," I said as I released his hand slowly and started to walk away from him. He never took his eyes off me from the time I boarded the bus until he disappeared from my view. I would have hugged him for the last time, but I couldn't. We didn't want to be noticed.

Unforgettable Memories

The bus stopped to await the ferry at Prek Kdam. Papa, stepmother and I had waited here when he took us to Angkor Wat; it seemed to have happened in another lifetime. He had sent me to buy the crispy prawn cakes and then cracked jokes and teased stepmother. The prawn cakes were still made and sold in this same spot; girls still carried baskets of the local specialty through the crowds begging travelers, "Please buy my cakes. Please! Please! My mother will beat me if I don't sell all these cakes."

Now as I really looked at those girls and not at the cakes, I had to lower my head to hide my shame. I had hardly noticed the girls when I traveled as a fourteen year old 'princess' to Angkor Wat. Now I saw the people, not the cakes, and it broke my heart. They were so young to be doing this for a living just to help their family. Under the hot midday sun, I could see the sweat dripping from their foreheads, but they ignored the discomfort because street vending is very competitive and challenging, as I now understood all too well from my experiences with Auntie Princess.

The girls should have been at school; at their age, I never worried about anything but going to school, and dressing up and showing off to my friends. Look at these kids; they lived from day to day and meal to meal. If I didn't buy their wares, they would be sad or beaten by their mothers. But, I had no money for treats like prawn cakes. Suddenly, I saw Dararan; he had been following the bus, riding his Vespa.

"I miss you already, Honey. I don't want you to leave," he cried.

"I have to go. I want you to stay married to your wife and take care of your son. My life has to take a different turn. If you keep following me, I will not be able to go forward." These were my last words to him as the ferry arrived at the shore and our bus started to move forward, taking me away from my darling who was staring at me until I couldn't see him anymore. Our last look at each other was through a veil of tears.

The bus trip was long, hot and tiring and I was happy to arrive in Siem Reap. I urged Ty to hurry as rushed to *Baung* Sien's house to surprise her. I was sure she would be excited to see me and feel proud of me when she knew I would escape to Khao I Dang.

"*Baung* Sien! *Baung* Sien! It is me I ran up the steps so eager to see my dearest friend, my savior and hero but came to a high speed stop in front of *Baung* Sien who greeted me with wide eyes and panic written on her face. "What are you doing here?" she asked, in a voice that rose in pitch with every word. "Who will my daughter stay with? Why did you leave her?" My arms, open wide to hug her, dropped to my sides. "What?" I asked, completely confused and stricken with guilt although I had no idea what I was guilty of. I was astonished at this turn of events and I had no idea what to say.

Her voice became even shriller as she scolded me, "I just sent Thom to Phnom Penh to live with you."

From behind her came the voice of Ta, her youngest daughter, "I told you not to send her to but you are impatient."

"Shut up!" *Baung* Sien then turned her anger on her daughter who shrugged and turned away.

Now I felt guilty as though I had somehow been disrespectful. However my brain was searching for some way to protect myself even though I was shocked. "When did you tell me about your plan?" I blurted out.

Instead of answering to my question she continued, "Who would I send her to other than you?"

"What? You didn't tell me you were going to do this. I had no idea," I was astonished at this turn of events and stunned that she was blaming me.

"I sent her along with my nephew." She looked at Ty, but he didn't know any more than I did and backed away.

"Where is she now? I did not see her at all; when did you send her?" I looked at Ty also but he only shrugged his shoulders.

Baung Sien's hands started to shake, her eyes turned red and she started to cry. I was scared and guilty and angry all at the same time, "I didn't know. How could I know? You cannot be mad at me and you cannot blame me for ignoring Thom. I wouldn't do that to you." Tears welled in my eyes and rolled down my cheeks, I felt terrible.

When she saw me cry, she got control of herself and her attitude changed, "Oh Vicheara, don't cry, it is going to be fine. She will come back to Siem Reap if she can't find you. Why are you here?" She asked.

"I want to cross the border to Thailand," I said. My answer made her think.

"Really? I didn't know this was your plan. I hope Thom will be back in time to go with you!"

"Go with me? You know escaping is very risky. There are bandits and KR. There are mines all over the border area. To me, my life here is worthless and I have no future. If I fail, if I get caught or injured or raped or shot, then I will die. If I die, then I die and it will be over. But I cannot protect your daughter on this journey; if something happens to her, I will regret it the rest of my life and you will never forgive me. I can barely care for myself, how can I care for her?"

Now she was mad at me again. She seemed blind to the dangers and insisted that this would be her daughter's chance for a better life. Ty was no help and backed into a corner like a rat waiting for the cat to go away. After hearing how upset she was about her daughter, Ty suggested from his safe corner, "It is not a big problem. You will not cross the border tonight or tomorrow. We can wait for Thom."

That decision satisfied *Baung* Sien, but made me mad. If my plan failed and I could not get across the border because I had to wait for Thom, then I had put my entire life at risk for nothing. It would be a terrible problem for me to return to work.

Baung Sien worried, "I have not collected enough gold for Thom to take with her."

That told me I was stuck here until she got the gold ready for Thom. I took a deep breath and exhaled, trying to calm myself. "This woman is killing me," I said to myself.

We didn't talk to each other for a couple of hours. Ty went to the market to escape the stressful environment and I stayed outside on the balcony, watching people walking by on the street, buses running in different directions, and children playing. When I had calmed down enough, I went back inside looking for her to talk. I found her lying in the hammock, reading. One more time, I tried to convince her of my good intentions to Thom and of my innocence in the situation.

"I did not know you had sent Thom to live with me. I didn't have a plan to escape the country until the last minute. How could I possibly have thought you would send her to live with me?"

She stopped reading, looked at me for a moment, and then looked away. I could tell she was angry again. "Nobody is going to die. You are worried for nothing."

"What are you talking about?" I asked, as her statement really confused me.

Ty came back from the market and peeked through the curtain, smiling, "Can I come in now?"

"Idiot, come in. You don't have to ask my permission," *Baung* Sien answered, but remained in the hammock. She turned to me and continued, "I am talking about the escape. Earlier you said the escape was risky, yet I see people going back and forth to Thailand like going to the market so it can't be that dangerous. You are worried for nothing."

Ty shook his head and said, "*Baung*, you are seeing traders go back and forth every day. It is not so risky for them because the KR and the people at the border know them. But it is not the same for people who are trying to escape. They are often robbed and sometimes raped and even murdered. If they don't have a good guide, they can step on a mine. It can be very risky. I need to do one more business trip to the Thai border while you wait for Thom. I will come back with updated information about the KR situation and at the *Chumrum Thmey* camp, the last stop before crossing the Thai border."

"When will you come back? A couple of days? Next week? Next month?" *Baung* Sien pulled out her pocket again, and said, more to herself than to us, "Where is it? I have misplaced my money."

"I'll be back within a week. Let say, the trip to Thailand will take one day, then a week to go to Phnom Penh to sell all the merchandise, and then one day to get back here. OK, give me ten days. By that time, Thom will have returned home. I will stop by when I come back from Thailand if I learn anything new about the camp safety."

"Can you pay me first for the silver container?"

"Just wait until I come back. I don't have the gold now."

"Please don't forget to sell my silver pot for me, OK?" He left early in the next morning.

Bird in a Cage

Three days passed, then one week, then one month. He never came back; he lied to us. Now I was stuck in Siem Reap like a bird in a cage. The updated news from Khao I Dang never arrived. Thom did not return either. My relationship with *Baung* Sien was strained as she worried about her daughter. We had not heard from Thom and there was still no postal service, nor public phones. She had no one but me to blame although I had no responsibility for the problem.

I noticed that her business with *Bo Doy* had grown. Every morning, she left the house for a couple of hours and arrived back just before lunch. Like before, every day there many new *Bo Doy* who came for meals. High rank and low rank, they came and went like a hotel.

Ta, her youngest daughter, always looked bored. Her thin, red lips moved like a doll talking and her high pitched childlike voice made me laugh all the time. She was trying to imitate the accent of Siem Reap, but to me, it was funny. "What did your *Mak* do for living after I left you?" I asked as we snuggled in the hammock and she tickled me on the armpit.

"*Mak* is like a man. A lot of *Ong Leun* like her. I hate those *Ong Leuns*. They talk and talk until late night. They never want to go home."

I wanted to ask more questions but felt it was not my business – *Baung* Sien had rescued me from the princess. Sien still shared the house with the owner but then her room was now very crowded with her merchandise, a big sack of rice, and her clothes. There was also now a hammock in the corner of the room, with curtains for privacy.

"Who sleeps in the hammock?"

"It's for a Vietnamese military officer who comes to rest in it at lunch time," Ta answered. Hum, I thought, I've never seen him coming by.

About three months later, Ty showed up unexpectedly. My first question was about the camp, "Is the attack over in the *Chumrum Thmey* camp?"

"Attacks happen every day because the KR and Vietnamese try to intimidate each other, but it won't last very long. When an attack is over, the merchants come out to do business. They disappear when the attacks start again. This is the real life along the border." He laughed at me as if I had just asked a stupid question.

"Why didn't you come back like you promised? Are you still going to help me?"

"Maybe, maybe not, it depends on my business. Right now, I am broke. I have to stay here for a while to replace my losses."

"Broke? Uh….You have nothing at all to pay for my silver container? Will you pay …now? or later…? Or…never?"

"Don't worry I will pay you soon. I have one *damleng* left, just enough to restart my business."

"You are not broke. You need to pay me now; it's not your money. I will put a curse on you if you are dishonest."

Baung Sien seemed to be on my side as she said to him, "She means it; you'd better pay her so you can be safe on your next trip to the Thai border. Also, you need to prove that I am not wrong to see you as a good person. Are you going to go back to Phnom Penh?"

"I will, but not soon." Then he turned to me, "I suggest you go back home."

"Are you talking to me?"

"Yes, I met your boyfriend before we departed for Siem Reap. He wants you to go back," Ty pulled a letter from his pocket.

I went to a quiet place to open the envelope, excited to hear from my sweetheart again. My love for him swelled; I missed Dararan and still loved him. In his letter he said:

Honey,
I wish you would come back to finish your degree as the pharmacy school
reopens next month. I love and miss you always. Love, Dararan

The idea of going back to the pharmacy school was the deciding factor for me; I would postpone my escape across the Thai border, "I will go back home. I will go back to my own place."

"Who sent you the letter? What is in it? Is it from my daughter?" *Baung* Sien arrived looking happier than I had seen her for a while.

"No, it's from my boyfriend asking me to return and giving me important news: the pharmacy school at the University of Phnom Penh has reopened. I promised my father that I would finish my pharmacy degree but it was impossible with the school closed. I need to go back and finish my degree, but I am worried if it will be safe to go back after I have been gone for four months. I will find Thom and she can live with me." This made *Baung* Sien happy. I could tell by the way she looked at me with a big smile then walked away singing.

Ty left us while I was reading the letter. This worried me but he came back before dark with the gold. It was a band of two *chees* of 24K gold.

That night, as usual, *Bang* Sien received many guests, both Cambodian and Vietnamese. I saw many new faces coming to chat with her. They always stayed very late. In the candlelight, she looked very happy; she laughed and talked as if she had been drinking. She laughed comfortably. She introduced me to a Cambodian man, dark skin, and curly hair, handsome and charming. Unmarried, she said.

This man never stopped staring at me. Clever like a monkey, *Baung* Sien made a plan. When he got up to use the restroom, she whispered in my ear, "He likes you. He has a lot of money. He might pay your way back home." She rolled her eyes suggestively.

"He might, but then what would he want in return? You know men don't help women without expecting sex."

"Tell him the truth that you need help, but nothing else."

"I will."

When he returned, he continued to smile at me but said little. It was obvious he was attracted to me. "When will you go back to Phnom Penh?" his friend asked him as he sipped his tea.

"Day after tomorrow."

Baung Sien pinched my back to let me know the plan was perfect and whispered in my ear, "Let me take care of the conversation." She turned to him, smiled and asked, "Can I send my cousin with you to Phnom Penh? She needs to return now that the University is open but she has no money."

Who could say 'No' to her when she asked so directly? "Of course, of course, I would love to take her." He looked at me, "What is your name? Where do you want me to drop you off?"

Now that the ice was broken, he talked to me for the rest of the evening, until *Baung* Sien admitted she was tired and the party broke up. He left promising to come back in one day's time to pick me up. However, the next day, when *Baung* Sien came back from the market and found me in the kitchen, she said, "Vicheara, that man is not single. He is looking for a way to get rid of his wife."

"I don't care. I don't want him for more than just a friend. If he is a good person and takes me to Phnom Penh, I will appreciate and respect him as a person."

"Ok, good, I feel better now." She walked away, happily singing a love song.

As promised, the next day the man came to pick me up, and we rode to Phnom Penh in a Vietnamese truck. At that time, everybody bribed the Vietnamese military truck drivers for a ride. He never told me how much he had paid the soldier for both of us, and I didn't ask either. We sat together and chatted amiably during the long trip. He said nothing to make me uncomfortable. When we got to Phnom Penh, he escorted me to my cousin Phach's and told me that he would come to see me at the pharmacy school. I was a little suspicious about that but my suspicion was unfounded as I never heard from or saw him again.

After I left *Baung* Sien that day, I never saw her again and never found out what Thom did once she got to Phnom Penh and couldn't find me.

Unsuccessful Fugitive is Thrown Away

Once in Phnom Penh, happy as a bird drinking in a water fountain, I went to find Phach. To my disappointment, she was not at home.

"Oh, Auntie, you are back! *Mak* will be happy to see you. She is worried about you," my dearly niece Sivanna shouted happily; her husband just mutely looked at me with no emotion, like usual. He was an odd man.

"I never went anywhere. My guide ruined my escape plan so I had to come back. I feel guilty for leaving my work. I don't know what they will say when I go back." I put my clothes bag on her bed and then kissed her twin babies.

"It is not your time to escape yet. Don't worry; act like you have not done anything wrong," she said trying to reassure me and then laughed very loudly, startling the babies who began to cry.

Who should I see next? My mind immediately went to Dararan whom I missed so desperately. I decided I would surprise him. My heart beat fast at the thought of seeing him again. "Dear niece, I will be back. Don't tell your mom yet about me. I will surprise her." They both agreed to keep the secret.

I walked to the National Bank, where Dararan worked, intending to walk in and surprise him but that was not to be as the security guard wouldn't let me in until he received permission from Dararan. About three minutes later, my sweetheart appeared in front of me; he appeared very surprised, and instead of the romantic greeting I had dreamed of, took my arm and hustled me quickly to the corner, "Honey, wait for me here, I will be right back."

About ten minutes later, he came back, but was still rushed and obviously worried that someone was watching. "Honey, is everything alright? I missed you so much. I will see you tonight at cousin Phach's, all right?"

He rushed to go back inside, leaving me to figure out what was wrong with him. I expected him to be more excited than surprised. He seemed to be afraid of something.

I walked back to Dumex, meeting pharmacist friends along the way. I had anticipated that my return after four months would cause problems, but I was not prepared for the depth of fear that I encountered. I met my Leang's cousin, Professor Nim in the hallway but he would neither look at me, nor talk to me. Well, I hadn't escaped and I actually hadn't done anything wrong so I decided not to accept this behavior. I needed my job back and a place to live. I followed him, talking to his back, until he asked, "What happens now?"

He kept walking, making me chase after him like a fool. I didn't know what he meant but his expression told me that he was angry with me and wanted nothing to do with me. It wasn't just the Professor either; other pharmacists and all my close friends avoided me as well. It was a very scary and uncomfortable situation but it also made me mad. I was not a slave like in the KR. If I want to escape the country again, I will do it. I don't care if Mr. Nim dislikes me or not. If he talks to me, I will respond. If he smiles at me, I will greet him. If he ignores me, I will pretend he does not exist.

Finally, Professor Nim did give me my job back and offered me a place to live, but nothing like where I lived before. He only did it because I kept begging him and annoying him until I wore him down and he just wanted me out of his face. The home he assigned me was a one story brick row house which had been last inhabited by Chinese merchants, a lower class business family, four years ago. It was an awful place but it was located near my work at Dumex. There were only two old-fashioned windows - both with metal bars, one in the front next to the door, the other in the back but that one would not close. Next to this second window, the rear door opened to the three small compartments, the kitchen, bathroom, and the toilet.

The whole place, from floor to ceiling, was very filthy as it had been abandoned for years. It was also empty, no bed, no desk, nothing remained. The kitchen was covered with spider webs and rotten garbage that had piled up and smelled of dead rats. The toilet couldn't be used for now due to the smell of the rotten trash inside; the bathroom was moldy and infested with cockroaches that came and went as they pleased. They were crawling around the floor and all over the water tank. I accidently stepped on some of them and the crunching sound made my stomach roll. More dropped from the ceiling on my clothes. I gasped and left the building faster than the speed of light.

Outside, I shivered and shook my hair and then my shirt to make sure there were no cockroaches anywhere on me or inside my bra. My thoughts went back to the leeches in the flooded fields and I shivered again. I hated crawly things. I didn't want to go back into that apartment but I knew I had no choice. I had to clean it up; if I washed the tiles one at the time with a wire brush and disinfectant, I could get rid of the smell. Then a better idea formed in my mind, perhaps I could get someone to do it for me. I thought of asking my *Pou* Phan's son to help me. He wouldn't refuse the work if I paid him. It seemed a good plan and I decided to stop by *Pou* Phan's house, which was not far from me. As she often did, my aunt was sitting in front of the house, doing alterations by hand in the bright sunlight. I surprised her by stomping on the cement beside her, "Auntie, I am back."

She looked up at me calmly, taking off her reading glasses. "You didn't get very far, huh? Why did you come back?"

"I cannot hide from you. You can see clearly through me, like I was a crystal ball," I pulled another chair to sit next to her.

"You are stupid to come back. A lot of people have successfully escaped the country," she said, as she put her glasses back on and continued her work.

"I got a row house behind yours. It's going to be a lot of work. I hate cleaning up all the garbage and cockroaches."

"I will help you, Cousin," a boy's voice offered, as my little chow mien buddy came from the kitchen. "How much will you pay me?"

"Ha, you smell money, don't you, little boy?" said his mama.

"Let's work together on the weekend, OK? I will pay you when I get paid." He nodded and looked so happy at the prospect of earning some money.

After a long conversation about my unsuccessful escape, I left my Auntie and walked back to Cousin Phach's. That night, when my cousin returned from the market, she was happy to see me but disappointed that my plan to escape had failed, "I wish you would have succeeded and built a happy life in another country, but I am also happy to see you back safe. What is your plan now?" she asked, as she continued to prepare her merchandise to sell the next morning.

"Go to work in the same place and then clean up the horrible house they gave me."

"Did they take you back?"

"Yes, they did. But, I feel uncomfortable."

"I can understand why....you escaped, and then you came back. They didn't like it. It is just not your time to leave the country yet. Maybe you will have another chance when it is your time and then you will succeed."

"I don't have enough money to pay the guide. Someone else will have to take me for free or for less money. I have only two *chees* of gold." My cousin didn't respond, only sighed.

We stopped talking when I felt someone standing behind me. I turned and saw my sweetheart in person in front of me. *"Chum Reap Sour, Neak Baung,"* he said as he bowed to my Cousin. She bowed back and smiled.

"Honey, tell me what happened," he took my hand and we walked away from my cousin.

"Ty was not really committed to helping me. Actually, I was so lucky that I got stuck at *Baung* Sien's in Siem Reap. Can you imagine what would have happened if he left me in the middle of the jungle or somewhere else really dangerous?" I took a deep breath.

"Well, you needed to come back for me. I am happy to see you back, I missed you so much. After you left, I felt I had lost half of my body." I wanted to kiss him now, but not in front of my family.

"I did get my job back and a new place to live. I will show you my new place tomorrow if you want to see it. It is very dirty."

"Dinner time!!" said the gentle voice of my little Ngeb behind me. My dear cousin fed us a good meal and my boyfriend stayed with us until midnight.

Temporary Life

As the next weeks passed, I worked my butt off to clean the floor, the toilet and the bathroom. It was another humbling experience. My little volunteer kept checking on me often to see if I needed help. Each time he went home unhappy because I was unable to pay him until I got paid.

When Dararan came to visit me, nothing had changed his love for me. He found me a bed, a desk and an armoire. There was no electricity and no water came from the faucet. A single water pipe that supplied all the residents in that area was in front of the house and only had water at certain times. We all fought for water - first come, first served. Day and night, the temperature in the whole house was the same, hot. I dripped with sweat from head to toe.

Even with the furniture, I was too scared to stay there at night. I was afraid of both the living and the dead, as both robbers and ghosts menaced the city. My best choice to sleep with peace was my Cousin Phach's house where I was never alone. The neighbor on the left of my row house had committed suicide about a month before I arrived and Sothy, on the right, also left at night as did the people across the street.

The Pearl of Asia becomes a Rotting Eyesore

The market was open from 7 AM to 5 PM like before and was very busy. Next to the market, a pile of rotting garbage still grew daily. The disgusting site was the result of an increasing population and the lack of any sanitation services. The pile of garbage was made up of anything and everything from rotten food to worn clothes. Big, fat rats scurried in and out of the piles and dogs scavenged for anything to eat; when one found something edible, a fight ensued and the snarling was heard throughout the market. Dead rats increased the population of flies. The city administrators seemed unable to restore any basic sanitation services. Beautiful Phnom Penh, once the Pearl of Asia, was now a rotting eyesore.

The positive side was that there were more Chinese-Cambodian and Cambodian merchants arriving every day so the variety of available goods increased. The Cambodians sold tobacco, desserts, vegetables, fermented fish, and sometimes rice. A few Vietnamese sold freshly prepared foods like vegetable rolls and egg rolls. I was suspicious of them. Vietnamese? Why were they here? Were they encouraged by the Vietnamese leaders to come here?

Not many people used rice to pay for merchandise and food in the market anymore. Instead, they used dong and 24K gold. The price for goods was always quoted in gold; I also heard conversations about buying and selling the row houses and paying in gold. I thought about my family home; if I had stayed there when I first returned, I could have sold it by now. I made a poor decision but it was too late to go back to my house now. I needed to move on with no regrets and to learn from my mistakes and my choices.

Overestimate

Cousin Phach worked very hard to support her family. The oldest sons did little to help compared to the daughters. The younger daughters Ngeb (nine years old by now) and Bopha (14 years old) got up at 4 AM to help their mother take her merchandise to the market, and then back again at night. The youngest daughter, Suzette, about six years old, would wake up and walk to the market with her eyes closed to help her mother sell additional cakes whenever my cousin had time to make them. My dearest cousin never, ever asked me to help. I lived with her for free. Bopha and Ngeb also carried water from the market to fill up the water reservoir at home. Naith and Ridth, the oldest sons, helped a little to bring water up to their living quarters.

Seeing them all work so hard, I was mad at myself for not taking my house back. Now, I was broke and couldn't help. I wanted them to live in a nice house, with electricity and a reliable water supply. I did not want to see her working so hard from early morning to late at night. Worst of all was her worried face as she struggled to make ends meet. I was not happy to hear the kids complaining about the hard work when they were tired. I felt guilty that I could not help more than I did.

One day I made a terrible mistake when I was frustrated with them. Ngep worked harder than anybody else, but was also very stubborn and sassy. I had been watching her resisting her mother's rules for so long and, one day, I snapped and slapped her on the face. Her reaction to this was probably much as mine would have been at her age – rather than backing off, she screamed louder and looked to her mother for rescue. She also called me names. This made me furious and I screamed back.

My Cousin was so angry at me for hitting her daughter; she instantly came to her daughter's defense. All my nephews and nieces were quiet as their mother told me, "It is best that you not live with us anymore."

I had made a terrible mistake. This mistake taught me that an outsider has no business disciplining the children of others. Indeed, I should have known that mother and children, brothers and sisters, can fight with each other and forget it in two minutes but they will unite against anyone else.

This incident forced me to return to my lonely row house permanently; I would have to learn to live with the fear of ghosts and robbers. Now, the only family I frequently visited was *Pou* Chhun's. I spent most weekends with them to ease my loneliness. I missed Phach and her family so much but I couldn't go back due to my own poor judgment and bad temper. Am I like my Papa? I remembered my *Lok Tah* saying to me, 'Like father, like daughter'.

Promotion

As I waited for the pharmacy school to re-open, little changed in my life except for the weather. The oppressive heat and humidity gave way to the monsoon season. Late each morning, gray clouds heavy with rain, would begin to build as a warning of the approaching storm. The morning's heat dissipated; and cool, moist air began to gather energy as it whipped awnings and flags and redistributed the rubbish in the streets. Street merchants heard the wind's message and quickly packed their goods; pedestrians hurried to finish their errands and return home or find shelter. Everyone enjoyed the cool air as it circulated through the city and they prepared for the deluge that was to come. In case anyone had missed the message from the wind, lightning crackled and thunder roared like a lion in the sky warning that heavy rain was on its way.

I lay on my bed imagining the activities outside my house, pleased with the cool air but annoyed that my nap had been disturbed. I knew all the small children were shedding their clothes waiting for the lightning to stop and the rain to begin so they could race around and play naked in the downpour. Parents were busy looking for containers, as many as they could find, to catch the clean, pure rainwater. Now I heard the first heavy rain drops falling, hitting the roof of my house like small stones. The clatter competed with the delighted screaming of the children playing outside. I lay there looking at the ceiling, watching the water dripping through the cracks, running in a stream to the wall and pouring like a waterfall through the back window which would not close. Frustrated with my life and my loneliness, I didn't even bother to mop up the water; what was the point?

I heard someone knock on the door, "*Baung* (cousin), are you here?" I recognized this voice right away; it was my little volunteer boy. I unlocked the door and opened it a little as the rain splashed my face. He was soaked, but still smiled hopefully, "When are you going to need me again? I need money." I let him in.

"You come at the right time. I just got my pay yesterday. You can help me mop up all this the water. And don't forget to come back tomorrow to fill up the water tank for me. I will give you ten dong."

"OK." He was happy and reached for the mop.

"Hey, do the mopping after the rain, not now, silly head."

My little cousin laughed and played with the dripping water.

"No, go home. Come back later in two or three hours." I knew the monsoon would last at least that long.

After the rain, there was a flood in front of my house. I opened the door wide to let the cool air in, and watched the small naked kids enjoying the after-rain play. Then my little boy came back as promised, splashing happily through the flood. He was not a bad worker. Around six, as evening arrived and shadows gathered around me, I lit a candle and was about to go out to buy dinner when Dararan came to my door. He always changed my mood like a breath of fresh air. I pulled him inside of the house to savor the warmth of his arms and the sweetness of his kiss. "Any good news, Honey?"

"I was promoted."

I clapped my hands with joy, "What is your title now?"

"Bank Manager."

"Fantastic. What about our relationship?"

"Honey, listen," he walked me to the bed and we both sat down. He started to rub my hands, his voice was anxious and pitched higher than usual. "My mom knows we are still together. She wants to meet you." I could feel a blush bloom on my neck and move up my throat. I listened attentively for what he would say next. "She got a job working in the bank with me, too."

"She who? Your wife?" He nodded. "Oh, I understand now. When I went to see you at the bank, you rushed to push me to leave because you were afraid of her seeing me. Am I right?"

"Uh, Yeah. I wanted to protect you. I love you, Honey."

"Now, what do you want from me?"

"I want you to love me."

I pushed him away, "I am so sick of hearing this over and over."

"Wait, listen." He stopped me from getting up from the bed.

"If you don't make our wedding happen this time, I will not stay with you." I walked toward the window.

"We could have been married before, but because ......"

"No buts....I was very clear; I refuse to be your second wife."

"Honey, you know that all the legal documents were destroyed during the Year Zero. There is nothing left to prove anything regarding personal property or marriages. *Ong Leun* will recognize a marriage as legal if the partners submit government paperwork. She and I are considered to be legally married because we had our names documented with our employment office when we returned and were looking for work, way before I met you. I could only dissolve my marriage if I get agreement from *Ong Leun* and that's very tricky because the 'Father Boss' is very clear that a bad person is a bad worker or someone who is divorced. So a divorce will damage my reputation and my potential for job promotion. I might even lose this job because I am expected to be a role model to my employees. That makes it very tough for me to divorce my wife and for us to marry. The only hope we have to avoid this problem with job security is to have her leave me for another man because neither of us wants to stay married."

"Do you realize that I will be a pharmacist very soon? When I graduate, I will work and get paid more than you do. You can dissolve your marriage at that time and work somewhere else or start a trading business for a living in addition to my income."

"Honey, I cannot live my life running across the border like those people."

There was nothing to say. I still lived depending on circumstances I could not control, hoping something would work out and we could be together.

Re-Opening of the Pharmacy School

The first faculty of the University of Phnom Penh that reopened was Medicine and Pharmacy. Pharmacists who remained alive reorganized the schools with the help of doctors and a few organizations like OMS and UNICEF. A few more hospitals were also reopened. Nurses, medical equipment, medicine and other supplies were provided by foreign charity organizations. All the fourth year pharmacy students and fifth year medical students were asked to take accelerated courses in order to graduate as soon as possible because the need for trained medical professionals was so great. I enrolled in the fourth year of Pharmacy at the Faculty of Medicine in early 1981 at no cost to myself.

During the school year, we were all required to learn the Vietnamese alphabet and practice oral language skills with Vietnamese professors. We all had problems with this order. Why should we learn Vietnamese to pay respect to them? Are they really our saviors? Dr. Mey said we had only ourselves to blame. If a people do not take care of their own country, somebody else will. It appeared to me that someone had kept the promise very well.

About one hundred students had survived to return to the University. After I passed the written exam, I had to take an oral exam given by pharmacists and professors from the School of Medicine. One of these MDs was Dr. Yith, who used this opportunity to ask me to become his mistress. I was very taken aback by this suggestion as it was the last thing I expected from him. Rather than pushing me, he begged me to think about it and give him an answer. When I refused in no uncertain terms, I was very worried that he would cause me to fail the oral exam, but I passed.

I graduated on November 23, 1981. I am a pharmacist now, Papa! Are you proud of your daughter? I finished my degree as I promised you.

~FORTY ONE~

PROMISE KEPT

There were many more bicycles than cars on the roads in the city. During that time, whoever owned a bicycle had a better life than all the rest of us who had to walk everywhere. Not many people had private cars, only a few Cambodian business people could afford them. There were some official cars, donated by UNICEF, OMS and other organizations, which were used by state departments like Finance, the National Bank, Commerce, Education, Urban Development, and industries like Dumex, etc. All the pharmacy leaders, including Professor Nim, had cars with chauffeurs. I walked everywhere -sweating from head to toes.

All the newly graduated pharmacists were hired by either the hospital, the Red Cross, OMS or UNICEF. A classmate named Phear and I were offered positions as pharmacists working at the Epidemiology Institute with Dr. Sieng as our supervisor. Our offices were in a three story brick row house. The first floor had originally been a three car garage and still had a metal gate attached to one side of the wall that could be pulled straight to lock on the other side. Attached to the garage was a small room about a size of a master bedroom; it had a sturdy lock and was to be the pharmacy and medical storage. In the corner, a staircase led to the second floor, where two bedrooms had been turned into private offices, one for Dr. Sieng, the other for the payroll clerk. On the third floor, a center wall now bisected the open area that had been the living room and dining room and Phear and I each occupied one side. I was given a worn-out executive desk with a chair, as was Phear. She was assigned to do administrative work and public relations with the *Ong Leun*, while I was responsible for the pharmacy. Our office was fortunately located across the street from Dumex and the Health Ministry building. I appreciated this as we often had meetings there with the Health Minister and *Ong Leun*, and I had no transportation.

Poverty, Corruption

The rumor among the newly graduated pharmacists was that our pharmacist professors who had arrived in Phnom Penh right after liberation had ransacked the stock at every pharmacy in the city. They took all the imported drugs like Becozym (complex vitamin B) injectables, Bepanthene injectables and capsules and sold them on the black market for 24K gold. I had no idea if any of this was true but I knew we had very little stock and most of that we had was very old and expired. It was common knowledge among pharmacists that some of our colleagues made fake orders and

368

then kept the medicine for themselves. Big quantities of medicine were received from western organizations; however, it was all delivered to the main warehouse at the Health Ministry. All I knew was that the rich pharmacists were the ones who worked in the big warehouses like the one at the Health Ministry. Corruption was rampant. Once again, a Cambodian adage fit the situation, "*A Thom see thom, Ah Toch see toch* – The superior eats big, the inferior very small." Small pharmacists like me who did not kiss the superior's butt, stayed in the corner and ate the leftovers.

As a pharmacist, I was once again paid in dong and rice, no surprise. Because we could barely survive on our small incomes, each of us was allowed to take a limited amount of calcium syrup or Vitamin C injectables, and thirty tablets of anything that Dumex was producing locally. Employees could provide this medicine to their own family members or sell it on the black market.

Pharmacies provided great temptation for corruption. Having access to medicine was like having gold. Everywhere, everyone needed western medicine from injectables to tablets. There were rules about providing security for inventory but there was no government agency that actually audited anything so rules were up to the individual. Walking into my dark, dirty and dusty little pharmacy was like walking into a prison. I worked my butt off to clean it and placed the expired medicines in order. An electric line and a light bulb made a considerable difference. Dr. Sieng soon ordered me to do an audit on my expired medicines and to keep it locked all the time. He impressed upon me over and over not to lose the key.

Jealousy

One morning I was called to my supervisor's office. I was happy to have a one to one meeting with Dr. Sieng because I hoped I would be able to get a promotion to a better position. Dr. Sieng's eyes started to twitch on one side as he listened to my request. "I encourage you to stay firm in your position. I see a bright future ahead for you when the Epidemiology Institute merges with the Pasteur Institute." I nodded. "I will choose you to be the pharmacy director when the Pasteur Institute opens. I want you to be in charge of all the laboratories like bacteriology, hematology and microbiology. You will have more opportunity to advance than Phear because you are honest. Additionally, you speak fluent French. It will be very important for us to have good communication with the French guests helping at the Pasteur Institute. You are also liked by many Vietnamese friends, the top leaders. They always come and ask for you. I see you can also speak Vietnamese."

I blushed with this compliment. "How about Phear?" I asked him.

"She will be in charge of administrative work at the Pasteur Institute."

Over time, I heard rumors that Phear was jealous of me and tried to get me fired so that she could supervise the pharmacy rather than do administrative work where she had no access to medicines. I'm sure she thought I must be stealing a lot of medicine, even though she saw me asking for medicine from our superior just to survive. She obviously thought that I was hiding something and she needed more - more power and the superiority that the money from corruption would bring.

First, I heard from Dr. Yith, the gentleman who asked me to be his mistress during the oral exam, that Phear had complained about me. I was told that she said I was lazy and non-productive and that she could do both jobs, the pharmacy as well as the administrative work. The same afternoon, when I was busy doing the medicine stock inventory, Dr. Yith showed up at my desk. "Whoever said Vicheara is lazy must be wrong," he said loudly and then cleared his throat.

He startled me and I jumped, "Please don't sneak behind me. I am easily scared." I rubbed my chest like usual when I was scared. "Who said that?" I asked him.

He leaned closer and murmured, "Who else? Be smart and figure it out. Only people who work close to you would have an opinion."

"Uh…" I pretended to be thinking, putting my right hand on my head. "Phear?" He just smiled rather than answer. "Thanks for your comment."

The rumor was true. She liked to spend time at the Health Ministry so she could build up a strong network of colleagues that was to be her secret weapon to eliminate me indirectly. The more she knew people, the stronger and more powerful she felt she would be, so she soon was spending more time there than at her office. Her behavior toward me had changed; she didn't look me in the eye when she spoke to me and seemed to be avoiding me. Her behavior had been noticed by one of my employees who was brave enough to tell me that she was jealous of me because she couldn't get my position.

"Jealous? She is my friend. I cannot let this jealousy ruin our friendship. If she wants my position, I will let her take it."

"No, don't think with your heart at work. Think with your head. I had a meeting with Dr. Sieng to discuss this before we made the decision to choose you over her."

I tapped my foot on the floor to release my stress, "Why did you choose me?"

"You are not arrogant and you have a good heart."

"And, obviously, also am naïve." I pushed her to say more.

"*Chah*, you have been naïve about Phear. You are understanding, easy-going and honest. I agreed with Dr. Sieng that you should be in charge of the pharmacy because you have no family and therefore less need to steal."

"Less need to steal? If I steal, then I am not honest." We laughed.

"This is what we are looking for. Your personality and your profile have met our expectations. Phear is not happy in her home life as she married a peasant in KR time. She told me a long time ago that she wanted to get rid of him, but she couldn't. Then, when we looked at her private life before we made the decision, we found her husband does trading at the Thai border. That's illegal, of course, no matter how common it is."

"Well, I'm obviously not as smart as she and her husband are, since they earn a good living," I said and we both laughed ruefully.

As my employee rose to leave, we looked out the balcony window and saw the minivan stop in front of the office. We saw Phear getting out, carrying her black briefcase. Was she really the vicious competitor my employee described? I didn't want to accept it because I had believed we were good friends. I had trusted her based on her sincere manner and her sweet voice. My employee's advice 'don't think with your heart at work' made me remember when Papa cautioned me to not trust the sweet words of my mother -in-law. Papa was right. However, it took me a long time to accept that painful truth.

After work hours, I networked with other pharmacists to get extra imported medicine. At that time, the third wife of *Pou* Chhun was performing legal abortions at home. She was paid in 24 K gold, the amount determined by the difficulty of the procedure. I provided medicines to her and earned a little extra that way. When we were paid in gold, I saved it. I spent dong on restaurants and clothes.

Naïve

Phear's jealousy of me was growing each day. She was jealous of my style in clothes, my long straight hair and my fluency in French. She wanted to impress the foreign guests that she was more important than I, but no matter how hard she tried, it did not work because she was not fluent in French and she was married. I noticed that every time we met the French and Vietnamese male guests, they always checked to find out if we were single. They preferred to deal with single woman because they were always hoping for 'romance' but they were doomed to disappointment with me.

Her back-stabbing continued but I was still very surprised one morning when Dr. Sieng called me into his office and criticized my western style, my haircut, and make-up. It made me so angry and I retorted, "I wear a long *sampot* in traditional Cambodian style, my blouse is modest, and my hair is straight. I do not see anything wrong with that."

"I want you to change your personal style to fit into the new society, as Phear had done."

"This comparison doesn't make sense. My blouse covers my belly. Do you want me to change to a short blouse that shows the belly? My *sampot* is Khmer traditional style, straight and long, just above the ankle. Her's flare at the bottom and the waist is low, showing the belly. Her's is the new style, not mine."

I was outraged; how could Dr. Sieng say this? Even though he was my supervisor, his rank was not much different from mine. I expected him to respect me; why would he think he could criticize my attire and my personal style, was it just because he was a man? "I have nothing to change to fit to what you call 'this society'."

I left the unusual meeting happy that I stood up for myself but unhappy about the confrontation. The whole day, his words that I did not fit in 'this society' kept running through my mind over and over. At my desk, I kept working on my inventory list, but my mind kept searching for the answer on how to handle this issue. I pressed harder and harder on my pencil until it punctured the paper and broke on the wood. But I still couldn't find the answer.

"What is wrong?" Phear asked me from the other side of partition.

"Nothing bad, nothing good," I answered, without looking up.

"Dr. Sieng must have said something to upset you."

I stood to look at her, this time trying to see her two faces. She knew very well what he had said and she was playing with me. "Someone has told him that my outfits don't fit 'this society', but yours do. He wanted me to dress like you." I watched her for a reaction but she just turned quickly and walked back to her desk.

"Men have no right to say things like this to women. We are pharmacists; he is just an MD, he is not our superior. We are not his employees anyhow." I got up and walked to her desk to drop off my last words, "He said I will be the pharmacy manager, and you, the administrative manager," I said to her and watched for a reaction.

"I wouldn't want to work in the Pharmacy, eating shit there. We have nothing in our pharmacy except shit expired medicines that nobody wants. I heard from the Ministry of Health, someone in a high position, that our department won't have its own pharmacy in the future. There will be a communal pharmacy at the Ministry of Health. They are corrupt and can make that happen." She was now openly pissed at me and threw her file on the desk.

"I don't care. Since I don't fit in 'this society', I'm not staying here anyway." I walked away. The minute those words were out of my mouth, I knew I had made a mistake. I hoped she hadn't heard them.

I had nothing to feel worried about. I had no parents, no children, and no husband; no one depended on me. All I carried was a feeling of regret that I was not able to move into my paternal house right after liberation; if I had had transportation, I would have stayed there. Two years had flown by and it was now too late to claim my house back. There was no one to right this injustice, certainly not the government. It was not just me who lost her home; other pharmacists and doctors working at Dumex lost their property, too.

Training in Saigon – *Prey Nokor*, our Original Land

In April 1982, Phear and I were sent to Vietnam for training in bacteriology with French professors who came from Paris. We stayed for a week in Ho Chi Minh City. I remembered how this land had once been part of the ancient Khmer Empire and was called *Prey Nokor*. Out of curiosity, I took a pedicab to the big market, leaving Phear alone in the room. I saw for myself that Vietnam remained in good shape, despite the war. Buildings, markets, temples, banks, and schools were intact. The Vietnamese continued their life as usual, unlike in Cambodia where everything had been destroyed by KR. Both of these countries were overtaken by the communists, but the Vietnamese had not murdered half their population and destroyed their infrastructure as Cambodia did. What was the whole picture telling me? It was telling me their leaders were following Nam Tien strategy to take over the weaker countries, Cambodia and Laos. This plan started from Champa, which disappeared into Vietnam's hands in the seventeenth century, and then Kampuchea Krom in the nineteenth, next would be Cambodia and Laos. Pol Pot killed all the educated Khmers who would oppose him, and eliminated our culture, religion, and traditions; now it would be easy for Vietnam to penetrate Cambodia and take what was left. – Khmer leaders, please wake up. Don't help the Vietnamese to accomplish their plan.

Suddenly, a woman screaming in the middle of the market startled me. I looked in the direction of the screaming and saw a Vietnamese man beating his wife. Bang! I was hit by someone while I was distracted by the commotion and, before I knew what had happened, my pocket was picked by the kid who bumped me. That had never happened to me in Cambodia.

Stealing is a Job

The next day, Phear and I went to the same market again; I warned her to be careful near the small kids. I hid my money in my bra and was careful not to get bumped by any young boy or girl. In the center of the crowd, I felt just one unexpected hit and the money was gone from my bra. I told a Vietnamese woman in Vietnamese, "Catch that girl. She picked my money from my bra."

"I saw it too. I don't dare to get involved because the criminals are organized and if I report her to the police, she will come back and punish me," she explained. "Those kids have a job."

"What job?" I asked her, in Vietnamese.

"Stealing is their job," she said loudly.

"Wow, that's interesting." I walked away, regretting ever coming to the market. I went back to my place broke. Phear and I couldn't do anything besides laugh, "How did she know I hid the money in my bra?"

"She must have been following you for a long time, and you might have accidently checked the money and that was all she needed."

Make a Long Story Short - Go to Hanoi

The trip to Vietnam was a positive motivator for me. Changing the environment, meeting new people, eating different foods, all changed my attitude. The grey clouds that had hung over my mind disappeared gradually. I came back home with a new pair of high heeled shoes, new fashionable outfits, and new lipstick colors. I felt like I was a new person with new thinking. How stupid was I to let my boyfriend play with my heart? I had enough. I made the decision to end my ambiguous relationship with him.

As usual, Dararan showed up at my house the evening I returned. "Let's go have dinner at the restaurant," I said.

"I missed you a lot, Honey. You were gone for only a week, but it felt like a hundred years."

"For me, too," I smiled.

At the restaurant, we were seated and placed our order. While waiting for the waiter, my boyfriend took my hands and stared at me saying nothing. Then he asked, "Did you miss me a lot?"

"Yes, Honey,"

"I have to leave for Hanoi for three years of training," he said without any warning and looked at me as though he was afraid I would explode. I yanked my hands from his in shock. At first I was shocked and then I was annoyed as I had planned to be the one to leave, but now it was the other way around.

"Our relationship needs to be terminated before you leave," I pulled my hair to the side of my neck.

"No, Honey...No..." He grabbed my hand back.

"I just cannot continue to be a mistress, to commit adultery... it is not me."

"If I stay married to her, she won't let us be together. However, if I go to Hanoi, then she will believe that we have broken up and then she will leave me. So, please wait for me until I come back! The good news is that I know she is having an affair with a friend of mine."

I jumped up with anger when hearing this, "You are a liar. When are you going to leave?"

"In three days."

"Are you ready to order now?" We were interrupted by a waitress.

"Yes, please give me roasted duck and fried rice. How about you?" I looked at the menu instead of looking at Dararan.

"I'll have hot tea."

"Anything to eat?" the waitress laughed and covered her mouth.

"Oh, I forgot. I'll have wonton soup."

I was very conflicted. My problem was solved but not the way I had wanted. But maybe this way was better? I doubted he would ever come back to me; I felt I had seen him for the last time.

"Honey, I promise to send you a letter every week."

"How will you do that?" I pretended to read the menu.

"I know someone, my favorite chauffeur from work. I told him about us. He will bring the letter to you."

"Why did you agree to go?"

"Honey, if I accept this training, I have a guaranteed promotion; I do this for us."

"What?"

"Like I said, she has someone now. When I leave, she will be with that person. Whoever waits for me when I come back, will be my wife."

Hearing this last statement hardened my heart. "Oh, so now, you see yourself as a King," I replied coldly playing with the fork and spoon as I decided what to say. "I will not fight with your wife to win you. It is not my nature. I will not wait for you." We stared at each other silently.

"Honey, she will never leave me unless I go."

"I've had enough of the stupid love for you. I need to open up a new chapter in my life. This is the end for us."

"I will go find you and steal you from whoever takes you away from me."

"Not this time."

Food was served. Dararan stared at his bowl sadly.

"Do you need anything else, *Lok?*" He just shook his head negatively. We finished dinner quietly and returned to my home where we said good bye sadly.

I avoided him but pretending he did not exist was difficult after three years. My heart still thought of him every hour of every day and my memories of our sweet love tumbled in my mind. I knew he would probably be at my door before he left so I bought some toiletries that he would need in Hanoi, even though my mind kept telling my heart that I was stupid. On the last night before he left for Hanoi, he was at my door and my heart let him in. "I brought some things for you in case you don't have enough money to buy them in Hanoi."

He was quiet as he opened the package. "Honey! Only you would think of me and know what I need. One day when I have more money, I will pay you back."

"Will it be enough for at least a month's supply?"

"Two toothbrushes, five toothpaste, and soap; it will be good for at least six months." His eyes were red now. "I am not saying good bye to you. I will come back to see you in three years. Whatever happens to both of us, I will go find you to get you back." I turned my face away from him. "Honey, don't cry."

I cried because he still didn't believe I would leave him forever. Our last memorable kisses that night made me cry more. "Don't cry. I will send you a letter as soon as I arrive." I nodded. "Tonight, I cannot stay long with you. I need to finish packing and go to bed early." I didn't ask him the departure time, I didn't want to hear anything from him.

The next morning, when the sound of an airplane penetrated my office, I wondered how much I would miss him, since at the moment I missed him a lot. That night, I walked to the same restaurant for dinner, sat at the same place staring at the same chair that my sweetheart had sat in last night. Was this really the change I wanted? I finished my dinner and left with no plans to ever return. Then, like an answer from the universe, as I was walking along the street, not paying attention to where I was going, I saw Dararan's wife walking into a restaurant with a man. From their behavior, I knew he must be her boyfriend. Dararan was right. She had committed adultery and she was being mean and vindictive to us. She was selfish. I had to stop myself from confronting her and slapping her face. She seemed so happy with her boyfriend. Why was I once again alone and sad? That part of my life was over.

Weeks passed by; then a month. I never got a letter. His silence urged me to move on, forget about the past. Yet, it was so painful for my heart to give up the love I had wanted to keep forever. It was so hard to move on because my heart was missing him. I wanted to scream out to the whole world to give me an answer on how to cut off the pain, and stop loving him. At this moment, if Papa were still alive, I would cry to him to let out my pain, but I was alone. Who could I tell?

Training with Paul

I felt like a lost boat in the middle of the ocean, not knowing where I was going, moving only where the wind blew me. I felt I had no control over anything. I closed my heart to everybody. I became depressed and didn't care much about anything around me. I didn't care about Phear's jealousy or Dr. Sieng's advice. I needed a strong wind - someone free to love me but I had no hope that person existed. Papa's advice to me, "You are not going to die if you don't have a man," rang in my ears daily. My hurt from loving Dararan and losing him and then fighting myself to move on were too much all at once. I needed to love and be loved before I could move on.

Once again, a pharmacist friend encouraged me to find a foreigner to have an affair with. She said it was a safe relationship and I would have someone to fill the huge hole Dararan had left in my heart. I reasoned that it might be safe because I wouldn't have the stress and worry of an adulterous relationship, but it certainly was not safe politically because Cambodians were prohibited from having personal relationships with foreigners. However, I also knew that no matter how tough the law was, it still left a small chance for me to sneak out of the country with a support of the foreigner.

The more I thought about it, the more I thought, why not? As I mulled this over and over in my mind, a meeting with Dr. Sieng the next morning was fortuitous. He announced that a bacteriologist from France named Paul would be coming to Cambodia to help us organize the Pasteur Institute. Then he said, "There will be many more foreigners coming to assist in bacteriology."

"You never know, you might meet someone, Vicheara," said Phear, turning to me.

"Huh, are you jealous?"

Silence. A breeze swept through the open door behind her desk, rustling her beautiful curly hair. She looked away through the door, maybe looking for the right answer before turning to me and saying, "Yes, I wish I was single like you."

Was it her honest answer or her jealousy? There was no way I could read her mind, and I had no time to do it. The only way I could break the ice was to express my true feelings. "It's not fun being single and worse when one hasn't any family."

After a moment, Phear interrupted my thoughts, "You think because I am married that I have fun? I don't! There are too many problems to have fun. When you are single, you want to be married; when you are married, you long to be single again."

"Life. You just never know where it will take you," I agreed as I rested my chin on my intertwined fingers, "and you don't always want to go in the direction it is taking you."

A Brief Romance

The morning we were to meet the new visiting professor, I awoke filled with anticipation. We knew nothing about him except he was French and a bacteriologist. When he walked into the room, everyone was instantly silent because he was very, very tall, about 6'5", nice looking with a medium build. His complexion was as smooth as a baby's bottom. He wore a short-sleeved white lab coat and when I saw his hairy muscular arms, any remaining images of Dararan ceased to exist.

I was very attracted to him and wondered, "Do I think I like him because I hope he could be the foreigner I have been waiting for? Because, if things go my way, he could sponsor me to leave the country as his wife? Or, if I cannot marry this man, maybe he will give me enough money to pay for my escape? If nothing else, maybe I will have a good time with him and find the strength to move on with my life." All these thoughts raced around in my head and I hadn't even spoken to him!

He was very quiet. Was he shy? Timid? Married or single?" I needed to break the ice. As it turned out, the fact that I was fluent in French was the ice-breaker. During the class, he looked at me and gave me all his attention as I was asked to translate questions and answers for my classmates. This gave me an opportunity to talk to him all the time. This was the first step in getting close to him. At first, it was all about the curriculum. Then, as the days went by, the talks became about my life and my plans for the future. My loneliness must have been written on my face in neon lights because he grew compassionate and developed a special caring for me. He knew I needed to escape. He knew I needed money to pay the guide, as I explained to him. He knew I couldn't trust the political situation in Cambodia. Nor did he.

Outside of class, I went out to eat with him, and showed him the market and, eventually, the city. To the casual observer, I was only a professional translator. There were many male and female translators touring around the city with foreigners. Fortunately, I never encountered any trouble with the authorities.

One Sunday, a week before he finished the training, our group took him on a trip to Oudong Hill about 40 kilometers northwest of Phnom Penh. This had been the capitol of the Khmer Kings in the early seventeenth century. It has great historical, cultural and religious value in the history of the Khmer Empire. After climbing a long stairway to see a gigantic Buddha, I stopped to rest on a big rock away from the group. Soon he joined me there, pretending to look at the view. As I came close to him, he looked at me and smiled. I saw exactly what I wanted to see in his crystal clear green eyes....Romance! He took my hand for a mere moment, then we both let go, trying to keep our relationship professional. At least he was and I had to play the role. His curly, nut brown hair so perfectly matched his smiling green eyes. Who wouldn't fall in love with green eyes like his? His lips were almost similar to Dararan's.

"*Je t'aime* – I love you," he whispered. His hot breath sent shivers through my body.

"*Moi aussi* – I love you too."

"*Qu'est-ce-que tu fais demain après-midi* – What are you doing tomorrow afternoon? *Pourras-tu aller au cinéma avec moi* - Will you go to the movies with me?" I nodded my head. "*On vas diner ensemble* – Would you like to have dinner?" I nodded again. "*D'accord* – OK. A quelle heure – What time?"

"*À Cinq heure du soir* – 5 PM. *J'irai t'attendre devant le cinéma de Kirirom* – I'll wait for you in front of the Kirirom Theatre."

After going out with him a couple of times, our romance grew deeper. The first time I was alone with him in his room, he revealed a truth I had never wanted to hear again as long as I lived, "*J'suis marrié* – I'm married."

I can't say that I was shocked, but I was bitterly, bitterly disappointed. We were silent. What was there to say? Was this to be the story of my life?

"*T'as besoin de l'argent?* – do you need money?" He pulled one hundred dollars from his wallet. "*Tu en as besoin pour vivre. Ici, ç'est mon adresse. Ne pas dire à person que je t'ai donné de l'argent ainsi que mon adresse* – You need the money to survive. Here's my address. Don't tell anybody about the money or give out my address."

I put the little piece of paper in my purse as well as the money. This money would be saved for the escape fee as he told me. When the training was finished, we parted as friends and I kept in touch with him for a long time. His three month mission in Cambodia was over in March, 1982. A brief romance with him was ended - a closed book, but my mind and hope still remained open. I may need him later when I find my freedom.

The Fortune Teller

I started to save as much money as possible to prepare for my escape. I networked with pharmacist friends to get medicines that could be sold for a good profit. One day when meeting with my dear friend Khan, I met a woman who had been in the bacteriology training with Dr. Paul. As I chatted with her, she mentioned that she was on her way to see a fortuneteller. This was hard for me to resist as fortunetellers had been my best advisors and counselors all my life, so I asked, "I cannot go, but can I give you five dong to get a reading for me?"

"What do you want to know?"

"When will I be sent to Hanoi?"

At that time, all pharmacists were obligated to continue their education or training in any specialized area as needed by the government. Phear and I knew that sooner or later, one of us would be sent to Hanoi. Going to Hanoi was not my wish as it would disrupt my plans to escape the country but, who knew what might happen.

Anxious to hear what my life would be, I hurried back to meet my friend to hear my fortune. As soon as she saw me, she screamed with excitement, "Vicheara! The fortuneteller didn't see you going to Hanoi, but to the West. It must be Khao I Dang camp, and then to a third country."

"Shush.....you kill me when you scream like a thunderstorm. My God, let's find a place to talk." I pulled her to the parking lot. She repeated the same thing - that I wouldn't be going to Hanoi. It was with mixed feelings of fear and excitement that I heard this. I shook my head negatively, "Not going to happen. I do not have enough gold." To further cover my tracks, I lied to her and said that my boss planned to send me to Hanoi.

She persisted, "I don't know about that. I am just telling you what the fortuneteller saw in the cards. It could be right; a few pharmacists in my department have disappeared from work but we all know that they escaped. Doctors disappeared, too, as well as people from other departments."

"No, your fortuneteller is wrong. I cannot escape with empty pockets. No gold!"

"It could be true, Vicheara, because I didn't get the same reading as you; the fortuneteller told me that I cannot get out of the country. And I do have the gold that I could use for the escape. I don't know what to believe."

I left her, keeping up the pretense but I was excited, as I knew I would successfully escape in the future. However, at work, Dr. Sieng announced, "*Ong Leun* is working on sending you to Hanoi." This news was not what I wanted to hear.

"When will I be sent?"

"Soon," he said.

This pushed me to accelerate my plans to escape. After work, I went to see my friend Pat, who lived next to me. She was a petite, talkative widow with two adult children and, best of all, she was also a card reader. She frequently offered me a card reading when I was at her house. Later, when she became familiar with my private life with Dararan, I worried about what she would think of me. But she understood that life was complicated and never judged me for loving a married man. She had gone through the same problem.

This time I went to see her not about my broken heart but my future, "Will I go to Hanoi or the Khao I Dang camp? I am kind of scared to hear I will be sent to Hanoi. Despite what the other fortuneteller said, I know it is more likely that I will wind up in Hanoi than Thailand."

She said she would consult with a Malaysian man who used a crystal ball to see the future. She brought his answer the next day, "You will go to the West, not Hanoi. He said you were not born to stay in Cambodia for the rest of your life. There will be a big change in your life."

I now had the same message from two fortunetellers but I was not convinced so I decided to see one more. I spent ten dong on the next card reader. I was told the same thing - I would not live in Cambodia much longer. She saw me going to the West, which was Khao I Dang camp.

Everything Comes Together

I had not visited Cousin Phach for so long, not since the incident with Ngeb. However, I always went to the market where she sold her merchandise to check on her and her kids to make sure everybody was OK and sometimes, we ran into each other in other places. We still talked.

In early February, 1983, a month after the readings with the fortune tellers, I met her in the market and got good news, "Remember Many, your Aunt Pho's youngest son?"

"Yes, I remember him and my Aunt Pho, too. She was *Mak's* older sister. Your son told me Many is still alive."

"Yes, he is here now and looking for you."

"For me? Really?"

"He is now twenty six years old and married by *Angkar* to a girl that he is not in love with; they have three kids together. If you want to escape, he will help you."

"Escape? With no money? As the fortuneteller said?" I screamed with excitement.

"What? What about the fortuneteller?"

"I was told I would be going to a third country."

"Huh…with Many," she nodded confidently. "He knows the road and directions very well."

Many came to see me soon after Phach told him how to find me. He was excited to see me alive. We shared our sorrow about the losses of our families. Many in his family were executed by KR, even the small infants.

"I want to escape; I need to get away from my wife because I do not love her. She is too dark and ugly," he said, when we finally began to talk about the future.

"Many!! I have dark skin, too. What is so wrong with dark skin?"

"Her's is darker and not beautiful. Dark skin is not considered beautiful in Cambodia, don't you know that?"

"You are an asshole. What about the kids?"

He ignored my question and said, "Come to Khao I Dang with me. I guarantee that I will take care of you on the way to the Thai border and at the Khao I Dang camp. I have a business helping people get to Khao I Dang and have done it many times successfully. I know the way; it's like going to the market for me. All I need from you is one damleng of gold."

I took a deep breath and sighed, "I never can get that much gold."

"The main thing that I worry about is crossing the border where the KR hides!" Many lowered his voice as he said this to me.

"Why? What do you mean? Now I am scared. I do not want to go there," I said in alarm.

"It won't be a problem if you do what I say."

"Why is the KR there?" I wanted to make sure he was being honest with me. Ty had already told me much the same thing when I had talked to him about escaping.

"After 1979, when the KR were chased out by *Bo Doy*, they set up camp in-between the Cambodian and Thai borders to carry out guerilla warfare against the North *Bo Doy*. You will pass the Vietnamese troops at the Cambodian border first, then the KR lines, and then a third problem will be at the *Chum Rum Thmey* camp which is held by National Cambodians who claim that they are rescuing Cambodian victims of the North Vietnamese invasion."

After listening to this explanation, I took a deep, worried breath and said, "Hum.... It is very scary."

"Not a big deal. You can wait for another week or so until the attacks calm down."

"Attacks! What attacks?"

"There are attacks all the time along the border due to the fighting between the North Vietnamese, the KR and the security guards in the *Chum Rum Thmey* camp. They are constantly trying to intimidate each other. If either side violates the boundaries, the other will attack. Just come with me; life is worthless here. If you go to a third country, you will be happy and safer than here."

"I don't have enough gold."

"You are a pharmacist." He looked at me. I looked at him. "Do something with medicine to make money as quick as you can. Most pharmacists are rich, why aren't you?"

I knew what he was thinking – that I could steal all the medicine in my charge to pay for my escape. "Let me work on it," I said, but I was irritated that once again I was encouraged to steal.

"Do it quickly," he said, in a tone meant to let me know this offer would not last forever.

I went to see my *Pou* Chhun right away in case he or his wife could come up with any help. She told me the same thing - I would have to steal medicine from my pharmacy to make it happen.

"No, I would not do that and I couldn't."

A day later, Many came to check on me and insisted I make a decision.

"I do not have enough gold. My answer is still the same - that I will not steal."

"Then I have another solution. Find someone who has one *damleng* of 24 K gold and who wants to escape with you, so you can lean on her payment."

"Well, that's a good idea but, who is rich enough to have one *damleng* of gold?"

"Another idea is to sell your row house and the furniture for three *chees* of gold."

"Yes, with my savings that would make five *chees*."

"You don't have to come up with one *damleng*. Five *chees* will be good enough."

This idea seemed to be the best and most honest plan for me to get enough money. Many promised to find me a buyer for the house and furniture.

That same day, my neighbor Sothy called to through the open kitchen wall during siesta, "Vicheara, I had a dream that you said goodbye to me to go to a third country."

"Impossible," I replied casually, but, inwardly, I was excited because his dream confirmed the fortunetellers' predictions. I couldn't confide in him because I had to be careful with everyone around me so I wouldn't get into trouble with the law before I could escape.

One *Damleng* of Gold

The next day I was sent to the Health Ministry to bring the inventory list to Dr. Yith. He surprised me with good news about an old girlfriend, Sophal. "Guess what, Vicheara? Someone is looking for you. Do you remember Sophal? She is alive!"

"Sophal! Yes, she was my best friend years ago when we attended the same College."

He gave me her address and work phone number; I called her and we scheduled to meet for lunch. "Wow, you look the same, slim and beautiful," I told her, as we recognized each other in the noodle shop.

"She laughed, "You look the same too, a little bit chubbier, but still beautiful."

"You still have the same laugh; it has been so many years."

"I just arrived in the city a week ago and went straight to see Dr. Yith because he used to live in the same province as I did during the KR. I have a good job and a car that the office provides. Today, I want to go see my paternal home. Can you go with me after lunch?"

We found her house demolished, burned down to the ground, nothing left. Her house had been a wood two-story located on the Monivong Blvd. She was looking for photos of her wedding. "My husband was picked up by KR on the day we were expelled from Phnom Penh, and I believed he was executed. My father died during the KR due to sickness, as did my other sisters and brothers. The only family I have left is one older sister who now lives in Philadelphia."

"Do you have her address?"

"Of course, I remember it by heart. I wish I could leave the country and go find her."

Could this be happening? It seemed like I found gold after all. "I actually have a plan to escape the country soon," I said, throwing caution to the wind.

"Widows from KR should not stay in Cambodia anymore. We've had so much pain from the loss of our families. When there is no one left to miss us, we need to go. I have one damleng of gold in a belt around my waist. Do you know anybody who can take us to Khao I Dang?"

Standing in the ruins of her family home, we agreed to escape the country together as soon as we could. I described the plan Many had presented to me and told her what the fortunetellers had insisted was in my future. We looked at each other with amazement. Could this have really happened in the space of two hours?

"If we stay here, we will end up being mistresses to married men. It is better to face the unknown and hope for a better life," she said, and I could only nod with agreement. How well I knew what she meant.

My first priority was to sell my row house. I immediately began to ask my friends if they knew anyone who would want to buy it, and that, of course, brought up many questions about my intentions. I explained that I wanted to go live with my *Pou* Chhun.

I arranged for Many and Sophal to meet and he agreed to take us both for her one *damleng* of 24K gold. The timeline accelerated to full speed the next day when Many came to my house and announced, "We need to leave tomorrow. I have found a buyer for your house who will move in today!"

"Will he pay me three *chees* today, too?"

"Don't worry. He is my best friend. He has a lot of gold."

We looked at each other, "Are you sure he will pay me?"

He smiled. "Yes, I am sure he will pay." I felt confident it would work out. One day was very short notice and I was glad I had sold the house furnished and didn't have to dispose of the furniture. I could never have done it all so fast. As it was, I felt like everything was out of control. I called Sophal to come meet me at my house so we could go to Many's together before we got on the bus in the morning.

~FORTY TWO~

TIGER OPENS THE GATE

It was exciting to say goodbye to a place I disliked so much, to people who didn't care if I was around, to a job with no future, to a house that I hated living in. "It is time to leave the pain and hurt here, and move on in my new life," I told myself, as I carefully packed all I could carry into a cloth bag. I knew it would be on my back as I crossed the mountains. However, what should I do about the family members that I liked most, my *Pous* Chhun and Srun, and cousin Phach? Everything needed to be done fast, no time to wait. I made a decision to at least say good- bye to my uncles' families while I still had time. I borrowed a bike and hurried to Kbal Thnal where Auntie Nidd was distressed by such a sudden departure and insisted we go to a fortuneteller that she trusted.

"Let's go fast then before I run out of time. I have to see Cousin Phach before I leave."

The fortuneteller spread her cards on the table and drew a deep breath, "It is a good time for you to leave, there is no danger and you will successfully arrive at your destination." She paused dramatically and took a sip of her tea before continuing, "The tiger opens the gate for you now."(This translates that the door of opportunity is open for you. You will go through the gate with no danger or insurmountable obstacles. The tiger represents enemies, or danger.)

Auntie Nidd smiled but insisted, "Read carefully about my niece one more time."

"Yes, I guarantee she will have no danger or obstacles along the road. Her destiny is not in Cambodia."

"If my niece doesn't reach her destination, you will reimburse my money?"

"My readings are always right."

We hurried back to her house. I met my *Pou* at the door, he looked scared when I said goodbye. "I don't know what to say, what to think now," he said, his voice quavering. "You must keep us updated wherever you are. I will pray for you every day." As I ran down the stairs, he called after me, "You are making the right decision not to live in Cambodia, especially now under Vietnamese control. Pol Pot and this new regime are the same, just different names."

I went to say goodbye to *Pou* Srun who was still as sick as he had been five years ago. He wished me well and blessed me. This was the last time I ever saw my uncles.

I had no time left to see Phach; fortunately, she had heard from Many and was waiting at my house, her face wet with tears. I hugged her and said, "Your tears will stop me from moving on in my life."

"I wish only success for your dreams...I..do..," she sniffed back tears.

"I will be fine, cousin!! I have made up my mind and I have to make my own destiny. If I live and get to a third country, I will be back to see you and take care of you. However, if I die during this adventure, do not cry. I will be happy to be with Papa."

These words made her cry even more. "Are you sure you want to leave the country? I heard there was a big attack at the *Chum Rum Thmey* camp a week ago." Her eyes were red and swollen and she choked on the words.

"No, I am not scared. I am going. I do not belong here. I have no house, no family, and no real love."

Cousin Many, his friend who was buying my house, and Sophal all arrived at my house at the same time, just as it was getting dark. "Let me light a candle," I said.

"No, don't. I don't want anybody to see us," Many replied in a low voice. "Let's not create any suspicion."

I whispered to Many, "Your friend has not paid me for my house."

His friend heard me and pleaded, "*Baung,* I will send the money later with Many when he returns to Phnom Penh."

I chose not to argue with him because Many insisted that his friend wouldn't lie to me. I grabbed Papa's tooth and handkerchief, put them in a small plastic bag and hid them in my bra. Phach did not talk any more but she still wept silently. I turned back to her for the last time and encouraged her to wish me good luck in my adventure, "I love you so much!! I will be back to take care of you if I am alive and successful. If I don't come back, I will still be happy because my pain will end. Let me go. Do not cry!!"

As we left, I grabbed the cloth bag I had prepared but Many said, "No! Leave it. Don't take anything with you. I want just you and the gold. We cannot arouse suspicion and that is too much to carry. This is an escape, not a vacation." Many was calm but, as I walked out the door, my emotions got the best of me and I felt panic beginning to rise in my throat.

Leaving Phach was leaving all that had been good in my life. I kept walking forward without looking back to see my dearest Phach for the last time. I remembered what one of my old friends at the market told me, "If you cannot make a decision, you cannot be a king!" If I let my fears keep me from action, then I would be stuck for the rest of my life.

~FORTY THREE~

ESCAPE

Many took us to his wife's house on *Psar* O' Russey, about three blocks from my Cousin Phach's house. "You told me you wanted to leave her, why did you take us over here?" I asked.

"I was just kidding, Cousin; I wouldn't leave my kids. I want you to cut your hair shorter to change your appearance." Responded Many.

His wife didn't ask me anything, just gave me a haircut with a warm smile and said, "I hope you will be safe with my husband."

At 5 AM, Many woke us and rushed us to leave immediately for the bus station. When I resisted and said I at least had to wash my face, he just pushed me toward the door saying, "You will be fine. Now, don't talk and don't ask questions. We must not say anything that will make anyone suspicious. We will go to Battambang province first and from there to the border."

Sophal gave him one *damleng* from her belt and he took the two *chees* I had. I continued to press him about the money for the house, "How about my house? Will I get the money from your friend very soon?"

"Don't worry about it. I think at least the buyer did you a big favor by not spreading the news of your escape to other people."

"What do you mean?" He ignored my question and I decided not to press it for the moment.

"Let's move on."

After we arrived in Battambang province, we took a second bus to Svay Sisophon district near the Thai border and arrived around 2 PM. We had a quick stop at the market to get a new pair of sandals for each one of us. Then, Many hurried us to a house where we were once again told to change our clothes. Sophal changed to a black *sampot* and blouse and I was given an old pair of black pants and a worn and dirty man's shirt in light green. Many seemed quite anxious about our appearance, especially mine.

After we changed clothes, Many told us to rest, "Stay quiet inside the house; we will leave for the border at 10 PM tonight."

"OK, but I'm really hungry," I replied. "Can we eat something before we start on this long walk tonight?"

"Just look in the pot and eat whatever it has left. Are you ready for tonight?" he asked as he looked at me anxiously again. "Are you sure? You cannot back out once we start, there will be no one to take you back."

"What are you so worried about?"

"Your appearance is the main thing; you just don't look like a typical peasant trader. I'm worried you will draw too much attention and I'm not sure you will be strong enough for the climb up the mountain."

"I am not going back home," I insisted. "I am stronger than I look, I lived through the KR! Why do we have to wait until dark?"

"Cousin, be serious! Crossing the border is illegal! It is much easier to avoid problems with the Vietnamese patrols under the cover of darkness. At night, they usually stay in one place, leaving us plenty of space to cross the border. Also, there will be little moonlight tonight and that will help us; that's the main reason I wanted to go tonight and not wait even a day or two."

"Why?"

"No matter how quiet we are, a full moon can create shadows which the Vietnamese could notice."

"Oh. .....I see."

By 10 o'clock, we were prepared to leave. It was dark but there was enough light from the moon and the stars that we could see reasonably well. Before we left, Many rubbed charcoal powder on my forehead so the moonlight wouldn't reflect off my face and warned us again to be very, very quiet. We walked down a deserted road to join a group waiting for us; there were no introductions, I wasn't sure if they were merchants or guides. "You must stay hidden in this group," Many cautioned.

Tobacco Merchant

In the darkness it was impossible to see their faces but from their size, shape and energy, I guessed the group was all younger men. There were no children, nor any other women. There were about ten people, all dressed in black, all calm and confident. One of them gave Many two big sacks containing tobacco, and Sophal and I were each told to carry one. The men moved purposefully and I sensed none of the fear that I felt and I knew Sophal felt, as she was holding my hand in a death grip. I wondered if the others had done this trip many times and were familiar with the territory.

In a voice barely above a whisper, Many told us, "We are pretending to be peasant traders crossing back and forth over the border so both of you will carry a sack of tobacco, about 10 kilos, on your head. It is very important to walk single file and to follow the leader precisely because this area has land-mines. Do you understand?"

Now reality set in and I was truly afraid. My heart started to pound and my mouth was dry. I pulled Papa's handkerchief and tooth from my bra and kissed them to give me hope and courage. I told myself that Papa was always with me and protected me. I reminded myself that three fortunetellers said that I would make this journey successfully. I began to silently pray to Papa and to God to keep fear away from me. "Let's go."

Many walked behind me and Sophal behind him. We moved off the dirt road onto a narrow trail in the jungle and began to walk. About one hour in, Many pushed me from behind, "Walk faster," he said in an insistent whisper.

"The tobacco sack is getting really heavy," I whispered, as I stopped and turned to him.

He lifted it up little bit to gauge the weight and dropped it back on my head. "Go faster. Do you see the glow of those wood fires? The Vietnamese make those fires to chase away the foxes, so if there are fires, there are *Bo Doy*. To be safe, we need to arrive at the next stop by 6 AM - before they begin to patrol. Walk faster."

I couldn't see well under the dim starlight and I had no idea what terrain was ahead. The ground was very uneven and we seemed to be skirting the edge of a big field. From the stubble that poked my feet when I lost my balance, I guessed it was an abandoned rice field. After several more hours of walking, we moved into heavy bush with many big trees that loomed over us like giants watching our progress. The group leader didn't hesitate and our pace never slackened. Thankfully, it was relatively flat and I wondered when the mountains would begin to make the trek even harder. There was no way to ask such a question; just Many's whispered voice from behind me encouraging me to stay in line and to keep up. I was exhausted and terrified of stumbling out of line and onto a landmine. I didn't think I was crying but tears were rolling down my face. The tobacco sack grew heavier with every mile and sweat mingled with my tears as I struggled with the weight and the uneven ground.

I was surprised at how quiet the jungle was – no sounds of insects or nocturnal birds. Only our muffled footsteps broke the silence until the howling of a fox in the distance startled me. I remembered the howling of the foxes when my father died and the memories and the fear brought me to a halt. Many pushed me from behind, "It is just a fox, keep moving."

I pushed myself to keep going, praying to Papa with every single breath to keep me out of trouble. We walked non-stop from 10 PM until sometime in the early morning when we stopped for a five minute rest. I was deathly tired and thought my feet couldn't move anymore. "Are we near Khao I Dang yet?"

"No."

"I am tired. I am hungry and thirsty. I am overwhelmed. Leave me here and let me die because I have run out of energy. All night, we didn't take any breaks. I won't put this stupid tobacco sack on my head anymore." I kicked it away from me. "My head is hurting, my legs are hurting from the rough ground and you never helped me."

Many picked up the sack and carried it himself, "Please do not give up. We are almost at the *Chum Rum Thmey* camp where you will have a long rest. If you try hard just one more time, you will make it," he encouraged me. We got to our feet and started again.

You Cost a Lot of Money

The shadows of the group in front of us slowed and changed direction. The group assembled at some big boulders and the leader whispered that we were now in the KR territory and that their camp was not far. "We have arrived at the exact time we planned. We will rest here hidden in the boulders until daylight."

I knew we were in the same general area that I had been in during the 'Political Morality' training. The KR, hiding in the forest since 1979, were the same evil crows who had murdered and tormented the villagers who looked to us for help. This realization chilled me and I sank to the ground. Luckily my exhaustion overcame my terror and I passed out right away next to one of the big boulders.

Many woke me in what seemed like just minutes and whispered, "Cousin, it is time to go now."

It was 6 AM. I checked my bra to ensure Papa's handkerchief and tooth were there. I felt blessed to see I still had them. But, unaccountably, looking at his tooth scared me this time. I did not know why. Then, as I was wondering about this new fear, I heard the leader warning us to be very careful when crossing this territory. I decided to leave Papa's tooth next to the big rock where I was resting.

In the early morning light, we could see the KR camp in a valley ahead. The camp had been cut out of the jungle and was very rough. The earth had a reddish tinge and the cabins were made from the local trees and were close together. The camp was not very large and I didn't see many people around at this early hour. Some were obviously KR from their uniforms but others were dressed in casual clothes so it was hard to tell if they were the soldiers' families or maybe traders. As I peeked through a gap in the boulders, Many whispered in my ear and pointed out one KR soldier on the trail ahead.

The KR guard sat on a big rock at the entrance to the valley, a long rifle held upright in his left hand. He looked carefully at each person who passed by. Our leader gathered us together and whispered the plan, "We have to walk fast just like real merchants, this is no time to light a cigarette or chat, just walk past like you know where you are going and do this all the time. "You," he said to Many, "wait for me here, in this camp. Keep your people safe and quiet until I come back." Then he looked at me, "You will cost a lot of money."

I was almost fainted when I heard him say this. My heart started to pound as I had a feeling I would be caught. I looked at Many, then Sophal. She looked down instead of meeting my eyes. "What does he mean?" I asked with panic. "I cannot go back."

I turned to Many who took a good look at me in the daylight and cracked up, "I know why nobody wants you to be with them because, in the clear light of day, you look like a criminal with all that charcoal on your face." He laughed again and wiped my face clean.

"You put in on my forehead last night."

"You girlfriend is fine with her black outfit, but you, with these clothes?" Many shook his head, "Seriously, you don't blend with the group. The outfit makes you look like a beggar but your complexion is not weathered like someone out in the elements all day."

"You selected the clothes for me. What am I supposed to do now?"

My appearance, combined with the fact that some of the others in the group were merchants who passed here regularly and the KR knew their faces, made Many afraid the KR would notice me and then arrest all of us, including him and Sophal. I was seriously panicked by now and unable to control the fear on my face. All of these issues made me a bad risk and the group didn't want to be caught because of me, so they separated from me. The leader told them to break up into groups of two or three and proceed individually; each had their own story. One by one, small groups left the shelter of the boulders and entered the KR camp.

I was sick with fright when Many hissed at me, "Now, go…now….go…walk like a normal person, put the tobacco sack on your head, and keep your face turned away from the KR soldier if you can. Don't show any feelings that may catch his attention. Remember the story; if the KR soldier asks you, you are a tobacco merchant following your husband who has gone on ahead. Go now."

I did as he commanded, but turned at the last second to ask, "How about you? Will you come after me?" but it was too late; he and Sophal were gone.

I saw no-one else, only the KR guard that I would need to deal with. The other travelers were quickly making their way through the camp and into the jungle. I was scared to death but I had no choice - just go…go…go…as fast as I can. I will see what is going to happen.

I soon encountered two black-clad KR guards instead of one that I had seen earlier. When did that happen? Were my eyes blurred? I saw one, now two were checking everyone. I tried to walk calmly and with purpose as though I had done this many times. I adjusted the sack on my head with my hand so my face was partially blocked. I tried to walk quickly past them so they wouldn't have time to distinguish me from the other merchants. I held my breath but kept my ears open to hear if they suspected me. Life or death again. Again I remembered the old proverb and thought that crossing the border was just like going down to the water where you could be bitten by a crocodile, coming out of the water you could be bitten by a tiger. This time the tiger was the KR. As I got about three steps past the guards, I heard one call me, "Hey, you, woman, show me your identification."

I was frightened by the KR voice – a harsh voice that I had heard for four years, always with very bad results. A million thoughts swirled around in my head. Was this where my life would end? What are they going to do to me? Why do I look suspicious? Why weren't the others stopped and arrested? Why not Sophal, what is so different about me? Was I born to be unlucky?

They arrested me right there in the middle of the road. I told them exactly what I was instructed to say, but they said, "*Chè* (Sister in Chinese) does not look like a merchant."

I just stood there waiting for someone to rescue me. Where were the other people who walked with me last night? Where was Many? As my eyes searched to find someone to help me, I saw Many and Sophal hidden behind a big rock in the bushes, about 100 feet away from me. They were both chewing something. My cousin was watching and, as soon as I was trapped, he left his hiding spot and came to negotiate with the KR.

Finally, I was released but Many had to bribe them with two *chees* of gold (my gold). Instead of being grateful, I was angry that Many and my girlfriend had not only abandoned me but then ate breakfast without me. Where did they get something to eat that fast? When I scolded them, they warned me to not come close to them because I brought unwelcome attention. The fact that I was concerned about food after that encounter with the KR seems ridiculous now, but terror clouds your mind.

Many kept urging us to move quickly through the KR territory because they were unpredictable and without any discipline; they changed their minds all the time. As soon as they changed their minds, the negotiation wouldn't be very pleasant. Because the KR didn't control much territory, we passed through quickly and soon arrived at the new camp, called *Chum Rum Thmey*.

We were so happy to finally stop and rest on a bamboo bed, wipe the sweat from our brows and calm our nerves. As soon as I had breath, I again asked Many why he had abandoned me on the trail but he just laughed and replied, "We are fine now, don't worry about the past. We must think about escaping this camp and the sooner the better. The leader of this camp will keep you to work for him if he finds out you are a pharmacist." I could tell from his expression that he was serious with this last sentence. He then, said, "I have to keep moving around; talking to you too long will attract their attention."

"Wait." He was about to take off. "Who were those men from last night, where did they go?"

"Some were the guides, some merchants and the others were also escaping. The guides have your money, your's and Sophal's. They will lead the escape tonight also. I have only one *damleng* of gold left; I'm not sure if they will take you both for one *damleng*." I stayed quiet, but I knew I would be the one left behind if they would not take us both.

"What are we doing here?" Sophal wondered.

"Just relax and I will come back soon to place you." He took off.

You Cause Big Trouble

The camp was not very big; it was controlled by a new organization who called themselves *Khmer Romdos* (Cambodians rescued from Vietnamese). They had built rough cabins like those we lived in during the KR time, and they sold food and coffee to travelers. Other merchants sold *sarongs batik* (color printed *sarong* in cotton), laundry soap, stereos and other goods like watches. Now, I understood what my auntie and Papa's mistress meant when they talked about illegal trading businesses at the border. Traders arrived here with tobacco and other goods as well as gold, and then they bartered or paid in gold for merchandise to bring back to Cambodia. They bribed the KR for safe passage. *Chum Rum Thmey* was not a big camp. It was about the same size as the KR camp, but it was much busier.

Many's new plan was to have Sophal and me stay with a family in this camp until it was safe for us to move on towards Thailand. He warned us not to ask any questions, not to provide any information about ourselves or why we were there, and to make no friendships, not even with the owners of the cabin where we stayed.

We followed Many's rules but even without introducing ourselves, we still could talk a little bit. From the conversation, I learned that the man and wife had no children; she made and sold Cambodian noodles for a living. She and her husband lived under this roof and were protected by this Revolutionary Khmer group. Both of them talked about the rules and policy in the camp. They were dedicated to their leader, but I really didn't want to hear any more political fanaticism and didn't care about who the leader was.

Their cabin was a big one but had no walls. It was built of bamboo and covered with palm leaves and, to me, was just like the horrible places I lived in at the work camps. The wife explained that they all lived in open cabins to demonstrate their honesty to the Khmer group leader, which didn't make sense to me. They lived out in the open with no privacy so they could be watched at all times. They said people who have nothing to hide will hide nothing. I thought it was pathetic and ridiculous but I kept my mouth shut.

We rested as we were exhausted from our journey. As I lay on the bamboo bed, I decided to write a letter in French to send to *Pou* Chhun to let him know where I was and that I was safe. I intended to give this letter to Many in case he met someone returning to Phnom Penh who could deliver it. I stupidly did not register the obvious fact that this was suspicious behavior. The lady had been watching me and was, of course, going to report everything I did. Because she could not read French, or maybe read at all, she assumed that my letter might be a signal to an enemy to invade the camp. She forced me to give the letter to her. Luckily, she took it to Many before turning it into the leader of the camp.

Just a few minutes after she left, Many rushed to relocate us before she came back. "Hurry!! I told you to stay doing nothing. But, no, you had to write a letter in French. I warned you that this camp needs educated people like you to work with them. We have to relocate quickly because I assume that woman will go tell the group leader about you and the letter. I told you to just take a nap to regain your energy for the long walk tonight. Remember? Did you do that? No!" He was very angry with me.

"Where will we go now?" we asked him at the same time.

"We have to walk back to near the *Chum Rum Khmer Kraham* (KR camp) in order to cross the Thai border," Many said, as he looked back to ensure there was no one following us.

"A...g...ai..n? Wh...y? Sophal ran out of breath as she ran after Many.

"Why?" I asked him while trying to roll my *krama* around my head to cover my face.

"We are not supposed to come to *Chum Rum Thmey* camp. The directions are to pass this camp and walk straight to Khao I Dang. But, I had to hide you both here and wait until dark because you," he scowled at me, "stick out."

We both kept quiet; we were extremely lucky and passed no guards on the trail as we walked to a new place near the KR camp. It was 2 PM when we arrived at a rough cabin that was operating as a small restaurant selling noodle soup. Many met the Chinese owner and negotiated with him in sign language. He was around fifty and seemed very friendly; he came to greet us and offered me a place to rest, while Many took Sophal with him. My cousin ordered me not say anything to anyone, just stay hidden, and quiet! No questions, no answers.

I was put in a room bisected by a curtain. I lay down and dozed a little bit but woke up as I heard the voices of a man and woman talking on the other side of the curtain. They negotiated a price before they had sex. An hour later, my cousin came to find me and told me he had no idea he had left me in a brothel.

"Oh! Hell! I have been in worse places."

Many said that he, Sophal and I would rest until late afternoon, then we needed to keep moving, relocating frequently and as quickly as we could, so the KR would lose track of us. My cousin again bribed the owner of the restaurant to keep us secret until we left. The owner was a very nice man and gave us a big bowl of soup before we started the next leg of our journey.

A Mysterious Adventure

At 5 PM, we moved to a different house. Not long after our arrival, three new men appeared silently on bicycles; Many told us we would each ride with one. The men moved quickly and silently. No one spoke; everything went very fast and very quietly. Again - no questions, no answers. After several hours on the back of the bicycle over very rough ground, they dropped us at the base of a mountain where we were to walk across the border to the Khao I Dang camp in Thailand. The group of men we had been with earlier was already there but, as before, there was no talking, no introductions. There was also no talk of leaving me behind.

"Are you ready to take this trek over the mountain tonight?" Again, Many seemed to be more worried about me than Sophal, even though she, too, was now looking exhausted after the long, bumpy ride.

"Let's continue on! I am fine so far!" I assured him, but I didn't realize how bad my butt was bruised and aching from the non-stop bumps over the uneven, rocky road. I couldn't walk as fast as he expected and Many had to keep pushing me and urging me on as we started to walk up the mountain. Again, we walked single file and had to stay right in each other's footsteps to avoid mines or getting lost in the forest.

"It is going to get tougher later," Many warned me from behind. About an hour later, it started to get dark. It was not like the night before when we had a little starlight to help us see the path through the heavy jungle. Now, it was like a dark curtain had been pulled in front of us. Yet the guides seemed to know exactly where they were going because their pace never slowed - always moving forward and in the right direction. They seemed to know what they were doing and I used my ears rather than my eyes to stay right behind them. Their knowledge was certainly worth one *damleng* and I was grateful to be with them.

The only time they slowed down and remained hidden, listening to the sounds of the forest, was when we came to a place where bandits were known to ambush and prey on travelers. One guide slipped ahead to check the trail while we all waited. "The robbers are from the nearby villages; women have also been raped and robbed and left here by dishonest guides," Many whispered to me and Sophal, as we hid just off the trail.

"Everything is clear, let's move." Our guide had returned so silently we hadn't even heard him approach.

The ground was uneven, sometimes rough and firm like walking on rocks, sometimes slippery and covered with dropped leaves. Once in a while, I lost my balance, but Many was close behind and caught me. After about an hour, my cousin pulled my shirt to keep me from falling into in a mine crater. "I just saved your life," he whispered in my ear. I couldn't see any farther than the feet of the man walking in front of me; it was so hard to concentrate on staying in line and not slipping. We had been walking for hours over this rough ground when the guide asked us to speed up. Now the terrain became very rocky and gradually steeper. The steeper the incline, the more energy I spent keeping up with the man in front of me.

"We are climbing Khao I Dang Mountain now," Many whispered. Hearing these words re-energized me, the exhaustion lifted and I was filled with excitement. I didn't know how high the mountain was or how much longer we would climb but I was sure I could make it now.

About 3 AM, we arrived at the summit of the mountain. When we looked down, we saw the countryside lit up for miles. My cousin said, "Look! It is the Khao I Dang camp."

My heart filled and I could hardly breathe. I whispered to Sophal, "Look at the paradise!"

"Look at the lights of Khao I Dang camp! We dreamed about this!"

"We are safe. If all my cousins and *Pous* knew that I am here tonight, they would be very happy. Now, I understand the meaning of what the fortuneteller said: 'Tiger opens the gate!' It means we made it through without stepping on a landmine, no robberies or rapes while crossing the mountain at night, no arrest at KR camp."

Many urged me to breathe deeply and gather my strength, then be ready for the final push. The leader told us to stop and hide behind a big rock while he went down to "negotiate" with the Thai border guard. When he returned in about a half hour, he told us that we should be prepared to run to the barbed wire fence and slide under it when the spotlight was turned away from us. It never occurred to me to ask why we had to sneak into a refugee camp.

We started down the mountain; we had to be across the border before the guards changed their shift. We walked, slid, scrambled and ran down the slope as fast as we could. It was dark but the lights from the camp made the descent possible. As we neared the bottom, I could see the fence and hear the guide urging us forward. Fear and elation drove all thoughts of exhaustion from my mind. At the same time, I heard gunshots from the direction of the Thai guards. I was scared to death but I ran towards freedom. I ran and dove for the fence and suddenly I was inside the Khao I Dang camp.

I had made my escape. I was on my way to a new life. It was March of 1983. I was thirty one years old, not a penny or possession to my name and dressed in filthy rags; but I was free – free of the Khmer Rouge and free of the Vietnamese communists. I was free to start again.

EPILOGUE

I made my way to the United States in 1985. I had survived genocide by the Khmer Rouge in my Cambodian homeland, but at a terrible cost. The only physical reminder of my young life in Cambodia is the handkerchief that covered my father's face after he drew his last breath and the "Lecreucet" pot. I still weep for him; I still miss him. His parenting left a lot to be desired and the harsh physical discipline I suffered as a young person was very damaging emotionally and physically. This abusive discipline was acceptable in our culture and he was not strong enough to find a better way. Yet, I know that he loved me. He made mistakes; he was human.

I wonder how different my life would have been if he had lived, if he had sent me out of Cambodia, if the Genocide didn't happen, if, if, if…. But, such thinking is pointless. Life goes on, do not look back. But there will always be an icy drop of sorrow and loneliness that just keeps running through my veins. I grieve for my life that might have been, the loss of my home and my culture, for my husband, my parents and family members and for all the innocents who perished.

I believe that things happen for a reason. I understand why Papa would not send me to France, no matter how hard I fought. It was not my destiny to leave him. I had to stay with him to learn to appreciate the love of the parents and others. I returned that love to him up to the time of his last breath. Even during the worst times as we struggled with starvation, I always put him first and never gave in to the temptation to hide food and save myself. I did not fight with him or disrespect him as I saw so many others do to their family members.

For this real love and caring for my dad, God blessed me with miracles and allowed me to survive. God saved my life, right in the nick of time, when I was to be beaten by the KR leader for stealing crab in the forced labor camp. God saved me from being detected by the dog in the rice warehouse; he sent an angel to save me from being swept away and drowned in the water canal; and saved me by setting up a rice grinder next to the Cemetery Hospital when I was fighting with death every day.

All the jewelry and other material things that I valued so much as a young woman were traded for a bowl of rice in the end. Dealing with betrayal and the loss of material possessions taught me to not be so naïve but the real lesson was that, as Papa said, 'only education can never be stolen'. After all these experiences, I realize that all these people, good and evil, have shaped my being. The loss of my parents and my extended family is still hard to deal with and I still struggle to understand God's purpose but I know he has one. He has given me the gifts of bravery, intelligence, an analytical nature and intuition. I am to figure it out.

Glossary

Angkar Leu: Superior Angkar in Khmer Rouge word.

Angkor: Holy city. The Angkorian period was dated from 802 A.D until 1431 A.D.

Akimbo: means standing with both hands on your hips, arms bent at the elbow.

Aun: Younger brother, younger sister, Honey, Darling.

Banteay **Longvek** or *Banteay* **Lovek.** Military base of Longvek located in Kompong Chhnang province, 66 km from Phnom-Penh. The base had been protected by thick bamboo and many lakes. The base was about three km in length and two km in width. It said that two sacred statues "Preah Keo" and "Preah Koh or sacred bull" were kept in Longvek. In 1593, Longvek was defeated by the Thais. The statues were taken by Thais as well as more records regarding the Khmer religion, and culture.

Baung: Older brother, older sister, Honey, Darling.

Bat: Yes for men

Chah: Yes for women

Chao: Granddaughter. Grandson

District of Preah Netr Preah: After the war, in 1988, five districts including Preah Netr Preah were separated from Battambang province into a new province of Banteay Mean Chey.

Ho Chi Minh: the original name was Prey Nokor and it was a Khmer city. According to history, in 1620, Cambodian King Chey, Chettha II married a Vietnamese woman, a daughter of Nguyen, Phuc Nguyen. To please his Vietnamese wife or perhaps as a dowry, King Chey, Chetta allowed the Vietnamese to settle Prey Nokor. At the end of 1975, the city, then known as Saigon, came under the control of the North Vietnamese and was renamed for their leader.

Keo: Refer to an aunt in Chinese in the father side

Kdouy mehr mee kaun aut mehr : Bad Insult

Kdouy mehr vear : Bad insult

Khmer Krom also called *Kampuchear Krom:* "Lower Cambodia or Cochin China". This land is known as a part of Khmer Empire, the oldest land in Southeast Asia. French colonialists had divided this land from the motherland, the Kingdom of Cambodia, and transferred it to Vietnam as a colony in June of 1949.

Krama: means multicolor hand-woven cloth, 3 meters long and half a meter wide. Krama can be cotton, lace or silk. A cotton krama is used to wrap around the body when women or men take a bath, also to wrap around the head for protection from the sun. Hand-woven silk and lace kramas are used for special occasions and wrap around the chest and finish on the left shoulder, held by a pin.

Kratié province: It was known as the region of pre-Angkorian Cambodia. It is situated north of Phnom Penh.

Lok krou: Male teacher

Lok Tah: Grandpa. Refer to an old person respectfully.

Lok Yey: Grandma. Refer to an old person respectfully.

Neak : *Mother.* Name used to call mother in the East and Northeastern Cambodia, like Kompong Cham, and Kratié provinces.

Mehr: Mother. Common name to call mother for the farmers and peasants.

Neak krou: *Female teacher*

Ong Leun: *Superior Angkar in Vietnamese word.*

Phachum Ben is the Gathering of Ancestors festival: the fifteen day of the tenth month of the Khmer Calendar is the time we believe that the spirits of our ancestors will be temporarily released from punishment, if they had done many bad things during their lifetime. The punished spirits will walk the earth to get food and blessings. For this reason, it is very important for us, as children and grandchildren to offer food to the monks. In return, the monks will forward the blessings to the punished spirit. This aspect of Khmer culture and religion had been eliminated during the Pol Pot regime.

Pakee: Multiple purpose use on the farm as a basket. It is made out of young shredded bamboo to transport mud and other heavy things.

Professor: Female or Male teacher.

Pouk: Father. It is common for farmers call father this way.

Samak Mit: Comrade

Samak Mit phone: Comrade Young Brother

Sampot: Solid color in silk, or other textile, 2 meters in length and 1 meter in width. Both ends are finished.

Sampot Chang Kben: used at a special traditional occasion. Colors are varied based on the day of the week.

1- Sunday: Red (Cambodian = *Kra ham*)
2- Monday: Orange (Cambodian = *Leung Tom*)
3- Tuesday: Violet (Cambodian = *Svay*)
4- Wednesday: Greenish yellow (Cambodian = *Kar Tear*)
5- Thursday: Green (Cambodian= *Bey Tang*)
6- Friday: Dark blue (Cambodian = *Kheo*)
7- Saturday: Dark purple (Cambodian = *Pring Toom*)

Sarong: The difference between a *sarong* and a *sampot* is that the *sarong* is manually wrapped around the waist while the *sampot* has a sewn waist and is wrapped to the side of the hip, then attached with a hook. The *sampot* is worn outside of the house.

Tah: Grandpa. Refer to an old person casually

Tonlé Bassac: it starts in Phnom Peng, and runs crossing the border into Vietnam near Châ ĐỐc.

Tonlé Sap Lake: There are nine provinces that are surrounding *Tonlé Sap*: Banteay Meanchey, Battambang, Kampong Chhnang, Kompong Thom, Preah Vihear, Pursat, Siem Reap, Otdar Meanchey and Krong Pailin.

FATHER'S FAMILY SIDE

THE PUTH FAMILY

Puth, Suy ♂ (grand pa ●[1 bio grand mohter] (unknown name)

    Suy, Kim Houn ♂(**d/c in KR**)●[1] Bio mother:Duch Siphol ♀ (d/c 36y)

        Houn, Vicheara ♀● Leang ♂ (**executed 1978**)

      ●[2 step mother]:Te, Siv Phek ♀ (d/c in KR)

    Puth, Chhay Leng♀ (in France)

●[2 Step grandmother]:Nong, Kong (**d/c in KR**)

    Puth, Eng Srun ♂ (d/c after liberation) ● Puth, Eng Hour (**d/c in KR**)

    Puth, Ly Chun ♂

    Puth, Chhay Or nick name Va ♂ (**died in KR**)

    Puth, Sichour ♀ ● Phan ♂ survived in KR

    Puth, Sithour ♀ (**committed suicide during Pol Pot reign**) ● Heng, Lay ♂

    Puth, Bun Than ♂ ● married to teacher –2 kids

    Puth, Sunthary ♂ (**d/c during Pol Pot**)

Puth, Horn ♀ (d/c) ● grandfather Dauck

    Dauk, Met ♀ ● Thor, Thay Vaun ♂ (**d/c in hospital during KR invasion**)

        Thor, Peng Thong ♂- Dauck, Siv Leng ♀ (**all d/c in KR**)

        Thor, Peng Ly (**family died in KR** except 4 children

MOTHER'S FAMILY TREES

THE DUCH FAMILY

Duch. ♂ ● Grandmother Sem ♀ (d/c 2005 in Phnom Penh). They were, both cousin.

    Duch, Sathan ♂ ● Duch, Thoeun

        Duch Mong San

        Duch, Peach

    Duch, Phan ♀ (d/c before KR) ● Nam, Chhay ♂ (d/c after KR liberation)

        Nam, Chheng On ♂(**family d/c in KR**)

        Nam, Chheng Un ♂(**family d/c in KR**)

        Nam, Chheng Or ♂ (**d/c in KR**)

        Nam, Chheng Orth ♂ (survived in KR)

        Nam, Chheng Em ♂(survived in KR)

    Duch, Sipho ♀ ● Long, Det ♂(d/c after KR liberation)

        Long, Lady, nick name "Deun" (**family d/c in KR**)

        Long, Lathol (**d/c in KR**)

        Long, Nol (**family d/c in KR**)

        Long, Many ♂ changed then to Chheng Ny, then Lon

        Duch, Siphol ♀(my mother, d/c 1960) ● Suy, Kim Houn (**my Papa: d/c in KR**)

        Houn, Vicheara

        Duch, Soro ♀(d/c during labor) ● Chhin, Chhorn ♂

        Chhin, Phach ♀(survived in KR) ● Mao, Heng Bun ♂(d/c in KR)

Glossary

Angkar Leu: Superior Angkar in Khmer Rouge word.

Angkor: Holy city. The Angkorian period was dated from 802 A.D until 1431 A.D.

Akimbo: means standing with both hands on your hips, arms bent at the elbow.

Aun: Younger brother, younger sister, Honey, Darling.

Banteay **Longvek** *or Banteay* **Lovek.** Military base of Longvek located in Kompong Chhnang province, 66 km from Phnom-Penh. The base had been protected by thick bamboo and many lakes. The base was about three km in length and two km in width. It said that two sacred statues "Preah Keo" and "Preah Koh or sacred bull" were kept in Longvek. In 1593, Longvek was defeated by the Thais. The statues were taken by Thais as well as more records regarding the Khmer religion, and culture.

Baung: Older brother, older sister, Honey, Darling.

Bat: Yes for men

Chah: Yes for women

Chao: Granddaughter. Grandson

District of Preah Netr Preah: After the war, in 1988, five districts including Preah Netr Preah were separated from Battambang province into a new province of Banteay Mean Chey.

Ho Chi Minh: the original name was Prey Nokor and it was a Khmer city. According to history, in 1620, Cambodian King Chey, Chettha II married a Vietnamese woman, a daughter of Nguyen, Phuc Nguyen. To please his Vietnamese wife or perhaps as a dowry, King Chey, Chetta allowed the Vietnamese to settle Prey Nokor. At the end of 1975, the city, then known as Saigon, came under the control of the North Vietnamese and was renamed for their leader.

Keo: Refer to an aunt in Chinese in the father side

Kdouy mehr mee kaun aut mehr : Bad Insult

Kdouy mehr vear : Bad insult

Khmer Krom also called *Kampuchear Krom:* "Lower Cambodia or Cochin China". This land is known as a part of Khmer Empire, the oldest land in Southeast Asia. French colonialists had divided this land from the motherland, the Kingdom of Cambodia, and transferred it to Vietnam as a colony in June of 1949.

Krama: means multicolor hand-woven cloth, 3 meters long and half a meter wide. Krama can be cotton, lace or silk. A cotton krama is used to wrap around the body when women or men take a bath, also to wrap around the head for protection from the sun. Hand-woven silk and lace kramas are used for special occasions and wrap around the chest and finish on the left shoulder, held by a pin.

Kratié province: It was known as the region of pre-Angkorian Cambodia. It is situated north of Phnom Penh.

Lok krou: Male teacher

Lok Tah: Grandpa. Refer to an old person respectfully.

Lok Yey: Grandma. Refer to an old person respectfully.

Neak : *Mother.* Name used to call mother in the East and Northeastern Cambodia, like Kompong Cham, and Kratié provinces.

Mehr: Mother. Common name to call mother for the farmers and peasants.

Neak krou: *Female teacher*

Ong Leun: *Superior Angkar in Vietnamese word.*

Phachum Ben is the Gathering of Ancestors festival: the fifteen day of the tenth month of the Khmer Calendar is the time we believe that the spirits of our ancestors will be temporarily released from punishment, if they had done many bad things during their lifetime. The punished spirits will walk the earth to get food and blessings. For this reason, it is very important for us, as children and grandchildren to offer food to the monks. In return, the monks will forward the blessings to the punished spirit. This aspect of Khmer culture and religion had been eliminated during the Pol Pot regime.

Pakee: Multiple purpose use on the farm as a basket. It is made out of young shredded bamboo to transport mud and other heavy things.

Professor: Female or Male teacher.

Pouk: Father. It is common for farmers call father this way.

Samak Mit: Comrade

Samak Mit phone: Comrade Young Brother

Sampot: Solid color in silk, or other textile, 2 meters in length and 1 meter in width. Both ends are finished.

Sampot Chang Kben: used at a special traditional occasion. Colors are varied based on the day of the week.

    1- Sunday: Red (Cambodian = *Kra ham*)
    2- Monday: Orange (Cambodian = *Leung Tom*)
    3- Tuesday: Violet (Cambodian = *Svay*)
    4- Wednesday: Greenish yellow (Cambodian = *Kar Tear*)
    5- Thursday: Green (Cambodian= *Bey Tang*)
    6-Friday: Dark blue (Cambodian = *Kheo*)
    7- Saturday: Dark purple (Cambodian = *Pring Toom*)

Sarong: The difference between a *sarong* and a *sampot* is that the *sarong* is manually wrapped around the waist while the *sampot* has a sewn waist and is wrapped to the side of the hip, then attached with a hook. The *sampot* is worn outside of the house.

Tah: Grandpa. Refer to an old person casually

Tonlé Bassac: it starts in Phnom Peng, and runs crossing the border into Vietnam near Châ ĐỐc.

Tonlé Sap Lake: There are nine provinces that are surrounding *Tonlé Sap*: Banteay Meanchey, Battambang, Kampong Chhnang, Kompong Thom, Preah Vihear, Pursat, Siem Reap, Otdar Meanchey and Krong Pailin.

CPSIA information can be obtained at www.ICGtesting.com
Printed in the USA
BVOW11s1639030614

355266BV00003BA/5/P